Programming "Indigo": Code Name for the Unified Framework for Building Service-Oriented Applications on the Microsoft® Windows® Platform, Beta Edition

David Pallmann

PUBLISHED BY
Microsoft Press
A Division of Microsoft Corporation
One Microsoft Way
Redmond, Washington 98052-6399

Library of Congress Control Number 2005925788

Printed and bound in the United States of America.

2 3 4 5 6 7 8 9   QWT   8 7 6 5

Distributed in Canada by H.B. Fenn and Company Ltd. A CIP catalogue record for this book is available from the British Library.

Microsoft Press books are available through booksellers and distributors worldwide. For further information about international editions, contact your local Microsoft Corporation office or contact Microsoft Press International directly at fax (425) 936-7329. Visit our Web site at www.microsoft.com/mspress. Send comments to mspinput@microsoft.com.

Microsoft, Active Directory, ActiveX, Hotmail, IntelliSense, JScript, Microsoft Press, MSDN, Tahoma, Visual Basic, Visual C#, Visual J#, Visual Studio, Webdings, Windows, Windows NT, Windows Server, and WinFX are either registered trademarks or trademarks of Microsoft Corporation in the United States and/or other countries. Other product and company names mentioned herein may be the trademarks of their respective owners.

The example companies, organizations, products, domain names, e-mail addresses, logos, people, places, and events depicted herein are fictitious. No association with any real company, organization, product, domain name, e-mail address, logo, person, place, or event is intended or should be inferred.

This book expresses the author's views and opinions. The information contained in this book is provided without any express, statutory, or implied warranties. Neither the authors, Microsoft Corporation, nor its resellers, or distributors will be held liable for any damages caused or alleged to be caused either directly or indirectly by this book.

Acquisitions Editor: Ben Ryan
Project Editor: Kristine Haugseth
Copy Editors: Ina Chang and Lisa Pawlewicz
Proofreaders: Catherine Cooker and Sandi Resnick
Indexer: Lynn Armstrong

Body Part No. X11-15616

Table of Contents

Part II   Developing in Microsoft Code Name "Indigo"

Acknowledgments

This book took a year to write, to my great surprise. It was a mammoth undertaking to learn and write about the full breadth of Microsoft Code Name "Indigo" while it was still undergoing change. It was only through the contributions of many people that this book happened at all.

Time with my family really suffered during the writing of this book, so I would like to thank them first. When I emerged from my year of typing, I was pleased to see that my wife Becky and three children—Susan, Debra, and Jonathan—had not abandoned me. We're getting reacquainted, starting with a vacation. I did have some interaction with my one-and-a-half-year-old Jonathan, who must have climbed over, around, or under me several thousand times as I attempted to write on my laptop. If there are any bizarre typographical errors in the book that somehow escaped detection, there's a good chance he contributed them.

Just about every person on the Indigo product team contributed to my understanding of some facet of Indigo. In particular, I would like to thank the people who took time to perform a technical review despite their very busy schedules. I am deeply indebted to Venkat Chilakala, Carlos Figueira, Vijay Gajjala, Kirill Gavrylyuk, Kavita Kamani, Craig McLuckie, Vadim Meleshuk, Andy Milligan, Martin Petersen-Frey, Anand Rajagopalan, Scott Seely, David So, Krish Srinivasan, Richard Turner, Mike Vernal, and Alex Weinert. Thank you for pointing out inaccuracies, filling in the gaps in my knowledge, and making great suggestions.

There would be no book at all without the fine team of people at Microsoft Press who turned my raw content into readable content. Project editor Kristine Haugseth, who is simply wonderful, left no stone unturned in championing accuracy, clarity, and consistency. Important contributions to the book were also made by copy editors Ina Chang and Lisa Pawlewicz; proofreaders Sandi Resnick and Catherine Cooker; indexers Patty Masserman and Lynn Armstrong; artists Bill Teel and Joel Panchot; and compositors Ellie Fountain, Carl Diltz, Elizabeth Hansford, and Dan Latimer. Ben Ryan was at the helm, as has been the case with all of my prior books. Thank you all.

Introduction

Microsoft Code Name "Indigo" is an advanced infrastructure and programming model for creating connected applications. It's like nothing that has come before. That's a bold statement, so allow me to put it in perspective for you.

I wrote my first communication program over 20 years ago and remember it well. It was a lengthy program written in assembly language that ran on a minicomputer. It allowed files to be transferred over a phone line at 300 baud. The program was able to communicate with only a handful of other minicomputers equipped with the same software. I had to handle every detail of communication, including sending commands to the modem, creating a protocol for transferring chunks of data, and devising a strategy for handling errors. I was proud of this program: every bit of functionality had required discrete work on my part.

In the years that followed, communication programming changed a lot but didn't necessarily get much easier. Networking and the Internet and broadband gave us more capabilities, but developers now had to contend with a frightful number of protocols and formats that wouldn't stand still. Security complicated things further but was critically important. Standards meant to be simple, such as XML, became complex over time. Even as technologies such as Web applications, distributed objects, message queuing, and interoperable Web services arrived to shoulder more of the load, the sheer number of technologies that developers had to master became a problem in itself. These technologies didn't always integrate well and were sometimes at odds with one other. Communication programming simply hasn't been easy—until now.

A few moments ago, I wrote a communication program using Indigo on a PC. It is written in C# and is a mere 20 lines in length. It can stream data over networks and the Internet at high speed, potentially to millions of destinations. Although I wrote no code to deal with the intricacies of communication, the program is a marvel of sophisticated connectivity. It is transport neutral and is able to use HTTP, TCP, or named pipes to communicate. It uses advanced Web services standards that allow it to interact with other platforms. The receiving end can accept multiple transfers in parallel. It reliably transfers information and is able to resume in the face of a communication disruption. The program is also secure, positively identifying its destination and encrypting messages for confidentiality. I'm also proud of what this program can do, and I'm delighted that it took less than five minutes to write.

Clearly, this is a departure from the past. Indigo breaks free of the supposed truism that more functionality comes at the cost of more complexity for the developer.

Why Indigo?

We've seen many communication technologies come (and go) over the years. You might already be comfortable with several and wonder why you should bother to get acquainted with another one. Is Indigo for you? It is, if any of the following applies to you:

- **You need to create connected applications.**   Connectivity has become a top consideration in how distributed systems are architected. Service orientation (SO) champions this approach. When you create modern connected applications, you can benefit greatly from using tools and infrastructure designed for SO. Indigo is designed from the ground up with SO in mind.

- **You yearn for a unified programming model.**   Too often, developers of connected applications have had to master a multitude of technologies, each with a unique programming model. You might employ one technology for remote procedure calls, another for queuing, another for transacted components, and still another for interoperable communication across platforms. This technology fragmentation has gotten out of hand. Each technology is a world in itself, forcing developers to constantly switch between paradigms as they work. Indigo provides a single programming model for an extensive collection of communication capabilities and enterprise services.

- **You're tired of technologies that don't integrate well.**   Identifying and mastering individual technologies with the capabilities you need is only half the battle: can you also get them to work together? For example, using communication technology and transaction technology in the same program doesn't necessarily give you transacted communication. In contrast, integrated technologies that can work together seamlessly are a pleasure to use. Indigo communication and enterprise technologies are well integrated and work together automatically.

- **You require broad interoperability.**   Platform independence is a must these days. Interoperability preserves your development options and allows you to communicate with the entire world. Today's interoperability needs extend beyond mere communication—enterprises want a spectrum of platform-independent functionality. Indigo uses industry standard protocols that allow it to interoperate with any platform that also supports those protocols.

- **You don't want to sacrifice enterprise-strength features for interoperability.**   Interoperability has often come at the expense of features the enterprise needs, such as security, reliability, transactions, and performance. Enterprises need the benefits of interoperability but simply can't afford to give up these other features. This interoperability doesn't come at the expense of important enterprise features.

- **You want to concentrate on writing your application, not creating infrastructure.**   Building software is hard work. You should be free to concentrate on developing your application without having to worry about the mechanics of communication and coordination.

An infrastructure for communication and enterprise services should do the heavy lifting for you. The Indigo programming model stays out of your way. You can achieve a great deal with a small amount of code. Many capabilities can be enabled simply through declarative attributes and require no explicit code.

- **You want richer communication options.**   Different methods of communication serve different needs. Past technologies have often given you only one communication paradigm, such as message queuing or remote procedure calls. Ideally, you'd like to be able to employ synchronous, asynchronous, one-way, two-way, request-reply, queued, or streamed communication with equal ease. Having more communication options eases your solution design, allowing you to use the messaging approach that best fits a given problem. Indigo is a superset of prior communication technologies. It gives developers more choices, allowing them to apply the most natural communication method to a given problem.

- **You don't want to get locked into a dead-end technology.**   Technologies change all the time. How can you select communication technology that will stand the test of time? You don't want to find yourself with a dinosaur technology because transport methods, data formats, or security schemes have changed. You want an infrastructure that anticipates change and can be modularly upgraded. Indigo is designed with the long term in mind. Transport methods, message formats, security implementations, and many other areas can be extended or upgraded.

- **You need scale invariance.**   Your distributed solution needs to scale well, whether you are scaling up, out, down, or in. Your distributed solution should accommodate increased demand easily, even though it can be difficult to know in advance which direction that demand will come from. You also want a solution that's efficient and resource-conscious in smaller configurations.

We'll properly explore the capabilities of Indigo in Chapter 1, but this should serve to whet your appetite.

About the Book

The purpose of this book is to give you the practical information you need to program Indigo and apply it effectively. My intent is to equip you for maximum success in designing and building connected applications.

This is a how-to book, and you'll find that much of the material in these pages resembles a cookbook. This task-oriented organization allows you to easily look up something you need to do and see how to accomplish it with Indigo. Each task is explained conceptually and then followed by a code example. The code examples can also be downloaded (as explained shortly).

Target Audience

Developers of all kinds should find this book to be a useful reference. Regardless of your experience and skills, learning a new technology involves ramp-up, especially when you're learning one with as many capabilities as Indigo. Even seasoned professionals can use some help when taking on a new task. My hope is that this reference saves you time, points you in the right direction, and makes you fully aware of your options.

Application developers and independent software vendors sometimes program at very different levels. For this reason, this book presents high-level and low-level versions of some tasks.

What the Book Covers and Doesn't Cover

This book is about applied Indigo programming. It includes concise programming guidance and code examples for hundreds of tasks. Conceptual information is provided, along with sample applications that illustrate Indigo programming in real-world scenarios.

Let's also be clear on what the book is *not*. This is not an exhaustive reference to the Indigo object model; the Indigo documentation does a great job of describing that. Nor is this a guide to the inner workings of Indigo under the hood. Migration strategies from other technologies are not covered. Lastly, this book doesn't cover extensibility points such as adding a custom transport method to Indigo.

> **Note**   This book reflects the Beta 1 release of Indigo. Indigo could certainly change in subsequent releases as Microsoft refines the design and feature set in response to customer feedback.

Code Examples

When a code example can be implemented in more than one way, I've chosen the approach that is the most straightforward and most in the spirit of Indigo. Often this means using the Indigo service model (declarative attributes and configuration file settings) rather than writing explicit code. Microsoft recommends using the service model unless you have a specific reason not to, and I've followed that advice.

The code examples can be downloaded from the Microsoft Learning Web site at this URL:

http://www.microsoft.com/mspress/companion/0-7356-2151-9

To build and run the code examples, you should have Indigo and the Microsoft .NET Framework 2.0 installed on a supported operating system. Microsoft Visual Studio .NET 2005 is the recommended development environment.

Book and Chapter Organization

This book is divided into four parts:

- Part I: Preparing for Microsoft Code Name "Indigo"
- Part II: Developing in Microsoft Code Name "Indigo"
- Part III: Deploying Microsoft Code Name "Indigo" Solutions
- Part IV: Case Studies

Let's examine the theme and chapter organization of each part.

Part I: Preparing for Microsoft Code Name "Indigo"

Part I covers the material you need to know before you start writing code in Indigo. The chapters introduce Indigo, explain essential concepts, introduce the programming model, and walk you through creating a sample application.

- Chapter 1, "Microsoft Code Name 'Indigo', the Microsoft Runtime for Services," explains what service orientation means and provides a guided tour of Indigo features and functionality.
- Chapter 2, "Fundamental Concepts," covers the essential information every Indigo developer needs to know.
- Chapter 3, "The Programming Model," introduces the programming model and explains how Indigo solutions are created, built, deployed, and debugged. It also walks you through creating and running several "Hello, World" programs. This chapter provides you with a working knowledge of the development process and the experience of actually building and running an Indigo application.

Part II: Developing in Microsoft Code Name "Indigo"

Part II is the heart of the book. Each chapter focuses on a specific feature area of Indigo, beginning with a presentation of key concepts and a discussion of relevant elements of the programming model. This is followed by programming information and code examples, organized by task. Finally, each chapter contains a sample application that illustrates the chapter's programming information at work.

- Chapter 4, "Addresses and Bindings," describes how to specify the location, communication details, and security settings of endpoints.
- Chapter 5, "Contracts," describes how to use contracts to define service interfaces, data structures, and message format.
- Chapter 6, "Clients," describes how to define and implement clients, the programs that make requests of services.

- Chapter 7, "Services," covers defining and implementing services and controlling their run-time behavior.

- Chapter 8, "Security," covers security features, including client and server authentication, message confidentiality and integrity, and security profiles.

- Chapter 9, "Interoperability and Integration," describes how to create clients and services that can interoperate with other platforms or integrate with other technologies.

Part III: Deploying Microsoft Code Name "Indigo" Solutions

Part III addresses issues related to deploying your solution after it has been built. The chapters address hosting, management, deployment, and troubleshooting.

- Chapter 10, "Hosting," describes the hosting of services, with an emphasis on using Microsoft Internet Information Services (IIS) to host, activate, and monitor the health of services.

- Chapter 11, "Management," covers manageability features such as activity tracing and message logging.

- Chapter 12, "Deployment and Troubleshooting," covers deployment issues, including installation, configuration, and upgrading of applications.

Part IV: Case Studies

Part IV contains several case studies. In each chapter, an application is created from start to finish, showing many of the book's tasks working together in a distributed application. Business, peer-to-peer, and real-time applications are described.

- Chapter 13, "Case Study: Enterprise Order Processing," traces the design and development of an enterprise e-commerce solution.

- Chapter 14, "Case Study: Digital Whiteboard," describes a peer-to-peer application, tracing its design and development.

- Chapter 15, "Case Study: Elevator Control System," traces the design and development of a real-time application that simulates an elevator control system.

Getting the Most from the Book

It's been my observation that developers consume technical books in one of two ways: sequentially, reading the entire book from cover to cover to digest each and every detail and deeply understand the subject matter, or through random access, turning to a specific section of the book as needed to get something accomplished and showing more interest in *how* than *why*.

I've tried to accommodate both types of readers. Random access readers will find that the task-oriented organization of this book makes it easy to quickly locate information on a specific topic. Cross-references lead to related subjects elsewhere in the book.

The book's organization should also suit sequential readers. The chapters form an orderly progression of subject matter, with conceptual information to complement the practical information.

Support

Every effort has been made to ensure the accuracy of this book and companion content. Microsoft Learning provides corrections for books through the Web at the following address:

http://www.microsoft.com/learning/support/

To connect directly to the Microsoft Knowledge Base and enter a query regarding a question or an issue, go to:

http://www.microsoft.com/learning/support/search.asp

If you have comments, questions, or ideas regarding the book or companion content, or if you have questions that are not answered by querying the Knowledge Base, please send them to Microsoft Press using either of the following methods:

E-mail:

mspinput@microsoft.com

Postal mail:

Microsoft Press

Attn: Programming Indigo Editor

One Microsoft Way

Redmond, WA 98052-6399

Please note that product support is not offered through these addresses. For support information, please visit the Microsoft Product Support Web site at:

http://support.microsoft.com

It's also possible that Indigo will change over time. This book targets Indigo version 1.0, which is nearing beta release at the time of this writing. Be forewarned that there might be changes to the Indigo feature set or programming model between now and release.

I'm always interested in hearing comments from readers. Feel free to contact me at *dpall-mann@hotmail.com* with your feedback.

Have fun programming Indigo, and start thinking about how you're going to spend all of that free time.

Part I
Preparing for Microsoft Code Name "Indigo"

In this part:

Chapter 1

Microsoft Code Name "Indigo," the Microsoft Runtime for Services

> *"It will be hard," they say, "to find*
> *Another service such as this."*
>
> —Alfred, Lord Tennyson, In Memoriam

In this chapter, we will first explore the core principles behind Indigo service orientation (SO). A familiarity with SO will help you better understand and apply Indigo. Then we'll introduce Indigo itself and survey its capabilities.

After completing this chapter, you will:

- Understand the principles of service orientation.
- Be familiar with the capabilities of Indigo.

Understanding Service Orientation

The drive to connect people, organizations, and devices in new and better ways seems to be never-ending. In the business world, enterprises are demanding seamless communication with their partners and customers without sacrificing essential features such as security, transactions, reliability, and performance. At the consumer level, connectivity is finding its way into everything from wristwatches to automobiles. Distributed systems are becoming the norm. Simply put, the modern application is a connected application.

In response to these trends, connectivity has moved to center stage in software development. **Service orientation** (SO) is an approach to software design and development that champions this view, and it is an idea whose time has come. In SO, message-oriented programs called services are the building blocks from which solutions are created.

Indigo is the Microsoft service-oriented communication infrastructure and programming model. You can think of Indigo as the Microsoft runtime for services.

Designing and building good software is somewhat like wearing bifocals. It's important to focus on the big picture first and get that right before examining the finer details of the solution. Architecture is all about figuring out that big picture by separating the important parts of a solution from the less important parts. In service-oriented design, architecture has communication at its heart.

The change in focus makes sense because of the prominent role connectivity is now taking in applications. It's hard to think of an application today that doesn't talk to something else. Everyone and everything needs to be connected, including people and organizations and their devices and data centers. This means communication needs to be a primary design consideration, not an afterthought.

Service Orientation vs. Object Orientation

Why do we need a different approach to software development when object-oriented design and programming have served us so well for decades? In one sense, we don't: service orientation (SO) is a complement to object orientation (OO), not a *replacement* for it. Object orientation remains very important in software development, but objects aren't the best way to tie together the programs in a distributed solution.

The primary distinction between SO and OO is in how applications are viewed. In a solely object-oriented approach, an application is a tightly coupled collection of programs built from class libraries that have dependencies on each other. Figure 1-1 shows an object-oriented distributed solution. Parts of the system interact by calling distributed objects. This system is tightly coupled. For the parts to interact, they must all share a common type system.

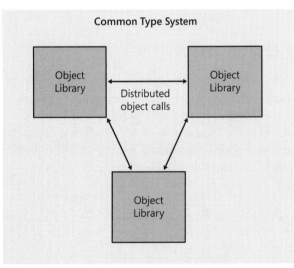

Figure 1-1   Object-oriented distributed solution

An SO application is a different entity entirely, composed of loosely coupled, autonomous service programs. Figure 1-2 shows a service-oriented distributed solution. The parts of the system communicate with messages. This system is loosely coupled. The parts can interact regardless of platform differences.

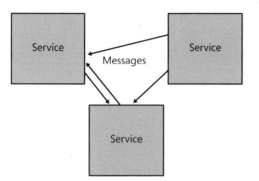

Figure 1-2   Service-oriented distributed solution

SO plus OO is a winning combination. You use message-oriented services to build a distributed solution and create those services with object orientation.

The Four Tenets of Service Orientation

There are four principles behind SO, known as the four tenets:

1. Boundaries are explicit.

2. Services are autonomous.

3. Services share schemas and contracts, not classes and types.

4. Compatibility is policy-based.

A true service-oriented solution follows all of these tenets faithfully. Let's see what they're all about.

Boundaries Are Explicit

In SO, services interact by sending messages across boundaries. Those boundaries are formal and explicit. No assumptions are made about what is behind boundaries, and this preserves flexibility in how services are implemented and deployed. Modeling services in this way allows them to be distributable, meaning they can be deployed anywhere, and composable, meaning they can call each other freely. Managing large, complex projects becomes simpler when formal boundaries are explicit.

Crossing a boundary can be expensive at times. If services interact across an implementation boundary, a trust domain boundary, or a geographic boundary, there might be a price to pay in terms of processing overhead, performance penalties, or communication costs. For this reason, SO urges discipline in what is exposed to a boundary. It's important to call services only when necessary and to do so as simply and efficiently as possible.

When you use objects instead of services to create a distributed system, little distinguishes a local object call from a remote object call: the whole idea of distributed objects is to make remote objects look like local objects. This can lead to an overuse of calls to distributed objects, where the expense is not obvious to a developer. In SO, you can't fall into this trap: accessing a service is distinctly different from accessing a local object.

The key take-aways from the "Boundaries Are Explicit" tenet are:

- Each service interaction is a boundary crossing.
- Crossing service boundaries can have costs.
- SO makes interaction formal, intentional, and explicit.

Services Are Autonomous

Distributed systems must tolerate change. Some systems are built in incremental stages, and services come online slowly over time. Any system might be subject to new requirements that result in the addition, upgrading, or removal of services. It should be possible to change a service without disrupting the overall system.

In SO, the topology of a distributed system is expected to change over time, and its services are designed to be deployed, managed, and versioned independently. There's no controlling authority to manage these changes, so services have to be robust enough to survive when other parts of the system are offline. Even though a service might depend on other services to perform its function, it should not fail when they are temporarily unavailable.

In a distributed object solution, the parts of an application often have to be deployed as an atomic unit, which can be terribly inconvenient in a production environment. Making a change to an application might require the entire solution to be rebuilt, redeployed, and restarted. Upgrading a server can require upgrading all clients. In SO, modifying a service's implementation doesn't cause a problem for the other services because they're loosely coupled.

The key take-aways from the "Services Are Autonomous" tenet are:

- The topology of a system evolves over time.
- There is no controlling authority.
- Services in a system are deployed, managed, and versioned independently.
- Services should not fail when dependent services are unavailable.

Share Schemas and Contracts, Not Classes and Types

ins implementation independence between services by being careful about what nge. Services use agreed-upon schemas to pass data and contracts to specify behav- don't pass classes or types. Services have no knowledge of each other's execution ent—and have no need to know—because the information they exchange is com- tform neutral.

st, in a distributed object solution, types and classes are passed across endpoints, e same type system on all parties. This makes for a tightly coupled system and holds hostage to the same execution environment.

should expose data and behavior relevant to their capabilities, not their implementa- ness actions and business documents are likely to remain stable. A service's interface qually stable if that's what it models.

The key take-aways of the "Services Share Schemas and Contracts" tenet are:

- Services interact solely on schemas for data and contracts for behaviors.
- Services do not combine data and behavior.
- Contracts and schemas remain stable over time.

Compatibility Is Policy-Based

Services don't just blindly access each other. They need to determine areas of compatibility and agree on how they will interact. Every service provides a **policy**, a machine-readable description of its capabilities and requirements. Policy allows services to find common ground.

Using policy allows the behavior of a service to be separated from the constraints for accessing the service. Imagine moving a service to a different environment where the parties allowed to access it are different. The policy changes to reflect this. The service behavior doesn't change at all.

When sophisticated services talk to each other, policy is used to determine the advanced capabilities that are mutual. When a very limited service is in the mix, policy is used to find a reduced set of capabilities that both services can support. Policy is what allows services designed according to SO principles to interoperate with traditional Web services, which have limited capabilities in comparison.

Key take-aways from the "Compatibility Is Policy-Based" tenet are:

- Policy separates the interactions the service can have from the constraints on those interactions.
- Service capabilities and requirements are expressed in terms of a policy expression.

The Benefits of Service Orientation

In a service-oriented solution, services are **loosely coupled**, which means all parties make very few assumptions about each other. Loosely coupled solutions have many compelling benefits:

- **Services are isolated.**   Changing the internals of one service doesn't force matching changes, rebuilding, or restarting of other services.

- **Services are location independent.**   Whether a service you need is on the same machine or halfway around the world, you access it in the same way.

- **Services are transport neutral, protocol neutral, and format neutral.**   The communication details between parties are flexible, not fixed.

- **Services are platform independent and implementation independent.**   A service doesn't need to know anything about another service's execution environment in order to interact with it.

- **Services are scale invariant.**   Services scale well in all directions. For example, a service can be scaled out by fronting it with a router service that distributes traffic among a farm of services.

- **Services can be time independent.**   If services make use of queue-based communication, they don't have to be online at the same time to interact.

- **Services can be address agnostic.**   If services employ a discovery mechanism, they can locate each other without any prior notion about where they reside.

- **Behavior is separated from constraints.**   Restricting, relocating, or outsourcing a service requires changes only in policy, not to the service itself.

Loosely coupled systems have excellent prospects for longevity. They are flexible and adaptive.

Services vs. Web Services

How do *services* compare to *Web services*? They are related but not identical. You can think of services as the successor to Web services. Like Web services, services make use of SOAP, XML, XSD, WSDL, and other standard protocols. Unlike Web services, services aren't limited to HTTP request-reply communication: they're free to use other transports and other message exchange patterns. Services are also more mature than Web services, providing enterprise-class features such as security, transactions, reliability, and performance. Services haven't forgotten their Web service roots, however. Through the use of policy, services and Web services can interoperate.

A Service-Oriented Example

Let's take a brief look at a service-oriented solution. Figure 1-3 shows a simplified customer support solution based on three primary services: a Help Desk service, a Dispatch service, and a Parts service.

When a customer reports a problem, the Help Desk service assigns the problem to a support representative. Most problems can be resolved over the phone by the help desk. If the help desk can't resolve a customer's problem, it escalates the problem to an on-site visit. A message is sent to the Dispatch service requesting a technician be sent to the customer.

If an on-site technician determines that a part needs to be replaced, a message is sent to the Parts service with a parts order. The Parts service sends a message to one of several vendors, depending on the specific part that has been ordered.

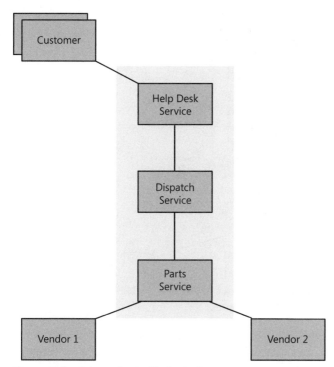

Figure 1-3   A hypothetical help desk system

Now let's see how this solution holds up as time goes by and conditions change. Over time, the volume of customer activity increases until it is no longer practical for the Help Desk service to handle the volume with a single server. Also during this time, company policy changes, requiring technicians to obtain approval from the Accounting department before placing orders for parts. Lastly, the number of parts vendors increases.

Figure 1-4 shows the solution after some time has passed with these changes addressed. The increased volume of customer activity has been accommodated by fronting the Help Desk service with a Routing service that distributes traffic among multiple instances of the Help Desk service. An Approval service has been inserted between the Dispatch service and the Parts service to approve or decline parts orders, with the same interface as the Parts service. The Parts service now works with a wider selection of vendors.

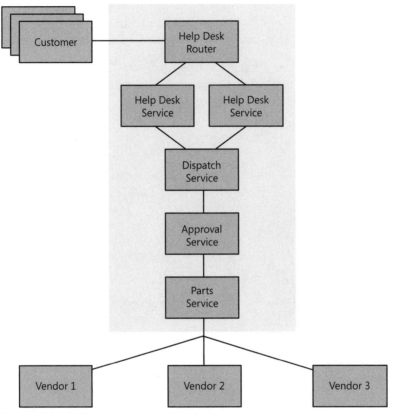

Figure 1-4   Help desk system with enhancements

Each of these changes was simple, isolated, and not disruptive to the rest of the system. Customers still send requests to what they believe is the Help Desk service, unaware that it is now actually a router. The Dispatch service still sends out parts orders in the same way, unaware that an Approval service is intercepting them. No other part of the system is aware—or affected by—the fact that the Parts service now supports additional vendors. Despite the improvements to the solution, the original services' interfaces and relationships haven't changed at all.

Let's imagine a more dramatic change-management problem in which changes to one service do affect other services. Perhaps it is no longer sufficient for the Approval service to match the Parts service; the Approval service really needs its own unique interface. If the Approval service changes its interface, the Dispatch service, which calls it, must also change. One approach is to upgrade the Dispatch and Approval services at the same time, so the rest of the solution is not disrupted. Another approach is to add a new interface to the Approval service but continue to support the original interface. This allows the services to be updated at different times: the updated Approval service is deployed first, and the updated Dispatch service follows.

We've seen that the fabric of a service-oriented solution allows for constant change without constant headache. Now that we have a good feel for the principles of SO and the flexible nature of services, it's time to turn to the subject of this book, Indigo.

Introducing Indigo

Indigo is the Microsoft platform for creating connected applications. It was designed from the ground up with SO in mind. The result is a powerful infrastructure for integrated communication and enterprise services with a simple programming model. Indigo has been described in several ways:

- Sockets for the 21st century
- The next generation of Web services
- The Microsoft runtime for services
- A single programming model for communication and enterprise features

Each of these characterizations is a valid way to think about Indigo.

Key Characteristics

Indigo was created with very specific goals in mind. There's a lot to Indigo, but it isn't some random collection of features. Every bit of functionality is there deliberately to give Indigo the characteristics described in the following sections.

Unified Programming Model

Indigo brings together a vast set of capabilities. Some of these capabilities are new, while others were formerly available as separate technologies. These capabilities are now accessible in a single unified programming model. The programming model gives developers one way of doing things. It's no longer necessary to switch gears as you go from one technology to another.

Rich Communication

Indigo provides a wealth of communication features. Developers have a lot to choose from: there are multiple transports, multiple message formats, and multiple messaging patterns. Developers can thus use the right messaging tools for the right job.

Broad Interoperability

Interoperability is *the* fundamental characteristic of Indigo. Indigo's communication is fully platform independent and its services are self-describing. All Indigo messages are SOAP envelopes containing XML payloads. Indigo follows the Web Services Architecture and uses established standards in its communication, including the WS-* protocols. Service descriptions are expressed using WSDL, XSD, WS-Policy, and WS-MetaExchange.

Enterprise-Ready Features

In the past, interoperability has often come at the expense of features important to enterprises. The benefits of ubiquitous Web services had to be weighed against the consequences of compromised security, transactions, reliability, and performance. Indigo overcomes this problem, providing interoperability and enterprise-strength features at the same time. Services can coordinate many sophisticated activities through the use of Web Service Architecture standards, including security, transactions, and reliable messaging. These standards are composable, allowing them to be intermixed. Indigo makes use of them as needed based on what your program is doing.

Transport, Protocol, and Format Neutrality

Indigo is transport neutral, protocol neutral, and format neutral. For example, services are free to make use of HTTP, TCP, named pipes, and any other transport mechanisms for which there is an implementation. Developers are free to add new transport providers. These details never affect the way you write your services. Indigo isolates your program code from communication specifics. This allows services to support a spectrum of communication methods without any extra work on your part.

Scale Invariance

Services written with Indigo are scale invariant. Services can scale up, out, down, and in. Services can scale *up* through deployment on more powerful servers, where Indigo can leverage more resources. Services can scale *out* through routing and server farms, distributing traffic to multiple instances of services. Services can scale *down* by interacting with service-oriented devices such as printers and cameras. Services can scale *in* using efficient cross-process transports. Scale invariance maximizes the deployment options for your application.

Architecture

The Indigo architecture is depicted in Figure 1-5. Services describe themselves at the contract layer. The service runtime layer loads and runs services, managing many behaviors such as instancing and concurrency. The messaging layer provides the communication infrastructure, which includes various composable communication channels for transport, reliable messaging, security, and queuing. The activation and hosting layer allows services to run in a variety of environments, ranging from a self-hosted EXE to automatic activation and hosting by Microsoft Internet Information Services (IIS).

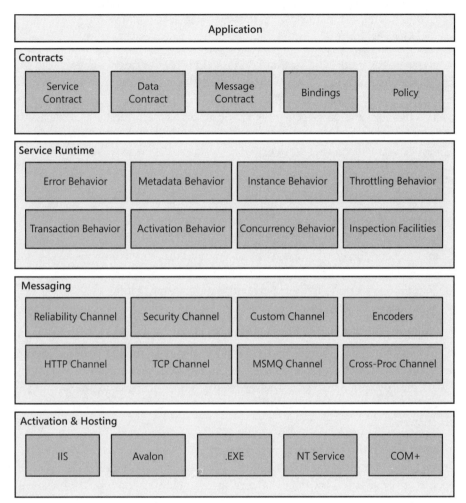

Figure 1-5   Indigo architecture

This architecture permits programmers to work at several levels. High-level programming leverages the service runtime and doesn't require developers to directly work with messages at all, unless they want to. At the other end of the spectrum, developers can program to the messaging layer and take charge of communication activities.

A Tour of Indigo's Capabilities

It's time to get acquainted with Indigo's primary features.

The Programming Model

Indigo makes service programming easy. Developers can take a "code-first" or "contract-first" approach to development. Tools assist development by generating code from service descriptions and vice versa.

The programming model allows common tasks to be performed with very little code yet allows developers full control when they want it. Although there are hundreds of classes in the complete object model, developers primarily work with a few high-level objects such as services, channels, and messages. Indigo code is compact, easy to write, and easy to understand. For example, in the following code fragment, notice how little code it takes to initiate communication with another service.

```
TradingSystemProxy proxy = new TradingSystemProxy();
price = proxy.GetQuote(symbol);
```

Programming Methods   The programming model offers developers three methods for writing programs: declarative programming using attributes, imperative programming using code and objects, and configuration-based programming through application configuration file settings. Developers typically declare contracts and service behaviors using attributes; configure endpoints, security, and management features using .config files; and implement service operations in code.

Several levels of programming are possible. **Typed services** contain service operations that are similar to functions, with parameters and return values that might be simple or complex data types. **Untyped services** contain service operations that accept and return messages. Developers work directly with messages at this level. Programming against the **messaging layer** is the lowest level of all, giving developers precise control over communication activities such as creating channels.

The Service Model   The programming model includes a collection of declarative attributes that can be used in place of explicit code, known as the **service model**. The service model gives you attribute-based control over many areas, including communication, security, transactions, instancing, and error handling. To get a sense for this, take a look at the following code fragment, in which a service contract specifies details about session, communication, and transaction behavior through the use of attributes.

```
[ServiceContract(Session=true)]
[ServiceBehavior(InstanceMode=InstanceMode.PrivateSession)]
public class MyService
{
    [OperationContract(IsOneWay=false)]
    [OperationBehavior(AutoEnlistTransaction=true)]
    string DebitAccount(string accountNo, double amount)
    {
        ...
    }
}
```

Many service model capabilities can also be specified as configuration settings, allowing deployment-time decisions to be made about communication, security, and run-time behavior. The Service Model allows you to focus on what's important: your application. In an Indigo program, most of the code will be your application code.

Communication

Indigo communication can be synchronous or asynchronous and one-way or two-way and can use datagram, duplex, or request-reply messaging patterns. The transport for communication can be HTTP, TCP, or named pipes (for cross-process communication). It is possible to add new transports by writing a transport provider.

Indigo programs exchange messages. A message can contain any digital information, from a simple string to a business data structure to video content. Messages are represented in memory as SOAP envelopes and can be rendered in text, binary, or Message Transmission Optimization Mechanism (MTOM) format for transmission. Messages can be buffered (transferred in entirety) or streamed.

Developers specify their communication, reliability, and security requirements (called *bindings*), and Indigo builds the appropriate types of communication channels in response. Over a dozen pre-defined "bindings" define the combinations needed for common scenarios, but developers are free to create their own custom bindings. Bindings can be specified in code or configuration files.

Reliable Sessions

On top of the core communication capabilities, a feature known as reliable sessions provides robust messaging, with automatic retry and recovery if communication is disrupted. With reliable sessions, your program can determine for sure whether messages make it to their destinations successfully. Developers specify the assurances they need, such as exactly-once, in-order delivery. Reliable sessions also provide the mechanics for clients and services to maintain sessions.

Queuing

Queuing provides first-in/first-out (FIFO) messaging. Queuing allows programs to work with a pull model rather than a push model. The queuing service integrates with Microsoft Message Queue (MSMQ). Queuing allows messages to be stored durably—an important capability for building reliable, recoverable messaging solutions. Queuing also allows programs to be time independent of each other in their communication.

Run-Time Behaviors

The service runtime manages the execution of services. Developers can specify run-time behaviors through attributes or configuration settings. Instancing behavior determines how many instances of a service are created for clients (for example, one per client session). Concurrency behavior controls thread synchronization. For example, a service can indicate that its instances are not thread-safe. Throttling behavior allows you to put limits on the number of connections, sessions, and threads. Error handling behaviors control how errors are handled and reported to clients.

Serialization

Even though service orientation discourages the use of objects as a way to connect programs, object-oriented programming remains important to developers. Indigo treats objects as first-class citizens. Serialization converts objects to and from XML. Serialization honors the "no classes and types" tenet of service orientation by converting objects to XML schema for transmission. Deserialization performs the reverse steps on the receiving side. When typed services are accessed, the serialization and deserialization of parameters and return values is completely automatic. Developers can also explicitly perform serialization on demand in code.

Security

Indigo provides comprehensive security features. These include client authentication, server authentication, message integrity, message confidentiality, replay detection, and role-based access control. Message integrity ensures that messages aren't tampered with. Message confidentiality makes sure that only authorized parties can read the messages. Replay detection prevents a hacker from capturing and retransmitting messages. Multiple security mechanisms are supported, including X.509 and integrated Windows security (Kerberos/NTLM).

Services indicate their security needs through declarative attributes, code, or configuration settings. Security environment information such as certificate locations is determined at runtime through configuration files. For common security configurations, developers can take advantage of turnkey security by specifying predefined bindings for common scenarios.

Transactions

Transactions ensure that related operations occur as an atomic unit, in which everything succeeds or everything fails. Indigo provides a centralized transaction system. In the past, transaction technologies were available for database processing and components, but there were too many ways of doing things. Indigo provides a single transaction system that supports traditional transactional work, such as database processing and transacted communication.

The programming model makes transactions easy to use. Developers create or enlist in transaction scopes to group operations transactionally. The following code fragment shows the use of a transaction around communication with two services.

```
using (TransactionScope scope = new TransactionScope())
{
    mortgageService.SubmitMortgageApplication(mortgageApp);
    insuranceService.SubmitInsuranceApplication(insuranceApp);
    scope.Complete();
}
```

Services can flow transactions to other services. This allows enterprises to perform transactional work across platforms.

Hosting

Indigo services can be hosted in many environments, including Windows Forms applications, console applications, and Windows service applications (also called Windows NT Services). They can also be hosted by Microsoft Internet Information Services (IIS).

Hosting in IIS allows services to be registered for automatic activation the first time a client attempts to access them. When a message arrives for a service that is not already running, it is launched automatically. IIS hosting also provides a reliable environment for services. Services are restarted if they enter an unhealthy state. If a service is updated, IIS hosting brings the new version online gracefully.

Summary

Modern applications are connected applications. Service orientation (SO) treats connected applications as a cooperating set of message-oriented programs called services. Service-oriented solutions are loosely coupled, which provides many benefits. The four tenets of SO are:

1. Boundaries are explicit.
2. Services are autonomous.
3. Services share schemas and contracts, not classes and types.
4. Compatibility is policy-based.

Services expose service descriptions in WSDL and a collection of endpoints. Services contain contracts, bindings, and endpoints. Service contracts define the operations a service can perform. Bindings define how a service communicates with the outside world. Endpoints define the access points to a service.

Indigo is the Microsoft platform for creating connected applications and is based on SO. Its key characteristics are a unified programming model, rich communication, broad interoperability, enterprise-strength features, communication neutrality, and scale invariance.

Indigo's primary feature areas are its programming model, the service model, communication, reliable sessions, queuing, run-time behaviors, serialization, security, and transactions. These features collaborate to give Indigo its key characteristics.

In Chapter 2, we'll cover the fundamental concepts in Indigo.

Chapter 2

Fundamental Concepts

We cannot live only for ourselves. A thousand fibers connect us with our fellow men; and among those fibers, as sympathetic threads, our actions run as courses, and they come back to us as effects.

—Herman Melville

The first step in learning Indigo is to understand the fundamental concepts presented in this chapter. They will give you the context to make sense of Indigo's features, programming model, and terminology.

After completing this chapter, you will:

- Understand the anatomy of services and the types of messaging programs that can be created.
- Be familiar with the structure of messages and the available message exchange patterns.
- Know the purpose of channel stacks, transports, encodings, reliable sessions, and security.
- Understand levels of interoperability and the roles of contracts, bindings, and end-points.
- Be familiar with the types of service behaviors available at runtime.

Types of Messaging Programs

Indigo programs communicate through the exchange of messages. There are three distinct kinds of messaging programs:

- **Clients**   Programs that initiate messages
- **Services**   Programs that respond to messages
- **Intermediaries**   Programs that are waypoints for messages en route

Each of these program types has a different role, is programmed somewhat differently, and can take advantage of unique features in Indigo. The typical application developer will write clients and services, not intermediaries.

One other kind of program is worth mentioning: extensions to Indigo. Indigo contains a number of extensibility points that allow developers to add such things as new transports or custom security mechanisms. Extensions are not covered in this book.

> **Important**   Although all communication takes place using messages, your programs do not have to work directly with messages. For example, a client can access a service's operations by calling its "methods," passing parameters to functions, and receiving results. Indigo developers work directly with messages only if they specifically want to work at that level.

Clients

Clients are programs that initiate messaging. A client sends a message to a service program to trigger some processing. Figure 2-1 shows a client sending a message to a service. When the service receives the message, it takes some action.

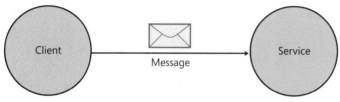

Figure 2-1   A client and a service

Clients can also receive messages. For example, a service might send a reply back to a client in response to a request. Because they are initiators, clients are very much in control of their messaging activity. A client determines which services it connects to and when it communicates with them.

Services

Services are programs that react to messages. An incoming message causes code to execute, performing some behavior. That behavior might include more messaging, such as sending a reply back to the source of the incoming message. Due to their passive nature, services aren't in control of communication the way clients are. A service can't determine in advance which clients will attempt communication, when that communication will occur, or what the volume of communication will be.

Services with Multiple Clients

Typically, a service is accessed by multiple clients. Well-used services with many clients can be hosted on servers to provide adequate capacity. A service is likely to have a longer lifetime, whereas clients are likely to have shorter lifetimes. Figure 2-2 shows a service interacting with multiple clients, accepting incoming messages, and responding with outgoing messages. Like a Web server, a service can maintain sessions for clients.

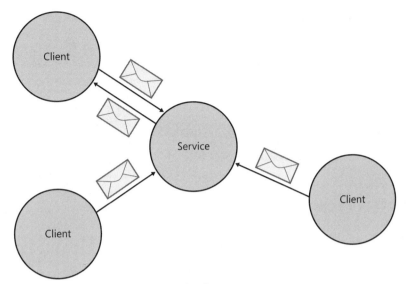

Figure 2-2   A service with multiple clients

Chains of Services

A service can also be a client at the same time. As a service reacts to an incoming message, it can send outgoing messages to other services, acting as a client. Figure 2-3 shows a chain of services communicating. When program A sends a message to program B, part of program B's response behavior is to send a message to program C. A is clearly a client, and C is clearly a service. B has the characteristics of both a service and a client.

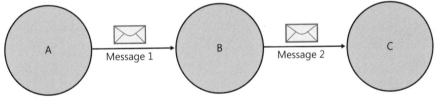

Figure 2-3   A chain of services

Messaging across a chain of services can have a cascading effect. For example, consider an emergency response service that sends dispatch messages to fire, police, and medical departments, which in turn perform additional messaging within their organizations to respond to an emergency. The original single-client message reporting the incident results in many messages, a great deal of physical activity, and the saving of lives!

Intermediaries

The communication between a client and a service might pass through another program, called an **intermediary**. An intermediary is invisible to the clients and the services it sits between. Intermediaries can perform many useful tasks, including the following:

- Acting as a firewall, preventing an unwanted message from reaching a service

- Routing a message to one of several destination services

- Acting as a gateway, bridging between two networks

- Monitoring activity

Figure 2-4 shows an intermediary between a client and a service. The intermediary is part of the communication path, but neither the client nor the service needs to be aware of it. There can be multiple intermediaries in a message path.

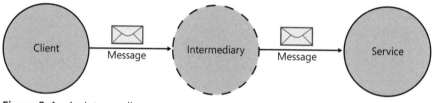

Figure 2-4   An intermediary

Intermediaries have to follow some rules. They are not message consumers—they're merely waypoints for messages en route to their destinations. Although there might be some information in a message that intermediaries look for or modify, the body of the message—the payload—is reserved for the ultimate recipient. Consider a secure message with an encrypted payload. The message remains encrypted as it passes through intermediaries, and only the final recipient can access the decrypted payload.

Logically speaking, a message traveling from a sender to a receiver is a single communication, even though there might be many message transfers across intermediaries along the way. Don't confuse an intermediary with a service that is also a client. In Figure 2-3, shown earlier, service B consumed a message and then sent a new message to service C. In Figure 2-4, the same message is passed along by the intermediary.

Messages

Indigo programs of all kinds—clients, services, or intermediaries—communicate through the exchange of **messages**. We need to understand some things about messages in order to use them effectively.

Structure of a Message

Figure 2-5 shows the structure of a message. The outer **envelope** contains the two significant parts of a message: **headers** and a **body**. The body is the payload of the message and is usually created and consumed by clients or services that application developers write. The headers section is a collection of information items, each called a header, which can be used by application developers as well as messaging infrastructures. A message always has one body but might have any number of headers.

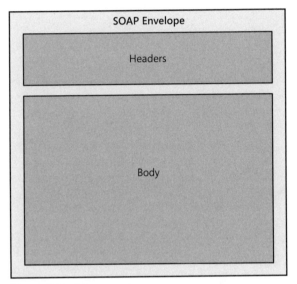

Figure 2-5   Message structure

All Indigo messages are represented as XML, specifically SOAP envelopes (version 1.1 or 1.2) containing XML Infosets. Although SOAP is often associated with textual XML and HTTP, you are not constrained to one format or one transmission method for messages. Indigo is format and transport neutral, capable of formatting SOAP messages in several encodings (text, binary, or Message Transmission Optimization Mechanism [MTOM]) and transmitting them over a variety of transports (HTTP, TCP, MSMQ, and named pipes).

Let's look at some actual Indigo messages. Imagine you have a client program accessing a calculator service. After establishing a connection to the service, the client calls an operation named *Add* with two double parameters and receives back a double result using the following code:

```
double result = proxy.Add(100.00D, 15.99D);
```

Listing 2-1 shows the request message that is sent from the client to the service.

Listing 2-1   Sample Request Message

```
<s:Envelope xmlns:s="http://www.w3.org/2003/05/soap-envelope"
    xmlns:a="http://schemas.xmlsoap.org/ws/2004/08/addressing">
  <s:Header>
    <a:Action s:mustUnderstand="1">http://tempuri.org/ISampleContract/Add
        </a:Action>
    <a:MessageID>uuid:1966fac9-6145-4583-a2a3-8bc106c50cd8;id=0</a:MessageID>
    <a:To s:mustUnderstand="1">http://localhost:8000/Selfhost/</a:To>
    <a:ReplyTo>
      <a:Address>http://schemas.xmlsoap.org/ws/2004/08/addressing/role/anonymous
          </a:Address>
    </a:ReplyTo>
  </s:Header>
  <s:Body>
    <Add xmlns="http://tempuri.org/">
      <n1>100</n1>
      <n2>15.99</n2>
    </Add>
  </s:Body>
</s:Envelope>
```

This particular message is quite small. There is one header, identifying the service operation
to be performed, and a simple payload, containing the two double parameters for the *Add*
operation.

The service responds with the reply message shown in Listing 2-2.

Listing 2-2   Sample Reply Message

```
<s:Envelope xmlns:a="http://schemas.xmlsoap.org/ws/2004/08/addressing"
    xmlns:s="http://www.w3.org/2003/05/soap-envelope">
  <s:Header>
    <a:Action s:mustUnderstand="1">http://tempuri.org/ISampleContract/AddResponse
        </a:Action>
  </s:Header>
  <s:Body>
    <AddResponse xmlns="http://tempuri.org/">
      <AddResult>115.99</AddResult>
    </AddResponse>
  </s:Body>
</s:Envelope>
```

The reply message is equally simple and straightforward. The body contains the result from
the *Add* operation.

Messaging Patterns

Programs can exchange messages in three basic patterns:

- **Simplex**   One-way messaging
- **Duplex**   Asynchronous two-way messaging
- **Request-reply**   Synchronous two-way messaging

More elaborate messaging patterns can be built from these intrinsic types. For example, it's not difficult to implement list-based publish-subscribe messaging using duplex messaging and a small amount of custom code.

Simplex

The simplest message pattern is **simplex**: one-way messaging in which single messages called **datagrams** are sent between programs. Figure 2-6 shows a client sending a datagram to a service.

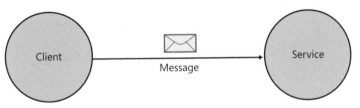

Figure 2-6   Simplex communication

Simplex communication permits a "fire-and-forget" style of messaging. This is the loosest, most asynchronous form of messaging. Fire-and-forget communication allows for the possibility of "write-only" services, which are kind of like black holes: they accept messages that come their way but generate no messages themselves.

Duplex

The **duplex** messaging pattern is two-way communication in which the two sides can be communicating freely in either direction without synchronization of any kind. Figure 2-7 shows a client and a service in duplex communication.

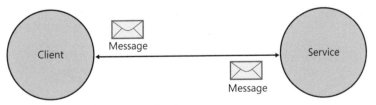

Figure 2-7   Duplex communication

An example of duplex communication is a remotely controlled robotic vehicle. Commands are sent to the vehicle to make it do something, such as move forward or make a turn. The vehicle communicates in the other direction to report its position as it changes.

Request-Reply

Two-way communication in which a request is paired with a reply is the **request-reply** messaging pattern. A client makes a request and waits for a reply. Figure 2-8 shows a client and a service communicating in request-reply fashion.

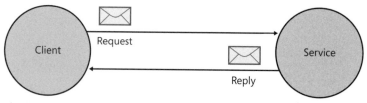

Figure 2-8   Request-reply communication

The request-reply pattern is familiar to just about everybody, thanks to the World Wide Web. Many traditional communication technologies are based on request-reply, including remote procedure calls and distributed objects. An example of request-reply communication is submitting an order to a business, in which the request message is the order and the reply is a confirmation or rejection of the order.

Channels

Channels are the highways over which messages travel. Before two programs can exchange messages, a channel must be established between them. The base Indigo channel types implement simplex input, simplex output, duplex, and request-reply messaging patterns. A client creates a channel to a service endpoint, specifying the type of channel desired and an address. If a service is listening at that same address, a channel can be established and messaging can take place. Once communication is completed, the channel can be torn down. Figure 2-9 is a sequence diagram showing the creation, use, and destruction of a request-reply channel.

Note that the channel is not actually established until the first message is sent. The first message from client to service is special in a number of ways: the channel is actually established at this time, and any negotiation needed for security features also takes place. For these reasons, the first message a client sends to a service can take longer to process than subsequent messages.

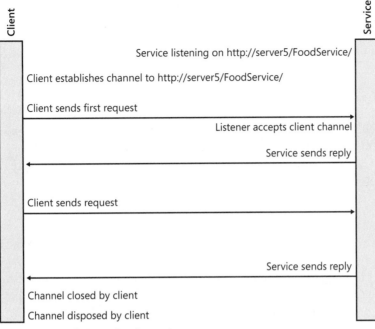

Figure 2-9 Lifetime of a channel

Tip A channel isn't really established until the first message is sent. If it's important to test communication up front before sending production messages, you can build a Ping operation into your service so that the client has a way to establish communication, verify the availability of a service, and negotiate security early on.

Channel Stacks

Channels are best thought of as pipelines: a message is sent on one end of the pipe and pops out of the other end. Different kinds of pipes can be connected to form **channel stacks**. When an Indigo program specifies some combination of needed features, the requested channel stack is created by combining the appropriate mix of channels. Figure 2-10 shows a channel stack. In this case, a request-reply channel has been combined with a binary message encoder, a TCP transport channel, a reliable sessions channel, and a Microsoft Windows security channel. The resulting channel stack provides this composed behavior but can be treated as an atomic unit.

Figure 2-10 Channel stack

Not every possible combination of channel stack features can be used with all messaging patterns. For example, duplex communication is not possible without a reliable session channel.

Let's visit some of the key features that can be composed to form a channel stack.

Transports

Transports are the method of communication a channel uses. The four transports built into Indigo are HTTP, TCP, MSMQ, and named pipes. It's possible to extend this list by writing a custom transport provider. Some transports have secure editions, such as HTTPS. The named pipes transport is intended for cross-process communication and can't be used to communicate across machines.

Encodings

Messages can be encoded over the wire in text, binary, or MTOM format. It's possible to extend this list by writing a custom message encoder. Text encoding is the least efficient but is highly interoperable. Binary encoding is more efficient but requires Microsoft .NET platforms on both ends of the conversation. MTOM uses attachments to provide highly optimized messages that are interoperable with other platforms that also support MTOM.

Security

Security features can include transport security, such as that provided by HTTPS and TCPS. There is also SOAP message security. Message security can provide authorization, authentication, auditing, message confidentiality, message integrity, and replay detection. Several security mechanisms are available, including X.509 security, Windows NTLM/Kerberos security, and username/password authentication. Message security is based on secure tokens. It's possible to add new security implementations by writing extensions such as a custom token provider.

Reliable Sessions

Reliable session channels provide two important capabilities, **reliable messaging** and **sessions**. Reliable messaging retries communication in the face of failure and provides delivery assurances, such as messages arriving in order. Sessions allow services to maintain state for clients over a series of interactions. These features are provided at the SOAP message level, which allows them to be used even if an underlying transport doesn't support reliability or sessions.

Messaging Patterns

The messaging patterns available depend on how a channel stack is constructed. The three core patterns—simplex, duplex, and request-reply—aren't all necessarily available. For example, the MSMQ transport doesn't support request-reply communication.

Interoperability

The ingredients in a channel stack affect how interoperable the channel stack is with other platforms. For example, using a .NET binary format makes communication very efficient, but this choice reduces interoperability with other platforms. There are several levels of interoperability to consider:

- **Basic Profile interoperability**   Represents the most interoperable mode for services. Compliance with the WS-I Basic Profile allows Indigo programs to communicate with first-generation Web services. This broad interoperability comes at a price: the other party can't be assumed to support reliable messaging, security, or transactions.

- **WS-* interoperability**   Targets interoperability with other platforms that also use the next-generation WS-* protocols. Programs can do more than just communicate—they can also coordinate reliability, security, and transactions.

- **.NET interoperability**   Takes advantage of .NET platforms on both ends of communication. Highly performant features such as binary message encoding can be used.

- **MSMQ interoperability**   Allows an Indigo program to interoperate with a non-Indigo deployment of MSMQ.

Anatomy of Services

To understand the make-up of services, we'll start by examining what a service exposes externally, and then we'll look under the hood.

Services from the Outside

Figure 2-11 shows the external view of a service. A service exposes a **service description** and a collection of **endpoints**. The service description tells what the service can do and how it can be accessed. The endpoints are the access points to the service.

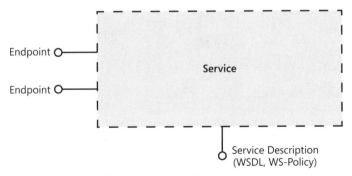

Figure 2-11   Outside view of a service

Service Descriptions

A service description provides essential information about how the service can be used. Service descriptions are expressed and communicated using several standards. This keeps service descriptions compatible with first-generation Web services while allowing more sophisticated descriptions for modern services.

- **Web Services Description Language (WSDL)**   The data format used to describe what a service can do, how a service is to be accessed, and where the service is located.

- **XML Schema (XSD)**   The data format used to describe complex data structures passed in messages.

- **WS-Policy**   The data format used to describe a service's **policies**. Policies can describe such things as the type of security mechanisms that must be satisfied, schedules of availability, and the quality of service provided.

- **WS-Metadata Exchange (or WS-MEX)**   The access protocol for asking a service to describe itself. Using WS-MEX, a client can ask a service for its WSDL and WS-Policy metadata.

Listing 2-3 shows a WSDL service description for a stock quote service.

Listing 2-3   WSDL Service Description

```xml
<?xml version="1.0"?>
<definitions name="StockQuote" targetNamespace="http://example.com/stockquote.wsdl"
        xmlns:tns="http://example.com/stockquote.wsdl"
        xmlns:xsd1="http://example.com/stockquote.xsd"
        xmlns:soap="http://schemas.xmlsoap.org/wsdl/soap/"
        xmlns="http://schemas.xmlsoap.org/wsdl/">

    <types>
        <schema targetNamespace="http://example.com/stockquote.xsd"
                xmlns="http://www.w3.org/2000/10/XMLSchema">
          <element name="TradePriceRequest">
            <complexType>
                <all>
                    <element name="tickerSymbol" type="string"/>
                </all>
            </complexType>
          </element>
          <element name="TradePrice">
            <complexType>
                <all>
                    <element name="price" type="float"/>
                </all>
            </complexType>
          </element>
        </schema>
    </types>
```

```
<message name="GetLastTradePriceInput">
    <part name="body" element="xsd1:TradePriceRequest"/>
</message>

<message name="GetLastTradePriceOutput">
    <part name="body" element="xsd1:TradePrice"/>
</message>

<portType name="StockQuotePortType">
    <operation name="GetLastTradePrice">
        <input message="tns:GetLastTradePriceInput"/>
        <output message="tns:GetLastTradePriceOutput"/>
    </operation>
</portType>

<binding name="StockQuoteSoapBinding" type="tns:StockQuotePortType">
    <soap:binding style="document"
        transport="http://schemas.xmlsoap.org/soap/http"/>
    <operation name="GetLastTradePrice">
        <soap:operation soapAction="http://example.com/GetLastTradePrice"/>
        <input>
            <soap:body use="literal"/>
        </input>
        <output>
            <soap:body use="literal"/>
        </output>
    </operation>
</binding>

<service name="StockQuoteService">
    <documentation>My first service</documentation>
    <port name="StockQuotePort" binding="tns:StockQuoteBinding">
        <soap:address location="http://example.com/stockquote"/>
    </port>
</service>

</definitions>
```

Services from the Inside

Let's go inside a service to see how it is structured. Figure 2-12 shows a cross-section of a service. Services contain endpoints, bindings, contracts, and implementation code. **Contracts** describe a service's behavior, structures, or message format. **Bindings** describe how a service is accessed. **Endpoints** associate a contract and a binding with an address.

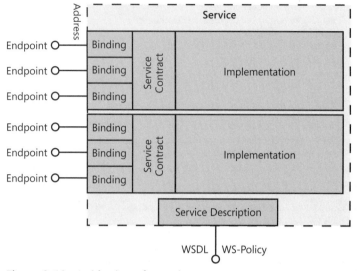

Figure 2-12   Inside view of a service

Contracts

There are three kinds of contracts in Indigo services: service contracts, data contracts, and message contracts.

- **Service contracts**   A service contract describes what a service does. Service contracts have names and define a set of related actions called **service operations**. For example, a service contract for a travel service might be named *TravelService* and define *Search-Flights*, *ReserveSeats*, and *MakePayment* service operations. A service must contain at least one service contract and might contain more than one. Services also contain the code that implements their service contracts.

  Service contracts map easily to object-oriented constructs. Service contracts are much like interfaces. The service operations in a service contract have names, can accept parameters, and can return results, much like methods can. The implementation code for a service contract is a class implementing an interface.

- **Data contracts**   Data contracts define custom data structures. If you wanted to pass a *PurchaseOrder* structure to a service operation, you could use a data contract to define its structure. In case you're wondering why you can't just pass an object to a service operation, recall that passing a type would violate the tenets of service orientation. With data contracts, your data can be passed to and from services in XML Schema form.

- **Message contracts**   Message contracts define the message formats passed to and from service operations. When you need to change where things go in a message, message contracts provide fine control. For example, data that normally goes in the body of a message can be reassigned to a header using a message contract.

Bindings

Bindings describe how a service communicates with the outside world. They specify such details as transport method, encoding format, reliability requirements, and security requirements. Indigo creates a channel stack to satisfy the binding you want to use. A service contract must be related to at least one binding in order to be accessible and can be related to multiple bindings.

Indigo includes nine predefined standard bindings that cover common scenarios. If none of these fits your needs, you can create your own custom binding with the mix of functionality you need. Table 2-1 shows the standard bindings.

Table 2-1   Standard Bindings

Binding Name	Interop	Transport	Encoding	Secure	Sessions	Reliable	Transactions	Messaging Patterns
BasicProfile-Binding	Basic Profile	HTTP or HTTPS	Text	Yes	No	No	No	Simplex, Request-Reply
WSProfileBinding	WS-*	HTTP or HTTPS	Text or MTOM	Yes	Yes	Yes	Yes	Simplex, Request-Reply
WSProfileDual-HttpBinding	WS-*	HTTP	Text or MTOM	Yes	Yes	Yes	Yes	Simplex, Request-Reply, Duplex
NetProfileTcp-Binding	.Net	TCP	Binary	Yes	Yes	Yes	Yes	Simplex, Request-Reply, Duplex
NetProfileDual-TcpBinding	.Net	TCP	Binary	Yes	Yes	Yes	Yes	Simplex, Request-Reply, Duplex
NetProfile-NamedPipe-Binding	.Net	Named pipe	Binary	Yes	Yes	Yes	Yes	Simplex, Request-Reply, Duplex
NetProfileMsmq-Binding	.Net	MSMQ	Binary	Yes	Yes	Yes	Yes	Simplex, Duplex
Msmq-Integration-Binding	MSMQ	MSMQ	Text	No	Yes	Yes	Yes	Simplex
Intermediary-Binding	n/a	HTTP, TCP, or named pipe	n/a	n/a	n/a	n/a	n/a	n/a

Bindings are described in more detail in Chapter 4.

Endpoints

Endpoints describe where a service is, associating an address with a service contract and binding. A service must provide at least one endpoint in order to be accessible and can have multiple endpoints.

> **Tip**   A useful mnemonic for remembering the elements of an endpoint is **ABC: A**ddress, **B**inding, and **C**ontract.

The simplest possible service has a single endpoint, a single service contract, and a single binding. A complex service can contain multiple endpoints, service contracts, and bindings. An endpoint's address and binding must be unique, but its service contract can be shared by more than one endpoint. Figure 2-13 shows a service with four endpoints.

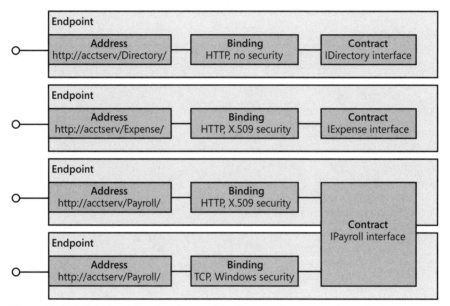

Figure 2-13   Relationship of addresses, bindings, and contracts in endpoints

In this example, endpoints allow a single service to offer a range of functions and access methods: directory services without security, expense services over HTTP with X.509 security, and payroll services with two access methods—HTTP with X.509 security as well as TCP with Windows security. Notice that the second and third endpoints share the same kind of binding but have different service contracts. Conversely, the third and fourth endpoints share the same service contract but have different bindings.

In addition to providing the endpoints for accessing its operations, a service can also provide another kind of endpoint whose purpose is to describe the service: a MEX (metadata exchange) endpoint. When a MEX endpoint is accessed, it returns metadata describing the service. MEX endpoints are provided automatically for services with HTTP endpoints.

Addresses

Service endpoints are exposed through addresses. The format of an endpoint address is affected by several factors, including the transport in use and whether Microsoft Internet Information Services (IIS) is helping to host the service. Table 2-2 shows the address formats used for different transports and sample addresses.

Table 2-2   Address Formats

Transport	Prefix	Address Form	Example
HTTP	http	*server*[:*port*]/*path*/	http://www.adventure-works.com:8000/SkiReport/
TCP	net.tcp	*server*[:*port*]/*path*	net.tcp://www.adventure-works.com:9000/SkiReport/
Named pipes	net.pipe	*server*/*path*/	net.pipe://localhost/SkiReport/
MSMQ	net.msmq	*server*/*path*/	net.msmq://localhost/private$/SkiReport/

If a service is hosted in IIS, addressing follows a different form. Services hosted in IIS use virtual directories that have addresses of the form *prefix://server/virtual-directory/svc-file*, as in *http://www.adventure-works.com/SkiReport/report.svc*. An .svc file contains information about the service, including source code or a reference to compiled code.

Addresses are described in more detail in Chapter 4.

Relating Service Concepts to WSDL

Many of the service concepts just presented directly correlate to Web Services Description Language (WSDL) but with different terminology. Table 2-3 relates Indigo service concepts to WSDL element names.

Table 2-3   Service Concepts and WSDL Elements

Service Concept	WSDL Element
Service contract	*<portType>*
Message contract	*<message>*
Data contract	*<type>*
Operation	*<operation>*
Binding	*<binding>*
Endpoint	*<port>*

Services at Runtime

When an Indigo service executes, the service description and implementation code are turned into a running common language runtime (CLR) instance. As messages are received by the service, they are dispatched to instances of the service implementation.

Figure 2-14 shows how a service is represented at runtime. The master runtime object for a service is called a *ServiceHost*. Via *ServiceHost*, the service's description, behaviors, endpoints, and runtime instances can be accessed. Some aspects of a service can be dynamically changed at runtime, such as adding an additional endpoint.

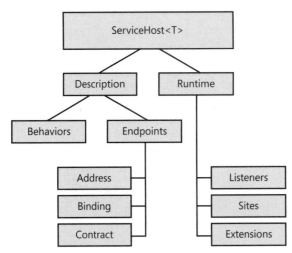

Figure 2-14   Runtime representation of a service

A service can be in any of six states at runtime: Created, Opening, Opened, Closing, Closed, or Faulted.

Service Behaviors

A service can execute code using the following kinds of runtime behaviors:

- **Instancing**   Instancing determines how instances of the service implementation class are created. The four instancing modes are **singleton** (one instance handling all clients), **per call** (one instance per service operation called), **private session** (one instance per client session), and **shared session** (one instance per session, but clients can share sessions).

- **Concurrency**   Concurrency controls how threads and instances relate. A developer can write a service implementation class to be thread safe or can require only one thread at a time to access the instance. The three concurrency modes are **single** (only one thread at a time accesses an instance), **multiple** (multiple threads can access an instance at the same time), and **reentrant** (threads can call into each other).

- **Throttling**   Throttling sets a limit on the number of messages, instances, or threads a service can process simultaneously. This makes it possible to establish an upper limit on resource consumption.

- **Error handling**   When an error occurs in a service, a developer can process the error directly or let it be handled by the framework. Developers can also control whether errors are reported back to the client.

- **Metadata**   Services can be self-describing, providing metadata on request.

- **Lifetime**   Services can control the lifetime (start and end) of client sessions by specifying some service operations as initiating a session and some as terminating a session.

- **Security**   Services can specify security behaviors, which can include message confidentiality, message integrity, authentication, authorization, auditing, and replay detection. Security can be realized via X.509, user/password, Kerberos, SAML, XrML, or custom security implementations. You can find out more about security behaviors in Chapter 8.

- **Transactions**   A client can flow a transaction to a service so that the service can participate in the transaction. A developer controls whether a service will accept a transaction. The client controls the scope and lifetime of the transaction.

Exercise: Designing a Service

We won't start writing program code until the next chapter, but it's useful to bring all of this information together and go through the exercise of designing a simple service. In this exercise, we will design a pizza-ordering service for Contoso, Ltd., a local pizzeria that likes to stay on the cutting edge of technology. Customers will order a series of food items for pick-up or delivery and confirm their order. Delivery orders will be accepted only from customers within 5 miles of the pizza shop, and customers will pay when they receive their pizza. We're only designing the service in this exercise, not implementing it.

Service Contract Design

To design the service contract, we must identify the service operations needed and think through how clients will use the service. We'll call this service contract *IPizza*. We could design the contract in WSDL, but it's generally easier to do it in code. As we design this contract, we'll show it the way you would code it in C# with Indigo.

The sequence of ordering generally involves starting an order, adding items to the order, and completing the order. Because we will decline orders if the customer is too far away, we should begin with a *StartOrder* service operation in which we learn the customer's delivery/pick-up option, location, and phone number. We can return a Boolean result to indicate whether the order can proceed.

```
bool StartOrder(bool Delivery, string address, string postalCode, string phone);
```

Once an order is started, the customer can order food items. We can have a single service operation for ordering food items or several, depending on the range of choices. Here, the only items offered are small, medium, large, and extra-large pizzas with toppings, so a single

AddItem service operation will suffice. What parameters should the *AddItem* service operation have? There are many choices for pizza toppings, and they might change over time, so listing each topping as a parameter seems like a poor idea. Instead, we can define a *Pizza* class in which the size and toppings will be specified. This makes *AddItem* very simple. We'll define the *Pizza* class itself shortly.

```
bool AddItem(Pizza pizza);
```

The customer will want to know the final price of the order before confirming it. This means two service operations, one to present an order's total for the customer's review and another to confirm (or cancel) the order. We'll call these *TotalOrder* and *ConfirmOrder*.

```
decimal TotalOrder();
void ConfirmOrder(bool);
```

Our service contract looks like this so far:

```
[ServiceContract]
public interface IPizza
{
    [OperationContract]
    bool StartOrder(bool Delivery, string address, string postalCode, string phone);
    [OperationContract]
    bool AddItem(Pizza pizza);
    [OperationContract]
    decimal TotalOrder();
    [OperationContract]
    void ConfirmOrder(bool placeOrder);
}
```

Most of these service operations return a result, so request-reply makes sense as a messaging pattern for this service. This service contract design requires the use of sessions: as a client builds an order, the order state must be maintained between calls.

Data Contract Design

As we noted during the service contract design, pizzas can be ordered in many variations. Rather than have many Boolean parameters in the service operations, we will use a *Pizza* structure. Our *Pizza* structure needs to store the pizza size and toppings desired. We can define a *PizzaSize* enumeration for pizza sizes and a *Topping* enumeration for pizza toppings. To allow customers to specify toppings for a half or full pizza, we'll store three topping arrays: one that applies to the first half of the pizza, one that applies to the second half, and one that applies to the entire pizza.

```
public enum PizzaSize { Small, Medium, Large, ExtraLarge }

public enum Topping
{
```

```
      Anchovies, Bacon, Beef, Chicken, ExtraCheese,
      Ham, Mushrooms, Olives, Onions, Pepperoni,
      Peppers, Pineapple, Sausage
}

[DataContract]
public class Pizza
{
      [DataMember]  public PizzaSize Size;
      [DataMember]  public Topping[] FirstHalfToppings;
      [DataMember]  public Topping[] SecondHalfToppings;
      [DataMember]  public Topping[] Toppings;
}
```

Binding Selection

A single binding will suffice for this scenario because we're dealing with a single pizza shop and one type of client, the pizza customer. To determine the binding details, we need to consider each of the possible binding characteristics against our scenario:

- **Transport**   Customers will order over the Internet, so HTTP is the logical transport.

- **Security**   No money changes hands through the service, and the information being communicated is not overly sensitive, so there isn't a strong security requirement.

- **Encoding**   The message size isn't terribly large and the volume of activity isn't high, so text encoding is acceptable and will preserve our options for interoperability.

- **Sessions**   Clients will be making multiple calls to the service to build their order, so sessions are necessary to maintain the state of a customer's order between calls.

- **Interoperability**   We want to be as interoperable as possible, but some of the other requirements, such as sessions, can't be met using Basic Profile interoperability. The WS-* interoperability mode is the right choice here.

An HTTP transport binding with reliable sessions and WS-* interoperability is indicated. Naturally, our binding decisions would be quite different if the service were a centralized point of ordering for a national or regional pizza chain or if payment information were being communicated. The *WSProfileDualHttp* standard binding meets our requirements. We will specify the binding in the service's configuration file when we define an endpoint.

Endpoint Design

With contracts in place and a binding selected, we can designate an endpoint for the service. This involves choosing an address, such as *http://www.contoso.com/pizza/*, and associating it with the *IPizza* service contract and binding we've selected. This can be specified in the service's configuration file.

```
<endpoint
    address="http://www.contoso.com/pizza/"
    bindingSectionName="wsProfileDualHttpBinding"
    contractType="ProgrammingIndigo.IPizza" />
```

Service Behaviors

We won't implement the code for the service operations in this exercise, but we can think about how we want the service to behave at runtime.

The main behavior we need to have is support for sessions so that client state is maintained between calls. The service must remember the details of a customer's order as the order is created through multiple calls. Customer orders must be kept separate from each other if multiple clients are accessing the service at the same time. This behavior is known as *PrivateSession* instancing.

The class that implements the service needs a separate instance for each session to track a client's order details.

```
[ServiceBehavior(InstanceMode=InstanceMode.PrivateSession)]
public class PizzaService : IPizza
{
    //TODO: implement service
}
```

Putting It All Together

Congratulations—we have just designed a service together! Let's put the service contract, data contract, service behavior, binding, and endpoint together to see how this looks in a program. The binding and endpoint information will be defined separately in a configuration file. Listing 2-4 shows how our service would look in C# code, minus the implementation details of the service operations.

Listing 2-4   PizzaService.cs

```
using System;
using System.ServiceModel;
using System.Runtime.Serialization;

namespace ProgrammingIndigo
{
    [ServiceContract]
    public interface IPizza
    {
        [OperationContract]
        bool StartOrder(bool Delivery, string address, string postalCode,
            string phone);
        [OperationContract]
        bool AddItem(Pizza pizza);
```

```
    [OperationContract]
    decimal TotalOrder();
    [OperationContract]
    void ConfirmOrder(bool placeOrder);
}

public enum PizzaSize { Small, Medium, Large, ExtraLarge }

public enum Topping
{
    Anchovies, Bacon, Beef, Chicken, ExtraCheese,
    Ham, Mushrooms, Olives, Onions, Pepperoni,
    Peppers, Pineapple, Sausage
}

[DataContract]
public class Pizza
{
    [DataMember]  public PizzaSize Size;
    [DataMember]  public Topping[] FirstHalfToppings;
    [DataMember]  public Topping[] SecondHalfToppings;
    [DataMember]  public Topping[] Toppings;
}

[ServiceBehavior(InstanceMode=InstanceMode.PrivateSession)]
public class PizzaService : IPizza
{
    public bool StartOrder(bool Delivery, string address, string postalCode,
        string phone)
    {
        //TODO: implement
        return true;
    }

    public bool AddItem(Pizza pizza)
    {
        //TODO: implement
        return true;
    }

    public decimal TotalOrder()
    {
        //TODO: implement
        return 0.00M;
    }

    public void ConfirmOrder(bool placeOrder)
    {
        //TODO: implement
    }
}
}
```

A minimal configuration file for this service is shown in Listing 2-5. This is where the endpoint and binding are specified.

Listing 2-5   PizzaService.exe.config

```xml
<?xml version="1.0" encoding="utf-8" ?>
<configuration xmlns="http://schemas.microsoft.com/.NetConfiguration/v2.0">
    <system.serviceModel>
        <services>
            <service serviceType="ProgrammingIndigo.PizzaService">
                <endpoint
                    address="http://www.contoso.com/pizza/"
                    bindingSectionName="wsProfileDualHttpBinding"
                    contractType="ProgrammingIndigo.IPizza" />
            </service>
        </services>
    </system.serviceModel>
</configuration>
```

In the next chapter, we'll write complete services.

Summary

This chapter presented fundamental Indigo concepts. There are three kinds of Indigo programs: programs that initiate messaging, programs that respond to messaging, and programs that act as intermediaries. The available messaging patterns include one-way simplex, two-way duplex, and request-reply.

Messages are structured as SOAP envelopes that contain a collection of headers and a body. The body is for use by application developers. Headers are used by messaging infrastructures as well as application developers.

Messages are sent over channels. Clients establish channels to services. The actual communication and security negotiation take place when the first message is sent. Channels are stackable, allowing basic messaging patterns to compose with transport, encodings, security, and reliable sessions. Different channel stacks have different levels of interoperability.

From the outside, services expose a service description and a collection of endpoints. Internally, services contain contracts, bindings, endpoints, and implementation code. Service contracts define sets of related operations. Data contracts define data structures. Message contracts allow precise control over message format. Endpoints associate an address with a binding and contract (easily remembered as *ABC*).

At runtime, service descriptions and implementation code are turned into running CLR instances. The master runtime object for a service is *ServiceHost*. Developers can specify many runtime behaviors for services, including instancing, concurrency, throttling, error handling and reporting, security, and transactions.

The exercise for this chapter involved designing a simple service for a pizza shop.

In Chapter 3, we'll look at the programming model and start writing programs in Indigo.

Chapter 3

The Programming Model

It claims to be fully automatic, but actually you have to push this little button here.
—Gentleman John Killian

In Chapter 2, you learned about the fundamental concepts behind Indigo. Now it's time to introduce you to the programming model. The best way to learn a platform is to use it, so let's plunge in and start writing some code.

After completing this chapter, you will:

- Know how to set up Indigo on your computers.
- Be familiar with the development process.
- Understand the Indigo programming model.
- Have created your first "Hello, world" Indigo programs.

Setting Up for Indigo

To set up for Indigo development, you must install Indigo and its prerequisites. Indigo is part of WinFX, the Microsoft Windows managed code development framework. You need all of the following to program with Indigo:

- An operating system that supports Indigo
- Microsoft .NET Framework 2.0
- Windows Application Pack (WAP)
- A development environment

If you have WAP and Microsoft Visual Studio 2005 installed, you already have all of the preceding items.

Supported Operating Systems

Indigo is part of the Microsoft "Longhorn" wave of technologies and will be included with future versions of Windows. As of this writing, you can also use Indigo with all editions of the following earlier operating systems:

- Windows XP SP2
- Microsoft Windows Server 2003

Indigo is not compatible with versions of Windows earlier than these. You can check which version of Windows a computer is running by opening System in Control Panel. The Windows version is displayed on the General tab.

> **Caution**   The version and edition of Windows that you use might limit the communication functionality of your programs. For example, Windows XP Home and Professional Editions limit simultaneous connections from other computers to 5 and 10, respectively.

.NET Framework 2.0

Indigo requires the .NET Framework 2.0. If the framework is not present on your operating system, you can download it from Microsoft at *http://msdn.microsoft.com/netframework*. Another way to obtain the .NET Framework is to install Visual Studio 2005 as your development environment.

If you're not sure what version of the .NET Framework is on your computer, you can find out by opening Add Or Remove Programs in Control Panel. If you don't see Microsoft .NET Framework 2.0 listed, you need to install the framework.

While installing the framework, you can also install the MSDN documentation library, which is highly recommended. This book assumes that you have access to both the .NET Framework documentation and the MSDN documentation.

Windows Application Pack

Indigo is part of WinFX, the managed code framework for Windows development. It includes Indigo as well as other technologies. WinFX will be included with the "Longhorn" edition of Windows but is also available as a download for supported operating systems as part of WAP.

You can check whether WAP is installed (and its version, if it is installed) by opening Add Or Remove Programs in Control Panel and examining the list of installed software.

WAP can be downloaded at *http://msdn.microsoft.com/webservices*.

Visual Studio .NET 2005

The recommended environment for Indigo development is Visual Studio .NET 2005. Visual Studio provides unparalleled support for Web, desktop, and device development in multiple languages. Its integrated development environment (IDE) includes a full-featured code editor, Microsoft IntelliSense, visual designers, and visual debugging. Visual Studio is integrated with Indigo, providing a rich and seamless development experience.

The Development Process

Solution development in Indigo combines traditional elements of object-oriented programming with some new considerations. The chief skill you need is the ability to think in a service-oriented manner. To enjoy the benefits discussed in Chapter 1, you should avoid design decisions that violate the tenets of service orientation (SO).

Service Design

To design a service properly, you must take into account its role in relation to other services. Some key questions to answer include the following:

- Does your service have a well-defined role as part of a distributed solution?

- What are the target audiences for your service? Who will be consuming it?

- What dependencies does your service have? What other services will your service access?

- What boundaries will be crossed to access your service, and what are the implications?

- What contracts and schemas should your service implement?

- What message exchange patterns should your service support?

- What are your service's security requirements?

- What are your service's interoperability requirements?

If you can answer these questions concretely, you are ready to begin designing your service.

A fundamental part of service design is determining contracts. Service contracts describe the operations a service can perform. Data contracts define information structures passed to and from service operations. Message contracts customize the organization of messages, which might be necessary for interoperability. You must define contracts, bindings, and endpoints for the services you create, and you must be aware of the contracts, bindings, and endpoints of other services you plan to access.

Development Approach

Developers can choose which part of a service to create first, the code or the contract. In the **code-first** approach, the service implementation code is written before the metadata (WSDL and XSD) is created. In the **contract-first** approach, the metadata is the starting point and the code follows. Each approach has its implications. Developers willing to work at a lower level have a third option, contractless or late-bound development.

Code-First Development

In the code-first approach, you begin by writing the implementation code for your service. The contract results from how you write your code. Once your code is complete, you can generate metadata describing your service. The metadata can be provided live by the service itself through a metadata exchange (MEX) endpoint, or you can create WSDL and XSD files from the service.

Not all class types can be converted to XSD schema, which illustrates one disadvantage of the code-first approach: if you choose types carelessly, you might prevent a smooth transition to WSDL and then XSD. You can find out more about Indigo conversions between types and XSD in Chapter 5.

Contract-First Development

In the contract-first approach, you begin with service metadata (WSDL and XSD) and the code follows. You might be implementing the service itself or creating a client to access the service. In either case, you can generate code from the service metadata, which then gives you a big helping hand in writing your program.

You can obtain service metadata in several ways. Ideally, you can retrieve metadata from a running service's MEX endpoint. Alternatively, you can obtain WSDL and XSD files via the Web or e-mail.

Contractless or Late-Bound Development

Another choice for developers is to not bother with contracts at all. You can choose this route if you are willing to work directly with messages. If your service operations just send and receive messages, Indigo does not have to make assumptions about the kind of messages your service works with. This requires your programs to work at a lower level than is usually necessary. You have to create messages to send and interpret messages that are received. You might use this technique for a service that accepts any kind of message for processing, such as a router.

Code Generation: The Svcutil Tool

Whether you use code-first or contract-first development, you can benefit from code generation. Most developers find metadata such as WSDL and XSD complex and cumbersome to work with directly, so it's desirable to have tools to read or write this information. Indigo provides a command-line tool named Svcutil that imports and exports service metadata. Svcutil can:

- Generate program code from service metadata retrieved from a running service's MEX endpoint.

- Generate program code from service metadata read from WSDL and XSD files.

- Generate service metadata WSDL and XSD files from a service assembly.

Svcutil has quite a few command-line options. Run *svcutil /?* for a list of them. You can also find a Svcutil reference in Appendix D, which is downloadable from the Web, as described in the Introduction.

Generating Program Code from a MEX Endpoint

Svcutil can read metadata from a service's MEX endpoint and generate program code. To generate code from a service's metadata, specify the MEX endpoint for the service on the Svcutil command line. The MEX endpoint address for a service is usually the same as the service's HTTP base address or HTTP endpoint address.

```
svcutil http://localhost/MyService
```

The code generated contains the client's contracts and a proxy class for accessing the service. Code can be generated in a variety of programming languages, including C# and Microsoft Visual Basic .NET.

Generating Program Code from WSDL and XSD Files

Svcutil can read metadata from WSDL and XSD files to generate program code. To generate code from a metadata file, specify the metadata file(s) for the service on the Svcutil command line. You can specify multiple files and use wildcards.

```
svcutil MyService.wsdl *.xsd
```

The code generated contains the client's contracts and a proxy class for accessing the service. Again, you have a choice of languages.

Generating WSDL and XSD Files from a Service Assembly

Once your service is compiled into a .NET assembly, Svcutil can generate metadata files from it. To generate WSDL and XSD files from a service assembly, specify the assembly file on the Svcutil command line:

```
svcutil MyService.dll
```

Self-Describing Services

You can make a service self-describing by providing a MEX endpoint. This does not require the Svcutil tool. Metadata is provided live, on demand, by your running service.

Program Implementation

Indigo is a managed code platform, so if you've ever programmed with .NET, you'll find your-self in familiar territory. Table 3-1 shows the primary Indigo namespaces and library assem-blies. Your programs must reference these assemblies.

Table 3-1   Indigo Namespaces and References

Namespace	Assembly Reference	Description
System.ServiceModel	System.ServiceModel.dll	Core library
System.Runtime.Serialization	System.Runtime.Serialization.dll	Serialization library
System.Security.Authorization	System.Security.Authorization.dll	Security library
System.Transactions	System.Transactions.dll	Transaction library

Indigo also includes a number of tools for such tasks as metadata import and export and viewing traces. Table 3-2 lists the tools.

Table 3-2   Tool Programs

Tool	Description
Comsvcutil.exe	Configures COM+ integration with services
Dc.exe	Import/export tool for converting between data contract types and XML schema documents
Svcutil.exe	Import/export tool for converting between service metadata and code
TraceViewer.exe	Management tool for viewing end-to-end traces and logged messages

Indigo programming involves the use of an object model, declarative attributes, and configu-ration settings. Listings 3-1 and 3-2 show a small example of client code in which all three are in use. In this example, attributes are used to describe a service contract, objects are used to access the service, and the service endpoint and access method are specified in a configura-tion file rather than in the program itself.

Listing 3-1   Example of Attributes and Object Model

```
using System;
using System.ServiceModel;

[ServiceContract]
interface ITaxService
{
    [OperationContract]
    double ComputeTax(double amount, double taxRate);
}

public class Client
{
    public static void Main()
```

```
    {
        using (TaxServiceProxy proxy = new TaxServiceProxy("DefaultEndpoint"))
        {
            double subtotal, tax, total;
            subtotal = 1500.00D;
            tax = proxy.ComputeTax(subtotal, 7.75D);
            total = subtotal + tax;
            proxy.Close();
        }
    }
}
```

Listing 3-2   Example of Configuration Settings

```xml
<?xml version="1.0" encoding="utf-8" ?>
<configuration xmlns="http://schemas.microsoft.com/.NetConfiguration/v2.0">
    <system.serviceModel>
        <client>
            <endpoint
                configurationName="DefaultEndpoint"
                address="http://localhost/Tax/service.svc"
                bindingSectionName="wsProfileBinding"
                contractType="ITaxService" />
        </client>
    </system.serviceModel>
</configuration>
```

As for where to put your code and what it compiles to, you have some choices. You can host your service in Internet Information Services (IIS), or you can write a small amount of extra code to host a service yourself. You can self-host a service from just about any environment that supports managed code, including a WinForms application, console application, library assembly (DLL), or Microsoft Windows NT Service. We'll talk more about this shortly.

Debugging Applications

Connected applications can be more challenging to test and debug than standalone applications, due to their distributed nature. Indigo provides two features to help with these tasks: end-to-end tracing and message logging.

End-to-end tracing results in a log of a service's activities. With a trace log, you can follow the sequence of events as services interact. You enable and control end-to-end tracing through a program's configuration file.

Message logging involves storing copies of messages for your inspection as XML files on disk. You enable message logging in an application's configuration file. Listing 3-3 shows a logged message.

Listing 3-3   A Logged Message

```
<MessageTraceRecord Time="05/28/2004 22:05:11"
  ChannelType="System.ServiceModel.Channels.HttpChannelProviderBase+HttpRequestChannel"
  xmlns="http://schemas.microsoft.com/mb/2002/07/management/messagetrace">
  <s:Envelope xmlns:s="http://www.w3.org/2003/05/soap-envelope">
  <s:Header />
    <s:Body xmlns:s="http://www.w3.org/2003/05/soap-envelope">
      <amount xmlns="">752.00</amount>
      <accountNumber xmlns="">441234435312324</accountNumber>
      <expDate xmlns="">01/07</expDate>
      <nameOnAccount xmlns="">JOHN Q PUBLIC</nameOnAccount>
    </s:Body>
  </s:Envelope>
</MessageTraceRecord>
```

You can relate events in the end-to-end trace log to logged messages. A message correlation ID allows you to follow a message's route from one service to another.

You can learn more about these management features in Chapter 11.

Deploying Applications

Indigo is hosting agnostic, which means you can write an Indigo program from any environment that supports managed code. The hosting environment you use generally has no effect on how you write code to create clients or services. As with other .NET code, you can put Indigo code into many kinds of programs and contexts, such as a console window program, a graphical WinForms application, a Windows NT service, or a Microsoft ASP.NET Web application. Both clients and services can be hosted this way. In each of these cases, you deploy your program in the usual manner. Configuration information is defined in an App.config or Web.config file. If you host in these environments, you must provide a few lines of code to create and start your service, for example:

```
ServiceHost<MyService> serviceHost = new ServiceHost<MyService>();
serviceHost.Open();
```

Another option is to host your services using IIS. In IIS hosting, your service doesn't have to be started up in advance; it is launched the first time an incoming message is received from it. In addition to automatic activation, hosting in IIS provides health monitoring and automatic process recycling in the event of unhandled exceptions. When your service is hosted in IIS, you don't have to write any hosting code.

Hosting in IIS is similar to working in ASP.NET. Applications are mapped to a virtual directory created in IIS Manager. An.svc file in the virtual directory describes the service. Your service code can either appear directly in the .svc file, where it is compiled on demand, or it can reside in an assembly. Hosting in IIS does not limit you to HTTP communication, but an Indigo listener service must be running for non-HTTP transports. You can find more information about IIS hosting in Chapter 10.

The Programming Model

The Indigo programming model stresses unification, simplicity, and interoperability. The capabilities of predecessor communication technologies such as COM, DCOM, COM+, Enterprise Services, MSMQ, and .NET Remoting are united under a single programming model. The programming model is rich and capable yet simple to use. Because it is backed by a service-oriented runtime, what you develop with the programming model can interoperate with other platforms.

Reconciling Object Orientation and Service Orientation

In Chapter 1 we went to great lengths to draw distinctions between service orientation (SO) and object orientation (OO). You should use OO to build programs but use SO to connect programs. This raises the question of how SO and OO meet up and what that means to developers.

In Indigo, objects are treated as first-class citizens. You define contracts and service implementations by writing interfaces and classes. Attributes are used to make the associations. Table 3-3 shows the relationship between SO and OO concepts in the programming model and the attributes that link them.

Table 3-3   Relationship of SO Entities to OO Entities

SO Entity	OO Entity	Attribute
Service contract	interface	Annotate interface with *[ServiceContract]*
Service operation	method	Annotate interface method with *[OperationContract]*
Implementation class	class	Annotate class with *[ServiceBehavior]* and derive from service contract interface
Implementation method	method	Annotate method with *[OperationBehavior]*
Data contract	class	Annotate class with *[DataContract]* and members with *[DataMember]*
Message contract	interface	Annotate service or data contracts with *[MessageContract]* and members with *[MessageHeader]* and *[MessageBody]*

To get a sense of this, study the following C# code, which defines a service contract by annotating an interface with attributes. The developer defines something familiar, an interface. Attributes relate the interface to a service contract and its methods to service operations.

```
[ServiceContract]
public interface IStockTrading
{
    [OperationContract]    bool Buy(string symbol, int shares);
```

```
    [OperationContract]     bool Sell(string symbol, int shares);
}
```

Similarly, the implementation code for the service can be defined as a class that implements the interface, again using attributes. An attribute identifies the class as a service implementation class.

```
[ServiceBehavior]
public class StockTrading : IStockTrading
{
    [OperationBehavior]
    public bool Buy(string symbol, int shares)
    {
        ...implementation...
    }
    [OperationBehavior]
    public bool Sell(string symbol, int shares)
    {
        ...implementation...
    }
}
```

This SO-to-OO mapping makes things convenient for the developer. Interfaces and classes are familiar entities from the object-oriented world. Annotating them with attributes defines corresponding entities in the service-oriented world. Using generated code from the Svcutil tool, a client can access this service's operations in an object-like manner:

```
StockTradingProxy proxy = new StockTradingProxy();
proxy.Buy("MSFT", 100);
```

This fusion of SO and OO means developers can use a paradigm they're already used to—object orientation—yet still enjoy all of the benefits of service orientation. Despite the familiar look of the code, what's sent over the wire is interoperable messages, not objects. The use of attributes in contracts gives developers explicit control over what is exposed to other programs.

Programming Approaches

The Indigo programming model supports three methods of programming:

- Declarative programming, in which you specify attributes
- Imperative programming, in which you work with the Indigo object model in code
- Configuration-based programming, in which you specify behavior in application configuration files

This is not to say that everything in Indigo can be done in three ways, but there are quite a few things you can do in more than one way. To illustrate the versatility this gives you, consider the task of specifying an endpoint for a service, which can be done via configuration file settings or in code, as you prefer. Here's an endpoint defined in a configuration file:

```
<endpoint
    address="http://localhost:8000/"
    bindingSectionName="wsProfileBinding"
    contractType="IMyContract" />
```

The same endpoint definition in code looks like this:

```
serviceHost = new ServiceHost<MyService>();
serviceHost.AddEndpoint(typeof(IMyContract), new WSProfileBinding(),
    "http://localhost:8000/MyService/");
```

If it's important to provide deployment-time control of the endpoint to IT deployment person-nel, specifying an address in a configuration file is the way to go.

These three programming approaches are not mutually exclusive. Developers can intermix attributes, the object model, and configuration files. In the appropriate chapters in this book, we'll identify the pertinent attributes, objects, and configuration settings.

Declarative Programming: Attributes

Declarative attributes are used to define contracts and specify service behaviors. The following code shows a data contract in C#.

```
[DataContract]
public class Contact
{
    [DataMember]    public string LastName;
    [DataMember]    public string FirstName;
    [DataMember]    public string Phone;
    [DataMember]    public string Email;
}
```

Note   Declarative attributes in C# take the form *[keyword]* or *[keyword(param=value, ...)]*. They can appear on the same line or precede the statements they apply to.

The equivalent code looks like this in Visual Basic .NET:

```
<DataContract> Public Class Contact
    <DataMember>    Public LastName As String
    <DataMember>    Public FirstName As String
    <DataMember>    Public Phone As String
    <DataMember>    Public Email As String
End Class
```

Note   Declarative attributes in Visual Basic .NET take the form *<keyword>* or *<key-word(param:=value, ...)>*. If you want the attributes to appear on separate lines from the state-ments they apply to, you must indicate line continuation with the underscore character.

Attributes can specify parameters that modify details of their requirements or behavior. The following service contract specifies session requirements and service operation direction using parameters.

```
[ServiceContract(Session=true)]
public interface IStockTrading
{
    [OperationContract(IsOneWay=false)]
    bool Buy(string symbol, int shares);
    [OperationContract(IsOneWay=false)]
    bool Sell(string symbol, int shares);
}
```

If you omit the parameters in an attribute, you must be aware of what they default to. By convention, Boolean parameters in attributes usually default to false.

You'll find a concise summary of attributes and parameters in Appendix B, which is downloadable from the Web, as described in the Introduction.

Imperative Programming: The Object Model

The object model, or application programming interface (API), is the collection of classes and interfaces that provide developers with the deepest level of access to Indigo. With the object model, developers can use object-oriented programming to create and access services. Of the three forms of programming supported by Indigo, the object model is the most extensive. When you need the most granular level of control over Indigo, you should use the object model.

The object model is managed code. If you've ever programmed with .NET, you'll find yourself in familiar territory. The following code, which creates and starts a service, shows the object model at work.

```
serviceHost = new ServiceHost<MyService>();
serviceHost.AddEndpoint(typeof(IMyContract), new WSProfileBinding(),
    "http://localhost:8000/MyService/");
serviceHost.Open();
```

Clients use the object model as well. Here a client creates a typed channel to a service using the object model and accesses the service.

```
IOrderProcessing orderProcessingService = ChannelFactory.CreateChannel
    <IOrderProcessing>(new EndpointAddress(uri), binding);
string orderID = orderProcessingService.SubmitOrder(order);
```

Client code is simplified if proxy code is generated using the Svcutil tool. A client can create a proxy this easily using generated code:

```
OrderProcessingProxy proxy = new OrderProcessingProxy("DefaultEndpoint");
string orderID = proxy.SubmitOrder(order);
```

Indigo has hundreds of classes, but application developers typically need to access only a small subset on a regular basis. The object model is described in the remaining chapters of this book. You'll find a summary of the object model classes of interest to application developers in Appendix A, which is downloadable from the Web, as described in the Introduction.

Configuration-Based Programming

Configuration-based development permits part of an application's behavior to be specified in configuration files. You can make such things as addresses, bindings, security details, service behavior, and tracing changeable without having to modify and recompile the program code. The following application configuration file defines a service endpoint.

```
<configuration xmlns="http://schemas.microsoft.com/.NetConfiguration/v2.0">
    <system.serviceModel>
        <services>
            <service serviceType="SampleService">
                <endpoint
                    address=http://localhost:8000/SampleService/
                    bindingSectionName="basicProfileBinding"
                    contractType="ISampleContract" />
            </service>
        </services>
    </system.serviceModel>
</configuration>
```

By specifying addresses, bindings, and behaviors in a configuration file, you can make deploy-time decisions about services that don't require any modification to the service programs themselves.

Configuration settings are described in the remaining chapters of this book. You'll find a concise list of configuration settings in Appendix C, which is downloadable from the Web, as described in the Introduction.

Order of Precedence in Indigo

You might be wondering who "wins" if declarative, imperative, and configuration-based programming are used in contradictory ways. For example, what happens if the same endpoint is defined in more than one place? Here's the order of precedence in Indigo:

1. Attributes are applied.

2. Configuration settings are applied (possibly overriding some definitions).

3. Code executes (possibly overriding some definitions).

The Service Model

Programming in Indigo is delightfully straightforward. With all of Indigo's many capabilities, you might expect the API to be enormous—and it's true that there are hundreds of classes and interfaces. Fortunately, you have to be familiar with only a small subset of them for typical application development tasks. What makes this possible is a carefully designed system of classes, declarative attributes, and configuration settings collectively known as the **service model**.

Most application developers will use the service model; there's no reason not to. Using the service model doesn't box you into a corner: if you occasionally want to do something at a lower level, you simply add some code. This is one of the nicest things about the Indigo API because you don't have to worry about going down a wrong path.

> **Tip**   The service model is your friend. Take advantage of it.

What Service Programs Look Like

Service programs contain four elements:

- **Contract definitions**   A service must have at least one service contract, and it might contain multiple service contracts, data contracts, or message contracts.

- **Implementation code**   The service contracts in a service need code to implement their service operations.

- **Hosting code**   Some code is needed to create and start the service.

- **Endpoint definitions**   One or more address–binding–contract endpoints must be declared.

Listing 3-4 shows a simple service hosted in a C# console program, and Listing 3-5 shows its accompanying configuration file. Take a moment to note the contract definitions, implementation code, hosting code, and endpoint definition.

Listing 3-4   Sample Service Program

```
using System;
using System.ServiceModel;

namespace Microsoft.Samples.Indigo.Samples
{
    [ServiceContract]
    public interface ISampleContract
    {
        [OperationContract]
        double Add(double n1, double n2);
        [OperationContract]
        double Subtract(double n1, double n2);
        [OperationContract]
        double Multiply(double n1, double n2);
        [OperationContract]
        double Divide(double n1, double n2);
    }
```

```
[ServiceBehavior]
public class SampleService : ISampleContract
{
    public double Add(double n1, double n2)
    {
        return n1 + n2;
    }

    public double Subtract(double n1, double n2)
    {
        return n1 - n2;
    }

    public double Multiply(double n1, double n2)
    {
        return n1 * n2;
    }

    public double Divide(double n1, double n2)
    {
        return n1 / n2;
    }

    public static void Main()
    {
        using (ServiceHost<SampleService> serviceHost =
            new ServiceHost<SampleService>();
        {
            serviceHost.Open();
            Console.WriteLine("Press ENTER to shut down service.");
            Console.ReadLine();
            serviceHost.Close();
        }
    }
}
```

Listing 3-5   Sample Service Configuration File

```xml
<?xml version="1.0" encoding="utf-8" ?>
<configuration xmlns="http://schemas.microsoft.com/.NetConfiguration/v2.0">
    <system.serviceModel>
        <services>
            <service serviceType="Microsoft.Samples.Indigo.Samples.SampleService">
                <endpoint
                    address="http://localhost:8000/SampleService/"
                    bindingSectionName="basicProfileBinding"
                    contractType="Microsoft.Samples.Indigo.Samples.ISampleContract" />
            </service>
        </services>
    </system.serviceModel>
</configuration>
```

Contracts

You define service contracts, data contracts, and message contracts by using declarative attributes.

You define service contracts by annotating an interface with *[ServiceContract]*. You identify service operations by annotating methods with *[OperationContract]*. The following service contract defines four service operations: Add, Subtract, Multiply, and Divide.

```
[ServiceContract]
public interface ISampleContract
{
    [OperationContract]
    double Add(double n1, double n2);
    [OperationContract]
    double Subtract(double n1, double n2);
    [OperationContract]
    double Multiply(double n1, double n2);
    [OperationContract]
    double Divide(double n1, double n2);
}
```

You define data contracts by annotating a class with *[DataContract]* and its members with *[DataMember]*. The following data contract defines a structure for contact information.

```
[DataContract]
public class Contact
{
    [DataMember]    public int ContactType;
    [DataMember]    public string LastName;
    [DataMember]    public string FirstName;
    [DataMember]    public string Address;
    [DataMember]    public string City;
    [DataMember]    public string Region;
    [DataMember]    public string Phone;
    [DataMember]    public string EMail;
}
```

You define message contracts by annotating a class or interface with *[MessageContract]* and its members with *[MessageBody]* and *[MessageHeader]*. The following class uses *MessageContract* attributes to specify which members of the class belong in the message body or its headers.

```
[MessageContract]
class MyMessage
{
    [MessageBody]
    public string MyData;
    [MessageHeader]
    public int MyHeader;
}
```

The service model attributes are described in the remaining chapters of this book.

Service Implementation Code

Implementation code is provided in a class that inherits from a service contract interface. The class is annotated with a *[ServiceBehavior]* attribute. The service operations in the contract are implemented in this class.

```
[ServiceBehavior]
public class SampleService : ISampleContract
{
    public double Add(double n1, double n2)
    {
        return n1 + n2;
    }
    ...
}
```

Service behaviors are also controlled using the *[ServiceBehavior]* attribute. The following attribute specifies *Singleton* instancing so that there is just one instance of the service implementation class regardless of the number of clients accessing the service.

```
[ServiceBehavior(InstanceMode=InstanceMode.Singleton)]
public class SampleService : ISampleContract
{
    ...
}
```

You can also specify behaviors for operations using the *[OperationBehavior]* attribute. *[Service-Behavior]* and *[OperationBehavior]* are optional: you don't need to specify them unless you need to specify a behavior setting.

Endpoints

Endpoints can be defined in code or in a configuration file. The following code defines an endpoint.

```
serviceHost = new ServiceHost<MyService>();
serviceHost.AddEndpoint(typeof(IMyContract), new WSProfileBinding(),
    "http://localhost:8000/MyService/");
```

The same endpoint can be defined in a configuration file:

```
<endpoint
    address="http://localhost:8000/MyService/"
    bindingSectionName="wsProfileBinding"
    contractType="IMyContract" />
```

What Client Programs Look Like

Client programs must contain contracts that match the service they are accessing. The recommended approach is to generate client code from a service using the Svcutil tool. Svcutil not only generates contract code, but it also provides a proxy class for accessing the service. Clients create a new instance of the proxy, and they can then access the service through the proxy.

Client programs contain three elements:

- **Proxy creation**   A client must create a proxy, which establishes a channel to the service.
- **Service access code**   Through the proxy, the client interacts with the service.
- **Endpoint definitions**   The client declares an address-binding-contract endpoint for the service.

Listing 3-6 shows a simple client implemented as a console program, and Listing 3-7 shows its .config file. Take a moment to see if you can locate the proxy creation, service access code, and endpoint definition.

Listing 3-6   Sample Client Program

```
using System;
using System.ServiceModel;

namespace Microsoft.Samples.Indigo.Samples
{
    class Client
    {
        static void Main()
        {
            using (SampleContractProxy proxy = new SampleContractProxy("SampleEndpoint")
            {
                double value1 = 100.00D;
                double value2 = 15.99D;
                double result = proxy.Add(value1, value2);

                value1 = 145.00D;
                value2 = 76.54D;
                result = proxy.Subtract(value1, value2);

                value1 = 9.00D;
                value2 = 81.25D;
                result = proxy.Multiply(value1, value2);

                value1 = 22.00D;
                value2 = 7.00D;
                result = proxy.Divide(value1, value2);

                proxy.Close();
            }
        }
    }
}
```

Listing 3-7 Sample Client Configuration File

```xml
<?xml version="1.0" encoding="utf-8" ?>
<configuration xmlns="http://schemas.microsoft.com/.NetConfiguration/v2.0">
    <system.serviceModel>
        <client>
            <endpoint
                configurationName="SampleEndpoint"
                address="http://localhost:8000/SampleService/"
                bindingConfiguration="SampleBinding"
                bindingSectionName="basicProfileBinding"
                contractType="ISampleContract" />
        </client>
        <bindings>
            <basicProfileBinding>
                <binding configurationName="SampleBinding" />
            </basicProfileBinding>
        </bindings>
    </system.serviceModel>
</configuration>
```

Proxy Creation

If the client makes use of code generated by Svcutil from the service's metadata, you can establish a connection to a service by simply creating a new instance of a proxy class. You can specify the name of a .config location where the service endpoint is defined.

```
using (SampleContractProxy proxy = new SampleContractProxy("SampleEndpoint")
{
    ...
}
```

Service Access

Once a proxy is created, all it takes to interact with a service is to call its service operations via the proxy. Working with the proxy feels similar to .NET Remoting or other distributed object technologies.

```
double result = proxy.Add(value1, value2);
```

Endpoints

Clients can also define endpoints in code or in a configuration file.

Levels of Programming

Several levels of programming are available to developers:

- **Typed service** Contains service operations that are like functions, where parameters and return values can be simple or complex data types

- **Untyped service**   Similar to a typed service, but the parameters and return values are messages

- **Messaging-layer programming**   Gives the developer precise control over communication

Typed Services

Typed services are the highest level of service programming and are likely to be the choice of most application developers. Service operations resemble functions. Parameters and return types can be simple or complex data types. Data contracts define complex data types. The following code connects to an order entry service and submits a purchase order.

```
OrderEntryProxy orderEntry = new OrderEntryProxy("OrderEntryEndpoint");
orderID = orderEntry.SubmitOrder(purchaseOrder);
```

Working with typed services feels similar to RPC-style distributed object technologies such as .NET Remoting. Interoperable SOAP messages are sent over the wire, but the developer doesn't have to think in these terms. Serialization and deserialization of parameters and return values to and from messages is automatic. If you need to, you can customize where these items go in a message by using a message contract.

You can use *ref* and *out* parameters in typed services. The ComputeTax service operation shown here returns a tax amount and updates a *ref* parameter with an order total. Being able to use *ref* and *out* is convenient, but it's important to keep in mind that all information is passed by value.

```
public double ComputeTax(double subtotal, double taxRate, ref orderTotal)
{
    double taxAmount = subtotal * (taxRate / 100.00D);
    orderTotal = subtotal + taxAmount;
    return taxAmount;
}
```

Untyped Services

Untyped services give developers direct access to messages. Like typed services, untyped services contain service operations that are like functions, but the parameters and return types are messages rather than data types. The following client code connects to an order entry service, creates a message from a purchase order, and submits it to the service.

```
OrderEntryProxy orderEntry = new OrderEntryProxy();
Message message = Message.CreateMessage("http://schemas.microsoft.com/OrderEntry",
    purchaseOrder);
orderEntry.SubmitOrder(message);
```

You might use an untyped service instead of a typed service if you have to handle a lot of variation in messages. For example, you might want an order entry service to accept several purchase order formats. An untyped service can examine received messages in code to decide how to interpret them.

Messaging-Layer Programming

Programming against the messaging layer is the lowest level of all. Developers take charge of communication details and explicitly create and work with messages and channels. The following client code creates an HTTP channel factory, creates and opens a channel, creates a message from a purchase order, and sends the message over the channel.

```
HttpChannelFactory channelFactory = new HttpChannelFactory();
channelFactory.Open();
IOutputChannel channel = channelFactory.CreateChannel<IOutputChannel>
    ("http://AcctgServer/OrderEntryService");
channel.Open();
Message message = Message.CreateMessage("http://schemas.microsoft.com/OrderEntry",
    purchaseOrder);
channel.Send(message);
```

To create intermediaries (such as routers or proxies) or extensions to Indigo (such as new transport channels or encoders), you must program at this level.

Programming Exercise: "Hello, World"

By longstanding tradition, the first program in a new language or platform is "Hello, world." Let's write "Hello, world" in Indigo. Our objective is simple: to give you experience creating, building, and running a service and a client. As discussed in the preceding section, the Indigo programming model provides more than one way to do this. To get a proper appreciation for the versatility of the programming model, we'll create two versions of "Hello, world." Table 3-4 describes how they differ. Hello World #1 is a bare-bones service that does everything in code. Hello World #2 takes advantage of contract-first programming, Svcutil-generated client proxy code, and .config files.

Table 3-4   "Hello, World" Programs

Program	Approach	Generated Code	Configuration File	Hosting
Hello World #1	Code-first	No	No	Console application
Hello World #2	Contract-first	Yes	Yes	Internet Information Services (IIS)

Each program comprises a service that performs simple calculator functions and a client that accesses the service. As you're about to see, you can write this service in different ways in Indigo.

You can download all of the code samples in this book from the Web, as described in the Introduction, but you'll get more from the experience if you actually enter, build, and run these samples from scratch. Don't be concerned when you encounter new and unfamiliar terminology, classes, and attributes—we'll explain them throughout the rest of the book.

It's time to write some code. Let's get started!

Hello World #1

In this programming exercise, you will create a service and a client. Both will be console applications. Imperative programming will be emphasized through heavy use of the object model—we'll use code wherever we can. The service performs Add, Subtract, Multiply, and Divide calculator functions.

This exercise has six development steps:

1. Create the service.
2. Add a reference to System.ServiceModel.dll.
3. Build the service.
4. Create the client.
5. Add a reference to System.ServiceModel.dll.
6. Build the client.

Step 1: Create the Service

To create the service program, launch your development environment and create a new C# console application project named *service*. Enter the code in Listing 3-8.

To perform these tasks using Visual Studio:

1. Choose File, New, Project.
2. Under Project Type, select Windows under Visual C#. Under Templates, select Console Application.
3. In the Name box, type **service**, in the Location box, type any path you want, and in the Solution Name box, type **hello1**. Click OK to generate and open the new project.
4. Replace the generated code in Program.cs with the code shown in Listing 3-8.

Listing 3-8   Hello1 Service: Program.cs

```
using System;
using System.ServiceModel;

namespace ProgrammingIndigo
{
    //Contract definition.
```

```
[ServiceContract]
public interface IHello
{
    [OperationContract]
    double Add(double n1, double n2);
    [OperationContract]
    double Subtract(double n1, double n2);
    [OperationContract]
    double Multiply(double n1, double n2);
    [OperationContract]
    double Divide(double n1, double n2);
}

// Service implementation.

public class HelloService : IHello
{
    public double Add(double n1, double n2)
    {
        Console.WriteLine("Add called");
        return n1 + n2;
    }

    public double Subtract(double n1, double n2)
    {
        Console.WriteLine("Subtract called");
        return n1 - n2;
    }

    public double Multiply(double n1, double n2)
    {
        Console.WriteLine("Multiply called");
        return n1 * n2;
    }

    public double Divide(double n1, double n2)
    {
        Console.WriteLine("Divide called");
        return n1 / n2;
    }

    // Host the service.

    public static void Main()
    {
        // Create a ServiceHost.

        using (ServiceHost<HelloService> serviceHost =
            new ServiceHost<HelloService>())
        {
            // Add an endpoint.

            WSProfileBinding binding = new WSProfileBinding();
            Uri uri = new Uri("http://localhost:8000/hello1/");
            serviceHost.AddEndpoint(typeof(IHello), binding, uri);
```

```
            // Open the service.

            serviceHost.Open();

            // The service can now be accessed.
            // Hold it open until user presses ENTER.

            Console.WriteLine("The service is ready");
            Console.WriteLine();
            Console.WriteLine("Press ENTER to shut down service.");
            Console.WriteLine();
            Console.ReadLine();

            // Close the service.

            serviceHost.Close();
        }
      }
    }
  }
```

We'll go through the code statement by statement later on.

Step 2: Add a Reference to System.ServiceModel.dll

Add a reference to System.ServiceModel.dll.

To perform the task using Visual Studio:

1. Right-click References in the Solution Explorer window and select Add Reference.

2. In the Add Reference dialog box, on the .NET tab, select System.ServiceModel.dll and click OK.

Step 3: Build the Service

Build the service program to make Service.exe. Resolve any typographical errors.

To perform the task using Visual Studio, select Build Solution from the Build menu to generate Service.exe.

Step 4: Create the Client

Create the client program. Add a second C# project named *client* to the solution. Enter the code in Listing 3-9.

To perform these tasks using Visual Studio:

1. Choose File, New, Project.

2. Under Project Type, select Windows under Visual C#. Under Templates, select Console Application. In the Name box, type **client**, in the Location box, type any path you want, and in the SolutionName box, type **Add To Solution**. Click OK to generate and open the new project.

3. Replace the generated code in Program.cs with the code shown in Listing 3-9.

Listing 3-9   Hello1 Client: Program.cs

```
using System;
using System.ServiceModel;

namespace ProgrammingIndigo
{
    //Contract definition.

    [ServiceContract]
    public interface IHello
    {
        [OperationContract]
        double Add(double n1, double n2);
        [OperationContract]
        double Subtract(double n1, double n2);
        [OperationContract]
        double Multiply(double n1, double n2);
        [OperationContract]
        double Divide(double n1, double n2);
    }

    //Client implementation code.

    class Client
    {
        static void Main()
        {
            // Create a proxy.
            WSProfileBinding binding = new WSProfileBinding();
            Uri uri = new Uri("http://localhost:8000/hello1/");
            IHello proxy = ChannelFactory.CreateChannel<IHello>(uri, binding);
            try
            {
                // Call the Add service operation.
                double value1 = 100.00D;
                double value2 = 15.99D;
                Console.WriteLine("Calling Add({0},{1})", value1, value2);
                double result = proxy.Add(value1, value2);
                Console.WriteLine("  Result: {0}", result);

                // Call the Subtract service operation.
                value1 = 145.00D;
                value2 = 76.54D;
                Console.WriteLine("Calling Subtract({0},{1})", value1, value2);
```

```
        result = proxy.Subtract(value1, value2);
        Console.WriteLine("  Result: {0}", result);

        // Call the Multiply service operation.
        value1 = 9.00D;
        value2 = 81.25D;
        Console.WriteLine("Calling Multiply({0},{1})", value1, value2);
        result = proxy.Multiply(value1, value2);
        Console.WriteLine("  Result: {0}", result);

        // Call the Divide service operation.
        value1 = 22.00D;
        value2 = 7.00D;
        Console.WriteLine("Calling Divide({0},{1})", value1, value2);
        result = proxy.Divide(value1, value2);
        Console.WriteLine("  Result: {0}", result);
    }
    finally
    {
        ((IChannel)proxy).Close();
        ((IChannel)proxy).Dispose();
    }

    Console.WriteLine();
    Console.WriteLine("Press ENTER to shut down client");
    Console.ReadLine();
        }
      }
    }
```

Step 5: Add a Reference to System.ServiceModel.dll

Add a reference to System.ServiceModel.dll.

To perform the task using Visual Studio:

1. Right-click References (under the client project) in the Solution Explorer window and select Add Reference.

2. In the Add Reference dialog box, on the .NET tab, select System.ServiceModel.dll and click OK.

Step 6: Build the Client

Build the client program to make Client.exe. Resolve any typographical errors.

To perform the task using Visual Studio, select Build Solution from the Build menu to generate Client.exe.

Deployment

We're now ready to try things out. Launch the service and client as follows:

1.   Run Service.exe from a command window.

2.   Wait for the service to initialize and display "Press ENTER to shut down service."

3.   Run Client.exe from another command window.

In the client window, you should see output like that shown in Figure 3-1. The service window will also display confirmation as client requests are serviced.

Figure 3-1   Hello World #1 client

Press ENTER on the client to shut it down. Press ENTER on the service to shut it down. Congratulations on successfully completing your first Indigo program!

Understanding the Service Code

The service program is shown in its entirety in Listing 3-8. The service contract for this service is named *IHello*. It is defined by creating an interface marked with the *[ServiceContract]* attribute. There are four service operations, defined by specifying four methods on the interface marked with *[OperationContract]* attributes.

```
[ServiceContract]
public interface IHello
{
    [OperationContract]
    double Add(double n1, double n2);
    [OperationContract]
    double Subtract(double n1, double n2);
    [OperationContract]
    double Multiply(double n1, double n2);
    [OperationContract]
    double Divide(double n1, double n2);
}
```

The *HelloService* class implements the service contract. The class derives from the *IHello* interface. Each service operation in the contract is implemented as a method.

```
public class HelloService : IHello
{
    public double Add(double n1, double n2)
    {
        Console.WriteLine("Add called");
        return n1 + n2;
    }
    ...
}
```

The service in this example is self-hosted. That is, the program takes responsibility for creating the service and maintaining it over its lifetime. The code for this is in the static *Main* startup function. To host a service, the code in the *Main* function creates an instance of *ServiceHost<T>*, specifying the service's implementation class. The service host is discarded when the *using* block exits.

```
public static void Main()
{
    // Create a ServiceHost.

    using (ServiceHost<SampleService> serviceHost = new ServiceHost<SampleService>())
    {
        ...
    }
}
```

An endpoint is added to the service host. An endpoint must specify an address, a binding, and a contract. Here, the address is *http://localhost:8000/hello1/*, the binding is a standard *WSProfileBinding*, and the contract is *IHello*.

```
WSProfileBinding binding = new WSProfileBinding();
Uri uri = new Uri("http://localhost:8000/hello1/");
serviceHost.AddEndpoint(typeof(IHello), binding, uri);
```

The service must be opened before it will accept requests. The code opens the service by calling the service host's *Open* method. The service is held open until the user presses ENTER. The program calls the service host's *Close* method to close the service.

```
// Open the service.

serviceHost.Open();

// The service can now be accessed. Hold it open until user presses ENTER.

Console.WriteLine("The service is ready");
Console.WriteLine();
Console.WriteLine("Press ENTER to shut down service.");
Console.WriteLine();
Console.ReadLine();
```

```
// Close the service.

serviceHost.Close();
```

Although we stressed the use of the object model in this example, we couldn't get away completely from service model declarative attributes. They were necessary to define the service contract and the service implementation class.

Understanding the Client Code

The client program is shown in its entirety in Listing 3-9. The client must agree with the service about address, binding, and contract, or communication is not possible. Because we are using code-first development and avoiding code generation tools in this example, the client's contract code is simply the result of a copy and paste from the service code.

```
[ServiceContract]
public interface IHello
{
    [OperationContract]
    double Add(double n1, double n2);
    [OperationContract]
    double Subtract(double n1, double n2);
    [OperationContract]
    double Multiply(double n1, double n2);
    [OperationContract]
    double Divide(double n1, double n2);
}
```

The client creates a proxy channel to the service using the *ChannelFactory* class's static *Create-Channel<T>* method, specifying the contract name (*IHello*), address (*http://localhost:8000/ hello1*), and the *WSProfileBinding* standard binding. Once the client is finished accessing the service, the proxy is closed and discarded. It's necessary to cast the proxy object–defined merely as something supporting the *IHello* interface in our program–to an *IChannel* in order to access the *Close* and *Dispose* functions.

```
static void Main()
{
    // Create a proxy.
    WSProfileBinding binding = new WSProfileBinding();
    Uri uri = new Uri("http://localhost:8000/hello1/");
    IHello proxy = ChannelFactory.CreateChannel<IHello>(uri, binding);
    try
    {
        ...
        ((IChannel)proxy).Close();
    }
    finally
    {
        ((IChannel)proxy).Dispose();
    }
}
```

The client's access to the service is straightforward. You can call the service's operations by using the proxy channel.

```
// Call the Add service operation.
double value1 = 100.00D;
double value2 = 15.99D;
Console.WriteLine("Calling Add({0},{1})", value1, value2);
double result = proxy.Add(value1, value2);
Console.WriteLine("  Result: {0}", result);

// Call the Subtract service operation.
value1 = 145.00D;
value2 = 76.54D;
Console.WriteLine("Calling Subtract({0},{1})", value1, value2);
result = proxy.Subtract(value1, value2);
Console.WriteLine("  Result: {0}", result);
...
```

Hello World #2

Our second "Hello, world" program will be functionally identical to the first one but will be written quite differently. The programming approach will be contract first. Client code will be generated from the service's metadata using the Svcutil tool. The service will be hosted by IIS. The client and the service will define endpoints and bindings in .config files rather than in code.

This exercise has 10 development steps:

1. Create the service.

2. Build the service.

3. Create the .svc file.

4. Create a configuration file for the service.

5. Create a virtual directory for the service.

6. Test the service with a browser.

7. Create the client.

8. Generate proxy code for the client.

9. Create a configuration file for the client.

10. Build the client.

Step 1: Create the Service

Create a service program that compiles to a DLL library assembly. Launch your development environment and create a new C# console application project named *service*. Enter the code in Listing 3-10.

To perform these tasks using Visual Studio:

1. Choose File, New, Project.

2. Under Project Type, select Windows under Visual C#. Under Templates, select Console Application. In the Name box, type **service**, in the Location box, type any path you want, and in the Solution Name box, type **hello2**. Click OK to generate and open the new project.

3. Replace the generated code in Program.cs with the code shown in Listing 3-10.

Your service project will need to reference System.ServiceModel.dll.

To perform the task using Visual Studio:

1. Right-click References in the Solution Explorer window and select Add Reference.

2. In the Add Reference dialog box, on the .NET tab, select System.ServiceModel.dll and click OK.

Listing 3-10   Hello2 Service: Program.cs

```csharp
using System;
using System.ServiceModel;
using System.Diagnostics;

namespace ProgrammingIndigo
{
    // Contract definition.

    [ServiceContract]
    public interface IHello
    {
        [OperationContract]
        double Add(double n1, double n2);
        [OperationContract]
        double Subtract(double n1, double n2);
        [OperationContract]
        double Multiply(double n1, double n2);
        [OperationContract]
        double Divide(double n1, double n2);
    }

    // Service implementation.

    [ServiceBehavior]
    public class HelloService : IHello
    {
        public double Add(double n1, double n2)
        {
            return n1 + n2;
        }
```

```
public double Subtract(double n1, double n2)
{
    return n1 - n2;
}

public double Multiply(double n1, double n2)
{
    return n1 * n2;
}

public double Divide(double n1, double n2)
{
    return n1 / n2;
}

    }
}
```

Step 2: Build the Service

Build the service program to make Service.dll. Resolve any typographical errors.

To perform the task using Visual Studio, choose Build Solution from the Build menu to generate Service.dll.

Step 3: Create the .svc File

An .svc file is needed to identify the Indigo service to IIS. Using an editor or development environment, create a text file named Service.svc. Enter the code in Listing 3-11.

To perform these tasks using Visual Studio:

1. Right-click the service project and select Add, New Item.

2. Select Text File, and click Add. Rename the text file Service.svc.

3. Type the code in Listing 3-11 into Service.svc.

Listing 3-11   Hello2 Service: Service.svc

```
<%@Service language=c# Debug="true" class="ProgrammingIndigo.HelloService" %>
<%@Assembly Name="service" %>
```

Step 4: Create a Configuration File for the Service

A Web.config file is needed to specify endpoints and bindings for the service. Using an editor or development environment, create a text file with the code shown in Listing 3-12. Save the code under the name Web.config in the same folder in which the service program and .svc file are located.

To perform these tasks using Visual Studio:

1. Right-click the service project and select Add, New Item.

2. Select Application Configuration File, and click Add.

3. Name the file Web.config.

4. Type the code in Listing 3-12 into Web.config.

Listing 3-12   Hello2 Service: Web.config

```
<?xml version="1.0" encoding="utf-8" ?>
<configuration xmlns="http://schemas.microsoft.com/.NetConfiguration/v2.0">
    <system.serviceModel>
        <services>
            <service
                serviceType="ProgrammingIndigo.HelloService">
                <endpoint
                    address=""
                    bindingSectionName="wsProfileBinding"
                    contractType="ProgrammingIndigo.IHello, service" />
            </service>
        </services>
    </system.serviceModel>
    <system.web>
        <compilation debug="true" />
    </system.web>
</configuration>
```

Step 5: Create a Virtual Directory for the Service

Like ASP.NET applications, Web-hosted services reside in virtual directories. Follow this procedure to set up a virtual directory for the service.

1. **Create a directory.** Create a folder on your computer named *hello2*.

2. **Create a virtual directory.** From the Start menu, launch Control Panel. Select Administrative Tools, Internet Information Services. Navigate to Web Sites, Default Web Sites. Right-click and select New, Virtual Directory. Specify the name **hello2** and associate it with the hello2 folder created in step 1. Before exiting IIS Manager, check step 3.

3. **Enable anonymous access.** While in IIS, navigate to Web Sites, Default Web Sites. The hello2 folder should be listed. Right-click hello2 and select Properties. On the Directory Security tab, click Edit. An Authentication Methods dialog box appears. Anonymous Access should be selected; if it is not, select it. Close all dialog boxes by clicking OK, and close IIS.

4. **Deploy the service.** Copy the Service.svc file to the hello2 folder. Underneath hello2, create a bin subdirectory and copy Service.dll into it. You should have the following directory-file structure.

```
\hello2
  service.svc
    \bin
      service.dll
```

Step 6: Test the Service with a Browser

Before going on to the client, we must test to make sure the service can be accessed. Launch Internet Explorer. On the address bar, specify the URL *http://localhost/hello2/service.svc* and press ENTER. If the resulting page does not list any errors, proceed to step 7. If there are problems, check the following:

- If the page returned by the browser describes compilation errors, check the code entered in the preceding steps. The compilation error display should highlight the offending code.

- If the resulting page describes HTTP errors, make sure your system has IIS enabled. You should be able to access *http://localhost* in a browser without receiving an error. If IIS seems to be properly enabled, review the virtual directory setup in step 5. If this also fails, look for clues in Control Panel, Administrative Tools, Event Log or try an *IISRESET*.

The service is now ready. Next we need a client program to access it.

Step 7: Create the Client

Create the client program. Launch your development environment and create a new C# console application project named *client*. Enter the code in Listing 3-13.

To perform these tasks using Visual Studio:

1. Select New, Project from the File menu.

2. Under Project Type, select Windows under Visual C#. Under Templates, select Console Application. In the Name box, type **client**, in the Location box, type any path you want, and in the Solution Name box, type **hello2**. Click OK to generate and open the new project.

3. Replace the generated code in Program.cs with the code shown in Listing 3-13.

Your client project will need to reference System.ServiceModel.dll.

To perform the task using Visual Studio:

1. Right-click References in the Solution Explorer window and select Add Reference.

2. In the Add Reference dialog box, on the .NET tab, select System.ServiceModel.dll and click OK.

Build the client, which will create Client.exe.

Listing 3-13 Hello2 Client: Program.cs

```csharp
using System;
using System.ServiceModel;

namespace ProgrammingIndigo
{
    class Client
    {
        static void Main(string[] args)
        {
            // Create a proxy.
            Console.WriteLine("Creating proxy to service");
            using (HelloProxy proxy = new HelloProxy("HelloEndpoint"))
            {
                // Call the Add service operation.
                double value1 = 100.00D;
                double value2 = 15.99D;
                Console.WriteLine("Calling Add({0},{1})", value1, value2);
                double result = proxy.Add(value1, value2);
                Console.WriteLine("  Result: {0}", result);

                // Call the Subtract service operation.
                value1 = 145.00D;
                value2 = 76.54D;
                Console.WriteLine("Calling Subtract({0},{1})", value1, value2);
                result = proxy.Subtract(value1, value2);
                Console.WriteLine("  Result: {0}", result);

                // Call the Multiply service operation.
                value1 = 9.00D;
                value2 = 81.25D;
                Console.WriteLine("Calling Multiply({0},{1})", value1, value2);
                result = proxy.Multiply(value1, value2);
                Console.WriteLine("  Result: {0}", result);

                // Call the Divide service operation.
                value1 = 22.00D;
                value2 = 7.00D;
                Console.WriteLine("Calling Divide({0},{1})", value1, value2);
                result = proxy.Divide(value1, value2);
                Console.WriteLine("  Result: {0}", result);

                proxy.Close();
            }

            Console.WriteLine();
            Console.WriteLine("Press ENTER to shut down client");
            Console.ReadLine();
        }
    }
}
```

Step 8: Generate Proxy Code for the Client

We will now generate client proxy code by accessing the service's MEX endpoint with the Svcutil tool:

1. In a command window, change the directory to the location where your client project and source files reside. Run the following Svcutil command:

   ```
   svcutil http://localhost/hello2/service.svc
   ```

   The file Out.cs will be generated, containing the service contract and a proxy class for accessing the service. It should match the code in Listing 3-14.

2. Add Out.cs to your client project. In Visual Studio, right-click the project in the Solution Explorer window and select Add, Existing Item.

3. In the File Open dialog box, select Out.cs and click OK. Out.cs is added to the client project.

Listing 3-14   Hello2 Client: Out.cs

```
//----------------------------------------------------------------------------
// <auto-generated>
//      This code was generated by a tool.
//      Runtime Version:2.0.50105.0
//
//      Changes to this file may cause incorrect behavior and will be lost if
//      the code is regenerated.
// </auto-generated>
//----------------------------------------------------------------------------


[System.ServiceModel.ServiceContractAttribute()]
public interface IHello
{

    [System.ServiceModel.OperationContractAttribute(Action =
        "http://tempuri.org/IHello/Add", ReplyAction =
        "http://tempuri.org/IHello/AddResponse")]
    [return: System.ServiceModel.MessageBodyAttribute(Name = "AddResult",
        Namespace ="http://tempuri.org/")]
    double Add([System.ServiceModel.MessageBodyAttribute(Namespace =
        "http://tempuri.org/")] double n1,
        [System.ServiceModel.MessageBodyAttribute(Namespace =
        "http://tempuri.org/")] double n2);

    [System.ServiceModel.OperationContractAttribute(Action =
        "http://tempuri.org/IHello/Subtract", ReplyAction =
        "http://tempuri.org/IHello/SubtractResponse")]
    [return: System.ServiceModel.MessageBodyAttribute(Name = "SubtractResult",
        Namespace = "http://tempuri.org/")]
    double Subtract([System.ServiceModel.MessageBodyAttribute(Namespace =
        "http://tempuri.org/")] double n1,
```

```csharp
        [System.ServiceModel.MessageBodyAttribute(Namespace =
            "http://tempuri.org/")] double n2);

    [System.ServiceModel.OperationContractAttribute(Action =
        "http://tempuri.org/IHello/Multiply", ReplyAction =
        "http://tempuri.org/IHello/MultiplyResponse")]
    [return: System.ServiceModel.MessageBodyAttribute(Name = "MultiplyResult",
        Namespace = "http://tempuri.org/")]
    double Multiply([System.ServiceModel.MessageBodyAttribute(Namespace =
        "http://tempuri.org/")] double n1,
        [System.ServiceModel.MessageBodyAttribute(Namespace =
        "http://tempuri.org/")] double n2);

    [System.ServiceModel.OperationContractAttribute(Action =
        "http://tempuri.org/IHello/Divide", ReplyAction =
        "http://tempuri.org/IHello/DivideResponse")]
    [return: System.ServiceModel.MessageBodyAttribute(Name = "DivideResult",
        Namespace = "http://tempuri.org/")]
    double Divide([System.ServiceModel.MessageBodyAttribute(Namespace =
        "http://tempuri.org/")] double n1,
        [System.ServiceModel.MessageBodyAttribute(Namespace =
        "http://tempuri.org/")] double n2);
}

public interface IHelloChannel : IHello, System.ServiceModel.IProxyChannel
{
}

public partial class HelloProxy : System.ServiceModel.ProxyBase<IHello>, IHello
{

    public HelloProxy()
    {
    }

    public HelloProxy(string configurationName)
        :
            base(configurationName)
    {
    }

    public HelloProxy(System.ServiceModel.Binding binding)
        :
            base(binding)
    {
    }

    public HelloProxy(System.ServiceModel.EndpointAddress address,
        System.ServiceModel.Binding binding)
        :
            base(address, binding)
    {
    }

    public double Add(double n1, double n2)
```

```
        {
            return base.InnerProxy.Add(n1, n2);
        }

    public double Subtract(double n1, double n2)
        {
            return base.InnerProxy.Subtract(n1, n2);
        }

    public double Multiply(double n1, double n2)
        {
            return base.InnerProxy.Multiply(n1, n2);
        }

    public double Divide(double n1, double n2)
        {
            return base.InnerProxy.Divide(n1, n2);
        }
}

[System.ServiceModel.ServiceContractAttribute(Name =
    "WS-MetadataExchange", Namespace = "http://schemas.xmlsoap.org/ws/2004/08/mex")]
public interface WSMetadataExchange
{

    [System.ServiceModel.OperationContractAttribute(Action =
        "http://schemas.xmlsoap.org/ws/2004/08/mex/GetMetadata/Request", ReplyAction =
        "http://schemas.xmlsoap.org/ws/2004/08/mex/GetMetadata/Response")]
    [return: System.ServiceModel.MessageBodyAttribute(Name = "GetMetadataResult",
        Namespace = "")]
    System.ServiceModel.Message GetMetadata([System.ServiceModel.MessageBodyAttribute
        (Namespace = "")] System.ServiceModel.Message request);

    [System.ServiceModel.OperationContractAttribute(Action =
        "http://schemas.xmlsoap.org/ws/2004/08/mex/Get/Request", ReplyAction =
        "http://schemas.xmlsoap.org/ws/2004/08/mex/Get/Response")]
    [return: System.ServiceModel.MessageBodyAttribute(Name = "GetResult",
        Namespace = "")]
    System.ServiceModel.Message Get([System.ServiceModel.MessageBodyAttribute
        (Namespace = "")] System.ServiceModel.Message request);
}

public interface WSMetadataExchangeChannel : WSMetadataExchange,
    System.ServiceModel.IProxyChannel
{
}

public partial class WSMetadataExchangeProxy : System.ServiceModel.ProxyBase
    <WSMetadataExchange>, WSMetadataExchange
{

    public WSMetadataExchangeProxy()
        {
        }
```

```
   public WSMetadataExchangeProxy(string configurationName)
       :
           base(configurationName)
   {
   }

   public WSMetadataExchangeProxy(System.ServiceModel.Binding binding)
       :
           base(binding)
   {
   }

   public WSMetadataExchangeProxy(System.ServiceModel.EndpointAddress address,
      System.ServiceModel.Binding binding)
       :
           base(address, binding)
   {
   }

   public System.ServiceModel.Message GetMetadata(System.ServiceModel.Message request)
   {
       return base.InnerProxy.GetMetadata(request);
   }

   public System.ServiceModel.Message Get(System.ServiceModel.Message request)
   {
       return base.InnerProxy.Get(request);
   }
}
```

Step 9: Create a Configuration File for the Client

A Client.exe.config file is needed to specify the service endpoint and binding to use. Using an editor or development environment, create a text file with the code shown in Listing 3-15. Save the code under the name Client.exe.config.

To perform these tasks using Visual Studio:

1. Right-click the service project and select Add, New Item.

2. Select Application Configuration File, and click Add.

3. Name the file App.config. (It will be copied to Client.exe.config at build time.)

4. Enter the code in Listing 3-15 into App.config.

Listing 3-15   Hello2 Client: App.config

```xml
<?xml version="1.0" encoding="utf-8" ?>
<configuration xmlns="http://schemas.microsoft.com/.NetConfiguration/v2.0">
    <system.serviceModel>
        <client>
```

```
            <endpoint
                configurationName="HelloEndpoint"
                address="http://localhost/hello2/service.svc"
                bindingConfiguration="helloBinding" bindingSectionName="wsProfileBinding"
                contractType="IHello" />
        </client>
        <bindings>
            <wsProfileBinding>
                <binding configurationName="helloBinding" />
            </wsProfileBinding>
        </bindings>
    </system.serviceModel>
</configuration>
```

Step 10: Build the Client

Build the client program to make client.exe. Resolve any typographical errors.

To perform the task using Visual Studio, select Build Solution from the Build menu to generate Client.exe.

Deployment

We're now ready to try things out. Run the client from your development environment or from a command line. You should see output like that shown in Figure 3-2. Notice that there's no need to launch the service; services hosted in IIS compile and activate when they are accessed. If the program fails, check that you've properly and fully carried out each of the preceding steps.

Figure 3-2   Hello World #2 client

Press ENTER on the client to shut it down. Congratulations on successfully completing your second Indigo program!

Understanding the Service Code

The service program code is shown in Listing 3-10. The service contract for this service is named *IHello*. This is the same contract used in the Hello World #1 example and is defined in the same way, by annotating an interface with attributes.

```
[ServiceContract]
public interface IHello
{
    [OperationContract]
    double Add(double n1, double n2);
    [OperationContract]
    double Subtract(double n1, double n2);
    [OperationContract]
    double Multiply(double n1, double n2);
    [OperationContract]
    double Divide(double n1, double n2);
}
```

The *HelloService* class implements the service contract. The class is marked with a *[ServiceBehavior]* attribute and derives from the *IHello* interface. Each service operation in the contract is implemented as a method. The implementation classes for Hello World #1 and #2 implement service operations identically.

```
[ServiceBehavior]
public class HelloService : IHello
{
    public double Add(double n1, double n2)
    {
        return n1 + n2;
    }
    ...
}
```

The service in this example is hosted by IIS, so there is no need for the hosting code required in Hello World #1. IIS launches the service when a message comes in. The Service.svc file, shown in Listing 3-11, defines the service for IIS. The *Service* directive identifies the service class, ProgrammingIndigo.HelloService. The *Assembly* directive identifies the assembly in which the service class resides, Service.dll.

```
<%@Service language=c# Debug="true" class="ProgrammingIndigo.HelloService" %>
<%@Assembly Name="service" %>
```

The endpoint for the service and the binding it uses are defined in the Web.config file shown in Listing 3-12. This is different from Hello World #1, in which these elements were defined in code. The service endpoint has the address *http://localhost/hello2/service.svc*, a standard *wsProfileBinding* binding, and the contract *IHello*. The endpoint address for this service is quite different from Hello World #1 due to hosting by IIS. The virtual directory (hello2) and .svc filename (Service.svc) form part of the address.

```
<system.serviceModel>
    <client>
        <endpoint
            configurationName="HelloEndpoint"
            address="http://localhost/hello2/service.svc"
            bindingConfiguration="helloBinding"
            bindingSectionName="wsProfileBinding"
            contractType="IHello" />
    </client>
    <bindings>
        <wsProfileBinding>
            <binding configurationName="helloBinding" />
        </wsProfileBinding>
    </bindings>
</system.serviceModel>
```

Understanding the Client Code

The client must agree with the service about address, binding, and contract, or communication will not be possible. Because we are using contract-first development for this client, client proxy code was generated from the service using the Svcutil tool. The generated program code is shown in Listing 3-14. The code generated includes both the service contract, *IHello*, and a class for accessing the service, *HelloProxy*.

The client program code is shown in Listing 3-13. The client creates a proxy to the service by creating a new instance of the generated *HelloProxy* class. The string specified in the constructor, *HelloEndpoint*, specifies a configuration section in which the endpoint for the service is defined. The client configuration file is shown in Listing 3-15. The proxy is created in a *using* statement; when the *using* statement block exits, the proxy is discarded.

```
using (HelloProxy proxy = new HelloProxy("HelloEndpoint"))
{
    ...
}
```

The client's access to the service is straightforward. The service's operations can be called using the proxy channel. When the client is finished communicating with the service, the proxy is closed.

```
// Call the Add service operation.
double value1 = 100.00D;
double value2 = 15.99D;
Console.WriteLine("Calling Add({0},{1})", value1, value2);
double result = proxy.Add(value1, value2);
Console.WriteLine("  Result: {0}", result);
```

```
// Call the Subtract service operation.
value1 = 145.00D;
value2 = 76.54D;
Console.WriteLine("Calling Subtract({0},{1})", value1, value2);
result = proxy.Subtract(value1, value2);
Console.WriteLine("  Result: {0}", result);

...
proxy.Close();
```

A Tale of Two Services: Comparing Hello World #1 and Hello World #2

Hello World #1 was created with code-first programming, whereas the client for Hello World #2 was created with contract-first programming. In the code-first case, this meant copying the service's contract into the client code. In the contract-first case, the contract was generated by pointing the Svcutil tool to the service's MEX endpoint.

The service in Hello World #1 is self-hosted, requiring the program to create an instance of *ServiceHost*, open it, and maintain it while the service is accessed. The service in Hello World #2 requires no hosting code thanks to IIS. The Hello World #1 service must be launched before a client can access it; the Hello World #2 service is launched upon the first client request.

Creating the client was much simpler in Hello World #2 because there was a generated proxy class to use. In Hello World #1, we had to write code to create a channel.

Endpoint and binding definitions for Hello World #1's service and client are defined in code. In Hello World #2 they are defined in .config files.

Summary

This chapter introduced the Indigo programming model, starting with how to set up Indigo on your computer. To develop in Indigo, you need WinFX, a supported operating system, the Microsoft .NET Framework 2.0, and a development environment. Visual Studio 2005 is the recommended development environment because it integrates well with Indigo to provide a richer experience for developers.

Our overview of the development process described service design, development approaches, program implementation, application deployment, hosting, and debugging.

This chapter also introduced the programming model, describing how object orientation (OO) and service orientation (SO) are reconciled. Three programming approaches were identified: declarative programming through service model attributes, imperative programming through the object model, and configuration file–based programming through application .config files. Web hosting eliminates the need to write code to create and start up a service.

We created two "Hello, world" Indigo programs, each comprising a service and a client. Hello World #1's service is self-hosted and created with code-first programming, and it emphasizes doing everything in code. Hello World #2's service is hosted in Internet Information Services, its client was created with contract-first programming, and it emphasizes heavy use of .config file settings to define endpoints and bindings.

The chapters that follow explore Indigo programming by topic, starting with addresses and bindings in Chapter 4 and contracts in Chapter 5.

Part II
Developing in Microsoft Code Name "Indigo"

Chapter 4
Addresses and Bindings

Every path serves a purpose.

—Gene Oliver

As we learned in Chapter 2, endpoints are made up of three parts: addresses, bindings, and contracts. Addresses identify where a service is. Bindings specify how to talk to a service. Contracts define what a service can do. In this chapter, we'll explore addresses and bindings. Then we'll go on to cover contracts in Chapter 5.

After completing this chapter, you will:

- Know how service endpoint addresses are formatted.
- Know the names, purposes, and characteristics of standard bindings.
- Know how to construct a custom binding.
- Understand how to specify and customize bindings in code and configuration files.

Understanding Addresses

Addresses represent the location of a service endpoint. The information in an address includes the following:

- The transport protocol to use
- The name of the target machine where the service is running
- A path on the target machine that identifies the specific service to be accessed

Types of Addresses

There are several kinds of addresses. An **endpoint address** is the address of a service endpoint that a client can access to use the service, such as *http://localhost:8000/MyService/*. A client talks to an endpoint address to use a service.

A **MEX address** is the address of a metadata exchange (HTTP) endpoint address that can be accessed to get information about the service—for example, *http://localhost:8000/MyService*. A client talks to a MEX address to learn about a service.

A **base address** is a primary address associated with a service. By using a base address, you can specify endpoint addresses as relative addresses. For example, in the case of a service with a base address of *http://localhost:8000/MyService*, specifying endpoints Service1 and Service2 establishes endpoints at *http://localhost:8000/MyService/Service1* and *http://localhost:8000/MyService/Service2*.

Address Formats

The address format depends on the transport used. The first part of an address, its **scheme**, identifies the transport. The hosting environment can also impose rules on how addresses are formatted.

The person developing or deploying a service chooses the address for the service's endpoints. A client must know a service's endpoint address to consume the service. Addresses can be specified in code or in a configuration file.

HTTP Addresses

Self-hosted HTTP addresses take the following form:

```
http:// machine-name [:port] [/path/[.../]]
```

Here is an example:

http://www.adventure-works.com:8000/SkiReport/

These are the parts of the address:

- **Scheme**   The *http:* scheme identifies the HTTP protocol.
- **Machine name**   This part is normally a fully qualified domain name. You can use the name *localhost* if all parties communicating are on the same machine.
- **Port number**   This part is optional and is specified as *:port* after the machine name. The port defaults to 80 if omitted. Example: *localhost:8000*.
- **Path**   Paths are one or more names, delimited by forward slashes. Example: */Accounting/*.

If you're using Microsoft Internet Information Services (IIS) 5.1, it's a good idea to specify a port number and avoid port 80 in your addresses because there would be conflicts on port 80. Most examples in this book use port 8000, but there's no special significance to this number.

HTTPS Addresses

HTTP can be made secure using Secure Sockets Layer (SSL). HTTP addresses secured with SSL use the *https:* scheme but otherwise follow the same rules described earlier for HTTP addresses.

Here is an example:

https://www.adventure-works.com:8000/SkiReport/

To use HTTPS, you must obtain a certificate for the server.

TCP Addresses

TCP addresses use the *net.tcp:* scheme but otherwise follow the same rules described earlier for HTTP addresses. Here is an example:

net.tcp://www.adventure-works.com:8000/SkiReport/

The default port for TCP addresses is 808.

Named Pipe Addresses

Named pipe addresses use the *net.pipe:* scheme but otherwise follow most of the rules described earlier for HTTP addresses. There are two differences to be aware of. First, named pipe communication cannot be cross machine. Second, port numbers are not meaningful in named pipe addresses. Here is an example:

net.pipe://localhost/SkiReport/

MSMQ Addresses

MSMQ addresses use the *net.msmq:* scheme and specify a machine name, queue type, and queue name:

```
net.msmq:// machine-name/queue-type/queue-name
```

Here is an example:

net.msmq://localhost/private$/SkiReport

Here are the parts of an MSMQ address:

- **Scheme** The *net.msmq:* scheme identifies the MSMQ protocol.
- **Machine name** Normally a fully qualified domain name. You can use the name *localhost* if all parties communicating are on the same machine.

- **Queue type**   For a private queue, this is */private$*. For a public queue, a queue type is not specified.

- **Queue name**   The name of the queue.

Private queues are available on a local machine, and they can be accessed directly. Public queues are located through Active Directory.

IIS-Hosted Addresses

Services hosted in IIS use Microsoft ASP.NET and follow a different addressing scheme. The address must include a virtual directory name and an.svc filename.

IIS-hosted HTTP addresses take the following form:

```
http:// machine-name [:port] [/vdirpath] filename.svc
```

Here is an example:

http://www.adventure-works.com/SkiReport/service.svc

These are the parts of the address:

- **Scheme**   The *http:* scheme identifies the HTTP protocol.

- **Machine name**   Normally a fully qualified domain name. You can use the name *localhost* if all parties communicating are on the same machine.

- **Port number**   The optional port number is specified as *:port* after the machine name. The port defaults to 80 if omitted. You're free to use port 80 with IIS hosting.

- **Virtual directory name**   Example: */Accounting/*.

- **.svc filename**   In IIS hosting, an .svc file defines the service.

For more information about IIS hosting, see Chapter 10.

Understanding Bindings

A **binding** describes how a service endpoint wants to be communicated with. The communication transport to be used is a key part of the binding. Bindings also specify the following:

- The transport method to be used for communication

- The encoding format

- Security requirements

- Reliable session requirements

- Transaction requirements

Binding Elements

A binding is made up of composable binding elements. Whether you use a standard binding or create your own custom binding, it is made up of a collection of binding elements. Figure 4-1 shows the *BasicProfile* binding and the associated binding elements.

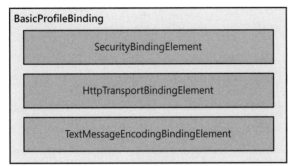

Figure 4-1   Bindings are composed of binding elements.

Standard Bindings

Indigo provides nine predefined **standard bindings**, which are listed in Table 4-1. For common scenarios, one of the standard bindings will usually do the job. Standard bindings can be fine-tuned. For example, many of the standard bindings default to Microsoft Windows security, but you can specify an alternative security schema, such as X.509. If a standard binding doesn't meet your needs, you can create a custom binding.

Table 4-1   Standard Bindings

Binding Name	Interoperability	Encoding	Transport	Data-gram	Request-Reply	Duplex
BasicProfileBinding	Basic Profile	Text	HTTP, HTTPS	Yes	Yes	No
WSProfileBinding	WS Profile	Text, MTOM	HTTP, HTTPS	Yes	Yes	No
WSProfileDualHttpBinding	WS Profile	Text, MTOM	HTTP	Yes	Yes	Yes
NetProfileTcpBinding	.Net Profile	Binary	TCP	Yes	Yes	Yes
NetProfileDualTcpBinding	.Net Profile	Binary	TCP	Yes	Yes	Yes
NetProfileNamedPipeBinding	.Net Profile	Binary	Named pipe	Yes	Yes	Yes
NetProfileMsmqBinding	.Net Profile	Binary	MSMQ	Yes	No	No
MsmqIntegrationBinding	MSMQ	Text	MSMQ	Yes	No	No
IntermediaryBinding	N/A	N/A	HTTP, TCP, named pipe	N/A	N/A	N/A

BasicProfile Binding

The *BasicProfile* binding provides the broadest interoperability. It is the only standard binding that is compatible with first-generation Web services as well as next-generation services. The interoperability of the *BasicProfile* binding comes at some expense: Simple Object Access Protocol (SOAP) security, reliability, and transaction features are not available. The *BasicProfile* binding does allow HTTPS transport security, however. It uses the HTTP or HTTPS transports, and messages have a text encoding. The messaging patterns available are datagram and request-reply. Figure 4-2 shows the transmission of text encoded messages over HTTP or HTTPS using *BasicProfile* binding.

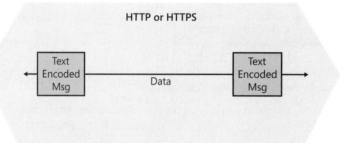

Figure 4-2   *BasicProfile* binding

Table 4-2 lists the characteristics of the *BasicProfile* binding.

Table 4-2   *BasicProfile* **Binding**

Interop Level	Basic Profile
Encoding	Text
Distance	Cross-machine
Transport	HTTP or HTTPS
Security	Transport
Client Authentication	HTTP or BSP
Transport Session	No
Reliable Session	No
Transactions Allowed	No
Datagram Messaging	Yes
Request-Reply messaging	Yes
Duplex Messaging	No

WSProfile Binding

The *WSProfile* binding is compatible with other next-generation Web services (platforms that also implement the same Web Services Architecture standards). It provides full access to

SOAP security, reliability, and transaction features. *WSProfile* uses the HTTP or HTTPS transport, and messages have a text or Message Transmission Optimization Mechanism (MTOM) encoding. The messaging patterns available are datagram and request-reply. Figure 4-3 shows the transmission of a text encoded messages over HTTP or HTTPS using *WSProfile* binding

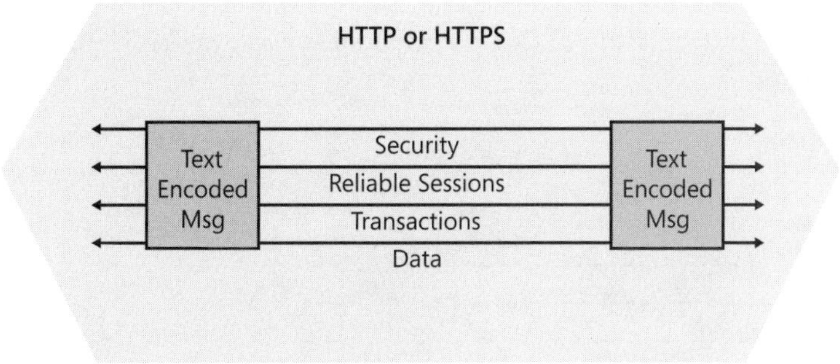

HTTP or HTTPS

| Text Encoded Msg | Security / Reliable Sessions / Transactions / Data | Text Encoded Msg |

Figure 4-3 *WSProfile* binding

Table 4-3 lists the characteristics of the *WSProfile* binding.

Table 4-3 *WSProfile* **Binding**

Interop level	WS-Profile
Encoding	Text or MTOM
Distance	Cross-machine
Transport	HTTP or HTTPS
Security	Transport or WS-Security
Client Authentication	Transport or WS-Security
Transport Session	No
Reliable Session	Yes
Transactions Allowed	Yes
Datagram messaging	Yes
Request-reply messaging	Yes
Duplex messaging	No

WSProfileDualHttp Binding

The *WSProfileDualHttp* binding is compatible with other next-generation Web services (platforms that also implement the same Web Services Architecture standards). This binding provides full access to SOAP security, reliability, and transaction features. *WSProfile* uses the HTTP transport, and messages have a text or MTOM encoding. The messaging patterns available are datagram, request-reply, and duplex.

There are three key differences between *WSProfile* and *WSProfileDualHttp*:

- Only *WSProfile* supports HTTPS transport security.

- Only *WSProfileDualHttp* supports duplex messaging.

- In *WSProfileDualHttp*, reliable sessions are always on. In *WSProfile*, reliable sessions can be enabled or disabled and are off by default.

Figure 4-4 illustrates the transmission of text encoded messages over HTTP or HTTPS using *WSProfileDualHttp* binding.

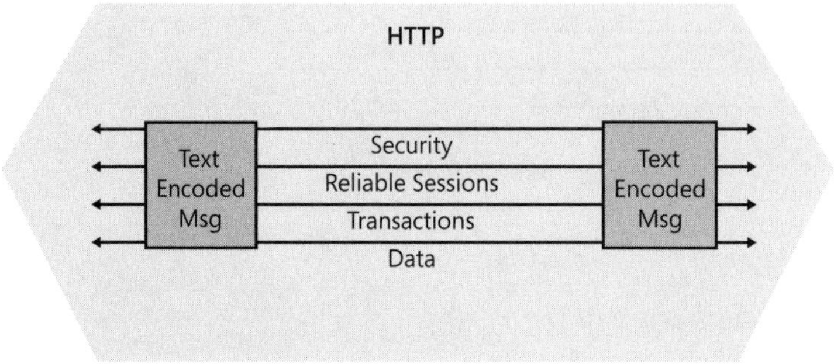

Figure 4-4   *WSProfileDualHttp* binding

Table 4-4 lists the characteristics of the *WSProfileDualHttp* binding.

Table 4-4   *WSProfileDualHttp* Binding

Interop Level	WS-Profile
Encoding	Text or MTOM
Distance	Cross-machine
Transport	HTTP
Security	WS-Security
Client Authentication	Transport or WS-Security
Transport Session	No
Reliable Session	Yes
Transactions Allowed	Yes
Datagram Messaging	Yes
Request-Reply Messaging	Yes
Duplex Messaging	Yes

NetProfileTcp Binding

The *NetProfileTcp* binding provides efficient communication in a .NET-to-.NET environment. This binding provides full access to SOAP security, reliability, and transaction features. *NetProfileTcp* uses the TCP transport, and messages have a binary encoding. The messaging patterns available are datagram and request-reply. Figure 4-5 shows the transmission of text encoded messages over HTTP using *NetProfileTcp* binding.

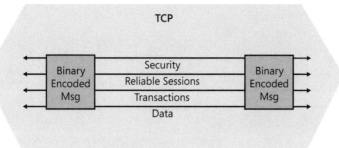

Figure 4-5   *NetProfileTcp* binding

Table 4-5 lists the characteristics of the *NetProfileTcp* binding.

Table 4-5   *NetProfileTcp* **Binding**

Interop Level	.Net Profile
Encoding	Binary
Distance	Cross-machine
Transport	TCP
Security	Transport or WS-Security
Client Authentication	Transport or WS-Security
Transport Session	Yes
Reliable Session	Yes
Transactions Allowed	Yes
Datagram Messaging	Yes
Request-Reply Messaging	Yes
Duplex Messaging	No

NetProfileDualTcp Binding

The *NetProfileDualTcp* binding provides efficient communication in a .NET-to-.NET environment. This binding provides full access to SOAP security, reliability, and transaction features. *NetProfileDualTcp* uses the TCP transport, and messages have a binary encoding. The messaging patterns available are datagram, request-reply, and duplex.

There are two key differences between *NetProfileTcp* and *NetProfileDualTcp*:

- *NetProfileTcp* can use the TCP transport or SOAP to provide security and sessions, whereas *NetProfileDualTcp* can provide this only via SOAP.

- Only *NetProfileDualTcp* supports duplex messaging.

Figure 4-6 shows the transmission of binary encoded messages over TCP using *NetProfile-DualTcp* binding.

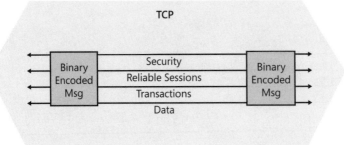

Figure 4-6 *NetProfileDualTcp* binding

Table 4-6 lists the characteristics of the *NetProfileDualTcp* binding.

Table 4-6 *NetProfileDualTcp* Binding

Interop Level	.Net Profile
Encoding	Binary
Distance	Cross-machine
Transport	TCP
Security	WS-Security
Client Authentication	WS-Security
Transport Session	No
Reliable Session	Yes
Transactions Allowed	Yes
Datagram Messaging	Yes
Request-Reply Messaging	Yes
Duplex Messaging	Yes

NetProfileNamedPipe Binding

The *NetProfileNamedPipe* binding provides efficient cross-process communication in a .NET-to-.NET environment. This binding provides full access to SOAP security, reliability, and transaction features. *NetProfileNamedPipe* uses the named pipe transport, and messages have a binary encoding. *NetProfileNamedPipe* cannot cross machines. The messaging patterns available are datagram, request-reply, and duplex. Figure 4-7 shows the transmission of a binary encoded message over TCP using *NetProfileNamedPipe* binding.

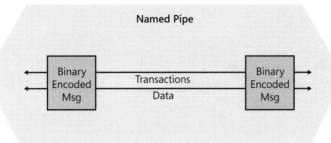

Figure 4-7 *NetProfileNamedPipe* binding

Table 4-7 lists the characteristics of the *NetProfileNamedPipe* binding.

Table 4-7 *NetProfileNamedPipe* Binding

Interop Level	.Net Profile
Encoding	Binary
Distance	Cross-process
Transport	Named pipe
Security	Transport
Client Authentication	Transport
Transport Session	Yes
Reliable Session	No
Transactions Allowed	Yes
Datagram Messaging	Yes
Request-Reply Messaging	Yes
Duplex Messaging	Yes

NetProfileMsmq Binding

The *NetProfileMsmq* binding provides queued communication in a .NET-to-.NET environment. It uses the MSMQ transport, and messages have a binary encoding. Queues can be durable, which allows for time-disconnected operation (or **temporal isolation**): a client and service don't have to be online at the same time. The messaging pattern available is datagram. Figure 4-8 shows the transmission of a binary encoded message over MSMQ using *NetProfile-Msmq* binding.

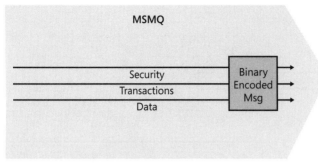

Figure 4-8   *NetProfileMsmq* binding

Table 4-8 lists the characteristics of the *NetProfileMsmq* binding.

Table 4-8   *NetProfileMsmq* **Binding**

Interop Level	.Net Profile
Encoding	Binary
Distance	Cross-machine
Transport	MSMQ
Security	Transport or WS-Security
Client Authentication	Transport or WS-Security
Transport Session	Yes
Reliable Session	No
Transactions Allowed	Yes
Datagram Messaging	Yes
Request-Reply Messaging	No
Duplex Messaging	No

MsmqIntegration Binding

The *MsmqIntegration* binding provides integration between an Indigo program and direct MSMQ. This is very different from *NetProfileMsmq* binding, where MSMQ is used as a transport but the client and service both use Indigo. You use the *MsmqIntegration* binding to allow an Indigo program to communicate with an existing MSMQ deployment that you don't want to modify to communicate with Indigo. The messaging pattern available is datagram. Figure 4-9 shows the transmission of a text encoded message over MSMQ using *MsmqIntegration* binding.

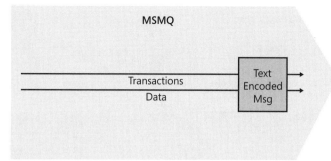

Figure 4-9 *MsmqIntegration* binding

Table 4-9 lists the characteristics of the *MsmqIntegration* binding.

Table 4-9 *MsmqIntegration* **Binding**

Interop Level	MSMQ integration
Encoding	Text
Distance	Cross-machine
Transport	MSMQ
Security	None
Client Authentication	None
Transport Session	No
Reliable Session	Yes
Transactions Allowed	Yes
Datagram Messaging	Yes
Request-Reply Messaging	No
Duplex Messaging	No

Intermediary Binding

The *Intermediary* binding is an intermediary that sits between a client and a service. It can communicate via the HTTP, TCP, or named pipe transport. Figure 4-10 shows the transmission of a message over HTTP, TCP, or a named pipe using *Intermediary* binding.

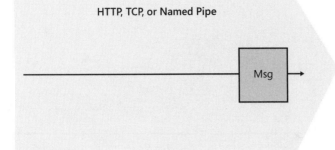

Figure 4-10   *Intermediary* binding

Table 4-10 lists the characteristics of the *Intermediary* binding.

Table 4-10   *Intermediary* Binding

Interop Level	N/A
Encoding	N/A
Distance	Cross-machine or cross-process
Transport	HTTP, TCP, or named pipe
Security	N/A
Client Authentication	N/A
Transport Session	N/A
Reliable Session	N/A
Transactions Allowed	N/A
Datagram Messaging	N/A
Request-Reply Messaging	N/A
Duplex Messaging	N/A

Programming Addresses

The programming tasks in this section involve working with addresses. In addition to performing the most common task of specifying endpoint addresses, developers can define base addresses and work with MEX endpoints.

Exposing a MEX Endpoint

A MEX endpoint provides a way for clients or tools to learn about your service. Indigo creates a MEX endpoint for your service if a base address is specified for it. (The next section explains how to specify a base address.) If your service is hosted in IIS, a base address is already known for your service.

When an HTTP base address is defined for a service, a MEX endpoint is also created with the same address. An HTTP base address is implicitly defined for services hosted in IIS. In a self-hosted service, you need to define an HTTP base address explicitly in order to have a MEX endpoint.

Specifying a Base Address

Self-hosted services create an instance of the *ServiceHost* instance. The base address for a service can be specified in the *ServiceHost<T>* constructor as a URI. The following code creates a *ServiceHost* and specifies a base address for the service.

```
Uri baseAddress = new Uri("http://localhost:8000/MyService");
ServiceHost<MyService> ServiceHost = new ServiceHost<MyService>(baseAddress);
```

Services can have more than one base address. With more than one endpoint, more than one transport might be in use. For example, if a service offers both an HTTP and a TCP endpoint, you can specify a base address for each transport. The *ServiceHost* constructor accommodates this by accepting any number of URIs. The following code specifies three base addresses for a service. You can't have more than one base address for the same transport.

```
Uri uri1 = new Uri("http://localhost:8000/MyService");
Uri uri2 = new Uri("net.tcp://localhost:9000/MyService");
Uri uri3 = new Uri("net.pipe://localhost/private$/MyService");
ServiceHost<MyService> ServiceHost = new ServiceHost<MyService>(uri1, uri2, uri3);
```

Once a service has one or more base addresses defined, you can specify endpoints for the service by using relative addresses (in code or in a configuration file).

If you specify a base address for a service, a MEX endpoint is created for the service.

Learning Service Endpoint Addresses

If you know the MEX address for a service, you can learn the addresses of the service's endpoints using the Svcutil tool. On the Svcutil command line, you specify the MEX address and */config:filename* to generate a .config file. The generated file will include endpoint definitions for the service, including addresses.

```
svcutil http://localhost:8000/SomeService /config:service.config
```

Specifying Endpoint Addresses

Endpoint addresses can be specified in code or in configuration settings. An endpoint address can be absolute or relative to a base address.

Specifying Endpoint Addresses in Code

You can specify addresses in several ways in code. Various classes and constructors in Indigo accept addresses as *string*, *Uri*, or *EndpointAddress* types. The following code adds an endpoint to a service using the *Uri* class.

```
Uri address = new Uri("http://localhost:8000/Server/Math/");
ServiceHost<MathService> service = new ServiceHost<MathService>();
service.AddEndpoint(typeof(IMath), binding, address);
```

Specifying Endpoint Addresses in a Configuration File

Clients and services can define endpoints in configuration files. The *address* attribute of the *endpoint* element is where the address is specified.

```
<endpoint
    configurationName="SampleEndpoint"
    address="http://localhost/MyService/service.svc"
    bindingSectionName="wsProfileDualHttpBinding"
    contractType="ISampleContract" />
```

Specifying Relative Endpoint Addresses

Endpoint addresses can be absolute, as in the code just shown, or relative if a service has a base address. The following configuration file, for an IIS-hosted service, specifies a relative address.

```
<endpoint
    configurationName="SampleEndpoint"
    address="ThisEndpoint"
    bindingSectionName="wsProfileDualHttpBinding"
    contractType="ISampleContract" />
```

Note that a relative address can be empty, which means the endpoint address is the same as the service's base address. If the base address for this service is *http://localhost/MyVdir/MyService.svc*, the following code defines an endpoint whose address is the same as the base address, *http://localhost/MyVdir/MyService.svc*.

```
<endpoint
    configurationName="SampleEndpoint"
    address=""
    bindingSectionName="wsProfileDualHttpBinding"
    contractType="ISampleContract" />
```

Programming Bindings

Developers can make use of standard bindings or define their own custom bindings. Bindings can be defined, configured, and specified in code or configuration settings.

Specifying Endpoints

Both clients and services have to define endpoints. Services do so to create endpoints, and clients do so to access endpoints. Whenever a client or service defines an endpoint, an address, binding, and contract must be specified. This information can be specified in code or in .config settings. You can find out more about how clients and services specify endpoints in Chapters 6 and 7.

Table 4-11 shows the class names and configuration file keywords for the standard bindings.

Table 4-11   Binding Classes and Configuration File Keywords

Binding	Class	Configuration File Name
BasicProfile	*BasicProfileBinding*	*basicProfileBinding*
Custom	*CustomBinding*	*customBinding*
Intermediary	*IntermediaryBinding*	*intermediaryBinding*
MsmqIntegration	*MsmqIntegrationBinding*	*msmqIntegrationBinding*
NetProfileDualTcp	*NetProfileDualTcpBinding*	*netProfileDualTcpBinding*
NetProfileMsmq	*NetProfileMsmqBinding*	*netProfileMsmqBinding*
NetProfileNamedPipe	*NetProfileNamedPipeBinding*	*netProfileNamedPipeBinding*
NetProfileTcp	*NetProfileTcpBinding*	*netProfileTcpBinding*
WSProfile	*WSProfileBinding*	*wsProfileBinding*
WSProfileDualHttp	*WSProfileDualHttpBinding*	*wsProfileDualHttpBinding*

Specifying a Binding for an Endpoint in Code

When a binding for an endpoint is defined in code, a binding must be created from one of the binding classes. There are binding classes for each of the standard bindings as well as a *CustomBinding* class for standard bindings. You can tailor the binding if desired. For example, the following code creates an instance of the *BasicProfileBinding* class and specifies it as an endpoint that is added to a service.

```
BasicProfileBinding binding = new BasicProfileBinding();
service.AddEndpoint(typeof(ICounter), binding, address);
```

The binding classes are listed in Table 4-11. The constructors for the binding classes vary and are enumerated in the Indigo documentation.

We will look at how to create a binding in code shortly.

Specifying a Binding for an Endpoint in a Configuration File

When you define a binding for an endpoint in .config settings, you must specify a binding type. You do this using the *bindingSectionName* attribute of the *endpoint* element. For example, the following endpoint definition specifies the *WSProfile* binding.

```
<endpoint
    address="http://localhost/MyService/service.svc"
    bindingSectionName="wsProfileBinding"
    contractType="ISampleContract" />
```

The binding configuration names are listed in Table 4-11 (in a previous section). Notice that binding names in a configuration file use camel casing and begin with lowercase letters.

For details on how to create a binding in .config settings, see the section titled "Creating a Binding in a Configuration File" later in this chapter.

Creating a Binding in Code

Bindings in code are created using one of the standard binding classes listed in Table 4-11 (shown earlier). In the following code, a *WSProfile* binding is created by creating an instance of *WSProfileBinding* and is then used to add an endpoint to the service.

```
WSProfileBinding binding = new WSProfileBinding();
service.AddEndpoint(typeof(IMyService), binding, address);
```

Tailoring a Standard Binding in Code

Bindings in code can be tailored in two ways. You can customize certain constructors for the binding classes, or you can modify a binding's properties. The following code creates a *WSProfile* binding by creating an instance of *WSProfileBinding* and specifying a security mode in the constructor. Next, the message encoding is set and a proxy option is disabled using properties. At this point, the tailored standard binding is used to create an endpoint.

```
WSProfileBinding binding = new WSProfileBinding(WSProfileSecurityMode.WSSecurityOverHttp);
binding.MessageEncoding = WSMessageEncoding.Text;
binding.UseSystemWebProxy = false;
service.AddEndpoint(typeof(IMyService), binding, address);
```

Creating a Custom Binding in Code

Custom bindings are created with the *CustomBinding* class. The constructor to *CustomBinding* accepts a variable number of binding elements. The following code creates a custom binding with reliable sessions, composite duplex, and HTTP transport.

```
CustomBinding binding = new CustomBinding(new ReliableSessionBindingElement(),
    new CompositeDuplexBindingElement(), new HttpTransportBindingElement()));
service.AddEndpoint(typeof(IMyService), binding, address);
```

When creating a custom binding, you must add binding elements in a specific order:

1. Context flow

2. Reliable sessions

3. Security

4. Composite duplex

5. Transport

6. Message encoding

Creating a Binding in a Configuration File

In a .config endpoint definition, you specify a binding by using the *bindingSectionName* attribute of the *endpoint* element. You can specify a binding .config name from Table 4-11 (shown earlier). The following endpoint definition specifies the *BasicProfile* binding.

```
<endpoint
    address="http://localhost/MyService/service.svc"
    bindingSectionName="basicProfileBinding"
    contractType="ISampleContract" />
```

If you don't want to tailor the binding, this is all you have to do.

Tailoring a Standard Binding in a Configuration File

You can tailor a standard binding by adding a binding configuration to your .config file. You specify a **binding configuration** in a *<bindings>* area of the .config file that is separate from where endpoints are defined. A configuration name attribute links an endpoint to a binding configuration.

The bindings area contains a nested set of elements. The outermost element is *<bindings>*. Within that is an element with the binding type, such as *<wsProfileBinding>* or *<netProfileTcp-Binding>*. Within that, a *<binding>* section defines a binding configuration. The following partial .config file defines two *BasicProfileBinding* configurations and one *WSProfileBinding* configuration.

```
<system.serviceModel>
    ...
    <bindings>
        <basicProfileBinding>
            <binding ... />
            <binding ... />
        </basicProfileBinding>
        <wsProfileBinding>
            <binding ... />
        </wsProfileBinding>
    </bindings>
</system.serviceModel>
```

A binding configuration is in a different section of the .config file from the endpoint definitions, so how are they related? In the binding configuration, the *binding* element has a *configurationName* attribute that gives the configuration a name. This name is specified in an endpoint definition by using a *bindingConfiguration* attribute.

Let's see how this looks in practice. The following .config file shows a binding configuration named *SampleBinding* that enables transaction flow. Note that even when you specify a binding configuration for an endpoint with *bindingConfiguration*, the *bindingSectionName* parameter is still required.

```
<system.serviceModel>
    <services>
        <service serviceType="ProgrammingIndigo.SampleService">
            <endpoint address="http://localhost:8000/TransactedWork/"
                bindingConfiguration="SampleBinding"
                bindingSectionName="wsProfileBinding"
                contractType="ProgrammingIndigo.ISampleContract" />
        </service>
    </services>
    <bindings>
        <wsProfileBinding>
        <binding configurationName="SampleBinding" flowTransactions="Required" />
        </wsProfileBinding>
    </bindings>
</system.serviceModel>
```

Creating a Custom Binding in a Configuration File

Creating a custom binding is similar to tailoring a standard binding. In an endpoint definition, *bindingSectionName* is set to *customBinding*. The configuration file contains an area for binding configurations in which a *binding* element contains a *customBinding* element that contains one or more binding configurations. The binding configuration has a name, specified in the *configurationName* attribute of the *binding* element. This name is specified in an *endpoint* element's *bindingConfiguration* attribute. The following configuration file shows a custom binding named *MyBinding*.

```
<?xml version="1.0" encoding="utf-8" ?>
<configuration xmlns="http://schemas.microsoft.com/.NetConfiguration/v2.0">
    <system.serviceModel>
        <services>
            <service serviceType="ProgrammingIndigo.MyService">
                <endpoint address="http://localhost:8000/MyService/"
                    bindingSectionName="customBinding"
                    bindingConfiguration="MyBinding"
                    contractType="ProgrammingIndigo.IMyService" />
            </service>
        </services>
        <bindings>
            <customBinding>
                <binding configurationName="MyBinding">
                    <httpTransport />
                </binding>
            </customBinding>
        </bindings>
    </system.serviceModel>
</configuration>
```

The binding elements that make up the custom binding are specified within the binding configuration's *binding* element. In this example, the custom binding specifies just one binding element, HTTP transport.

Setting Standard Binding Properties

You can fine-tune the behavior of a standard binding by modifying its properties, which are described next. Not every binding contains each of these properties. To determine what properties a specific binding offers, see the section for that binding later in this chapter.

Some of these properties provide low-level technical control over HTTP and TCP communication that we cannot describe in detail in this book.

AddressingMode

The MSMQ transport can use several methods to resolve an endpoint address to a queue. The *AddressingMode* property can be set to *Native*, *DirectoryLookup*, *Srmp*, and *SecureSrmp*. The default value is *Native*.

- *Native*   The queue is addressed directly. The machine in which the queue is located is indicated in the endpoint address.

- *DirectoryLookup*   The queue is located through Active Directory.

- *Srmp*   The queue is accessed via HTTP using the SOAP Reliable Messaging Protocol (SRMP) protocol.

- *SecureSrmp*   The queue is accessed via HTTPS using the SRMP protocol.

BasicSecurityProfileAlgorithmSuite

The *BasicSecurityProfileAlgorithmSuite* property specifies the algorithm used for security encryption. This property can be set to *Default*, *Aes256*, *Aes192*, *Aes128*, or *TripleDes*.

BypassProxyOnLocal

If a proxy server is in use, the *BypassProxyOnLocal* property determines whether local addresses are routed through the proxy server. If *BypassProxyOnLocal* is *true*, requests to local Internet resources do not use the proxy server. If *BypassProxyOnLocal* is *false*, all requests are made through the proxy server.

ClientBaseAddress

The *ClientBaseAddress* property allows an address to be specified for the client. The default value is *null*, in which case an address is generated based on the transport in use.

DeadLetterQueue

For bindings that use the MSMQ transport, the *DeadLetterQueue* property identifies a queue to send messages that have expired or that fail transfer and delivery. The default value is the system dead letter queue, *net.msmq://localhost/System$;DeadXAct.*

Durable

For bindings that use the MSMQ transport, the *Durable* property identifies whether queued messages are durable or volatile. Durable messages are persisted to disk; volatile queue messages are not. Durable messages require delivery assurances and use of transactional queues. The default value is *true.*

FlowLocale

The *FlowLocale* property determines whether the client's locale should be flowed to the server. The property can be set to *NotAllowed*, *Allowed*, or *Required*. The default value is *NotAllowed*.

FlowLogicalThreadId

The *FlowLogicalThreadId* property determines whether the client's logical thread ID should be flowed to the server. The property can be set to *NotAllowed*, *Allowed*, or *Required*. The default value is *NotAllowed*.

FlowTransactions

The *FlowTransactions* property controls whether transactions can flow between programs via WS-Transactions. Possible values are *NotAllowed*, *Allowed*, and *Required*. The default value is *NotAllowed*.

- **NotAllowed**   A transaction must not flow from the client; if one does, the client will receive a fault.

- **Allowed**   A transaction can flow from the client; the service is fine whether or not a transaction is flowed.

- **Required**   A transaction must flow from the client; otherwise, the client will receive a fault.

HostnameComparisonMode

A computer can have more than one valid hostname. For example, *www.adventure-works.com* and *www.contoso.com* could map to the same IP address. The setting of the *HostnameComparisonMode* property determines how close a match is necessary for a message to be routed to your service. The possible values are *Exact*, *StrongWildcard*, and *WeakWildcard*. The default value for most bindings is *StrongWildcard*.

- *Exact*   A client can reach an endpoint only by specifying the same hostname as the endpoint.

- *StrongWildcard*   A client can reach an endpoint by specifying any valid hostname.

- *WeakWildcard*   Similar to *StrongWildcard*, but the endpoint receives only messages that no other endpoint would respond to.

HttpAuthentication

The *HttpAuthentication* property is used to configure HTTP authentication options. It applies only when the *HttpAuthenticationOverHttps* security mode is in use. The property references an object with the following properties:

- *HttpAuthenticationLevel*   The HTTP authentication level. This can be set to *None*, *MutualAuthRequested*, or *MutualAuthRequired*.

- *Scheme*   The authentication scheme in use. This can be set to *Digest*, *Negotiate*, *Ntlm*, *Basic*, or *Anonymous*.

- *ProxyScheme*   The proxy authentication scheme in use. This can be set to *Digest*, *Negotiate*, *Ntlm*, *Basic*, or *Anonymous*.

- *Realm*   A description string that defines a set of protected resources.

KeepAliveEnabled

The *KeepAliveEnabled* property determines whether TCP-level KeepAlive is used. If you are crossing intermediaries such as firewalls, Network Address Translators (NATs), or proxies, *KeepAlive* can be useful in preventing idle timeouts. The default value is *false*.

IPv6SocketProtectionLevel

The *IPv6SocketProtectionLevel* property configures the *IPV6_PROTECTION_LEVEL* option of the communication socket. Possible values are *Default*, *Restricted*, and *Unrestricted*. The default value is *Default*.

MaxBufferSize

The *MaxBufferSize* property specifies the amount of memory used to buffer incoming messages in memory. If more data is received than can be buffered, the data remains on the underlying socket until there is room in the buffer. The minimum value for *MaxBufferSize* is *MaxMessageSize*. The default value is *65536*.

MaxConnections

The *MaxConnections* property controls the maximum number of connections. The default is *10*.

MaxMessageSize

The *MaxMessageSize* property specifies the maximum size permissible for a message. The default value for most bindings is *65536*.

MaxRetries

For bindings that use the MSMQ transport, the *MaxRetries* property identifies the number of attempts made to deliver a message from its queue. If this value is reached, the message moves from its main application queue to a retry queue. The default value is *3*.

MaxRetryCycles

For bindings that use the MSMQ transport, messages that fail delivery and reach the *MaxRetries* setting enter a retry queue. When messages are moved into a retry queue, they remain there for a period of time controlled by the *RetryCycleDelay* property, and then they are moved back to the application queue to attempt delivery again. The *MaxRetryCycle* property determines how many times this can happen. The default value is *3*. If all retry attempts fail, the message is moved to a poison queue or a delivery failure is sent back to the sender of the message, based on the *RejectAfterLastRetry* property.

MessageEncoding

The *MessageEncoding* property determines the encoding used for messages. It can be set to *Binary*, *Text*, or *Mtom*.

- *Binary*   Encodes messages with the binary message encoder
- *Text*   Encodes messages with the text message encoder
- *Mtom*   Encodes messages with the MTOM encoder

MsmqAuthenticationMode

For bindings that use the MSMQ transport, the *MsmqAuthenticationMode* property controls whether identity is included in the message. It can be set to *None*, *Windows*, or *Certificate*. The default value is *Windows*. Including identity in the messages allows authentication to be used to limit access to the queue.

- *None*   No identity is included in the message.
- *Windows*   Identity is included in the message, and the user identity is mapped to a certificate in Active Directory. This mode allows authentication against an access control list (ACL).
- *Certificate*   Identity is included in the message, and the user identity is mapped to a certificate in a certificate store.

MsmqEncryptionLevel

For bindings that use the MSMQ transport, the *MsmqEncryptionLevel* property controls encryption and signing of messages. It can be set to *None*, *Sign*, or *EncryptAndSign*. The default value is *EncryptAndSign*.

OrderedSession

The *OrderedSession* property controls whether messages are guaranteed to be delivered in order. If true and reliable sessions are enabled (*ReliableSessionEnabled* is *true*), messages arrive in order. The default value is *true*.

ProxyAddress

The *ProxyAddress* property specifies the address of an HTTP proxy server to route requests through. The default value is *null*. If you set *ProxyAddress* to a non-null value, the *UseSystem-WebProxy* property must be *false*.

ReliableSessionEnabled

The *ReliableSessionEnabled* property controls reliable sessions. If it is set to *true*, reliable sessions are enabled and WS-ReliableMessaging is used to create sessionful channels. The default value is *false*.

RejectAfterLastRetry

For bindings that use the MSMQ transport, the *RejectAfterLastRetry* property determines what happens after retry attempts to deliver a message fail. A value of *true* means a message is rejected after the maximum number of retries fail. A value of *false* means the message is sent to a poison queue. The default value is *true*.

RetryCycleDelay

For bindings that use the MSMQ transport, the *RetryCycleDelay* property determines the delay between attempts to deliver a message. The default value is 10 minutes.

SecurityMode

The *SecurityMode* property sets the type of security to be used. The choices vary with the bindings. Most bindings default to Windows security. The possible values for this mode vary from one binding to another. Here are the possible values:

- *None*   Security is disabled.
- *HttpAuthentication*   HTTP authentication security is used.

- *BasicSecurityProfileMutualCertificate*   Basic Security Profile security with mutual certificates is used.

- *Https*   HTTPS transport security is used. This security mode provides message integrity, confidentiality, and server authentication. There is no client authentication.

- *HttpsWithClientCertificate*   HTTPS transport security with an X.509 certificate on the client side is used. This security mode provides message integrity, confidentiality, and mutual authentication.

- *HttpAuthenticationOverHttps*   HTTP authentication is used over HTTPS transport security. This security mode provides message integrity, confidentiality, and server authentication.

- *BasicSecurityProfileCertificateOverHttps*   Basic Security Profile security with certificate over HTTPS transport security is used.

- *BasicSecurityProfileUsernameOverHttps*   Basic Security Profile security with user name authentication over HTTPS transport security is used.

- *WSSecurityOverHttp*   WS-Security is used over HTTP. This security mode provides message integrity, confidentiality, and authentication.

- *TcpWithWindowsSecurity*   Windows security is used over TCP. This security mode provides message integrity, confidentiality, and mutual authentication.

- *TcpWithSsl*   SSL security is used over TCP. This security mode provides message integrity, confidentiality, and server authentication. There is no client authentication.

- *WSSecurityOverTcp*   WS-Security is used over TCP. This security mode provides message integrity, confidentiality, and authentication.

SerializationFormat

The *MsmqIntegration* binding allows selection of a serialization format. The possible values are *ActiveX*, *Binary*, *ByteArray*, *ByteStream*, and *Xml*. The default value is *Xml*.

- *ActiveX*   Uses the *ActiveXMessageFormatter* to serialize messages
- *Binary*   Uses the *BinaryMessageFormatter* to serialize messages
- *ByteArray*   Uses a byte array to serialize messages
- *ByteStream*   Uses a byte stream to serialize messages
- *Xml*   Uses the *XmlMessageFormatter* to serialize messages

SessionConnectTimeout

The *SessionConnectTimeout* property specifies the amount of time a session connect operation can take. The default value is 30 seconds.

SessionInactivityTimeout

The *SessionInactivityTimeout* property specifies the maximum amount of time a session can be idle before it is terminated. The default value is 5 minutes.

TcpPortSharingEnabled

The *TcpPortSharingEnabled* property controls whether services can share TCP ports. The default value is *false*, meaning a binding uses a TCP port exclusively. This property applies only to services, not clients.

TcpProtectionLevel

The *TcpProtectionLevel* property specifies the message protection level used with TCP security if the security mode is set to *TcpWithSsl* or *TcpWithWindowsSecurity*. Possible values are *None*, *Sign*, and *EncryptAndSign*. The default value is *EncryptAndSign*.

TcpProtectionLevel

The *TcpProtectionLevel* property specifies the message protection level used for TCP-based security if the security mode is *TcpWithSsl* or *TcpWithWindowsSecurity*. The default value is *EncryptAndSign*.

TextEncoding

The *TextEncoding* property specifies the character set encoding for messages. The default value is *utf-8*.

TimeToLive

For bindings that use the MSMQ transport, the *TimeToLive* property determines how long the message is held if the receiving application is not immediately available to read the message. For time-sensitive messages, you can use this property to specify how long messages will remain in the queue. Messages whose time to live has expired are moved to the dead letter queue. The default value is 24 hours.

TransferMode

The *TransferMode* property specifies whether messages are buffered or streamed. The possible values are *Buffered* and *Streaming*. The default value is *Buffered*. If you use *Streaming*, reliable sessions must not be enabled and the security mode must be *None*, *TcpWithSsl*, or *TcpWith-WindowsSecurity*.

TransferTimeout

The *TransferTimeout* property specifies the maximum amount of time a message transfer can take. The default value is *00:10:00* (10 minutes).

UseSystemWebProxy

The *UseSystemWebProxy* property allows the system's autoconfigured HTTP proxy to be used, if it is available. The default value is *true*.

WSSecurity

The *WSSecurity* property is used to configure the security behavior of the binding. When you use a *WSProfile* binding, if the security mode is *WSSecurityOverHttp*, the property references a *WSSecurityOverHttp* object. When you use a *NetProfile* binding and the TCP transport, if the security mode is *NetProfileSecurityMode*, the property references a *WSSecurityOverTcp* object.

Programming the *BasicProfile* Binding

You can specify and customize the *BasicProfile* binding in code or in a configuration file. Table 4-12 shows the properties of the *BasicProfile* binding.

Table 4-12   *BasicProfile* Binding Properties

Property	Default Value	Valid Values
BasicSecurityProfileAlgorithmSuite	Default	Default, Aes256, Aes192, Aes128, TripleDes
BypassProxyOnLocal	true	N/A
HostnameComparisonMode	StrongWildcard	Exact, StrongWildcard, WeakWildcard
MaxMessageSize	65536	N/A
MessageEncoding	Text	Text, MTOM
ProxyAddress	N/A	N/A
SecurityMode	None	None, HttpAuthentication, BasicSecurity-ProfileMutualCertificate, Https, HttpsWithClientCertificate, HttpAuthenticationOverHttps, BasicSecurityProfileCertificateOverHttps, BasicSecurityProfileUsernameOverHttps
TextEncoding	utf-8	N/A
TransferTimeout	00:10:00	N/A
UseSystemWebProxy	true	N/A

Specifying *BasicProfile* in a Configuration File

The *BasicProfile* binding is specified as part of a client or service endpoint definition. In an endpoint element, you set the *bindingSectionName* attribute to *"basicProfileBinding"*.

```
<endpoint
    address="http://www.contoso.com:8000/ExpenseReport"
    bindingSectionName="basicProfileBinding"
    contractType="IExpenseReport" />
```

If you're using the default configuration of the binding, this is all you need to do. The next section describes how to customize the binding.

Customizing *BasicProfile* in a Configuration File

To customize the *BasicProfile* binding, include a *bindingConfiguration* attribute in an endpoint definition that specifies a binding configuration name. Note that you use *bindingConfiguration* in addition to, not in place of, the *bindingSectionName* attribute that specifies the binding type.

```
<system.serviceModel>
    ...
    <service ...>
        <endpoint
            address="http://www.contoso.com:8000/ExpenseReport"
            bindingSectionName="basicProfileBinding"
            bindingConfiguration="MyCustomBinding"
            contractType="IExpenseReport" />
    </service>
</system.serviceModel>
```

The binding customization is done in a binding configuration that appears in a separate section of the configuration file. The binding configuration is defined in a *<binding>* element, which is contained within a *<basicProfileBinding>* section element, which in turn is contained in an outer *<bindings>* element. The binding configuration must have a name that matches the *bindingConfiguration* value specified in the endpoint.

```
<system.serviceModel>
    ...
    <bindings>
        <basicProfileBinding>
            <binding configurationName="MyCustomBinding" ... />
        </basicProfileBinding>
    </bindings>
</system.serviceModel>
```

Table 4-12, shown earlier, lists the binding properties that can be used in a *BasicProfile* binding configuration.

Listing 4-1 shows a configuration file that configures the *BasicProfile* binding. The values shown are the default values for the binding.

Listing 4-1   *BasicProfile* Binding Configuration

```xml
<?xml version="1.0" encoding="utf-8" ?>
<configuration xmlns="http://schemas.microsoft.com/.NetConfiguration/v2.0">
    <system.serviceModel>
        <client>
            <endpoint
                configurationName="MyEndpoint"
                address="http://localhost/myservice/service.svc"
                bindingSectionName="basicProfileBinding"
                bindingConfiguration="Binding1"
                contractType="IMyService" />
        </client>
        <bindings>
            <basicProfileBinding>
                <binding configurationName="Binding1"
                    hostnameComparisonMode="StrongWildcard"
                    transferTimeout="00:10:00"
                    maxMessageSize="65536"

                    messageEncoding="Text"
                    textEncoding="utf-8"

                    bypassProxyOnLocal="false"
                    useSystemWebProxy="true"
                    proxyAddress=""

                    securityMode="None"
                    basicSecurityProfileAlgorithmSuite="Default">
                </binding>
            </basicProfileBinding>
        </bindings>
    </system.serviceModel>
</configuration>
```

Specifying *BasicProfile* in Code

You can use the *BasicProfileBinding* class to create a *BasicProfile* binding in code. The following code uses *BasicProfileBinding* to add an endpoint to a service.

```csharp
Uri baseAddress = new Uri("http://localhost:8000/MyService/");
BasicProfileBinding binding = new BasicProfileBinding();
service.AddEndpoint(typeof(IMyService), binding, address);
```

Customizing *BasicProfile* in Code

The *BasicProfileBinding* class can be customized. After creating an instance of the class, you can adjust its properties before using it in endpoint construction. The following code creates an instance of *BasicProfileBinding*, changes the maximum message size, and uses the binding to create an endpoint.

```
Uri address = new Uri("http://localhost:8000/MyService/");
BasicProfileBinding binding = new BasicProfileBinding();
binding.MaxMessageSize = 200000;
service.AddEndpoint(typeof(IMyService), binding, address);
```

Table 4-12, shown earlier, lists the binding properties that can be used in a *BasicProfile* binding configuration.

Programming the *WSProfile* Binding

You can specify and customize the *WSProfile* binding in code or in a configuration file. Table 4-13 shows the properties of the *WSProfile* binding.

Table 4-13 *WSProfile* **Binding Properties**

Attribute	Default Value	Valid Values
BypassProxyOnLocal	*true*	N/A
FlowTransactions	*NotAllowed*	*Allowed, Ignore, NotAllowed, Required*
HostnameComparisonMode	*StrongWildcard*	*Exact, StrongWildcard, WeakWildcard*
HttpAuthentication.Level	*None*	*None, MutualAuthRequested, Mutual-AuthRequired*
HttpAuthentication.Scheme	*Anonymous*	*None, Anonymous, Basic, Digest, IntegratedWindowsAuthentication, Negotiate, Ntlm*
HttpAuthentication.ProxyScheme	*Anonymous*	*None, Anonymous, Basic, Digest, IntegratedWindowsAuthentication, Negotiate, Ntlm*
HttpAuthentication.Realm	N/A	N/A
MaxMessageSize	*65536*	N/A
MessageEncoding	*Text*	*Text, MTOM*
OrderedSession	*true*	N/A
ProxyAddress	N/A	N/A
ReliableSessionEnabled	*false*	N/A
SecurityMode	*WSSecurityOverHttp*	*None, Https, HttpsWithClientCertificate, HttpAuthenticationOverHttps, WSSecurityOverHttp*
SessionConnectTimeout	*30 seconds*	N/A
SessionInactivityTimeout	*5 minutes*	N/A
TextEncoding	*utf-8*	N/A
TransferTimeout	*00:10:00*	N/A
UseSystemWebProxy	*true*	N/A
WSSecurity.ProtectionLevel	*EncryptAndSign*	*None, Sign, EncryptAndSign*

Table 4-13 *WSProfile* **Binding Properties**

Attribute	Default Value	Valid Values
WSSecurity.UseNegotiation	*true*	N/A
WSSecurity.AuthenticationMode	*Windows*	*Windows, Anonymous, Username, Certificate*
WSSecurity.AlgorithmSuite	*Default*	*Default, Aes256, Aes192, Aes128, TripleDes*

Specifying *WSProfile* in a Configuration File

The *WSProfile* binding is specified as part of a client or service endpoint definition. In an endpoint element, you set the *BindingSectionName* attribute to *"wsProfileBinding"*.

```
<endpoint
    address="http://www.contoso.com:8000/ExpenseReport"
    bindingSectionName="wsProfileBinding"
    contractType="IExpenseReport" />
```

If you're using the default configuration of the binding, this is all you need to do. If you need to customize the binding, see the next section.

Customizing *WSProfile* in a Configuration File

To customize the *WSProfile* binding, include a *bindingConfiguration* attribute in an endpoint definition that specifies a binding configuration name.

```
<system.serviceModel>
    ...
    <service ...>
        <endpoint
            address="http://www.contoso.com:8000/ExpenseReport"
            bindingSectionName="wsProfileBinding"
            bindingConfiguration="MyCustomBinding"
            contractType="IExpenseReport" />
    </service>
</system.serviceModel>
```

The binding customization is done in a binding configuration that appears in a separate section of the configuration file. The binding configuration is defined in a *<binding>* element, which is contained within a *<wsProfileBinding>* section element, which in turn is contained in an outer *<bindings>* element. The binding configuration must have a name that matches the *bindingConfiguration* value specified in the endpoint.

```
<system.serviceModel>
    ...
    <bindings>
        <wsProfileBinding>
            <binding configurationName="MyCustomBinding" ... />
        </wsProfileBinding>
```

```
    </bindings>
</system.serviceModel>
```

Table 4-13, shown earlier, lists the binding properties that can be used in a *WSProfile* binding configuration. The *WSSecurity* attributes described earlier appear in a *<wsSecurity>* element, like this:

```
<binding configurationName="Binding1"
        useSystemWebProxy="true"
        bypassProxyOnLocal="false"
        securityMode="WSSecurityOverHttp">
    <wsSecurity authenticationMode="Windows"
                protectionLevel="EncryptAndSign"
                useNegotiation="true"
                algorithmSuite="Default" />
</binding>
```

Listing 4-2 shows a configuration file that configures the *WSProfile* binding. The values shown are the default values for the binding.

Listing 4-2   *WSProfile* Binding Configuration

```
<?xml version="1.0" encoding="utf-8" ?>
<configuration xmlns="http://schemas.microsoft.com/.NetConfiguration/v2.0">
    <system.serviceModel>
        <client>
            <endpoint configurationName="MyEndpoint"
                    address="http://localhost/myservice/service.svc"
                    bindingSectionName="wsProfileBinding"
                    bindingConfiguration="Binding1"
                    contractType="IMyService" />
        </client>
        <bindings>
            <wsProfileBinding>
                <binding configurationName="Binding1"
                        maxMessageSize="65536"
                        transferTimeout="00:10:00"
                        hostnameComparisonMode="StrongWildcard"
                        messageEncoding="Text"
                        textEncoding="utf-8"
                        proxyAddress=""
                        useSystemWebProxy="true"
                        bypassProxyOnLocal="false"
                        flowTransactions="NotAllowed"
                        reliableSessionEnabled="false"
                        orderedSession="true"
                        sessionInactivityTimeout="00:10:00"
                        securityMode="WSSecurityOverHttp">
                    <wsSecurity authenticationMode="Windows"
                                protectionLevel="EncryptAndSign"
                                useNegotiation="true"
                                algorithmSuite="Default" />
                </binding>
```

```
          </wsProfileBinding>
        </bindings>
      </system.serviceModel>
    </configuration>
```

Specifying *WSProfile* in Code

You can use the *WSProfileBinding* class to create a *WSProfile* binding in code. The following code uses *WSProfileBinding* to add an endpoint to a service in code.

```
Uri baseAddress = new Uri("http://localhost:8000/MyService/");
WSProfileBinding binding = new WSProfileBinding();
service.AddEndpoint(typeof(IMyService), binding, address);
```

Customizing *WSProfile* in Code

The *WSProfileBinding* class can be customized. After creating an instance of the class, you can adjust its properties before using it in endpoint construction. The following code creates an instance of *WSProfileBinding*, changes the maximum message size, and uses the binding to create an endpoint.

```
Uri address = new Uri("http://localhost:8000/MyService/");
WSProfileBinding binding = new WSProfileBinding();
binding.MaxMessageSize = 200000;
service.AddEndpoint(typeof(IMyService), binding, address);
```

Table 4-13, shown earlier, lists the binding properties that can be used in a *WSProfile* binding configuration.

Programming the *WSProfileDualHttp* Binding

The *WSProfileDualHttp* binding can be specified and customized in code or in a configuration file. Table 4-14 shows the properties of the *WSProfileDualHttp* binding.

Table 4-14   *WSProfileDualHttp* Binding Properties

Attribute	Default Value	Valid Values
BypassProxyOnLocal	true	N/A
ClientBaseAddress	N/A	N/A
FlowTransactions	NotAllowed	Allowed, Ignore, NotAllowed, Required
HostnameComparisonMode	StrongWildcard	Exact, StrongWildcard, WeakWildcard
HttpAuthentication.Level	None	None, MutualAuthRequested, MutualAuthRequired
HttpAuthentication.Scheme	Anonymous	None, Anonymous, Basic, Digest, IntegratedWindowsAuthentication, Negotiate, Ntlm

Table 4-14 *WSProfileDualHttp* Binding Properties

Attribute	Default Value	Valid Values
HttpAuthentication.ProxyScheme	Anonymous	None, Anonymous, Basic, Digest, IntegratedWindowsAuthentication, Negotiate, Ntlm
HttpAuthentication.Realm	N/A	N/A
MaxMessageSize	65536	N/A
MessageEncoding	Text	Text, MTOM
OrderedSession	true	N/A
ProxyAddress	N/A	N/A
SecurityMode	WSSecurityOverHttp	None, WSSecurityOverHttp
SessionConnectTimeout	30 seconds	N/A
SessionInactivityTimeout	5 minutes	N/A
TextEncoding	utf-8	N/A
TransferTimeout	00:10:00	N/A
UseSystemWebProxy	true	N/A
WSSecurity.ProtectionLevel	EncryptAndSign	None, Sign, EncryptAndSign
WSSecurity.UseNegotiation	true	N/A
WSSecurity.AuthenticationMode	Windows	Windows, Anonymous, Username, Certificate
WSSecurity.AlgorithmSuite	Default	Default, Aes256, Aes192, Aes128, TripleDes

Specifying *WSProfileDualHttp* in a Configuration File

The *WSProfileDualHttp* binding is specified as part of a client or service endpoint definition. In an endpoint element, you set the *BindingSectionName* attribute to *"wsProfileDualHttpBinding"*.

```
<endpoint
    address="http://www.contoso.com:8000/ExpenseReport"
    bindingSectionName="wsProfileDualHttpBinding"
    contractType="IExpenseReport" />
```

If you're using the default configuration of the binding, this is all you need to do. If you need to customize the binding, see the next section.

Customizing *WSProfileDualHttp* in a Configuration File

To customize the *WSProfileDualHttp* binding, you include a *bindingConfiguration* attribute in an endpoint definition that specifies a binding configuration name.

```
<system.serviceModel>
    ...
    <service ...>
        <endpoint
            address="http://www.contoso.com:8000/ExpenseReport"
```

```
                    bindingSectionName="wsProfileDualHttpBinding"
                    bindingConfiguration="MyCustomBinding"
                    contractType="IExpenseReport" />
        </service>
    </system.serviceModel>
```

The binding customization is done in a binding configuration that appears in a separate section of the configuration file. The binding configuration is defined in a *<binding>* element, which is contained within a *<wsProfileDualHttpBinding>* section element, which in turn is contained in an outer *<bindings>* element. The binding configuration must have a name that matches the *bindingConfiguration* value specified in the endpoint.

```
<system.serviceModel>
    ...
    <bindings>
        <wsProfileDualHttpBinding>
            <binding configurationName="MyCustomBinding" ... />
        </wsProfileDualHttpBinding>
    </bindings>
</system.serviceModel>
```

Table 4-14, shown earlier, lists the binding properties that can be used in a *WSProfileDualHttp* binding configuration. The *WSSecurity* attributes appear in a *<wsSecurity>* element, like this:

```
<binding configurationName="Binding1"
        useSystemWebProxy="true"
        bypassProxyOnLocal="false"
        securityMode="WSSecurityOverHttp">
    <wsSecurity authenticationMode="Windows"
                protectionLevel="EncryptAndSign"
                useNegotiation="true"
                algorithmSuite="Default" />
</binding>
```

Listing 4-3 shows a configuration file that configures the *WSProfileDualHttp* binding. The values shown are the default values for the binding.

Listing 4-3   *WSProfileDualHttp* Binding Configuration

```
<?xml version="1.0" encoding="utf-8" ?>
<configuration xmlns="http://schemas.microsoft.com/.NetConfiguration/v2.0">
    <system.serviceModel>
        <client>
            <endpoint configurationName="MyEndpoint"
                    address="http://localhost/myservice/service.svc"
                    bindingSectionName="wsProfileDualHttpBinding"
                    bindingConfiguration="Binding1"
                    contractType="IMyService" />
        </client>
        <bindings>
            <wsProfileDualHttpBinding>
                <binding configurationName="Binding1"
                        maxMessageSize="65536"
```

```
                transferTimeout="00:10:00"
                hostnameComparisonMode="StrongWildcard"
                messageEncoding="Text"
                textEncoding="utf-8"
                proxyAddress=""
                useSystemWebProxy="true"
                bypassProxyOnLocal="false"
                flowTransactions="NotAllowed"
                orderedSession="true"
                sessionInactivityTimeout="00:10:00"
                securityMode="WSSecurityOverHttp">
          <wsSecurity authenticationMode="Windows"
                      protectionLevel="EncryptAndSign"
                      useNegotiation="true"
                      algorithmSuite="Default" />
        </binding>
      </wsProfileDualHttpBinding>
    </bindings>
  </system.serviceModel>
</configuration>
```

Specifying *WSProfileDualHttp* in Code

You can use the *WSProfileDualHttpBinding* class to create a *WSProfileDualHttp* binding in code. The following code shows the use of *WSProfileDualHttpBinding* to add an endpoint to a service in code.

```
Uri baseAddress = new Uri("http://localhost:8000/MyService/");
WSProfileDualHttpBinding binding = new WSProfileDualHttpBinding();
service.AddEndpoint(typeof(IMyService), binding, address);
```

Customizing *WSProfileDualHttp* in Code

The *WSProfileDualHttpBinding* class can be customized. After creating an instance of the class, you can adjust its properties before using it in endpoint construction. The following code creates an instance of *WSProfileDualHttpBinding*, changes the maximum message size, and uses the binding to create an endpoint.

```
Uri address = new Uri("http://localhost:8000/MyService/");
WSProfileDualHttpBinding binding = new WSProfileDualHttpBinding();
binding.MaxMessageSize = 200000;
service.AddEndpoint(typeof(IMyService), binding, address);
```

Table 4-14, shown earlier, lists the binding properties that can be used in a *WSProfileDualHttp* binding configuration.

Programming the *NetProfileTcp* Binding

The *NetProfileTcp* binding can be specified and customized in code or in a configuration file. Table 4-15 shows the properties of the *NetProfileTcp* binding.

Table 4-15   *NetProfileTcp* Binding Properties

Attribute	Default Value	Valid Values
FlowLocale	NotAllowed	Allowed, Ignore, NotAllowed, Required
FlowLogicalThreadId	NotAllowed	Allowed, Ignore, NotAllowed, Required
FlowTransactions	NotAllowed	Allowed, Ignore, NotAllowed, Required
HostnameComparisonMode	StrongWildcard	StrongWildcard, WeakWildcard
IPv6SocketProtectionLevel	Default	Default, Restricted, Unrestricted
KeepAliveEnabled	False	N/A
MaxBufferSize	65536	N/A
MaxConnections	10	N/A
MaxMessageSize	65536	N/A
OrderedSession	true	N/A
ReliableSessionEnabled	false	N/A
SecurityMode	TcpWithWindowsSecurity	None, TcpWithWindowsSecurity, TcpWithSsl, WSSecurityOverTcp
SessionConnectTimeout	30 seconds	N/A
SessionInactivityTimeout	5 minutes	N/A
TcpPortSharingEnabled	False	N/A
TcpProtectionLevel	EncryptAndSign	None, Sign, EncryptAndSign
TransferMode	Buffered	Buffered, Streamed
TransferTimeout	00:10:00	N/A
WSSecurity.ProtectionLevel	EncryptAndSign	None, Sign, EncryptAndSign
WSSecurity.AuthenticationMode	Windows	Windows, Anonymous, Username, Certificate

Specifying *NetProfileTcp* in a Configuration File

The *NetProfileTcp* binding is specified as part of a client or service endpoint definition. In an endpoint element, you set the *BindingSectionName* attribute to "*netProfileTcpBinding*".

```
<endpoint
    address="http://www.contoso.com:8000/ExpenseReport"
    bindingSectionName="netProfileTcpBinding"
    contractType="IExpenseReport" />
```

If you're using the default configuration of the binding, this is all you need to do. If you need to customize the binding, see the next section.

Customizing *NetProfileTcp* in a Configuration File

To customize the *NetProfileTcp* binding, include a *bindingConfiguration* attribute in an endpoint definition that specifies a binding configuration name.

```
<system.serviceModel>
    ...
    <service ...>
        <endpoint
            address="net.tcp://www.contoso.com:8000/ExpenseReport"
            bindingSectionName="netProfileTcpBinding"
            bindingConfiguration="MyCustomBinding"
            contractType="IExpenseReport" />
    </service>
</system.serviceModel>
```

The binding customization is done in a binding configuration that appears in a separate section of the configuration file. The binding configuration is defined in a *<binding>* element, which is contained within a *<netProfileTcpBinding>* section element, which in turn is contained in an outer *<bindings>* element. The binding configuration must have a name that matches the *bindingConfiguration* value specified in the endpoint.

```
<system.serviceModel>
    ...
    <bindings>
        <netProfileTcpBinding>
            <binding configurationName="MyCustomBinding" ... />
        </netProfileTcpBinding>
    </bindings>
</system.serviceModel>
```

Table 4-15, shown earlier, lists the binding properties that can be used in a *NetProfileTcp* binding configuration.

The *WSSecurity* attributes described earlier appear in a *<wsSecurity>* element, like this:

```
<binding configurationName="Binding1"
    securityMode="WSSecurityOverHttp">
        <wsSecurity authenticationMode="Windows"
            protectionLevel="EncryptAndSign" />
</binding>
```

Listing 4-4 shows a configuration file that configures the *NetProfileTcp* binding. The values shown are the default values for the binding.

Listing 4-4   *NetProfileTcp* Binding Configuration

```xml
<?xml version="1.0" encoding="utf-8" ?>
<configuration xmlns="http://schemas.microsoft.com/.NetConfiguration/v2.0">
    <system.serviceModel>
        <client>
            <endpoint configurationName="MyEndpoint"
                      address="net.tcp://localhost:8000/myservice/"
                      bindingSectionName="netProfileTcpBinding"
                      bindingConfiguration="Binding1"
                      contractType="IMyService" />
        </client>
        <bindings>
            <netProfileTcpBinding>
                <binding configurationName="Binding1"
                         hostnameComparisonMode="StrongWildcard"
                         maxMessageSize="65536"
                         maxBufferSize="65536"
                         maxConnections="10"
                         transferTimeout="00:10:00"
                         transferMode="Buffered"
                         isKeepAliveEnabled="false"
                         tcpPortSharingEnabled="false"

                         flowLocale="NotAllowed"
                         flowLogicalThreadId="NotAllowed"
                         flowTransactions="NotAllowed"

                         reliableSessionEnabled="false"
                         orderedSession="true"
                         sessionInactivityTimeout="00:10:00"

                         securityMode="TcpWithWindowsSecurity"
                         tcpProtectionLevel="EncryptAndSign"
                         IPv6SocketProtectionLevel="Default">

                    <wsSecurity authenticationMode="Windows"
                        protectionLevel="EncryptAndSign" />

                </binding>
            </netProfileTcpBinding>
        </bindings>
    </system.serviceModel>
</configuration>
```

Specifying *NetProfileTcp* in Code

You can use the *NetProfileTcpBinding* class to create a *NetProfileTcp* binding in code. The following code shows the use of *NetProfileTcpBinding* to add an endpoint to a service in code.

```csharp
Uri baseAddress = new Uri("net.tcp://localhost:8000/MyService/");
NetProfileTcpBinding binding = new NetProfileTcpBinding();
service.AddEndpoint(typeof(IMyService), binding, address);
```

Customizing *NetProfileTcp* in Code

The *NetProfileTcpBinding* class can be customized. After creating an instance of the class, you can adjust its properties before using it in endpoint construction. The following code creates an instance of *NetProfileTcpBinding*, changes the maximum message size, enables reliable sessions, and uses the binding to create an endpoint.

```
Uri address = new Uri("net.tcp://localhost:8000/MyService/");
NetProfileTcpBinding binding = new NetProfileTcpBinding();
binding.MaxMessageSize = 200000;
binding.ReliableSessionEnabled = true;
service.AddEndpoint(typeof(IMyService), binding, address);
```

Table 4-15, shown earlier, lists the binding properties that can be used in a *NetProfileTcp* binding configuration.

Programming the *NetProfileDualTcp* Binding

The *NetProfileDualTcp* binding can be specified in code or in a configuration file. Table 4-16 shows the properties of the *NetProfileDualTcp* binding.

Table 4-16 *NetProfileDualTcp* **Binding Properties**

Attribute	Default Value	Valid Values
ClientBaseAddress	null	N/A
FlowLocale	NotAllowed	Allowed, Ignore, NotAllowed, Required
FlowLogicalThreadId	NotAllowed	Allowed, Ignore, NotAllowed, Required
FlowTransactions	NotAllowed	Allowed, Ignore, NotAllowed, Required
HostnameComparisonMode	StrongWildcard	Exact, StrongWildcard, Weak-Wildcard
KeepAliveEnabled	False	N/A
MaxBufferSize	65536	N/A
MaxConnections	10	N/A
MaxMessageSize	65536	N/A
OrderedSession	true	N/A
SecurityMode	WSSecurityOverTcp	None, WSSecurityOverTcp
SessionConnectTimeout	30 seconds	N/A
SessionInactivityTimeout	5 minutes	N/A
TcpPortSharingEnabled	False	N/A
TransferMode	Buffered	Buffered, Streamed

Table 4-16   *NetProfileDualTcp* **Binding Properties**

Attribute	Default Value	Valid Values
TransferTimeout	*00:10:00*	N/A
WSSecurity.ProtectionLevel	*EncryptAndSign*	*None, Sign, EncryptAndSign*
WSSecurity.AuthenticationMode	*Windows*	*Windows, Anonymous, User-name, Certificate*

Specifying *NetProfileDualTcp* in a Configuration File

The *NetProfileDualTcp* binding is specified as part of a client or service endpoint definition. In an endpoint element, you set the *BindingSectionName* attribute to *"netProfileDualTcpBinding"*.

```
<endpoint
    address="net.tcp://www.contoso.com:8000/ExpenseReport"
    bindingSectionName="netProfileDualTcpBinding"
    contractType="IExpenseReport" />
```

If you're using the default configuration of the binding, this is all you need to do. If you need to customize the binding, see the next section.

Customizing *NetProfileDualTcp* in a Configuration File

To customize the *NetProfileDualTcp* binding, you include a *bindingConfiguration* attribute in an endpoint definition that specifies a binding configuration name.

```
<system.serviceModel>
    ...
    <service ...>
        <endpoint
            address="http://www.contoso.com:8000/ExpenseReport"
            bindingSectionName="netProfileDualTcpBinding"
            bindingConfiguration="MyCustomBinding"
            contractType="IExpenseReport" />
    </service>
</system.serviceModel>
```

The binding customization is done in a binding configuration that appears in a separate section of the configuration file. The binding configuration is defined in a *<binding>* element, which is contained within a *<netProfileDualTcpBinding>* section element, which in turn is contained in an outer *<bindings>* element. The binding configuration must have a name that matches the *bindingConfiguration* value specified in the endpoint.

```
<system.serviceModel>
    ...
    <bindings>
        <netProfileDualTcpBinding>
            <binding configurationName="MyCustomBinding" ... />
        </netProfileDualTcpBinding>
    </bindings>
</system.serviceModel>
```

Table 4-16, shown earlier, lists the binding properties that can be used in a *NetProfileDualTcp* binding configuration.

The *WSSecurity* attributes appear in a *<wsSecurity>* element, like this:

```
<binding configurationName="Binding1"
        useSystemWebProxy="true"
        bypassProxyOnLocal="false"
        securityMode="WSSecurityOverHttp">
    <wsSecurity authenticationMode="Windows"
                protectionLevel="EncryptAndSign"
                useNegotiation="true"
                algorithmSuite="Default" />
</binding>
```

Listing 4-5 shows a configuration file that configures the *NetProfileDualTcp* binding. The values shown are the default values for the binding.

Listing 4-5 *NetProfileDualTcp* Binding Configuration

```
<?xml version="1.0" encoding="utf-8" ?>
<configuration xmlns="http://schemas.microsoft.com/.NetConfiguration/v2.0">
    <system.serviceModel>
        <client>
            <endpoint configurationName="MyEndpoint"
                      address="net.tcp://localhost:8000/myservice/"
                      bindingSectionName="netProfileDualTcpBinding"
                      bindingConfiguration="Binding1"
                      contractType="IMyService" />
        </client>
        <bindings>
            <netProfileDualTcpBinding>
                <binding configurationName="Binding1"
                         maxMessageSize="65536"
                         transferTimeout="00:10:00"
                         hostnameComparisonMode="StrongWildcard"
                         messageEncoding="Text"
                         textEncoding="utf-8"
                         flowTransactions="NotAllowed"
                         orderedSession="true"
                         sessionInactivityTimeout="00:10:00"
                         securityMode="WSSecurityOverHttp">
                    <wsSecurity authenticationMode="Windows"
                                protectionLevel="EncryptAndSign"
                                useNegotiation="true"
                                algorithmSuite="Default" />
                </binding>
            </netProfileDualTcpBinding>
        </bindings>
    </system.serviceModel>
</configuration>
```

Specifying *NetProfileDualTcp* in Code

The *NetProfileDualTcpBinding* class can be used to create a *NetProfileDualTcp* binding in code. The following code shows the use of *NetProfileDualTcpBinding* to add an endpoint to a service in code.

```
Uri baseAddress = new Uri("net.tcp://localhost:8000/MyService/");
NetProfileDualTcpBinding binding = new NetProfileDualTcpBinding();
service.AddEndpoint(typeof(IMyService), binding, address);
```

Customizing *NetProfileDualTcp* in Code

The *NetProfileDualTcpBinding* class can be customized. After creating an instance of the class, you can adjust its properties before using it in endpoint construction. The following code creates an instance of *NetProfileDualTcpBinding*, changes the maximum message size, and uses the binding to create an endpoint.

```
Uri address = new Uri("net.tcp://localhost:8000/MyService/");
NetProfileDualTcpBinding binding = new NetProfileDualTcpBinding();
binding.MaxMessageSize = 200000;
service.AddEndpoint(typeof(IMyService), binding, address);
```

Table 4-16, shown earlier, lists the binding properties that can be used in a *NetProfileDualTcp* binding configuration.

Programming the *NetProfileNamedPipe* Binding

The *NetProfileNamedPipe* binding can be specified in code or in a configuration file. It is limited to cross-process communication on the same machine. Table 4-17 shows the properties of the *NetProfileNamedPipe* binding.

Table 4-17   *NetProfileNamedPipe* Binding Properties

Attribute	Default Value	Valid Values
ConnectionTimeout	2 seconds	N/A
FlowLocale	NotAllowed	Allowed, Ignore, NotAllowed, Required
FlowLogicalThreadId	NotAllowed	Allowed, Ignore, NotAllowed, Required
FlowTransactions	NotAllowed	Allowed, Ignore, NotAllowed, Required
HostnameComparisonMode	Exact	Exact, StrongWildcard, Weak-Wildcard
MaxBufferSize	65536	N/A
MaxConnections	10	N/A

Table 4-17 *NetProfileNamedPipe* Binding Properties

Attribute	Default Value	Valid Values
MaxMessageSize	65536	N/A
NamedPipeProtectionLevel	*EncryptAndSign*	*None, Sign, EncryptAndSign*
TransferMode	*Buffered*	*Buffered, Streamed*
TransferTimeout	00:10:00	N/A

Specifying *NetProfileNamedPipe* in a Configuration File

The *NetProfileNamedPipe* binding is specified as part of a client or service endpoint definition. In an endpoint element, you set the *BindingSectionName* attribute to *"netProfileNamedPipeBinding"*.

```
<endpoint
    address="net.pipe://localhost/ExpenseReport"
    bindingSectionName="netProfileNamedPipeBinding"
    contractType="IExpenseReport" />
```

If you're using the default configuration of the binding, this is all you need to do. If you need to customize the binding, see the next section.

Customizing *NetProfileNamedPipe* in a Configuration File

To customize the *NetProfileNamedPipe* binding, you include a *bindingConfiguration* attribute in an endpoint definition that specifies a binding configuration name.

```
<system.serviceModel>
    ...
    <service ...>
        <endpoint
            address="net.pipe://localhost/ExpenseReport"
            bindingSectionName="netProfileNamedPipeBinding"
            bindingConfiguration="MyCustomBinding"
            contractType="IExpenseReport" />
    </service>
</system.serviceModel>
```

The binding customization is done in a binding configuration that appears in a separate section of the configuration file. The binding configuration is defined in a *<binding>* element, which is contained within a *<netProfileNamedPipeBinding>* section element, which in turn is contained in an outer *<bindings>* element. The binding configuration must have a name that matches the *bindingConfiguration* value specified in the endpoint.

```
<system.serviceModel>
    ...
    <bindings>
        <netProfileNamedPipeBinding>
            <binding configurationName="MyCustomBinding" ... />
```

```
        </netProfileNamedPipeBinding>
    </bindings>
</system.serviceModel>
```

Table 4-17, shown earlier, lists the binding properties that can be used in a *NetProfileNamed-Pipe* binding configuration.

Listing 4-6 shows a configuration file that configures the *NetProfileNamedPipe* binding. The values shown are the default values for the binding.

Listing 4-6   *NetProfileNamedPipe* Binding Configuration

```
<?xml version="1.0" encoding="utf-8" ?>
<configuration xmlns="http://schemas.microsoft.com/.NetConfiguration/v2.0">
    <system.serviceModel>
        <client>
            <endpoint configurationName="MyEndpoint"
                      address="net.pipe://localhost/MyService/"
                      bindingSectionName="netProfileNamedPipeBinding"
                      bindingConfiguration="Binding1"
                      contractType="IMyService" />
        </client>
        <bindings>
            <!--
                Following is the expanded configuration section for a
                NetProfileNamedPipeBinding.
                Each property is configured with the default value.
            -->
            <netProfileNamedPipeBinding>
                <binding configurationName="Binding1"

                    hostnameComparisonMode="StrongWildcard"
                    maxBufferSize="65536"
                    maxConnections="10"
                    maxMessageSize="65536"
                    transferMode="Buffered"
                    transferTimeout="00:10:00"

                    flowLocale="NotAllowed"
                    flowLogicalThreadId="NotAllowed"
                    flowTransactions="NotAllowed"

                    securityMode="NamedPipeWithWindowsSecurity"
                    namedPipeProtectionLevel="EncryptAndSign" />
            </netProfileNamedPipeBinding>
        </bindings>
    </system.serviceModel>
</configuration>
```

Specifying *NetProfileNamedPipe* in Code

You can use the *NetProfileNamedPipeBinding* class to create a *NetProfileNamedPipe* binding in code. The following code shows the use of *NetProfileNamedPipeBinding* to add an endpoint to a service in code.

```
Uri baseAddress = new Uri("net.pipe://localhost/MyService/");
NetProfileNamedPipeBinding binding = new NetProfileNamedPipeBinding();
service.AddEndpoint(typeof(IMyService), binding, address);
```

Customizing *NetProfileNamedPipe* in Code

The *NetProfileNamedPipeBinding* class can be customized. After creating an instance of the class, you can adjust its properties before using it in endpoint construction. The following code creates an instance of *NetProfileNamedPipeBinding*, changes the maximum message size, and uses the binding to create an endpoint.

```
Uri address = new Uri("net.pipe://localhost/MyService/");
NetProfileNamedPipeBinding binding = new NetProfileNamedPipeBinding();
binding.MaxMessageSize = 200000;
service.AddEndpoint(typeof(IMyService), binding, address);
```

Table 4-17, shown earlier, lists the binding properties that can be used in a *NetProfileNamed-Pipe* binding configuration.

Programming the *NetProfileMsmq* Binding

You can specify the *NetProfileMsmq* binding in code or in a configuration file. Unlike other Indigo transports, the *NetProfileMsmq* binding requires you to create queues before performing communication. Table 4-18 shows the properties of the *NetProfileMsmq* binding.

Table 4-18 *NetProfileMsmq* Binding Properties

Property	Default Value	Valid Values
AddressingMode	Native	DirectoryLookup, Native, SecureSrmp, Srmp
Assurances	ExactlyOnce	AtLeastOnce, AtMostOnce, Exactly-Once, None
DeadLetterQueue	net.msmq://localhost/System$;DeadXAct	N/A
Durable	true	N/A
HostnameComparisonMode	StrongWildcard	Exact, StrongWild-card, WeakWildcard
MaxMessageSize	65536	N/A
MaxRetries	3	N/A
MaxRetryCycles	3	N/A

Table 4-18   *NetProfileMsmq* Binding Properties

Property	Default Value	Valid Values
MsmqAuthenticationMode	*Windows*	*None, Windows, Certificate*
MsmqEncryptionLevel	*EncryptAndSign*	*None, Sign, EncryptAndSign*
RejectAfterLastRetry	*true*	N/A
RetryCycleDelay	*10 min*	N/A
TimeToLive	*24 hours*	N/A

Creating a Queue

Before an Indigo program can use the MSMQ transport, you must create a queue. You can do this manually or in code.

To create a queue manually, launch the Computer Management console by right-clicking My Computer and selecting Manage. Or you can choose Run from the Start menu and type **Compmgmt.msc.**

In Computer Management, expand the outline, and then find Message Queuing under Services And Applications. To add a private queue, right-click Private Queues, and then select New, Private Queue. To add a public queue, right-click Public Queues, and then select New, Public Queue.

Enter a queue name and be sure to select the transactional check box; if you fail to make the queue transactional, communication cannot take place.

Important   Make sure any queues you create are transactional.

To create a queue in code, add a reference to *System.Messaging* and use the static *Create* method of the *MessageQueue* class. Specify a queue name for the first parameter and specify *true* for the second parameter (to make the queue transactional).

The queue name is either a private queue name in the form *MachineName\Private$\Queue-Name* or a public queue name in the form *MachineName\QueueName*. Use a period (.) to indicate the local machine. You can use the *MessageQueue.Exists* function to test for the existence of a queue. Errors in queue creation can generate exceptions of type *MessageQueueException*. The following code creates a private queue named *Sample* on the local machine if it doesn't already exist.

```
using System.Messaging;
    ...
try
```

```
{
    string queueName = ".\\Private$\\Sample";
    if (!MessageQueue.Exists(queueName))
        MessageQueue.Create(queueName, true);
}
catch (MessageQueueException e)
{
    ...
}
```

Deleting a Queue

You can delete a queue manually or in code. To delete a queue manually, launch the Computer Management console by right-clicking My Computer and selecting Manage. Or you can choose Run from the Start menu and type **Compmgmt.msc**.

In Computer Management, expand the outline, and then find Message Queuing under Services And Applications. Navigate to Public Queues or Private Queues. Select the queue to be deleted. To delete the selected queue, press the Delete key or right-click and select Delete.

To delete a queue in code, add a reference to *System.Messaging* and use the static *Delete* method of the *MessageQueue* class. Specify a private queue name in the form *Machine-Name\Private$\QueueName* or a public queue name in the form *MachineName\QueueName*. Use a period (.) to indicate the local machine. You can use the *MessageQueue.Exists* function to test for the existence of a queue. Errors in queue deletion can generate exceptions of type *MessageQueueException*. The following code deletes a private queue named *Sample* on the local machine if it exists.

```
using System.Messaging;
    ...
try
{
    string queueName = ".\\Private$\\Sample";
    if (MessageQueue.Exists(queueName))
        MessageQueue.Delete(queueName);
}
catch (MessageQueueException e)
{
    ...
}
```

Specifying *NetProfileMsmq* in a Configuration File

The *NetProfileMsmq* binding is specified as part of a client or service endpoint definition. In an endpoint element, you set the *BindingSectionName* attribute to *"netProfileMsmqBinding"*.

```
<endpoint
    address="net.msmq://www.contoso.com/private$/ExpenseReport"
    bindingSectionName="netProfileMsmqBinding"
    contractType="IExpenseReport" />
```

The queue you use must have been created already. See the section titled "Creating a Queue" earlier in this chapter for the procedure.

If you're using the default configuration of the binding, this is all you need to do. If you need to customize the binding, see the next section.

Customizing *NetProfileMsmq* in a Configuration File

To customize the *NetProfileMsmq* binding, include a *bindingConfiguration* attribute in an end-point definition that specifies a binding configuration name.

```
<system.serviceModel>
    ...
    <service ...>
        <endpoint
            address="net.msmq://www.contoso.com/private$/MyService"
            bindingSectionName="netProfileMsmqBinding"
            bindingConfiguration="MyCustomBinding"
            contractType="IExpenseReport" />
    </service>
</system.serviceModel>
```

The binding customization is done in a binding configuration that appears in a separate section of the configuration file. The binding configuration is defined in a *<binding>* element, which is contained within a *<netProfileMsmqBinding>* section element, which in turn is contained in an outer *<bindings>* element. The binding configuration must have a name that matches the *bindingConfiguration* value specified in the endpoint.

```
<system.serviceModel>
    ...
    <bindings>
        <netProfileMsmqBinding>
            <binding configurationName="MyCustomBinding" ... />
        </netProfileMsmqBinding>
    </bindings>
</system.serviceModel>
```

Table 4-18, shown earlier, lists the binding properties that can be used in a *NetProfileMsmq* binding configuration.

Listing 4-7 shows a configuration file that configures the *NetProfileMsmq* binding. The values shown are the default values for the binding.

Listing 4-7 *NetProfileMsmq* Binding Configuration

```
<?xml version="1.0" encoding="utf-8" ?>
<configuration xmlns="http://schemas.microsoft.com/.NetConfiguration/v2.0">
    <system.serviceModel>
        <client>
            <endpoint configurationName="MyEndpoint"
```

```
                address="net.msmq://localhost/private$/myservice"
                bindingSectionName="netProfileMsmqBinding"
                bindingConfiguration="Binding1"
                contractType="IMyService" />
    </client>
    <bindings>
            <netProfileMsmqBinding>
                        <binding configurationName="Binding1"
                         addressingMode="Native"
                         assurances="ExactlyOnce"
                         deadLetterQueue="net.msmq://localhost/deadletter"
                         durable="true"
                         hostnameComparisonMode="StrongWildcard"
                         maxMessageSize="65536"
                         maxRetries="3"
                         maxRetryCycles="3"
                         messageAuthenticationMode="Windows"
                         messageProtectionLevel="EncryptAndSign"
                         msmqAuthenticationMode="Windows"
                         msmqProtectionLevel="EncryptandSign"
                         rejectAfterLastRetry="true"
                         retryCycleDelay="00:10:00"
                         timeToLive="24:00:00"/>
            </netProfileMsmqBinding>
        </bindings>
    </system.serviceModel>
</configuration>
```

Specifying *NetProfileMsmq* in Code

You can use the *NetProfileMsmqBinding* class to create a *NetProfileMsmq* binding in code. The following code shows the use of *NetProfileMsmqBinding* to add an endpoint to a service in code.

```
Uri baseAddress = new Uri("net.msmq://localhost/private$/MyService");
NetProfileMsmqBinding binding = new NetProfileMsmqBinding();
service.AddEndpoint(typeof(IMyService), binding, address);
```

Customizing *NetProfileMsmq* in Code

The *NetProfileMsmqBinding* class can be customized. After creating an instance of the class, you can adjust its properties before using it in endpoint construction. The following code creates an instance of *NetProfileMsmqBinding*, changes the maximum message size, sets durable queues, and uses the binding to create an endpoint.

```
Uri address = new Uri("net.tcp://localhost:8000/MyService/");
NetProfileMsmqBinding binding = new NetProfileMsmqBinding();
binding.MaxMessageSize = 200000;
binding.Durable = true;
service.AddEndpoint(typeof(IMyService), binding, address);
```

Table 4-18, shown earlier, lists the properties of the *NetProfileMsmq* binding.

Programming the *MsmqIntegration* Binding

The *MsmqIntegration* binding can be specified in code or in a configuration file. Table 4-19 shows the properties of the *MsmqIntegration* binding.

Table 4-19   *MsmqIntegration* Binding Properties

Property	Default Value	Valid Values
AddressingMode	Native	DirectoryLookup, Native, SecureSrmp, Srmp
Assurances	ExactlyOnce	AtLeastOnce, AtMostOnce, Exactly-Once, None
DeadLetterQueue	net.msmq://localhost/System$;DeadXAct	N/A
Durable	true	N/A
HostnameComparisonMode	StrongWildcard	Exact, StrongWild-card, WeakWildcard
MaxMessageSize	65536	N/A
MaxRetries	3	N/A
MaxRetryCycles	3	N/A
MsmqAuthenticationMode	Windows	None, Windows, Certificate
MsmqProtectionLevel	EncryptAndSign	None, Sign, EncryptAndSign
RejectAfterLastRetry	true	N/A
RetryCycleDelay	10 min	N/A
SerializationFormat	Xml	ActiveX, Binary, Byte-Array, Stream, Xml
TimeToLive	24 hours	N/A

Specifying *MsmqIntegration* in a Configuration File

The *MsmqIntegration* binding is specified as part of a client or service endpoint definition. In an endpoint element, you set the *BindingSectionName* attribute to *"msmqIntegrationBinding"*.

```
<endpoint
    address="net.msmq://www.contoso.com/private$/ExpenseReport"
    bindingSectionName="msmqIntegrationBinding"
    contractType="IExpenseReport" />
```

The queue you use must have been created already. (You can do this using the Microsoft Management Console.) If you're using the default configuration of the binding, this is all you need to do. If you need to customize the binding, see the next section.

Customizing *MsmqIntegration* in a Configuration File

To customize the *MsmqIntegration* binding, you include a *bindingConfiguration* attribute in an endpoint definition that specifies a binding configuration name.

```
<system.serviceModel>
    ...
    <service ...>
        <endpoint
            address="net.tcp://www.contoso.com:8000/ExpenseReport"
            bindingSectionName="msmqIntegrationBinding"
            bindingConfiguration="MyCustomBinding"
            contractType="IExpenseReport" />
    </service>
</system.serviceModel>
```

The binding customization is done in a binding configuration that appears in a separate section of the configuration file. The binding configuration is defined in a *<binding>* element, which is contained within an *<msmqIntegrationBinding>* section element, which in turn is contained in an outer *<bindings>* element. The binding configuration must have a name that matches the *bindingConfiguration* value specified in the endpoint.

```
<system.serviceModel>
    ...
    <bindings>
        <msmqIntegrationBinding>
            <binding configurationName="MyCustomBinding" ... />
        </msmqIntegrationBinding>
    </bindings>
</system.serviceModel>
```

Table 4-19, shown earlier, lists the binding properties that can be used in an *MsmqIntegration* binding configuration.

Listing 4-8 shows a configuration file that configures the *MsmqIntegration* binding. The values shown are the default values for the binding.

Listing 4-8 *MsmqIntegration* Binding Configuration

```
<?xml version="1.0" encoding="utf-8" ?>
<configuration xmlns="http://schemas.microsoft.com/.NetConfiguration/v2.0">
    <system.serviceModel>
        <client>
            <endpoint configurationName="MyEndpoint"
                      address="net.msmq://localhost/private$/myservice/"
                      bindingSectionName="msmqIntegrationBinding"
                      bindingConfiguration="Binding1"
                      contractType="IMyService" />
        </client>
        <bindings>
```

```
            <msmqIntegrationBinding>
                <binding configurationName="Binding1"
                        addressingMode="DirectoryLookup"
                        assurances="AtLeastOnce"
                        deadLetterQueue="net.msmq://localhost/service"
                        durable="true"
                        hostnameComparisonMode="StrongWildcard"
                        maxMessageSize="65536"
                        maxRetries="3"
                        maxRetryCycles="3"
                        msmqAuthenticationMode="None"
                        msmqProtectionLevel="None"
                        rejectAfterLastRetry="false"
                        retryCycleDelay="00:10:00"
                        serializationFormat="Xml"
                        timeToLive="24:00:00"/>
            </msmqIntegrationBinding>
        </bindings>
    </system.serviceModel>
</configuration>
```

Specifying *MsmqIntegration* in Code

You can use the *MsmqIntegrationBinding* class to create an *MsmqIntegration* binding in code. The following code shows the use of *MsmqIntegrationBinding* to add an endpoint to a service in code.

```
Uri baseAddress = new Uri("net.msmq://localhost/private$/MyService/");
MsmqIntegrationBinding binding = new MsmqIntegrationBinding();
service.AddEndpoint(typeof(IMyService), binding, address);
```

Customizing *MsmqIntegration* in Code

The *MsmqIntegrationBinding* class can be customized. After creating an instance of the class, you can adjust its properties before using it in endpoint construction. The following code creates an instance of *MsmqIntegrationBinding*, changes the maximum message size, and uses the binding to create an endpoint.

```
Uri address = new Uri("net.tcp://localhost:8000/MyService/");
MsmqIntegrationBinding binding = new MsmqIntegrationBinding();
binding.MaxMessageSize = 200000;
service.AddEndpoint(typeof(IMyService), binding, address);
```

Table 4-19, shown earlier, lists the properties of the *MsmqIntegration* binding.

Programming the *Intermediary* Binding

The *Intermediary* binding can be specified in code or in a configuration file. Table 4-20 shows the properties of the *Intermediary* binding.

Table 4-20 *Intermediary* **Binding Properties**

Property	Default Value	Valid Values
HostnameComparisonMode	Exact	Exact, StrongWildcard, WeakWildcard
MaxBufferSize	65536	N/A
MaxConnections	10	N/A
MaxMessageSize	65536	N/A
MessageEncoding	Text	Text, MTOM, Binary
TcpPortSharingEnabled	False	N/A
TextEncoding	utf-8	N/A
TransferMode	Buffered	Buffered, Streamed
TransferTimeout	10 minutes	N/A

Specifying *Intermediary* in a Configuration File

The *Intermediary* binding is specified as part of a client or service endpoint definition. In an endpoint element, you set the *BindingSectionName* attribute to *"IntermediaryBinding"*.

```
<endpoint
    address="net.msmq://www.contoso.com/private$/ExpenseReport"
    bindingSectionName="IntermediaryBinding"
    contractType="IExpenseReport" />
```

The queue you use must have been created already. (You can do this using the Microsoft Management Console.) If you're using the default configuration of the binding, this is all you need to do. If you need to customize the binding, see the next section.

Customizing *Intermediary* in a Configuration File

To customize the *Intermediary* binding, you include a *bindingConfiguration* attribute in an endpoint definition that specifies a binding configuration name.

```
<system.serviceModel>
    ...
    <service ...>
        <endpoint
            address="net.tcp://www.contoso.com:8000/ExpenseReport"
            bindingSectionName="IntermediaryBinding"
            bindingConfiguration="MyCustomBinding"
            contractType="IExpenseReport" />
    </service>
</system.serviceModel>
```

The binding customization is done in a binding configuration that appears in a separate section of the configuration file. The binding configuration is defined in a *<binding>* element, which is contained within an *<intermediaryBinding>* section element, which in turn is contained in an outer *<bindings>* element. The binding configuration must have a name that matches the *bindingConfiguration* value specified in the endpoint.

```
<system.serviceModel>
    ...
    <bindings>
        <intermediaryBinding>
            <binding configurationName="MyCustomBinding" ... />
        </intermediaryBinding>
    </bindings>
</system.serviceModel>
```

Table 4-20, shown earlier, lists the binding properties that can be used in an *Intermediary* binding configuration.

Listing 4-9 shows a configuration file that configures the *Intermediary* binding. The values shown are the default values for the binding.

Listing 4-9   *Intermediary* Binding Configuration

```
<?xml version="1.0" encoding="utf-8" ?>
<configuration xmlns="http://schemas.microsoft.com/.NetConfiguration/v2.0">
    <system.serviceModel>
        <client>
            <endpoint configurationName="MyEndpoint"
                    address="net.msmq://localhost/private$/myservice/"
                    bindingSectionName="intermediaryBinding"
                    bindingConfiguration="Binding1"
                    contractType="IMyService" />
        </client>
        <bindings>
                <intermediaryBinding>
                    <binding configurationName="Binding1"
                            hostnameComparisonMode="Exact"
                            maxBufferSize="65536"
                            maxConnections="10"
                            maxMessageSize="65536"
                            messageEncoding="Text"
                            tcpPortSharingEnabled="false"
                            textEncoding="utf-8"
                            transferTimeout="00:00:10"
                            transport="Tcp" />
                </intermediaryBinding>
        </bindings>
    </system.serviceModel>
</configuration>
```

Specifying *Intermediary* in Code

You can use the *IntermediaryBinding* class to create an *Intermediary* binding in code. The following code creates an *IntermediaryBinding* and uses it to add a TCP endpoint to a service in code.

```
Uri baseAddress = new Uri("net.tcp://localhost:9000/MyService/");
IntermediaryBinding binding = new IntermediaryBinding();
binding.Transport = IntermediaryTransport.Tcp;
service.AddEndpoint(typeof(IMyService), binding, address);
```

Customizing *Intermediary* in Code

The *IntermediaryBinding* class can be customized. After creating an instance of the class, you can adjust its properties before using it in endpoint construction. The following code creates an instance of *IntermediaryBinding*, sets a variety of properties, and uses the binding to create an endpoint.

```
Uri baseAddress = new Uri("net.tcp://localhost:9000/MyService/");
IntermediaryBinding binding = new IntermediaryBinding();
binding.HostnameComparisonMode = HostnameComparisonMode.WeakWildcard;
binding.MaxBufferSize = 200000;
binding.MaxConnections = 1000;
binding.MaxMessageSize = 65536;
binding.MessageEncoding = MessageEncoding.Mtom;
binding.TcpPortSharingEnabled = true;
binding.TextEncoding = Encoding.Unicode;
binding.TransferTimeout = TimeSpan.FromSeconds(10);
binding.Transport = IntermediaryTransport.Tcp;
service.AddEndpoint(typeof(IMyService), binding, address);
```

Table 4-20, shown earlier, lists the properties of the *Intermediary* binding.

Programming Exercise: A Service with Multiple Endpoints

In this programming exercise, we will create a service with multiple endpoints that can be accessed via HTTP, TCP, named pipes, or MSMQ. Each endpoint will have a unique address and binding definition. The service will collect weather information. Clients can report weather information for their local area using the transport of their choice. Both the service and client programs will be console applications.

We'll implement these four endpoints using these bindings:

■ For the HTTP endpoint, we'll use the *WSProfile* binding. We'll configure this binding for reliable sessions using a binding configuration.

■ For the TCP endpoint, we'll use the *NetProfileTcp* binding with default settings.

■ For the named pipes endpoint, we'll use the *NetProfileNamedPipe* binding with default settings.

■ For the MSMQ endpoint, we'll use the *NetProfileMsmq* binding with default settings.

This exercise has eight development steps:

1. Create the service program.

2. Create the service configuration file.

3. Build the service.

4. Create the client.

5. Generate proxy code for the client.

6. Create a configuration file for the client.

7. Build the client.

8. Create a queue.

Step 1: Create the Service Program

We'll now create the service program, which will compile to an EXE console program.

Launch your development environment and create a new C# console application project named *service*. Enter the code in Listing 4-10.

To perform these tasks using Microsoft Visual Studio:

1. Select New, Project from the File menu.

2. Under Project Type, Select Windows under Visual C#. Under Templates, select Console Application. In the Name box, type **service**, in the Location box, type any path you want, and in the Solution Name box, type **MultipleEndpoints**. Click OK to generate and open the new project.

3. Replace the generated code in Program.cs with the code shown in Listing 4-10.

4. Your service project must reference System.ServiceModel.dll. In Visual Studio, right-click References in Solution Explorer, and then select Add Reference.

5. In the Add Reference dialog box, on the .NET tab, select System.ServiceModel.dll, and then click OK.

Listing 4-10   Service Program.cs

```
using System;
using System.ServiceModel;
using System.ServiceModel.Design;

namespace ProgrammingIndigo
{
    // Service contract.

    [ServiceContract]
    public interface IWeather
    {
        [OperationContract(IsOneWay = true)]
        void WeatherReport(string region, int temperature, int windSpeed, int humidity,
            float pressure);
    }

    // Service implementation class.

    [ServiceBehavior]
    public class WeatherService : IWeather
    {
        public void WeatherReport(string region, int temperature, int windSpeed,
            int humidity, float pressure)
        {
            Console.WriteLine("{0,-15} {1,7} {2,11} {3,9} {4,9}",
                region, temperature, windSpeed, humidity, pressure);
        }

        // Host the service.
        // This service is a self-hosted EXE.
        // This code would be unnecessary in a service hosted by IIS.

        public static void Main()
        {
            Uri baseAddress = new Uri("http://localhost:8000/MultipleEndpoints/");
            using (ServiceHost<WeatherService> serviceHost =
                new ServiceHost<WeatherService>(baseAddress))
            {
                //Open the ServiceHost object.

                serviceHost.Open();

                // The service can now be accessed.

                Console.WriteLine("The service is ready");
                Console.WriteLine();
                Console.WriteLine("Press ENTER to shut down service.");
                Console.WriteLine();
                Console.WriteLine
                    ("Region        temperature  wind speed  humidity  pressure");
                Console.WriteLine
                    ("----------  -----------  ----------  --------  --------");
```

```
                    Console.ReadLine();
                    serviceHost.Close();
                }
            }
        }
    }
```

Step 2: Create the Service Configuration File

Next we need an App.config file to specify endpoints and bindings for the service.

Using an editor or development environment, create a text file with the code shown in Listing 4-11. Save the code under the name App.config in the same folder in which the service program and .svc file are located.

To perform these tasks using Visual Studio:

1. Right-click the service project, and then select Add, New Item.

2. Select Application Configuration File, and then click Add.

3. Name the file App.config.

4. Enter the code shown in Listing 4-11 into App.config.

Listing 4-11   Service App.config

```xml
<?xml version="1.0" encoding="utf-8" ?>
<configuration xmlns="http://schemas.microsoft.com/.NetConfiguration/v2.0">
    <system.serviceModel>

        <services>
            <service
                serviceType="ProgrammingIndigo.WeatherService">
                <endpoint
                    address="http://localhost:8000/Weather/"
                    bindingSectionName="wsProfileBinding"
                    bindingConfiguration="Binding1"
                    contractType="ProgrammingIndigo.IWeather" />
                <endpoint
                    address="net.tcp://localhost:9000/Weather/"
                    bindingSectionName="netProfileTcpBinding"
                    contractType="ProgrammingIndigo.IWeather" />
                <endpoint
                    address="net.pipe://localhost/Weather"
                    bindingSectionName="netProfileNamedPipeBinding"
                    contractType="ProgrammingIndigo.IWeather" />
                <endpoint
                    address="net.msmq://localhost/private$/Weather"
                    bindingSectionName="netProfileMsmqBinding"
                    contractType="ProgrammingIndigo.IWeather" />
            </service>
        </services>
```

```
    <bindings>
        <wsProfileBinding>
            <binding
                configurationName="Binding1"
                reliableSessionEnabled="true"
                orderedSession="true"/>
        </wsProfileBinding>
    </bindings>

    </system.serviceModel>
</configuration>
```

Step 3: Build the Service

Build the service program to make Service.exe. Resolve any typographical errors.

To perform the task using Visual Studio, select Build Solution from the Build menu to generate Service.exe.

The service is now ready. Next we need a client program to access it.

Step 4: Create the Client

Create the client program. Launch your development environment and create a new C# console application project named *client*. Enter the code in Listing 4-12.

To perform these tasks using Visual Studio:

1. Select New, Project from the File menu.

2. Under Project Type, select Windows under Visual C#. Under Templates, select Console Application. In the Name box, type **client**, in the Location box, type any path you want, and in the Solution Name box, type **MultipleEndpoints**. Click OK to generate and open the new project.

3. Replace the generated code in Program.cs with the code shown in Listing 4-12.

4. Your client project must reference System.ServiceModel.dll. In Visual Studio, right-click References in Solution Explorer, and then select Add Reference.

5. In the Add Reference dialog box, on the .NET tab, select System.ServiceModel.dll, and then click OK.

Build the client to create Client.exe.

Listing 4-12   Client Program.cs

```csharp
using System;
using System.ServiceModel;

namespace ProgrammingIndigo
{
    //Client implementation code.

    class Client
    {
        static void Main()
        {
            // Create a proxy.
            using (WeatherProxy proxy = new WeatherProxy("Endpoint1"))
            {
                Console.WriteLine("Sending weather reports");

                proxy.WeatherReport("Redmond, WA", 62, 5, 75, 30.03F);
                proxy.WeatherReport("Irvine, CA", 76, 10, 20, 32.09F);
                proxy.WeatherReport("Smithtown, NY", 41, 5, 50, 29.00F);
                proxy.WeatherReport("Reading, PA", 32, 7, 55, 33.20F);
                proxy.WeatherReport("Lubbock, TX", 90, 10, 88, 35.00F);

                proxy.Close();
            }

            Console.WriteLine();
            Console.WriteLine("Press ENTER to shut down client");
            Console.ReadLine();
        }
    }
}
```

Step 5: Generate Proxy Code for the Client

We will now generate client proxy code by accessing the service's MEX endpoint with the Svcutil tool. The service must be running for this step. Open a command window, change the current directory to the folder in which your service project and source files reside, and start Service.exe. Open another command window, change to the directory location where your client project and source files reside, and run the following Svcutil command:

```
svcutil http://localhost:8000/weather/out:proxy.cs
```

The file Proxy.cs will be generated, containing the service contract and a proxy class for accessing the service. It should match the code that is downloadable from the Web.

Next we'll add Proxy.cs to your client project.

1. In Visual Studio, right-click the project in Solution Explorer, and then select Add, Existing Item.

2. In the Open File dialog box, select Proxy.cs, and then click OK.

Proxy.cs is added to the client project.

Step 6: Create a Configuration File for the Client

A Client.exe.config file is needed to specify the service endpoint and binding to use. Using an editor or development environment, create a text file with the code shown in Listing 4-13. Save the code under the name Client.exe.config.

To perform these tasks using Visual Studio:

1. Right-click the service project, and then select Add, New Item.

2. Select Application Configuration File, and then click Add.

3. Name the file App.config. (It will be copied to Client.exe.config at build time.)

4. Enter the code in Listing 4-13 into App.config.

Listing 4-13   Client App.config

```xml
<?xml version="1.0" encoding="utf-8" ?>
<configuration>
    <system.serviceModel xmlns="http://schemas.microsoft.com/.NetConfiguration/v2.0">
        <client>
            <endpoint
                configurationName="Endpoint1"
                address="http://localhost:8000/weather/"
                bindingSectionName="wsProfileBinding"
                bindingConfiguration="Binding1"
                contractType="IWeather" />
            <endpoint
                configurationName="Endpoint2"
                address="net.tcp://localhost:9000/weather/"
                bindingSectionName="netProfileTcpBinding"
                contractType="IWeather" />
            <endpoint
                configurationName="Endpoint3"
                address="net.pipe://localhost/weather"
                bindingSectionName="netProfileNamedPipeBinding"
                contractType="IWeather" />
            <endpoint
                configurationName="Endpoint4"
                address="net.msmq://localhost/private$/weather"
                bindingSectionName="netProfileMsmqBinding"
                contractType="IWeather" />
        </client>
```

```
<bindings>
    <wsProfileBinding>
        <binding
            configurationName="Binding1"
            reliableSessionEnabled="true"
            orderedSession="true" />
    </wsProfileBinding>
</bindings>
    </system.serviceModel>
</configuration>
```

Step 7: Build the Client

Build the client program to make Client.exe. Resolve any typographical errors.

To perform the task using Visual Studio, select Build Solution from the Build menu to generate Client.exe.

Step 8: Create a Queue

One of the endpoints the service exposes uses MSMQ as a transport. You must create this queue in advance.

1. Right-click My Computer, and then select Manage.

2. In the outline pane, expand the Service And Applications node, and then navigate to Message Queuing.

3. Right-click on Private Queues, and then select New, Private Queue. When prompted for a queue name, type **Weather** and then click OK.

Deployment

We're now ready to try things out. Run the service from your development environment or from a command line. (You might already have it running from step 5.) Next, run the client from your development environment or from a command line. You should see output for the service like that shown in Figure 4-11. If the program fails, make sure you've properly carried out each of the preceding steps.

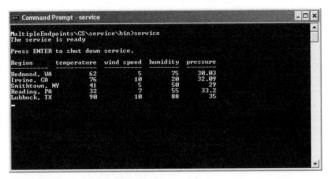

Figure 4-11   *MultipleEndpoints* service

Press ENTER on the client to shut it down, and then do the same for the service. Congratulations on successfully completing a service with multiple endpoints!

The client can communicate with the service over four different endpoints, each with its own binding and unique transport. To experiment with different bindings, change the endpoint name in the client from *Endpoint1* to *Endpoint2*, *Endpoint3*, or *Endpoint4*, and then rebuild and rerun the client.

When you test the *Endpoint4* (MSMQ) endpoint, it's possible for the client to communicate with the service without being active at the same time due to the use of queuing. You can run the client, let it send its messages, and shut it down before you start up the service. The other transports don't allow you to run disconnected in time.

If you want to run service and client on separate machines, replace *localhost* with the fully qualified domain name of the server machine in the service and client configuration files.

Understanding the Service Code

The service is self-hosted, so it must be explicitly launched, just like the client. The code in the static *main* function hosts the service. A *ServiceHost* object is created for the *WeatherService* class and opened.

Although the service gets its endpoints from the configuration file and supports multiple transports, an HTTP base address is specified when the *ServiceHost* is created. The reason for this is that self-hosted services get a MEX endpoint only if a base address is specified for the service. Otherwise, it is impossible to run the Svcutil tool and generate client proxy code.

```
// Host the service.
// This service is a self-hosted EXE.
// This code would be unnecessary in a service hosted by IIS.

public static void Main()
{
```

```
Uri baseAddress = new Uri("http://localhost:8000/MultipleEndpoints/");
using (ServiceHost<WeatherService> serviceHost =
    new ServiceHost<WeatherService>(baseAddress))
{
    //Open the ServiceHost object
    serviceHost.Open();
    // The service can now be accessed.

    Console.WriteLine("The service is ready");
    Console.WriteLine();
    Console.WriteLine("Press ENTER to shut down service.");
    Console.WriteLine();
    Console.WriteLine("Region         temperature  wind speed  humidity  pressure");
    Console.WriteLine("----------     -----------  ----------  --------  --------");
    Console.ReadLine();
    serviceHost.Close();
}
}
```

The service code contains the service contract and implementation code. The service contract has one-way service operations that require no response. The service implements the contract *IWeather*, which accepts weather reports from clients.

```
// Service contract.

[ServiceContract]
public interface IWeather
{
    [OperationContract(IsOneWay = true)]
    void WeatherReport(string region, int temperature, int windSpeed, int humidity,
        float pressure);
}
```

The *WeatherService* class implements the service, which accepts weather reports. The single-service operation, *WeatherReport*, merely displays what it receives on the console output.

```
// Service implementation class.

[ServiceBehavior]
public class WeatherService : IWeather
{
    public void WeatherReport(string region, int temperature, int windSpeed,
        int humidity, float pressure)
    {
        Console.WriteLine("{0,-15} {1,7} {2,11} {3,9} {4,9}",
            region, temperature, windSpeed, humidity, pressure);
    }
}
```

The configuration file for the service specifies four endpoints, each specifying a different standard binding: *WSProfile*, *NetProfileTcp*, *NetProfileNamedPipe*, or *NetProfileMsmq*. The format of each endpoint address reflects the transport in use. The contract is the same for all four endpoints, *IWeather*.

```xml
<?xml version="1.0" encoding="utf-8" ?>
<configuration xmlns="http://schemas.microsoft.com/.NetConfiguration/v2.0">
    <system.serviceModel>
        <services>
            <service
                serviceType="ProgrammingIndigo.WeatherService">
                <endpoint
                    address="http://localhost:8000/Weather/"
                    bindingSectionName="wsProfileBinding"
                    bindingConfiguration="Binding1"
                    contractType="ProgrammingIndigo.IWeather" />
                <endpoint
                    address="net.tcp://localhost:9000/Weather/"
                    bindingSectionName="netProfileTcpBinding"
                    contractType="ProgrammingIndigo.IWeather" />
                <endpoint
                    address="net.pipe://localhost/Weather"
                    bindingSectionName="netProfileNamedPipeBinding"
                    contractType="ProgrammingIndigo.IWeather" />
                <endpoint
                    address="net.msmq://localhost/private$/Weather"
                    bindingSectionName="netProfileMsmqBinding"
                    contractType="ProgrammingIndigo.IWeather" />
            </service>
        </services>
        ...
    </system.serviceModel>
</configuration>
```

The first endpoint specifies a binding configuration for the *WSProfile* binding named *Binding1*. The binding configuration enables reliable sessions, specifies exactly-once delivery assurances, and specifies in-order delivery of messages.

```xml
<?xml version="1.0" encoding="utf-8" ?>
<configuration xmlns="http://schemas.microsoft.com/.NetConfiguration/v2.0">
    <system.serviceModel>
        ...
        <bindings>
            <wsProfileBinding>
                <binding
                    configurationName="Binding1"
                    reliableSessionEnabled="true"
                    orderedSession="true" />
            </wsProfileBinding>
        </bindings>
```

```
        </system.serviceModel>
    </configuration>
```

For cross-machine communication, the references to *localhost* in the configuration file must be replaced by the fully qualified domain name of the server. Note that the *NetProfileNamedPipe* binding cannot be used cross-machine.

In this program, the four endpoints use standard bindings with default settings. If you had needed to alter those settings, you could have defined binding configurations in the .config file to allow fine-tuning.

Understanding the Client Code

In developing the client, we took advantage of the Svcutil tool to generate client proxy code from the service's MEX endpoint. The generated code, in Proxy.cs, includes the definition of the *IWeather* service contract and a *WeatherProxy* class for communicating with the service. Note that we could also have generated a configuration file for the client using this tool.

The client code in Client.cs creates a proxy using the generated *WeatherProxy* class. An endpoint configuration name of *Endpoint1* is specified in the *WeatherProxy* constructor. This causes the proxy to scan the client .config file for the endpoint definition with the name specified. If we were to change the endpoint configuration name to *Endpoint2*, *Endpoint3*, or *Endpoint4*, the proxy would select a different endpoint from the configuration settings.

```
// Create a proxy.
using (WeatherProxy proxy = new WeatherProxy("Endpoint1"))
{
    ...
}
```

Once the proxy is created, several weather reports are sent by calling the *WeatherReport* service operation. Once the client is finished communicating, the proxy is closed.

```
// Create a proxy.
using (WeatherProxy proxy = new WeatherProxy("Endpoint1"))
{
    Console.WriteLine("Sending weather reports");

    proxy.WeatherReport("Redmond, WA", 62, 5, 75, 30.03F);
    proxy.WeatherReport("Irvine, CA", 76, 10, 20, 32.09F);
    proxy.WeatherReport("Smithtown, NY", 41, 5, 50, 29.00F);
    proxy.WeatherReport("Reading, PA", 32, 7, 55, 33.20F);
    proxy.WeatherReport("Lubbock, TX", 90, 10, 88, 35.00F);

    proxy.Close();
}
```

The .config file for the client defines all four endpoints made available by the service. Like the service .config file, the client .config file contains a binding configuration for the first endpoint that enables reliable sessions.

```xml
<?xml version="1.0" encoding="utf-8" ?>
<configuration xmlns="http://schemas.microsoft.com/.NetConfiguration/v2.0">
    <system.serviceModel>
        <client>
            <endpoint
                configurationName="Endpoint1"
                address="http://localhost:8000/weather/"
                bindingSectionName="wsProfileBinding"
                bindingConfiguration="Binding1"
                contractType="IWeather, client" />
            <endpoint
                configurationName="Endpoint2"
                address="net.tcp://localhost:9000/weather/"
                bindingSectionName="netProfileTcpBinding"
                contractType="IWeather, client" />
            <endpoint
                configurationName="Endpoint3"
                address="net.pipe://localhost/weather"
                bindingSectionName="netProfileNamedPipeBinding"
                contractType="IWeather, client" />
            <endpoint
                configurationName="Endpoint4"
                address="net.msmq://localhost/private$/weather"
                bindingSectionName="netProfileMsmqBinding"
                contractType="IWeather, client" />
        </client>

        <bindings>
            <wsProfileBinding>
                <binding
                    configurationName="Binding1"
                    reliableSessionEnabled="true"
                    orderedSession="true"/>
            </wsProfileBinding>
        </bindings>
    </system.serviceModel>
</configuration>
```

For cross-machine communication, the references to *localhost* in the configuration file must be replaced by the fully qualified domain name of the server. The number of usable endpoints drops to three because the *NetProfileNamedPipe* binding cannot be used cross-machine.

When the client selects the *Endpoint1* endpoint configuration, it communicates with the service using the *WSProfile* binding. Communication takes place using the HTTP protocol, XML messages have a text encoding, reliable messaging provides delivery assurances, and no security is in place.

When the client selects the *Endpoint2* endpoint configuration, it communicates with the service using the *NetProfileTcp* binding. Communication takes place using the TCP protocol, XML messages have a binary encoding, and Windows security is on by default.

When the client selects the *Endpoint3* endpoint configuration, it communicates with the service using the *NetProfileNamedPipe* binding. Communication takes place using named pipes, XML messages have a binary encoding, and Windows security is on by default.

When the client selects the *Endpoint4* endpoint configuration, it communicates with the service using the *NetProfileMsmq* binding. Communication takes place using MSMQ, XML messages have a binary encoding, and Windows security is on by default. The use of queuing allows the client and the service to be time-disconnected from each other.

Summary

This chapter covered how to work with addresses and bindings. Addresses represent the location of a service endpoint. Bindings determine how a service endpoint is communicated with.

There are several types of addresses. An endpoint address is used to access a service. A MEX endpoint address is used to learn about a service. A base address allows endpoint addresses to be specified relatively. The address format depends on the transport in use.

Bindings determine transport method, encoding, and requirements for security, reliable sessions, and transactions. Bindings are composed of binding elements. You can create a custom binding, but for common scenarios a predefined standard binding usually suffices. The standard bindings are *BasicProfile*, *WSProfile*, *WSProfileDualHttp*, *NetProfileTcp*, *NetProfileDualTcp*, *NetProfileNamedPipe*, *NetProfileMsmq*, *MsmqIntegration*, and *Intermediary*. Standard bindings have properties that allow them to be customized. Bindings can be programmed in code or in a configuration file.

We covered how to specify and customize bindings in code and in a configuration file and also covered administrative tasks for the MSMQ transport.

The programming exercise developed a service with multiple endpoints. The endpoints and their bindings were defined in configuration settings.

In the next chapter, we'll look at contracts.

Chapter 5

Contracts

What usually comes first is the contract.

—Benjamin Disraeli

Contracts are what make interoperable services possible. In this chapter, we'll go into detail about the three kinds of contracts in Indigo: service contracts, data contracts, and message contracts.

After completing this chapter, you will:

- Understand the types of contracts available in Indigo and their purposes.
- Know how to define service contracts.
- Know how to define data contracts.
- Know how to define message contracts.

Understanding Contracts

Contracts are one of the fundamental concepts in Indigo. They allow clients and services to have a common understanding of available operations, data structures, and message structures while remaining loosely coupled and platform independent. Indigo includes three kinds of contracts:

- **Service contract**   Describes the operations a service can perform
- **Data contract**   Describes a data structure
- **Message contract**   Defines what goes where in a message

You define contracts by using familiar object-oriented constructs: interfaces and classes. By annotating interfaces and classes with attributes, you bestow contract status on them.

Figure 5-1 illustrates the relationship of the three contract types to the common language runtime (CLR).

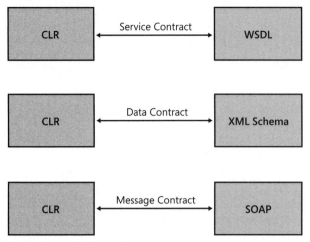

Figure 5-1   Relationship of contracts to the common language runtime

All three types of contracts translate between Microsoft .NET types used internally and the XML representations shared externally:

- A service contract converts between the CLR and Web Services Description Language (WSDL).

- A data contract converts between the CLR and XML Schema Definition (XSD).

- A message contract converts between the CLR and Simple Object Access Protocol (SOAP).

Understanding Service Contracts

A **service contract** describes the operations a service can perform. A service must have at least one service contract, and it can have more than one. You can think of a service contract as follows:

- It describes the client-callable operations (functions) your service provides.

- It maps the interface and methods of your service to a platform-independent description.

- It describes message exchange patterns that the service can have with another party. Some service operations might be one-way; others might require a request-reply pattern.

- It is analogous to the *<portType>* element in WSDL.

You define a service contract by annotating an interface (or class) with the *[ServiceContract]* attribute. You identify service operations by placing *[OperationContract]* attributes on the methods of the interface. The following service contract defines three service operations.

```
[ServiceContract]
public interface IReservation
{
    [OperationContract]
```

```
    string StartReservation(string lastName, string firstName);
    [OperationContract]
    bool ReserveRoom(string arriveDate, string departDate, int guests);
    [OperationContract]
    string ConfirmReservation(bool authorize);
}
```

Once you define a service contract using an interface, you can write a class to implement the interface. For example:

```
public class Reservation : IReservation
{
    public string StartReservation(string lastName, string firstName)
    {
        ...
    }
    public bool ReserveRoom(string arriveDate, string departDate, int guests)
    {
        ...
    }
    public string ConfirmReservation(bool authorize)
    {
        ...
    }
}
```

If you don't like using interfaces, you can instead define the service contract directly against the implementation class and skip the interface altogether. The following class both defines and implements a service contract.

```
[ServiceContract]
public class Reservation
{
    [OperationContract]
    public string StartReservation(string lastName, string firstName)
    {
        ...
    }
    [OperationContract]
    public bool ReserveRoom(string arriveDate, string departDate, int guests)
    {
        ...
    }
    [OperationContract]
    public string ConfirmReservation(bool authorize)
    {
        ...
    }
}
```

A service contract can specify requirements that must be satisfied by endpoint bindings. The *[BindingRequirements]* attribute specifies binding requirements for the contract. The following service contract specifies a requirement for ordered delivery of messages.

```
[ServiceContract]
[BindingRequirements(RequireOrderedDelivery=true)]
public interface IReservation
{
    [OperationContract]
    string StartReservation(string lastName, string firstName);
    [OperationContract]
    bool ReserveRoom(string arriveDate, string departDate, int guests);
    [OperationContract]
    string ConfirmReservation(bool authorize);
}
```

The *[ServiceContract]*, *[BindingRequirements]*, and *[OperationContract]* attributes contain many parameters for specifying service contract details. For detailed information on these attributes, see the section titled "Programming Service Contracts" later in this chapter.

Types of Services

There are three types of services: typed, untyped, and typed message. Typed services are the simplest. Service operations of this type resemble the methods of a class and can accept or return both simple and complex data types. This is often the logical type of service to use in application programming.

```
[OperationContract]
Contact LookupContact(string firstName, string lastName);
```

Untyped services allow developers to work at the message level. Service operations of this type accept or return *Message* objects. Use this type of service when you need to work directly with messages.

```
[OperationContract]
Message ProcessMessage(Message request);
```

Typed message services fall between typed services and untyped services. Service operations of this type accept or return information using custom message classes defined with message contracts. Use this type of service when you want to be able to treat requests and responses as messages and as structured data.

```
[OperationContract]
MyResponseMessage ProcessMessage(MyRequestMessage request);
```

Understanding Data Contracts

A **data contract** describes a data structure. If you're passing more than simple types to or from a service operation, you must define a data contract. You can think of a data contract in these ways:

- It describes the external format of information passed to and from service operations.
- It defines the structure and types of data exchanged in service messages.

- It maps a CLR type to an XML Schema.

- It defines how data types are serialized and deserialized.

- It is a versioning system that allows you to manage changes to structured data.

Serialization is the process of converting structured data such as an object into a sequence of bytes that can be transmitted over a network. Deserialization is the reverse process of reassembling structured data from a received sequence of bytes.

You define a data contract by annotating a class, structure, or enumeration with the *[Data-Contract]* attribute. You identify members of a data contract by placing *[DataMember]* attributes on the fields or properties of the class. The following code defines a data contract for a *Contact* class.

```
[DataContract]
public class Contact
{
    [DataMember] public string FirstName;
    [DataMember] public string LastName;
    [DataMember] public string Address;
    [DataMember] public string Address2;
    [DataMember] public string Phone;
    [DataMember] public string EMail;
}
```

Once a data contract is defined, you can use the type in service operations. The following code shows a service contract whose service operations send or receive the *Contact* structure described earlier.

```
[ServiceContract]
public interface IContact
{
    [OperationContract]
    Contact LookupContact(string lastName, string firstName);
    [OperationContract]
    void AddContact(Contact contact);
    [OperationContract]
    void UpdateContact(Contact contact);
    [OperationContract]
    void DeleteContact(Contact contact);
}
```

In a data contract, you must explicitly identify each member of the contract by using a *[Data-Member]* attribute. This requirement ensures that developers make a conscious choice to expose data externally. It is the sole determinant of whether data is shared externally; access modifiers such as *public* and *private* do not play a role.

Each data contract must have a unique name—a namespace and name that can be specified as parameters of the *[DataContract]* attribute. By default, the namespace and name are derived from the class.

The *[DataContract]* and *[DataMember]* attributes contain many parameters for specifying data contract details. For detailed information on these attributes, see the section titled "Programming Data Contracts" later in this chapter.

Explicit vs. Implicit Data Contracts

Data contracts can be explicit or implicit. You define an explicit data contract by using the *[DataContract]* and *[DataMember]* attributes.

Simple types have an implicit data contract. For example, you can use an int or a string in a service operation without having to define a data contract. Here are the types with an implicit data contract:

- *System.Boolean*
- *System.Byte*
- *System.Char*
- *System.DateTime*
- *System.Decimal*
- *System.Double*
- *System.Int16*
- *System.Int32*
- *System.Int64*
- *System.Object*
- *System.SByte*
- *System.Single*
- *System.String*
- *System.UInt16*
- *System.UInt32*
- *System.UInt64*
- Any delegate
- Any enum
- Any *ISerializable* type
- Any *[Serializable]* type
- Any array or generic of the preceding types

Serializable types also have an implicit data contract. Classes that implement .NET serialization using the *[Serializable]* attribute or the *ISerializable* interface can be passed to or from service operations without the need to specify data contract attributes.

Data Contract Compatibility

A data contract can be implemented in multiple ways. For a data contract to be considered compatible between two parties, its namespace, name, and list of members must match.

Consider the following simple data contract. The contract is named *Bid* and contains two members, *Lot* and *Amount*. By default, these names are taken from the class members.

```
[DataContract(Namespace="http://www.contoso.com")]
public class Bid
{
    [DataMember]
    public int Lot;
    [DataMember]
    public float Amount;
}
```

Another program might implement the same contract quite differently. The following class contains the same data contract but with different implementation details.

```
[DataContract(Namespace="http://www.contoso.com", Name="Bid")]
public class BidClass
{
    [DataMember(Name="Lot")]
    private string _lot;
    [DataMember(Name="Amount")]
    private double _amt;
    private int temp;
}
```

As in the first data contract, the contract name is *Bid* and the members are named *Lot* and *Amount*. Unlike in the first data contract, the contracts and members are explicitly given names that don't match the member names of the class. The data types and access modifiers are also different in this class. Despite these differences, the data contract is the same, and this information can be passed between two programs as a *Bid*.

It's perfectly acceptable for implementations to use different data types to implement data members, as long as a straightforward conversion exists. In the two contract implementations just shown, *Lot* and *Amount* are both implemented with different data types.

Data Contract Versioning

Data contracts support the concept of versioning. As data contracts are amended over time, you can use *[DataMember]* parameters to specify version numbers and control what happens if two parties are using different versions of a data contract. The following data contract has been amended several times.

```
[DataContract]
public class Book
{
    [DataMember]
    public string Title;
    [DataMember]
    public string Author;
    [DataMember]
    public string ISBN;
    [DataMember(VersionAdded=2, IsOptional=false, MustUnderstand=true)]
    public DateTime PublicationDate;
    [DataMember(VersionAdded=3, IsOptional=true, MustUnderstand=false)]
    public int Edition;
}
```

You can update a data contract without breaking compatibility by respecting the following versioning rules:

1. Don't change the namespace or name of the contract.

2. Don't change the names of the data members.

3. When adding new data members, specify a version number that is higher than previous version numbers.

4. Remove only data members that were defined to be optional.

Understanding Message Contracts

A **message contract** describes the structure of a message. Left to its own devices, Indigo makes its own decisions about what goes where in a SOAP message. Message contracts allow you to precisely control whether information goes in the message body or in message headers. One reason you might need this control is interoperability. Message contracts allow you to match the expectations of other systems concerning the structure of SOAP messages.

You define a message contract by annotating a class with the *[MessageContract]* attribute. You specify the message specifics for the class members by using the *[MessageBody]* and *[Message-Header]* attributes. The following code defines a simple message contract.

```
[MessageContract]
public sealed class OrderItemRequest
{
    [MessageHeader]
    public string orderNo;
    [MessageBody]
    public OrderItem orderItem;
}
```

A custom message class is called a **typed message**. Once you define a typed message, you can pass the message to or from service operations.

```
[ServiceContract]
public interface ISampleContract
{
    [OperationContract(IsOneWay=true)]
    void ProcessMessage(OrderItemRequest message);
}
```

Typed messages combine the benefits of typed services and untyped services. As with typed services, typed message programming provides ease of use, doesn't require you to manipulate a message's XML Infosets directly, and provides fine control over the mapping of the data to the message structure.

Another place where you can use message contract attributes is in service contracts. You might have noticed this if you've studied code generated by the Svcutil tool. The following code shows message contract attributes in a service contract.

```
[System.ServiceModel.ServiceContractAttribute()]
public interface ILibrary
{
    [System.ServiceModel.OperationContractAttribute(Action =
        "http://tempuri.org/ILibrary/FindBook", ReplyAction =
        "http://tempuri.org/ILibrary/FindBookResponse")]
    [return: System.ServiceModel.MessageBodyAttribute(Name = "FindBookResult",
        Namespace = "http://tempuri.org/")]
    int FindBook([System.ServiceModel.MessageBodyAttribute(Namespace =
        "http://tempuri.org/")] ProgrammingIndigo.Book book);
}
```

The *[MessageContract]*, *[MessageHeader]*, and *[MessageBody]* attributes contain many parameters for specifying message contract details. For detailed information on these attributes, see the section titled "Programming Message Contracts" later in this chapter.

Programming Service Contracts

You define a service contract by annotating an interface or class with the *[ServiceContract]* attribute. You indicate service operations by using *[OperationContract]* attributes on the methods of the interface. You can also specify a *[BindingRequirements]* attribute for the interface.

```
[ServiceContract]
public interface ISpellChecker
{
    [OperationContract]
    void OpenDocument(string documentText);
    [OperationContract]
    string[] CheckSpelling();
    [OperationContract]
    void MakeCorrection(int location, string replacementText);
    [OperationContract]
    string CloseDocument();
}
```

Service contracts can inherit from each other.

The *[ServiceContract]* Attribute

The *[ServiceContract]* attribute marks an interface or class as a service contract.

```
[ServiceContract(Session=true, FormatMode=XmlSerializer)]
public interface IMyService
{
    ...
}
```

You can specify the following parameters in any order for the *[ServiceContract]* attribute:

- *CallbackContract (type)*   References a client callback contract used for duplex communication. The default is no callback contract.

- *FormatMode (ContractFormatMode)*   Selects a serializer. A *serializer* is a class used to perform serialization and deserialization. You can set this property to *XmlFormatter* or *XmlSerializer*. The default is *XmlFormatter*.

- *Name (string)*   Specifies the name of the service contract. If this parameter is omitted, the default is the interface name.

- *Namespace (string)*   Specifies the namespace of the service contract. If this parameter is omitted, the default is the interface namespace.

- *Session (boolean)*   Indicates whether the contract requires a session. The default is *false*.

- *Style (ServiceOperationStyle)*   Determines how the WSDL metadata for the service is formatted. Possible values are *DocumentWrapped*, *DocumentBare*, and *Rpc*. The default is *DocumentWrapped*. This property also exists at the *[OperationContract]* level.

- *Use (ServiceOperationBindingUse)*   Determines whether the message format is literal or encoded. Possible values are *Literal* and *Encoded*. The default is *Literal*. This property also exists at the *[OperationContract]* level.

CallbackContract: Defining a Duplex Service Contract

When you use the duplex messaging pattern, both the service and the client implement a contract of service operations. The client's contract is called the **callback contract**. Thus, for duplex messaging a pair of contracts is always required.

To define a duplex contract pair, you define two sets of interfaces as service contracts and then link them. The *[ServiceContract]* attribute on the service contract should contain a *CallbackContract=typeof(type)* parameter that references the client callback contract.

```
[ServiceContract(CallbackContract=typeof(ISampleClientContract))]
public interface ISampleContract
{
    [OperationContract(IsOneWay=false)]
    void MoveForward(int units);
    [OperationContract(IsOneWay=false)]
```

```
    void MoveBackward(int units);
    [OperationContract(IsOneWay=false)]
    void TurnLeft();
    [OperationContract(IsOneWay=false)]
    void TurnRight();
}

public interface ISampleClientContract
{
    [OperationContract(IsOneWay=false)]
    void Position(int x, int y, string direction);
}
```

If the client and service implement identical contracts, there is no need to define a second contract. The service contract can reference itself in the *CallbackContract* parameter.

```
[ServiceContract(CallbackContract=typeof(IChat))]
public interface IChat
{
    [OperationContract]
    void Say(string from, string text);
}
```

FormatMode: Selecting a Serializer

The serialization of service operation parameters and return values to messages and the subsequent deserialization are handled by a serializer. The default serializer is *XmlFormatter*. The other choice is the .NET Framework's *XmlSerializer*.

You can specify a serializer in the *[ServiceContract]* attribute by using the *FormatMode* parameter. The choices are *ContractFormatMode.XmlFormatter* and *ContractFormatMode.XmlSerializer*. The following service contract attribute specifies *XmlSerializer*.

```
[ServiceContract(FormatMode=ContractFormatMode.XmlSerializer)]
```

If you serialize using *XmlSerializer*, only public members of classes are serialized.

Name and *Namespace*: Naming a Service Contract

By default, a service contract takes its name and namespace from the interface or class that the *[ServiceContract]* attribute is applied to. To set a different name, use the *Name* parameter of *[ServiceContract]*. To set a different namespace, use the *Namespace* parameter.

```
[ServiceContract(Namespace="http://tempuri.org", Name="IMyContract")]
interface IMyPrototypeContract
{
    ...
}
```

Session: Requiring Sessions

A service contract can indicate that sessions and message ordering must be supported by its binding. You set the *Session* parameter of *[ServiceContract]* to *true* to require sessions.

```
[ServiceContract(Session=true)]
public interface IStockAssistant
{
    [OperationContract(IsInitiating=true)]
    void StartSession(string account);
    [OperationContract]
    void Buy(string symbol, int shares);
    [OperationContract]
    void Sell(string symbol, int shares);
    [OperationContract(IsTerminating=true)]
    void EndSession();
}
```

Style: Controlling Metadata Style

The way WSDL formats metadata for the service can be set to document/wrapped, document/bare, or RPC message style. The default is document/wrapped. To change the style, use the *Style* parameter at the *[ServiceContract]* or *[OperationContract]* level. Possible values are *ServiceOperationStyle.DocumentWrapped*, *ServiceOperationStyle.DocumentBare*, and *Service-OperationStyle.Rpc*. The following code sets the metadata style to document/bare for the service contract in general, but one operation specifies the RPC style.

```
[ServiceContract(Style=ServiceOperationStyle.DocumentBare)]
public interface IMyService
{
    [OperationContract]
    int OperationA();
    [OperationContract]
    int OperationB();
    [OperationContract(Style=ServiceOperationStyle.Rpc)]
    int OperationC();
}
```

Use: Specifying Message Format

Messages can be in either literal or encoded format. In literal format, the body of a message conforms to an XSD. In encoded format, SOAP encoding is used. The default is literal. If you use the encoded setting, you must also specify *XmlSerializer*.

To change the message format, you set the *Use* parameter at the *[ServiceContract]* or *[Operation-Contract]* level. Possible values are *ServiceOperationBindingUse.Literal* and *ServiceOperation-BindingUse.Encoded*.

The following service contract attribute sets the message format to *Encoded* and specifies the *XmlSerializer* serializer.

```
[ServiceContract(Use=ServiceOperationBindingUse.Encoded, FormatMode=
    ContractFormatMode.XmlSerializer)]
```

The *[OperationContract]* Attribute

The *[OperationContract]* attribute marks a method as a service operation and makes it part of the service contract.

```
[ServiceContract(Session=true, FormatMode=XmlSerializer)]
public interface IMyService
{
    [OperationContract(IsOneWay=true)]
    void SubmitExpenseReport(ExpenseReport report);
}
```

The following parameters can be specified for the *[OperationContract]* attribute:

- *Action (string)*   Identifies the action to be performed by the service operation. If *Action* is not specified, the default is *http://tempuri.org/contract-name/operation-name*. In an untyped service, you can set *Action* to * to intercept all service operations.

- *AsyncPattern (boolean)*   Defines the service operation as synchronous or asynchronous. An asynchronous service operation is implemented as a *BeginX/EndX* pair in accordance with the general Async Pattern of the .NET Framework. The default is *false* (synchronous).

- *IsInitiating (boolean)*   Determines whether a service operation initiates a new channel on the service. The default is *true* (yes).

- *IsOneWay (boolean)*   Defines the service as one-way or two-way. A one-way service does not send a response and might not have a return type other than *void*. A two-way service is accessed in a request-reply pattern. The default is *false* (two-way).

- *IsTerminating (boolean)*   Determines whether a service operation will close and shut down the client channel after the service operation completes and replies. The default is *false* (no).

- *Name (string)*   Specifies the name of the service operation. The default is the method name of the service operation.

- *ReplyAction (string)*   Identifies the action of the response sent by the service operation. If *ReplyAction* is not specified, the default is *http://tempuri.org/contract-name/operation-nameResponse*.

- *Style (ServiceOperationStyle)*   Specifies how the WSDL metadata for the service is formatted. Possible values are *DocumentWrapped*, *DocumentBare*, and *Rpc*. The default is *DocumentWrapped*. This property also exists at the *[ServiceContract]* level and is described in that section of the chapter.

- *Use (ServiceOperationBindingUse)*   Specifies whether the message format is literal or encoded. Possible values are *Literal* and *Encoded*. *Use* defaults to *Literal*. This property also exists at the *[ServiceContract]* level and is described in that section of the chapter.

Action: Specifying Actions

Every service operation has a name in the service contract called an **action**. *Action* is a URI. If you don't specify an action for a service operation, the name will be *http://tempuri.org/contract-name/operation-name* (for example, *http://tempuri.org/IWeatherService/ReportLocalConditions*).

You can specify an action using the *Action=string* parameter of the *[OperationContract]* attribute. You can specify a simple operation name, like *RequestReply*, or a full URI.

```
[OperationContract(Action="http://tempuri.org/ISomeContract/SomeOperation")]
```

In an untyped service operation, you can set *Action* to * to intercept all messages.

```
[ServiceContract]
public interface IMyUntypedContract
{
    [OperationContract(IsOneWay=false, Action="*")]
    Message ProcessMessage(Message message);
}
```

AsyncPattern: Specifying Asynchronous Service Operations

Service operations can be synchronous or asynchronous. A client calling a two-way service operation synchronously blocks, waiting for the service operation to complete and send its response. A client calling a service operation asynchronously doesn't have to wait—it can start a service operation, do other work, and get the service operation result later.

Asynchronous service operations use the Async Pattern of the .NET Framework. Both clients and services can use the Async Pattern. For service operations, using *AsyncPattern* means breaking up the service operation into *Begin<operation>* and *End<operation>* operations. In the service contract, these two operations are defined under a single *[OperationContract]* attribute with an *AsyncPattern=true* parameter, like this:

```
[OperationContract(AsyncPattern=true)]
IAsyncResult BeginWeatherReport(string region, int temperature, int windSpeed, int humidity,
    float pressure, AsyncCallback callback, object state);
void EndWeatherReport(IAsyncResult ar);
```

The *Begin* operation has two additional parameters beyond what the service operation normally requires: *AsyncCallback* and a state object. The *Begin* operation returns an *IAsyncResult* rather than what the service operation would normally return. The *End* operation accepts an *IAsyncResult* parameter and returns the service operation result.

For information on using the Async Pattern in clients, see Chapter 6. For information on implementing the Async Pattern in service operations, see Chapter 7.

IsInitiating and *IsTerminating*: Controlling Session Lifetime

Services can provide session instancing, in which a separate instance of the class is maintained for each client channel. The *IsInitiating* and *IsTerminating* parameters allow you to control which service operations initiate or terminate a session instance. By default, all service operations initiate a session instance. In the following service contract, the *OpenAccount* service operation initiates the sessions and must be the first service operation a client calls. The *CloseAccount* service terminates the session.

```
[ServiceContract]
public interface IBanking
{
    [OperationContract(IsInitiating=true, IsTerminating=false)]
    void OpenAccount(account);
    [OperationContract(IsInitiating=false, IsTerminating=false)]
    void Deposit(decimal amount);
    [OperationContract(IsInitiating=false, IsTerminating=false)]
    void Withdraw(decimal amount);
    [OperationContract(IsInitiating=false, IsTerminating=true)]
    void CloseAccount();
}
```

IsOneWay: Setting Service Operation Direction

A service operation can be one-way or two-way. By default, a service operation is two-way, meaning that when a service operation is accessed there is both an incoming request communication and an outgoing reply communication. Even if a service operation has a return type of *void*, a reply takes place if it is two-way. When a client invokes a two-way service operation, it waits for the reply before continuing with its execution. When a client invokes a one-way service operation, it does not wait for a response.

To specify direction, use the *IsOneWay=boolean* parameter of the *[OperationContract]* attribute. A value of *true* indicates a one-way service; *false* indicates a two-way service. The following service contract specifies both one-way and two-way service operations.

```
[ServiceContract]
interface IWeatherReporting
{
    [OperationContract(IsOneWay=true)]
```

```
    void ReportTemperature(int region, float temp);
    [OperationContract(IsOneWay=true)]
    void ReportWindspeed(int region, int windspeed);
    [OperationContract(IsOneWay=false)]
    float GetTemperature(int region);
}
```

Name: Naming a Service Operation

By default, a service operation takes its name from the method name the *[OperationContract]* attribute is applied to. To set a different name, use the *Name* parameter of *[OperationContract]*.

```
[ServiceContract]
interface IMyPrototypeContract
{
    [OperationContract(Name="FunctionB")]
    void FunctionA();
}
```

ReplyAction: Specifying Actions

Just as the request message for a service operation specifies an action, a reply message specifies a reply action. A reply action is a URI. If you don't specify a reply action for a service operation, it will be named *http://tempuri.org/contract-name/operation-nameResponse* (for example, *http://tempuri.org/IWeatherService/ReportLocalConditionsResponse*).

You can specify a reply action by using the *ReplyAction=string* parameter of the *[OperationContract]* attribute. You can specify a simple operation name, like *RequestReplyResponse*, or a full URI.

```
[OperationContract(ReplyAction="http://tempuri.org/ISomeContract/SomeOperationResponse")]
```

The *[BindingRequirements]* Attribute

The *[BindingRequirements]* attribute specifies requirements for a service contract that bindings must meet. An error occurs if an attempt is made to create an endpoint whose binding doesn't match the requirements. Like the *[ServiceContract]* attribute, *[BindingRequirements]* is applied to the interface or class that defines the service contract.

```
[ServiceContract(Session=true)]
[BindingRequirements(
    CommunicationProfileRequirements=CommunicationProfileRequirements.DotNet,
    TransactionFlowRequirements=RequirementsMode.Require,
    QueuedDeliveryRequirements=RequirementsMode.Require,
    RequireOrderedDelivery=true)]
{
    ...
}
```

The following parameters can be specified for the *[BindingRequirements]* attribute:

- *CommunicationProfileRequirements (CommunicationProfileRequirements)*   Identifies a specific binding profile that must be used. Possible values are *BasicProfile, WS, DotNet,* and *None.* The default is *CommunicationProfileRequirements.None,* which allows bindings of any profile to be used.

- *QueuedDeliveryRequirements (RequirementsMode)*   Specifies whether queuing is required, prohibited, or permitted. Possible values are *Required, Disallowed,* and *Ignore.* The default is *RequirementsMode.Ignore,* which specifies no queuing requirements.

- *RequireOrderedDelivery (boolean)*   Specifies whether ordered delivery of messages is required. Possible values are *true* and *false.* The default is *false,* which means ordered delivery is not required.

- *TransactionFlowRequirements (RequirementsMode)*   Specifies whether transaction flow is required, prohibited, or permitted. Possible values are *Required, Disallowed,* and *Ignore.* The default is *RequirementsMode.Ignore,* which specifies no transaction flow requirements.

CommunicationProfileRequirements: Requiring a Profile

By default, bindings for a service contract can be of any profile: *BasicProfile, WSProfile, NetProfile,* or custom. To require a specific profile, use the *CommunicationProfileRequirements* parameter of *[BindingRequirements].* Possible values are *BasicProfile, WS, DotNet,* and *None.* The default is *None.*

```
[ServiceContract]
[BindingRequirements(CommunicationProfileRequirements=
   CommunicationProfileRequirements.DotNet)]
Public interface IMyContract
{
    [OperationContract]
    void DoSomething();
}
```

QueuedDeliveryRequirements: Queuing Control

By default, bindings for a service contract are free to use the MSMQ transport or not. To specifically require or disallow the use of queuing in a binding, use the *QueuedDeliveryRequirements* parameter of *[BindingRequirements].* Possible values are *Required, Disallowed,* and *Ignore.* The default is *Ignore.*

```
[ServiceContract]
[BindingRequirements(QueuedDeliveryRequirements=RequirementsMode.Required)]
Public interface IMyContract
{
    [OperationContract]
    void DoSomething();
}
```

RequireOrderedDelivery: Ordered Delivery Control

By default, bindings for a service contract can provide ordered delivery assurances or not. To specifically require or disallow ordered delivery, use the *RequireOrderedDelivery* parameter of *[BindingRequirements]*. Possible values are *true* and *false*. The default is *false*.

```
[ServiceContract]
[BindingRequirements(RequireOrderedDelivery=true)]
Public interface IMyContract
{
    [OperationContract]
    void DoSomething();
}
```

TransactionFlowRequirements: Transaction Flow Control

By default, bindings for a service contract are free to enable transaction flow or not. To specifically require or disallow transaction flow in a binding, use the *TransactionFlowRequirements* parameter of *[BindingRequirements]*. Possible values are *Required*, *Disallowed*, and *Ignore*. The default is *Ignore*.

```
[ServiceContract]
[BindingRequirements(TransactionFlowRequirements=RequirementsMode.Required)]
Public interface IMyContract
{
    [OperationContract]
    void DoSomething();
}
```

Defining Service Operations

There are three kinds of services:

- **Typed**   In a typed service, the parameters and return values of service operations are primitive or complex data types.

- **Untyped**   In an untyped service, the parameters and return values of service operations are messages.

- **Typed message**   In a typed message service, the parameters and return values of service operations are custom messages defined with message contracts.

Defining Typed Service Operations

A typed service operation is one that accepts simple or complex data as parameters and return values. Using a typed service operation feels very much like using a method of a class. The following service contract contains typed service operations.

```
[ServiceContract]
public interface IMeasurementConversion
```

```
{
    [OperationContract]
    float CalculateDistance(float x1, float y1, float x2, float y2);
    [OperationContract]
    int CalculateShippingZone(float x1, float y1);
}
```

Service operations can return values, as the preceding service operations do. But sometimes you might need to return more than one value or return a modified version of a parameter value. In these cases, you can use *ref* and *out* parameters, just as you would in object-oriented programming. In actuality, you are passing by value. The following service operations use *ref* and *out* parameters.

```
[ServiceContract]
public interface IMeasurementConversion
{
    [OperationContract]
    void MoveNorth(ref float x, ref float y, float distance);
    [OperationContract]
    void MoveSouth(ref float x, ref float y, float distance);
    [OperationContract]
    void MoveEast(ref float x, ref float y, float distance);
    [OperationContract]
    void MoveWest(ref float x, ref float y, float distance);
    [OperationContract]
    void CalculateDistance(float x1, float y1, float x2, float y2, out float distance);
}
```

In addition to simple types and arrays, typed service operations can also accept complex data structures as parameters or return them as results. This requires the use of data contracts. See the earlier section titled "Understanding Data Contracts" and the later section titled "Programming Data Contracts" for more information.

Defining Untyped Service Operations

An untyped service operation accepts a *Message* parameter, which allows it to accept any kind of incoming message. The service operation code is responsible for interpreting the message. If the service operation sends a reply, it is also of type *Message*. The following service contract contains an untyped service operation.

```
[ServiceContract]
public interface IMyUntypedContract
{
    [OperationContract(IsOneWay=true, Action="*")]
    void ProcessMessage(Message message);
}
```

Specifying the *Action="*"* parameter in the *[OperationContract]* attribute causes the service operation to receive all incoming messages regardless of the service operation name originally specified by the client.

For information on how to create messages to send or interpret received messages using *Message* objects, see Chapter 7.

Defining Typed Message Service Operations

A typed message service operation accepts a custom message parameter—a message contract class. The service operation code is responsible for interpreting the message. If the service operation sends a reply, the reply is also a custom message, but it does not have to be the same type as the request message. The following code contains a service contract with a typed message service operation and a message contract defining a custom message.

```
[ServiceContract]
public interface IMyTypedMessageContract
{
    [OperationContract(IsOneWay=true, Action="*")]
    void Register(Contact contact);
}

[MessageContract]
public class Contact
{
    [MessageHeader]
    string LastName;
    [MessageHeader]
    string FirstName;
    [MessageBody]
    string Phone;
    [MessageBody]
    string Email;
    [MessageBody]
    string Notes;
}
```

For information on how to create message contracts, see the section titled "Programming Message Contracts" later in this chapter. For information on how to implement typed message service operations, see Chapter 7.

Programming Data Contracts

You define a data contract by annotating a class with the *[DataContract]* attribute. Data contract members are indicated with *[DataMember]* attributes on the methods of the class.

```
[DataContract]
public class OrderItem
{
    [DataMember] public int Qty;
    [DataMember] public string PartNo;
    [DataMember] public string Description;
    [DataMember] public decimal Price;
}
```

The *[DataContract]* Attribute

The *[DataContract]* attribute marks a class as a data contract.

```
[DataContract]
public class ICustomer
{
    ...
}
```

The following parameters can be specified for the *[DataContract]* attribute:

- *Namespace (Uri)*   Specifies the namespace for the data contract. By default, the namespace for a data contract is derived from the CLR namespace.

- *Name (string)*   Specifies the name for the data contract. By default, the name for a data contract is derived from the name of the class.

Name and *Namespace*: Naming a Data Contract

By default, a data contract takes its name and namespace from the class or structure the *[DataContract]* attribute is applied to. To set a different name, use the *Name* parameter of *[DataContract]*. To set a different namespace, use the *Namespace* parameter.

```
[DataContract(Namespace="http://tempuri.org", Name="Customer")]
class CustomerClass
{
    ...
}
```

The *[DataMember]* Attribute

The *[DataMember]* attribute marks the field, property, or event of a class as a member of a data contract.

```
[DataContract]
public class Customer
{
    [DataMember]
    public string CustomerID;
    [DataMember]
    public string LastName;
    [DataMember]
    public string FirstName;
    ...
}
```

The following parameters can be specified for the *[DataMember]* attribute:

- *IsOptional (boolean)*   Controls what happens if data that is part of the receiving-side data contract is not present. If *IsOptional* is *false* and the member is not present in the incoming data, an error results. If *IsOptional* is *true*, no error results. The default is *false* (member required).

■ *MustUnderstand (boolean)*   Controls what happens if data is supplied that is not part of the receiving-side data contract. If *MustUnderstand* is *true* and the member is not part of the receiving side's data contract, an error results. If *MustUnderstand* is false, no error results. The default is *false*.

■ *Name (string)*   Specifies the name for the data contract. By default, the name for a data contract is derived from the name of the class.

■ *VersionAdded (int)*   Indicates the version of the data contract when the member was first added to the contract. The default is *1*.

■ *SerializeAs (SerializationReferenceMode)*   Controls what happens when two members of a data contract reference the same instance of an object. If *SerializeAs* is set to *SerializationReferenceMode.ReferenceType*, the result that is deserialized on the receiving side will likewise have two references to the same instance. If *SerializeAs* is set to *SerializationReferenceMode.ValueType*, reference semantics will be ignored and the receiving side will have references to two separate instances that have equal values. The default is *SerializationReferenceMode.ReferenceType*.

IsOptional: Requiring Data Members

To support versioning, data contract members can be optional or required. The *IsOptional* property controls what the receiving side does if a data member is not present. If *IsOptional* is false, an error occurs if the data member is missing in a message. The following code shows a data contract in which some members are required and some are optional.

```
[DataContract]
public class Contact
{
    [DataMember(IsOptional=false)]
    public string FirstName;
    [DataMember(IsOptional=true)]
    public string MiddleName;
    [DataMember(IsOptional=false)]
    public string LastName;
    [DataMember(IsOptional=false)]
    public string Address;
    [DataMember(IsOptional=true)]
    public string Address2;
}
```

Don't confuse *IsOptional* with *MustUnderstand*. Think of *IsOptional* as something the receiver specifies and *MustUnderstand* as something the sender specifies.

MustUnderstand: Requiring Data Members

A data contract can stipulate that the receiver must understand (expect) a data member. The *MustUnderstand* property controls what the receiving side does if a data member is present that is not part of its data contract. If *MustUnderstand* is *true*, an error occurs if the receiving side wasn't expecting the data member. The following code shows a data contract in which *MustUnderstand* is specified for some data members.

```
[DataContract]
public class Contact
{
    [DataMember(MustUnderstand=true)]
    public string FirstName;
    [DataMember(MustUnderstand=true)]
    public string MiddleName;
    [DataMember(MustUnderstand=true)]
    public string LastName;
    [DataMember(MustUnderstand=false)]
    public string Address;
    [DataMember(MustUnderstand=false)]
    public string Address2;
    [DataMember(MustUnderstand=true)]
    public string Phone;
}
```

Name: Naming a Data Member

By default, a data member takes its name from the field, property, or event the attribute is applied to. To set a different name, use the *Name* parameter of *[DataMember]*. The following data contract uses the *Name* parameter to specify several data member names.

```
[DataContract]
public class AirlineSeat
{
    [DataMember(Name="Column")]
    public char _column;
    [DataMember(Name="Row")]
    public int _row;
    [DataMember(Name="Class")]
    public CabinClass _class;
}
```

VersionAdded: Specifying a Version Number

To document the changes to a data contract, you can assign version numbers to data members. The default version number is 1. To specify a different version number, use the *Version-Added* parameter and specify an integer version number. The following code shows a data contract that is now at version 3.

```
[DataContract]
public class AirlineSeat
```

```
{
    [DataMember]
    public char _column;
    [DataMember(VersionAdded=2)]
    public int _row;
    [DataMember(VersionAdded=2)]
    public CabinClass _class;
    [DataMember(VersionAdded=3)]
    public CabinClass _class;
}
```

SerializeAs: Maintaining Reference Semantics

When a data contract class is serialized, more than one of its members might contain a reference to the same instance of an object. For example, a bill-to address and a ship-to address in a purchase order might reference the same address object. With the exception of strings, a data contract preserves CLR reference semantics, so the deserialized data contract will also have shared references. When you are communicating with another platform, this might be unwanted behavior. Use the *SerializeAs* property to enable or disable this behavior. Set *SerializeAs* to *SerializationReferenceMode.ReferenceType* to preserve reference semantics or set it to *SerializationReferenceMode.ValueType* to defeat reference semantics. The default is *ReferenceType*.

```
[DataContract]
public class AirlineSeat
{
    [DataMember(SerializeAs=SerializationReferenceMode.ValueType)]
    public Address BillToAddress;
    [DataMember(SerializeAs=SerializationReferenceMode.ValueType)]
    public Address ShipToAddress;
}
```

The *[KnownType]* Attribute

The serialization of data contracts usually contains all the information necessary for proper deserialization. But on occasion you might want to include more type information—for example, if you are using a dynamic array class such as *Hashtable*, which contains objects of other types. The definition of those other types won't be included in the serialization stream by default.

You use the *[KnownType]* attribute to make sure a type is included in the serialization stream. In the following code example, the *MediaCatalog* class contains a *Hashtable*. The types used with the *Hashtable*, *DVD* and *CD*, are identified to the data contract using *[KnownType]* attributes.

```
[DataContract]
public class DVD
{
    ...
```

```
}

[DataContract]
public class CD
{
    ...
}

[DataContract]
[KnownType(typeof(DVD))]
[KnownType(typeof(CD))]
public class MediaCatalog
{
    [DataMember]
    public Hashtable catalog;
}
```

[KnownType] in Service Operations

[KnownType] can be used in one other place: service contracts. You can specify *[KnownType]* attributes for a service operation when the type is not obvious. In the following code, the *UploadFile* service operation expects a *MediaFile* parameter. To permit the derived types *MusicMediaFile* and *VideoMediaFile* to also be used with the service operation, *[KnownType]* attributes are specified.

```
[ServiceContract]
public interface IMediaUploadService
{
    [OperationContract]
    [KnownType(typeof(MusicMediaFile))]
    [KnownType(typeof(VideoMediaFile))]
    void UploadFile(MediaFile file);
}
```

Programming Message Contracts

You define a message contract by annotating a class with the *[MessageContract]* attribute. The *[MessageBody]* and *[MessageHeader]* attributes are applied to class members.

```
[MessageContract]
public sealed class OrderItemRequest
{
    [MessageHeader]
    public string orderNo;
    [MessageBody]
    public OrderItem orderItem;
}
```

The *[MessageContract]* Attribute

The *[MessageContract]* attribute marks a class as a message contract.

```
[MessageContract]
public sealed class OrderItemRequest
{
    ...
}
```

The following parameters can be specified for the *[MessageContract]* attribute:

- *Action (string)*   Identifies the action part of the SOAP message. The default value is *, which means the message can target any service operation.

- *WrapperElementName (string)*   Specifies the name of the message body wrapper element. The wrapper element encloses the elements in the body of a message when the message is formatted in the document/wrapper style.

- *WrapperElementNamespace (string)*   Specifies the namespace of the message body wrapper element.

Action: Specifying an Action

The *Action* part of a SOAP message specifies the intended operation for the message. In typed messages, you can set the action to a specific string or to *, which means the message is suitable for any action. By default, a typed message has the action *.

```
[MessageContract(Action="http://SearchCatalog")]
class SearchCatalog
{
    ...
}
```

WrapperElementName and *WrapperElementNamespace*: Naming the Message Body Wrapper Element

The body of a message can be formatted in several styles. In the document/wrapper style, an outer XML element called the **wrapper element** surrounds the other elements in the body.

The *WrapperElementName* and *WrapperElementNamespace* properties allow you to set the name and namespace of the wrapper element, respectively. To set the name and namespace of the wrapper element, use the *WrapperElementName* and *WrapperElementNamespace* parameters of *[MessageContract]*. You specify the name and namespace as *strings*.

```
[MessageContract(WrapperElementName="Record", WrapperElementNamespace=
    "http://www.contoso.com/Record")]
```

```
public class RecordMessage
{
    ...
}
```

The *[MessageBody]* Attribute

The *[MessageBody]* attribute maps a message contract member to the body part of the message.

```
[MessageContract(Action="http://www.contoso.com/Contact")]
public class ContactMessage
{
    [MessageBody(Position=1)]
    public int Age;
    [MessageBody]
    public string Name;
}
```

The following parameters can be specified for the *[MessageBody]* attribute:

- *Name (string)*   Sets the name of the message contract member.

- *Namespace (string)*   Sets the namespace of the message contract member.

- *Position (int)*   Specifies where the message contract member appears in the body relative to other elements. This value influences only the order because more than one member can specify the same position number. The lowest possible position number is *0*, which is the default value.

- *ReferenceMode (SerializationReferenceMode)*   Controls what happens when two members of a data contract reference the same instance of an object. If *SerializeAs* is set to *SerializationReferenceMode.ReferenceType*, the result that is deserialized on the receiving side will likewise have two references to the same instance. If *SerializeAs* is set to *SerializationReferenceMode.ValueType*, reference semantics will be ignored and the receiving side will have references to two separate instances that have equal values. The default is *SerializationReferenceMode.ReferenceType*.

The *[MessageBodyArray]* Attribute

When you map an array to the message body, you can use the *[MessageBodyArray]* attribute instead of *[MessageBody]* to emit optimal XML. *[MessageBodyArray]* is similar to *[MessageBody]* and accepts the same parameters (*Name*, *Namespace*, and *Position*). It can be applied only to arrays.

```
[MessageBodyArray]
public OrderItem[] items;
```

The *[MessageHeader]* Attribute

The *[MessageHeader]* attribute maps a message contract member to a SOAP message header.

```
[MessageContract(Action="http://www.contoso.com/Contact")]
public class ContactMessage
{
    [MessageHeader(Position=1)]
    public int Age;
    [MessageHeader]
    public string Name;
}
```

[MessageHeader] accepts the same parameters as *[MessageBody]*. See the section titled "The *[MessageBody]* Attribute" earlier in this chapter for a description of these parameters. *[MessageHeader]* also accepts these additional parameters:

- *Actor (string)*   Sets the *Actor* property of a SOAP header
- *MustUnderstand (boolean)*   Sets the *MustUnderstand* property of a SOAP header
- *Relay (boolean)*   Sets the *Relay* property of a SOAP header

Actor: Addressing an Endpoint

SOAP headers have an *Actor* property that indicates that the header is meant for a specific endpoint as the message makes its way from sender to receiver. The *Actor* parameter of *[Message-Header]* sets the *Actor* property to a URI string.

```
[MessageContract]
public class MyMessage
{
    [MessageHeader(Actor="http://contoso.com/roleA", Relay="false")]
    public string HeaderA;
}
```

MustUnderstand: Making Headers Mandatory

SOAP headers have a *MustUnderstand* property. If the *Actor* property is set to *true*, the receiver indicated by the property must recognize the header in order to process the message. The *MustUnderstand* parameter of *[MessageHeader]* sets the *MustUnderstand* property.

```
[MessageContract]
public class MyMessage
{
    [MessageHeader(Actor="http://contoso.com/roleB", MustUnderstand="true")]
    public string HeaderB;
    ...
}
```

Relay: Message Relay to Downstream Endpoints

SOAP headers have a *Relay* property. If the *Relay* property is set to *true*, the endpoint indicated by the *Actor* property should pass the message to the next endpoint after processing the message. The *Relay* parameter of *[MessageHeader]* sets the *Relay* property.

```
[MessageContract]
public class MyMessage
{
    [MessageHeader(Actor="http://contoso.com/roleA", Relay="true")]
    public string HeaderA;
    [MessageHeader(Actor="http://contoso.com/roleB", Relay="false")]
    public string HeaderB;
}
```

Generating Client Code for Typed Messages

The Svcutil tool does not generate typed message classes by default. If your service uses typed messages, specify the */tm* switch on the Svcutil command line to generate the appropriate typed message classes.

```
svcutil http://localhost:8000/MyService/ /tm
```

Programming Exercise: Contracts

In this programming exercise, we will create a service with service, data, and message contracts. The service is a parcel-shipping service. It implements two service contracts, allowing clients to access the service using typed service operations or typed messages. A data contract will define a contact structure. A message contract will define a typed message class. Both the service and client programs will be console applications.

This exercise has six development steps:

1. Create the service program.
2. Create the service configuration file.
3. Build the service.
4. Create the client.
5. Create a configuration file for the client.
6. Build the client.

Step 1: Create the Service Program

We'll create the service program and compile it to an EXE console program. Launch your development environment and create a new C# console application project named *service*. Enter the code in Listing 5-1.

To perform these tasks using Microsoft Visual Studio:

1. Select New, Project from the File menu. Under Project Type, select Windows under Microsoft Visual C#. Under Templates, select Console Application. In the Name box, type **service**, in the Location box, type any path you want, and in the Solution Name box, type **Contracts**. Click OK to generate and open the new project.

2. Replace the generated code in Program.cs with the code shown in Listing 5-1.

Your service project will need to reference System.Runtime.Serialization.dll and System.ServiceModel.dll.

To perform these tasks using Visual Studio:

1. Right-click References in the Solution Explorer window, and then select Add Reference.

2. In the Add Reference dialog box, on the .NET tab, select System.Runtime.Serialization.dll, and then click OK.

3. Add another reference in the same manner for System.ServiceModel.dll.

Listing 5-1   Service: Program.cs

```
using System;
using System.Runtime.Serialization;
using System.ServiceModel;
using System.ServiceModel.Design;

namespace ProgrammingIndigo
{
    // Service contracts.

    [ServiceContract]
    public interface IParcelService
    {
        [OperationContract]
        void StartOrder();
        [OperationContract]
        void SetFrom(Contact contact);
        [OperationContract]
        void SetTo(Contact contact);
        [OperationContract]
        void SetWeight(int weight);
        [OperationContract]
        void FinishOrder();
    }

    [ServiceContract]
    public interface IParcelService2
    {
        [OperationContract]
        void PlaceOrder(OrderMessage orderMessage);
    }
```

```
// Data contract.

[DataContract]
public class Contact
{
    [DataMember]
    public string LastName;
    [DataMember]
    public string FirstName;
    [DataMember]
    public string Address;
    [DataMember]
    public string Address2;
    [DataMember]
    public string Phone;
}


// Message contract.

[MessageContract]
public class OrderMessage
{
    [MessageBody]
    public Contact From;
    [MessageBody]
    public Contact To;
    [MessageBody]
    public int Weight;
}

// Service implementation class.

[ServiceBehavior(InstanceMode=InstanceMode.PrivateSession)]
public class ParcelService : IParcelService, IParcelService2
{
    Contact from;
    Contact to;
    int weight;

    public void StartOrder()
    {
        Console.WriteLine("Start order");
    }

    public void SetFrom(Contact contact)
    {
        this.from = contact;
        Console.WriteLine("    From");
        Console.WriteLine("        " + contact.FirstName + " " + contact.LastName);
        Console.WriteLine("        " + contact.Address);
        Console.WriteLine("        " + contact.Phone);
    }

    public void SetTo(Contact contact)
    {
```

```csharp
        this.to = contact;
        Console.WriteLine("    To");
        Console.WriteLine("        " + contact.FirstName + " " + contact.LastName);
        Console.WriteLine("        " + contact.Address);
        Console.WriteLine("        " + contact.Phone);
    }

    public void SetWeight(int weight)
    {
        this.weight = weight;
        Console.WriteLine("Weight {0}", weight);
    }

    public void FinishOrder()
    {
        Console.WriteLine("Finish order");
        Console.WriteLine();
    }

    public void PlaceOrder(OrderMessage orderMessage)
    {
        Console.WriteLine("PlaceOrder");
        ShowOrder(orderMessage);
    }

    void ShowOrder(OrderMessage order)
    {
        Console.WriteLine("Order contains:");
        Console.WriteLine("    From");
        Console.WriteLine("        " + order.From.FirstName + " " +
            order.From.LastName);
        Console.WriteLine("        " + order.From.Address);
        Console.WriteLine("        " + order.From.Phone);
        Console.WriteLine("    To");
        Console.WriteLine("        " + order.To.FirstName + " " +
            order.To.LastName);
        Console.WriteLine("        " + order.To.Address);
        Console.WriteLine("        " + order.To.Phone);
        Console.WriteLine("    Weight: " + order.Weight);
        Console.WriteLine();
    }

    // Host the service.
    // This service is a self-hosted EXE.
    // This code would be unnecessary in a service hosted by IIS.

    public static void Main()
    {
        ServiceHost<ParcelService> serviceHost = new ServiceHost<ParcelService>();

        //Open the ServiceHost object.

        serviceHost.Open();

        // The service can now be accessed.
```

```
            Console.WriteLine("The service is ready");
            Console.WriteLine();
            Console.WriteLine("Press ENTER to shut down service.");
            Console.ReadLine();

            serviceHost.Close();
        }
    }
}
```

Step 2: Create the Service Configuration File

An App.config file is needed to specify endpoints and bindings for the service. Using an editor or development environment, create a text file with the code shown in Listing 5-2. Save the code under the name App.config in the same folder in which the service program is located.

To perform these tasks using Visual Studio:

1. Right-click the service project, and then select Add, New Item. Select Application Configuration File, and then click Add. Name the file App.config.

2. Enter the code in Listing 5-2 into App.config.

Listing 5-2   Service: App.config

```xml
<?xml version="1.0" encoding="utf-8" ?>
<configuration xmlns="http://schemas.microsoft.com/.NetConfiguration/v2.0">
    <system.serviceModel>

        <services>
            <service
                serviceType="ProgrammingIndigo.ParcelService"
                behaviorConfiguration="ParcelServiceBehavior">
                <endpoint
                    address="http://localhost:8000/ParcelService/"
                    bindingSectionName="wsProfileBinding"
                    bindingConfiguration="ParcelServiceBinding"
                    contractType="ProgrammingIndigo.IParcelService" />
                <endpoint
                    address="http://localhost:9000/ParcelService2/"
                    bindingSectionName="wsProfileBinding"
                    bindingConfiguration="ParcelServiceBinding"
                    contractType="ProgrammingIndigo.IParcelService2" />
            </service>
        </services>

        <bindings>
            <wsProfileBinding>
                    <binding configurationName="ParcelServiceBinding"
                             reliableSessionEnabled="true"/>
            </wsProfileBinding>
        </bindings>
```

```
        <behaviors>
            <behavior
                configurationName="ParcelServiceBehavior"
                returnUnknownExceptionsAsFaults="true" >
            </behavior>
            <behavior
                configurationName="ParcelServiceBehavior2"
                returnUnknownExceptionsAsFaults="true" >
            </behavior>
        </behaviors>

    </system.serviceModel>
</configuration>
```

Step 3: Build the Service

Build the service program to make Service.exe. Resolve any typographical errors.

To perform the task using Visual Studio, select Build Solution from the Build menu to generate Service.exe.

The service is now ready. Next we need a client program to access it.

Step 4: Create the Client

To create the client program, launch your development environment and create a new C# console application project named *client*. Enter the code in Listing 5-3.

To perform these tasks using Visual Studio:

1. Select New, Project from the File menu. Under Project Type, select Windows under Visual C#. Under Templates, select Console Application. In the Name box, type **client**, in the Location box, type any path you want, and in the Solution Name box, type **Contracts**. Click OK to generate and open the new project.

2. Replace the generated code in Program.cs with the code shown in Listing 5-3.

Your client project will need to reference System.Runtime.Serialization.dll and System.Service-Model.dll.

To perform these tasks using Visual Studio:

1. Right-click References in the Solution Explorer window, and then select Add Reference.

2. In the Add Reference dialog box, on the .NET tab, select System.Runtime.Serialization.dll; and then click OK.

3. Add another reference in the same manner for System.ServiceModel.dll.

4. Build the client to create Client.exe.

Listing 5-3 Client: Program.cs

```csharp
using System;
using System.Runtime.Serialization;
using System.ServiceModel;

namespace ProgrammingIndigo
{
    // Service contract.

    [ServiceContract]
    public interface IParcelService
    {
        [OperationContract]
        void StartOrder();
        [OperationContract]
        void SetFrom(Contact contact);
        [OperationContract]
        void SetTo(Contact contact);
        [OperationContract]
        void SetWeight(int weight);
        [OperationContract]
        void FinishOrder();
    }

    [ServiceContract]
    public interface IParcelService2
    {
        [OperationContract]
        void PlaceOrder(OrderMessage orderMessage);
    }

    [DataContract]
    public class Contact
    {
        [DataMember]
        public string LastName;
        [DataMember]
        public string FirstName;
        [DataMember]
        public string Address;
        [DataMember]
        public string Address2;
        [DataMember]
        public string Phone;
    }

    [MessageContract]
    public class OrderMessage
    {
        [MessageBody]
        public Contact From;
        [MessageBody]
        public Contact To;
        [MessageBody]
```

```csharp
        public int Weight;
}

//Client implementation code.

class Client
{
    static void Main()
    {
        Contact from = new Contact();
        from.FirstName = "Kim";
        from.LastName = "Akers";
        from.Address = "100 Main St";
        from.Address2 = "Redmond, WA 98052";
        from.Phone = "555-555-1001";

        Contact to = new Contact();
        to.FirstName = "Jeff";
        to.LastName = "Smith";
        to.Address = "1201 Flower St";
        to.Address2 = "New York, NY 98052";
        to.Phone = "555-555-1002";

        // Create a proxy.
        IParcelService proxy =
            ChannelFactory.CreateChannel<IParcelService>("ParcelServiceEndpoint");

        Console.WriteLine("Placing order 1 with ParcelService");
        Console.WriteLine("    Starting order");
        proxy.StartOrder();

        Console.WriteLine("    Setting From address");
        proxy.SetFrom(from);

        Console.WriteLine("    Setting To address");
        proxy.SetTo(to);

        Console.WriteLine("    Setting Weight");
        proxy.SetWeight(15);

        Console.WriteLine("    Finishing order");
        proxy.FinishOrder();

        Console.WriteLine("Order 1 is complete");
        Console.WriteLine();
        ((IChannel)proxy).Close();

        // Create a second proxy.
        IParcelService2 proxy2 =
            ChannelFactory.CreateChannel<IParcelService2>("ParcelService2Endpoint");

        Console.WriteLine("Placing order 2 with ParcelService2");

        Console.WriteLine("    Placing order");
        OrderMessage order = new OrderMessage();
```

```
                    order.To = to;
                    order.From = from;
                    order.Weight = 25;
                    proxy2.PlaceOrder(order);

                    Console.WriteLine("Order 2 is complete");
                    Console.WriteLine();
                    ((IChannel)proxy2).Close();

                    Console.WriteLine();
                    Console.WriteLine("Press ENTER to shut down client");
                    Console.ReadLine();
            }
        }
    }
```

Step 5: Create a Configuration File for the Client

A Client.exe.config file is needed to specify the service endpoint and binding to use. Using an editor or development environment, create a text file with the code shown in Listing 5-4. Save the code under the name Client.exe.config.

To perform these tasks using Visual Studio:

1. Right-click the service project, and then select Add, New Item. Select Application Configuration File, and then click Add. Name the file App.config. (It will be copied to Client.exe.config at build time.)

2. Enter the code in Listing 5-4 into App.config.

Listing 5-4   Client: App.config

```xml
<?xml version="1.0" encoding="utf-8" ?>
<configuration xmlns="http://schemas.microsoft.com/.NetConfiguration/v2.0">
    <system.serviceModel>
        <client>
            <endpoint
                configurationName="ParcelServiceEndpoint"
                address="http://localhost:8000/ParcelService/"
                bindingSectionName="wsProfileBinding"
                bindingConfiguration="ParcelServiceBinding"
                contractType="ProgrammingIndigo.IParcelService" />
            <endpoint
                configurationName="ParcelService2Endpoint"
                address="http://localhost:9000/ParcelService2/"
                bindingSectionName="wsProfileBinding"
                bindingConfiguration="ParcelServiceBinding"
                contractType="ProgrammingIndigo.IParcelService2" />
        </client>

        <bindings>
            <wsProfileBinding>
```

```
                <binding configurationName="ParcelServiceBinding"
                         reliableSessionEnabled="true"/>
            </wsProfileBinding>
          </bindings>
        </system.serviceModel>
      </configuration>
```

Step 6: Build the Client

Build the client program to make Client.exe. Resolve any typographical errors.

To do this using Visual Studio, select Build Solution from the Build menu to generate Client.exe.

Deployment

We're now ready to try things out. Run the service from your development environment or from a command line. You should see output for the service like that shown in Figure 5-2. If the program fails, double-check that you've properly carried out each of the preceding steps.

Figure 5-2   Contracts service

Press ENTER on the client to shut it down, and then do the same for the service. Congratulations on successfully completing a service with multiple endpoints!

The first order sent by the client accesses the typed service operations of the *IParcelService* contract. The second order sent by the client accesses the typed message of the *IParcelService2* contract.

If you want to run the service and the client on separate machines, replace *localhost* with the fully qualified domain name of the server machine in the client and service .config files.

Understanding the Service Code

The service is self-hosted, so it must be explicitly launched just like the client. The service program code is shown in Listing 5-1. The code in the static *Main* function hosts the service. A *ServiceHost* object is created for the *ParcelService* class and opened. Two endpoints for the service are defined in configuration settings, one for the *IParcelService* contract and one for the *IParcelService2* contract. The service configuration file is shown in Listing 5-2.

```
// Host the service.
// This service is a self-hosted EXE.
// This code would be unnecessary in a service hosted by IIS.

public static void Main()
{
    ServiceHost<ParcelService> serviceHost = new ServiceHost<ParcelService>();

    // Open the ServiceHost object.

    serviceHost.Open();

    // The service can now be accessed.

    Console.WriteLine("The service is ready");
    Console.WriteLine();
    Console.WriteLine("Press ENTER to shut down service.");
    Console.ReadLine();

    serviceHost.Close();
}
```

This service contains two service contracts. The service contract *IParcelService* is a typed service that uses sessions. A client must call a series of operations to place a shipping order with this contract. The second service contract, *IParcelService2*, is a typed message service. A client can place a shipping order by sending a single message with this contract.

```
// Service contracts.

[ServiceContract]
public interface IParcelService
{
    [OperationContract]
    void StartOrder();
    [OperationContract]
    void SetFrom(Contact contact);
    [OperationContract]
    void SetTo(Contact contact);
    [OperationContract]
    void SetWeight(int weight);
    [OperationContract]
    void FinishOrder();
}

[ServiceContract]
public interface IParcelService2
{
    [OperationContract]
    void PlaceOrder(OrderMessage orderMessage);
}
```

Some of the service operations in *IParcelService* accept a *Contact* structure. A data contract is defined for *Contact*.

```
// Data contract.

[DataContract]
public class Contact
{
    [DataMember]
    public string LastName;
    [DataMember]
    public string FirstName;
    [DataMember]
    public string Address;
    [DataMember]
    public string Address2;
    [DataMember]
    public string Phone;
}
```

The *IParcelService2* typed message service contract accepts a typed message named *OrderMessage*. A message contract is defined for *OrderMessage*.

```
// Message contract.

[MessageContract]
public class OrderMessage
{
    [MessageBody]
    public Contact From;
    [MessageBody]
    public Contact To;
    [MessageBody]
    public int Weight;
}
```

The *ParcelService* class implements the service operations for both the *IParcelService* and *IParcelService2* service contracts. The service operations echo their activity in the service console window.

```
// Service implementation class.

[ServiceBehavior(InstanceMode=InstanceMode.PrivateSession)]
public class ParcelService : IParcelService, IParcelService2
{
    ...
    public void SetFrom(Contact contact)
    {
        this.from = contact;
        Console.WriteLine("    From");
        Console.WriteLine("        " + contact.FirstName + " " + contact.LastName);
        Console.WriteLine("        " + contact.Address);
        Console.WriteLine("        " + contact.Phone);
```

```
    }
    ...
}
```

The typed message service operation, *PlaceOrder*, receives an *OrderMessage*. The client displays the order contents by calling a *ShowOrder* method. The typed message can be treated as a message and as an object.

```
public void PlaceOrder(OrderMessage orderMessage)
{
    Console.WriteLine("PlaceOrder");
    ShowOrder(orderMessage);
}

void ShowOrder(OrderMessage order)
{
    Console.WriteLine("Order contains:");
    Console.WriteLine("    From");
    Console.WriteLine("        " + order.From.FirstName + " " + order.From.LastName);
    Console.WriteLine("        " + order.From.Address);
    Console.WriteLine("        " + order.From.Phone);
    Console.WriteLine("    To");
    Console.WriteLine("        " + order.To.FirstName + " " + order.To.LastName);
    Console.WriteLine("        " + order.To.Address);
    Console.WriteLine("        " + order.To.Phone);
    Console.WriteLine("    Weight: " + order.Weight);
    Console.WriteLine();
}
```

Understanding the Client Code

The client contains the same contract definitions described earlier for the service. In this programming exercise, generated client code was not used, so there is no client proxy class. The client will use the *ChannelFactory* class to create proxy channels.

The client creates its first proxy to the service endpoint that implements the *IParcelService* contract. In the client configuration file, this endpoint is defined under the name *ParcelService-Endpoint*. Once the proxy is created, the client calls a series of service operations to submit a shipping order. After the order has been sent, the channel proxy is closed.

```
// Create a proxy.
IParcelService proxy =
    ChannelFactory.CreateChannel<IParcelService>("ParcelServiceEndpoint");

Console.WriteLine("Placing order 1 with ParcelService");
Console.WriteLine("    Starting order");
proxy.StartOrder();

Console.WriteLine("    Setting From address");
proxy.SetFrom(from);
```

```
Console.WriteLine("    Setting To address");
proxy.SetTo(to);

Console.WriteLine("    Setting Weight");
proxy.SetWeight(15);

Console.WriteLine("    Finishing order");
proxy.FinishOrder();

Console.WriteLine("Order 1 is complete");
Console.WriteLine();
((IChannel)proxy).Close();
```

Next the client creates a second proxy to the service endpoint that implements the *IParcel-Service2* contract. In the client configuration file, this endpoint is defined under the name *ParcelService2Endpoint*. Once the proxy is created, the client creates an *OrderMessage* typed message and submits an order in a single service operation. After the order has been sent, the channel proxy is closed.

```
// Create a second proxy.
IParcelService2 proxy2 =
    ChannelFactory.CreateChannel<IParcelService2>("ParcelService2Endpoint");

Console.WriteLine("Placing order 2 with ParcelService2");

Console.WriteLine("    Placing order");
OrderMessage order = new OrderMessage();
order.To = to;
order.From = from;
order.Weight = 25;
proxy2.PlaceOrder(order);

Console.WriteLine("Order 2 is complete");
Console.WriteLine();
((IChannel)proxy2).Close();
```

If communicating cross-machine, the references to *localhost* in the client and service configuration files must be replaced by the fully qualified domain name of the server.

Summary

This chapter described in detail the three types of contracts in Indigo: service contracts, data contracts, and message contracts. Contracts make interoperable, loosely coupled service orientation possible.

Service contracts describe the operations a service can perform and are behavioral in nature. A service contract is defined with the *[ServiceContract]* and *[OperationContract]* attributes. Binding requirements can be specified for the contract with a *[BindingRequirements]* attribute.

Data contracts describe data structures. A data contract is defined primarily with the *[Data-Contract]* and *[DataMember]* attributes.

Message contracts describe SOAP messages. A message contract is defined primarily with the *[MessageContract]*, *[MessageBody]*, and *[MessageHeader]* attributes.

The programming tasks in the chapter covered how to define service, data, and message contracts. The attributes used for defining contracts and their parameters were described.

The programming exercise developed a parcel shipping service with multiple service contracts, a data contract, and a message contract. The client was able to place orders by using a typed service and a typed message service.

In the next chapter, we'll cover clients.

Chapter 6
Clients

The most important thing in communication is to hear what isn't being said.

—Peter Drucker

This chapter describes how to develop clients, programs that consume services.

After completing this chapter, you will:

- Understand how to create client programs.
- Understand how to generate client code from service metadata.
- Know how to define client endpoints and bindings.
- Know how to enable reliable sessions.
- Know how to use transactions.

Understanding Clients

Services wouldn't be of any use without clients to access them. Clients trigger the processing in a service-oriented solution by initiating communication. Figure 6-1 shows clients accessing a service.

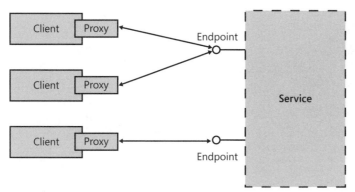

Figure 6-1   Clients accessing a service

Because services can call other services, client code can appear in both client and service programs. Any program that initiates messaging is acting as a client, even if that program is also a service.

Proxies

Clients talk to services via proxies. A proxy is an object that creates a channel to a service. A client accesses a service's operations by calling methods of the proxy. You can create proxies dynamically or by using a proxy class generated from service metadata.

Datagram Communication

In datagram communication, clients send request messages but there are no replies from the service. The client does not wait for the service operation to complete and continues executing. The client communicates with the service using a proxy. Figure 6-2 illustrates datagram communication.

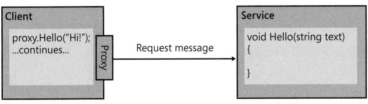

Figure 6-2 Datagram communication

Request-Reply Communication

In request-reply communication, clients send request messages and wait for reply messages from the service. The client waits for the service operation to complete and respond before it continues executing. The client communicates with the service using a proxy. Figure 6-3 illustrates request-reply communication.

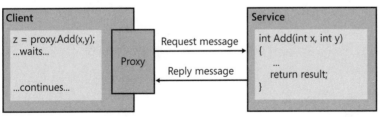

Figure 6-3 Request-reply communication

Duplex Communication

In duplex communication, clients and services can communicate bidirectionally. Clients send request messages to a service and can receive reply messages. Independently, the service can make requests of the client and receive reply messages. Figure 6-4 illustrates duplex communication.

The client implements a service contract just as the service does. The client accesses the service using a proxy. The service accesses the client using a callback. Duplex communication requires the use of reliable sessions.

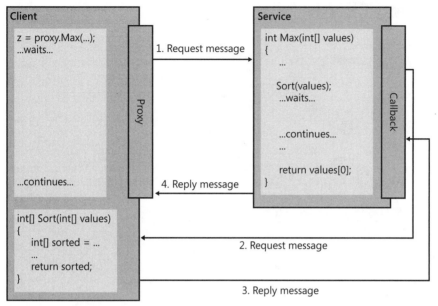

Figure 6-4   Duplex communication

Endpoints

A service exposes one or more endpoints. For a client to access a service, it must have one of those endpoints in mind. A client requires information about where a service is, how to communicate with it, and what the service can do. An endpoint definition provides this information by specifying an address, binding, and service contract. Endpoints can be specified in application .config files or in code.

Bindings

A binding determines how a client and service communicate. Bindings specify transports, security, reliable sessions, transaction, and encoding. To communicate successfully with a service, a client must use a binding that matches the service endpoint it is trying to access. A client can specify one of Indigo's predefined standard bindings or create a custom binding. For more information on bindings, see Chapter 4.

Generated Code

You can generate client code from service metadata by using the Svcutil tool. The generated code defines contracts and a proxy class for accessing the service. Svcutil can also generate the client configuration file for a service, which includes endpoint and binding definitions.

Programming Clients

Common client development tasks include generating proxy code, using proxies to access services, and specifying endpoints and bindings.

Creating Proxies

A proxy is an object you create that you use to communicate with a service. There are two ways to create a proxy:

1. If you have generated client code with the Svcutil tool, you can create a proxy by creating a new instance of the generated proxy class.

2. You can create a client channel using the *ChannelFactory* class.

For duplex clients, you need to perform additional work (described later).

The act of creating a proxy does not perform any communication in and of itself. Only when a client invokes a service operation does messaging take place.

Creating a Client Proxy from Generated Code

The Svcutil tool generates client code from service metadata. The generated code includes a proxy class. The proxy class has the same name as the service implementation class, with a suffix of *Proxy*. For example, the proxy class for *SampleService* is named *SampleServiceProxy*.

Generating a proxy from generated code couldn't be simpler. All you do is create a new instance of the proxy class and then start accessing the service through the proxy.

```
SampleServiceProxy proxy = new SampleServiceProxy("SampleEndpoint");
proxy.DoSomething();
proxy.DoSomethingElse();
proxy.Close();
```

In the constructor of the proxy, you must define a service endpoint. You can pass an endpoint configuration name, as just shown, or an address and binding in code, as follows. See "Defining Endpoints" later in this chapter for details.

```
EndpointAddress address = new EndpointAddress("http://localhost:8000/SampleService/");
BasicProfileBinding binding = new BasicProfileBinding();
SampleServiceProxy proxy = new SampleServiceProxy(address, binding);
```

```
proxy.DoSomething();
proxy.DoSomethingElse();
proxy.Close();
```

When the proxy is finished accessing the service, the proxy object can be closed and disposed. A compact way to code the proxy creation and disposal is by using the *using* statement:

```
using (SampleServiceProxy proxy = new SampleServiceProxy("SampleEndpoint"))
{
    proxy.DoSomething();
    proxy.DoSomethingElse();
    proxy.Close();
}
```

How does the generated proxy class actually create the proxy to the service? The proxy class creates a channel by calling *ChannelFactory*, as described in the next section.

Creating a Client Proxy Using *ChannelFactory*

You can create a client proxy by using the *CreateChannel* static method of the *ChannelFactory* class. *CreateChannel* requires a **generic** specifying the service contract name. The arguments to *CreateChannel* define the service endpoint to be accessed. You can specify the endpoint with a configuration name string or by supplying an address and binding, as shown here.

```
EndpointAddress address = new EndpointAddress("http://localhost:8000/SampleService/");
BasicProfileBinding binding = new BasicProfileBinding();
ISampleService proxy = ChannelFactory.CreateChannel<ISampleService>(address, binding);
proxy.DoSomething();
proxy.DoSomethingElse();
((IChannel)proxy).Close();
((IChannel)proxy).Dispose();
```

> **Note** In C#, a generic takes the form *<type>*. In Microsoft Visual Basic .NET, a generic takes the form *(Of type)*.

The result of *ChannelFactory.CreateChannel* is a channel object that implements the requested service contract. That's why we can assign it to *proxy* in the preceding code, whose type has been declared as *ISampleService*.

Once a proxy is created, the service's operations can be accessed via the proxy. For example, if the service has an operation called *DoSomething*, the client can call *proxy.DoSomething()* to access it.

```
ISampleService proxy = ChannelFactory.CreateChannel<ISampleService>(address, binding);
proxy.DoSomething();
proxy.DoSomethingElse();
```

When the proxy is finished accessing the service, the proxy object can be closed and then disposed. To close and dispose a proxy, you must cast the proxy to an *IChannel*.

```
((IChannel)proxy).Close();
((IChannel)proxy).Dispose();
```

Creating Duplex Proxies

Duplex clients differ from datagram clients and request-reply clients in that they must implement a callback service. The client can make requests of the service, but the service can also make requests of the client.

Service contracts for duplex services are paired up with a client callback contract. The service-side contract for the service has a *[ServiceContract]* attribute and specifies the name of the client callback contract with a *CallbackContract=typeof(contract)* parameter. The client callback service contract does not require a *[ServiceContract]* attribute. A sample pair of duplex contracts is shown here.

```
[ServiceContract(CallbackContract=typeof(ISampleClientContract))]
public interface ISampleContract
{
    [OperationContract(IsOneWay=false)]
    void MoveForward(int units);
    [OperationContract(IsOneWay=false)]
    void MoveBackward(int units);
    [OperationContract(IsOneWay = false)]
    void TurnLeft();
    [OperationContract(IsOneWay = false)]
    void TurnRight();
}

public interface ISampleClientContract
{
    [OperationContract(IsOneWay=false)]
    void Position(int x, int y, string direction);
}
```

Creating a Duplex Client Proxy from Generated Code

For duplex services, the Svcutil tool generates both the service and callback contracts from service metadata. The generated code includes a proxy class that can accommodate duplex communication. The proxy class has the same name as the service implementation class, with a suffix of *Proxy*. For example, the proxy class for *SampleService* is named *SampleServiceProxy*.

Normally, Svcutil preserves the original name of service contracts in the proxy code that is generated. For example, *ISample* is faithfully generated as *ISample*. This is not true for duplex client callback contracts, however. Regardless of the original contract name, the callback contract in the generated code is named after the service contract, followed by the name *Callback*.

The callback contract for *ISample* is *ISampleCallback*, for example, regardless of the original name of the callback contract.

> **Caution**   Svcutil doesn't preserve the original name of duplex client callback contracts in generated code.

To generate a proxy from generated code, first create a *ServiceSite* from an instance of the class implementing the client callback contract. Then create an instance of the proxy class, specifying the *ServiceSite* and an endpoint.

```
// Create a duplex proxy.
ServiceSite clientSite = new ServiceSite(null, new Client());
using (SampleContractProxy proxy = new SampleContractProxy(clientSite, "SampleEndpoint"))
{
    proxy.DoSomething();
    proxy.DoSomethingElse();
       ...
    proxy.Close();
}
```

In the constructor of the proxy, you must define a service endpoint. You can pass a configuration name, as just shown, or an address and binding in code, as shown next. See "Defining Endpoints" later in this chapter for details.

```
// Create a duplex proxy.
EndpointAddress address = new EndpointAddress("http://localhost:8000/SampleService/");
WSProfileDualHttpBinding binding = new WSProfileDualHttpBinding();
ServiceSite clientSite = new ServiceSite(null, new Client());
using (SampleContractProxy proxy = new SampleContractProxy(clientSite, address, binding))
{
    proxy.DoSomething();
    proxy.DoSomethingElse();
       ...
    proxy.Close();
}
```

The client must implement a callback service contract:

```
class Client : ISampleContractCallback
{
    static void Main(string[] args)
    {
        // Create a proxy.
        ServiceSite clientSite = new ServiceSite(null, new Client());
        using (SampleContractProxy proxy = new SampleContractProxy(clientSite,
            "SampleEndpoint"))
        {
            // Call a service operation.
            Console.WriteLine("Sending command: MoveForward(3)");
            proxy.MoveForward(3);
```

```
            . . .

        proxy.Close();
    }
}

public void Position(int x, int y, string direction)
{
    Console.WriteLine("Received notification: Position(" + x + "," + y + "," +
        direction + ")");
}

}
```

When the proxy is finished accessing the service, the proxy object can be closed and then disposed. A compact way to code the proxy creation and disposal is by using the *using* statement:

```
ServiceSite clientSite = new ServiceSite(null, new Client());
using (SampleServiceProxy proxy = new SampleServiceProxy(clientSite, "SampleEndpoint"))
{
    proxy.DoSomething();
    proxy.DoSomethingElse();
    proxy.Close();
}
```

While the client is connected to the service, the client's callback service operations might be called at any time. There is no synchronization between client calls to the service and service callbacks to the client.

How does the generated proxy class actually create the proxy to the service? The proxy class creates a channel by calling *ChannelFactory*, as described in the next section.

Creating a Duplex Client Proxy Using *ChannelFactory*

You can create a duplex client proxy by using the *CreateDuplexChannel* static method of the *ChannelFactory* class. *CreateDuplexChannel* requires a generic that specifies the service contract name. To create a duplex proxy, first create a *ServiceSite* from an instance of the class implementing the client callback contract. Then call *ChannelFactory.CreateDuplexChannel*, specifying the *ServiceSite* and an endpoint. You can specify the endpoint as a configuration name string or by providing an address and binding, as shown next. The proxy returned by *ChannelFactory* will be of the same type as the service contract interface. For example, in the following code, *CreateDuplexChannel* returns a proxy of type *ISampleService*.

```
EndpointAddress address = new EndpointAddress("http://localhost:8000/SampleService/");
BasicProfileBinding binding = new BasicProfileBinding();
ServiceSite clientSite = new ServiceSite(null, new Client());
ISampleService proxy = ChannelFactory.CreateDuplexChannel<ISampleService>(clientSite,
    address, binding);
proxy.DoSomething();
proxy.DoSomethingElse();
```

```
((IChannel)proxy).Close();
((IChannel)proxy).Dispose();
```

Once a proxy is created, the service's operations can be accessed via the proxy. When the proxy is finished accessing the service, the proxy object can be closed and then disposed. To close and dispose the proxy, you must cast the proxy to an *IChannel*.

Generating Client Code

The Svcutil tool can generate client code from service metadata. The code generated includes service contracts, data contracts, message contracts, and a proxy class for accessing the service. You can also opt to generate configuration settings for the client.

Generating Client Proxy Code from a Service MEX Endpoint

To generate client proxy code from a running service's MEX endpoint, run the Svcutil tool in a command window, specifying the MEX endpoint address on the command line. The MEX endpoint is an HTTP endpoint address or an HTTP base address that has been defined for the service.

```
svcutil http://localhost:8000/MyService/
```

By default, the code generation language is C# and the output file is named after the service contract namespace, such as tempuri.org.cs. You can override the language and output filename using the */language:language* and */out:filename.ext* command options. Table 6-1 lists the legal values for */language*.

```
svcutil http://localhost:8000/MyService/ /language:vb /out:proxy.vb
```

Table 6-1 Svcutil Code Generation Language Options

Option	Code Generation Language
c#, cs, csharp	C#
vb, visualbasic	Visual Basic .NET
js, jscript	Microsoft JScript
vj#, vjs, vjsharp	Microsoft Visual J#

Svcutil-generated code defines contracts for the service and defines a proxy class for accessing the service. Generated code tends to be more verbose than original code, primarily because generated code is very explicit.

It's a good idea to keep generated code and your own client code in separate source files. This practice allows you to regenerate the proxy code if needed without disturbing your own code.

Generating Client Proxy Code from a Service Assembly

An alternative to generating code from a live service MEX endpoint is to generate code from an assembly. This is a two-step process. To generate client proxy code from an assembly, you run the Svcutil tool in a command window and specify the assembly file on the command line.

```
svcutil MyService.dll
```

The output is the service metadata in the form of one or more .wsdl or .xsd files. To generate code from the metadata, run Svcutil again, this time specifying the .wsdl and .xsd files on the command line.

```
svcutil *.wsdl *.xsd
```

By default, the code generation language is C# and the output file is named Out.cs. You can override the language and output filename by using the */language:language* and */out:file-name.ext* command options. Table 6-1, shown earlier, lists the legal values for */language.*

Generating Client Configuration Files

When you generate client code with Svcutil, a configuration file is also generated. You can specify the output name of the configuration file by including a */config:filename* option on the Svcutil command line.

```
svcutil http://localhost:8000/MyService/ /config:MyClient.exe.config
```

The generated configuration file defines endpoints and bindings for accessing the service.

You can have the generated .config file merged with an existing .config file. The */config:filename1,filename2* option reads configuration settings from *filename1*, merges them with the generated .config file, and saves the result to *filename2*.

```
svcutil http://localhost:8000/MyService/ /config:MyTemplate.exe.config,MyClient.exe.config
```

Defining Endpoints

Endpoints specify the ABCs of access to a service: address, binding, and [service] contract. You can define an endpoint in code or in a configuration file.

Defining an Endpoint in Code

To define an endpoint in code, you specify an address, binding, and service contract when your proxy is created. If you are using a generated proxy class, the contract is already known. One form of the generated proxy constructor accepts an address and a binding. In the following code, an address is created using an *EndpointAddress* class, and a binding is created using the *BasicProfileBinding* class. A proxy is created, specifying the address and binding in the constructor. The generated proxy class already knows the service contract to use.

```
EndpointAddress address = new EndpointAddress("http://localhost:8000/SampleService/");
BasicProfileBinding binding = new BasicProfileBinding();
SampleServiceProxy proxy = new SampleServiceProxy(address, binding);
```

When you create a proxy channel directly with the *ChannelFactory* class's *CreateChannel* method, the address and binding are passed to the method. The service contract must also be specified, and you do this using a generic. In the following code, a proxy channel is created using *ChannelFactory.CreateChannel*. The service contract, *ISampleService*, is specified as a generic. The address and binding are provided as parameters to the *CreateChannel* method.

```
EndpointAddress address = new EndpointAddress("http://localhost:8000/SampleService/");
BasicProfileBinding binding = new BasicProfileBinding();
ISampleService proxy = ChannelFactory.CreateChannel<ISampleService>(address, binding);
```

The same code in Visual Basic .NET looks like this:

```
Dim address As EndpointAddress = New EndpointAddress("http://localhost:8000/SampleService/")
Dim binding As BasicProfileBinding = New BasicProfileBinding()
Dim proxy As ISampleService = ChannelFactory.CreateChannel(Of ISampleService)(address,
    binding)
```

Defining a Binding in Code

Each standard binding has a class associated with it. To create a standard binding, you create an instance of the appropriate class:

```
BasicProfileBinding binding = new BasicProfileBinding();
```

Once the binding is created, you can tune it by modifying its properties. The following code creates a standard binding and then modifies it to disable security and enable reliable sessions.

```
WSProfileBinding currentBinding = new WSProfileBinding();
currentBinding.SecurityMode = WSProfileSecurityMode.None;
currentBinding.ReliableSessionEnabled = true;
```

Defining an Endpoint in a Configuration File

Defining an endpoint in a configuration file gives you the freedom of making deployment-time decisions about addressing and binding. One form of the generated proxy constructor accepts an endpoint configuration name. In the following code, a proxy is created that specifies the endpoint configuration name *SampleEndpoint* in the constructor. The endpoint definition is loaded at runtime from the application configuration file.

```
SampleServiceProxy proxy = new SampleServiceProxy("SampleEndpoint");
```

When you create a proxy channel directly with the *ChannelFactory* class's *CreateChannel* method, an endpoint configuration name is passed to the method. The service contract is specified as a generic. The remainder of the endpoint definition comes from the specified endpoint configuration. In the following code, a proxy channel is created using *Channel-*

Factory.CreateChannel. The service contract, *ISampleService*, is specified as a generic. The endpoint definition is loaded at runtime from the endpoint configuration named *SampleEndpoint*.

```
ISampleService proxy = ChannelFactory.CreateChannel<ISampleService>("SampleEndpoint");
```

A client endpoint is defined in an *<endpoint>* element, which appears in the application configuration file in the *<configuration><system.serviceModel><client>* section. Here is a simple example of a client endpoint definition:

```
<configuration xmlns="http://schemas.microsoft.com/.NetConfiguration/v2.0">
    <system.serviceModel>
        <client>
            <endpoint
                configurationName="SampleEndpoint"
                address="http://localhost/RequestReply/service.svc"
                bindingSectionName="wsProfileBinding"
                contractType="ISampleContract" />
        </client>
    </system.serviceModel>
</configuration>
```

The client endpoint definition has four key attributes: *configurationName*, *address*, *bindingSectionName*, and *contractType*.

- *configurationName* is simply an identifier string. It allows the client program to specify which endpoint to use because multiple endpoints can be defined in a configuration file.

- *address* is the address of the service.

- *bindingSectionName* is the name of a standard binding, or *customBinding*. This can be accompanied by a *bindingConfiguration* attribute for a detailed binding definition.

- *contractType* identifies the service contract's type.

Defining a Binding Configuration in a Configuration File

If you want to fine-tune a binding by changing some of its settings, or if you want to create your own custom binding, you can define a binding configuration. You can link an endpoint definition to a binding configuration by using a *bindingConfiguration* attribute. In the following endpoint definition, the endpoint specifies a *WSProfileBinding* standard binding but indicates a binding configuration named *SampleBinding*.

```
<configuration xmlns="http://schemas.microsoft.com/.NetConfiguration/v2.0">
    <system.serviceModel>
        <client>
            <endpoint
                configurationName="SampleEndpoint"
                address="http://localhost/RequestReply/service.svc"
```

```
                bindingSectionName="wsProfileBinding"
                bindingConfiguration="SampleBinding"
                contractType="ISampleContract" />
        </client>
    </system.serviceModel>
    ...binding configuration must be defined...
</configuration>
```

A binding configuration is defined in an element named after the binding type (such as
<*wsProfileBinding*>). This element appears in the application configuration file in the <*configu-
ration*><*system.serviceModel*><*bindings*> section. A configuration file with a binding configuration follows. In this case, a standard *WSProfileBinding* binding has been configured to enable
the flow of transactions from client to service.

```
<configuration xmlns="http://schemas.microsoft.com/.NetConfiguration/v2.0">
    <system.serviceModel>
        <client>
            <endpoint
                configurationName="SampleEndpoint"
                address="http://localhost/RequestReply/service.svc"
                bindingSectionName="wsProfileBinding"
                bindingConfiguration="SampleBinding"
                contractType="ISampleContract" />
        </client>
        <bindings>
            <wsProfileBinding>
                <binding configurationName="SampleBinding">
                    <contextFlow transactions="Allowed" />
                </binding>
            </wsProfileBinding>
        </bindings>
    </system.serviceModel>
</configuration>
```

You can find out more about bindings in Chapter 4.

Invoking Service Operations

There are three kinds of services: typed services, untyped services, and typed message services. Each type of service has implications on how clients invoke service operations. For more
information on the distinction between types of services, see Chapter 7.

Invoking Service Operations for a Typed Service

In a typed service, a service operation is very much like the method of a class. It can accept
zero or more parameters and may return a result. Parameters and return types can be simple
types such as *int* and *string* or complex types such as *Customer* and *Order*. To invoke a service
operation, a client calls the method using a proxy. The following code is an example of a client
invoking several service operations against a typed service.

```
weatherProxy.ReportTemperature(region1, 75);
weatherProxy.ReportWindspeed(region1, 15);

float temp = weatherProxy.GetTemperature(region2);
int windSpeed = weatherProxy.GetWindspeed(region2);
```

Like object-oriented methods, service operations support the use of *ref* and *out* parameters. This permits a service operation to return multiple results. When using the *ref* parameter, keep in mind that all information is passed by value. The following code shows a client using *out* parameters to retrieve multiple results from a service operation.

```
double high, low, current;
int volume;
proxy.GetStockQuote(symbol, out high, out low, out current, out volume);
```

Invoking Service Operations for an Untyped Service

In an untyped service, developers work at the message level. The client creates and passes a *Message* object as the parameter to the service operation. If the service operation returns a result, it is also a *Message* object.

Creating a message to send is accomplished by calling the static *CreateMessage* method of the *Message* class. There are several editions of *CreateMessage*, which are described in the Indigo documentation. The following code uses a form of *CreateMessage* that creates a message from an object. The object is serialized into the body of the message.

```
OrderItem orderItem = new OrderItem();
orderItem.PartNo = "0001-002";
orderItem.Description = "No. 2 Pencil";
orderItem.Qty = 1;
orderItem.Price = 0.25D;
Message message = Message.CreateMessage("http://tempuri.org/ISampleContract/
    ProcessMessage", orderItem);
```

If a proxy receives a result from an untyped service operation, it is always a *Message* object. The message body can be deserialized to an object by calling the message object's *GetBody* method. The type to deserialize to is specified as a generic argument to the method. The following statement retrieves an *OrderItem* object from the body of a received message.

```
OrderItem orderItem = message.GetBody<OrderItem>();
```

Working with messages at this level gives developers a lot of control, but it also places more responsibility on them. In order to successfully pass messages to and from an untyped service, the client developer must have knowledge of what the service expects.

The following code shows a client accessing an untyped service with one-way service operations. Messages are created from order items.

```
using System;
using System.Runtime.Serialization;
```

```
using System.ServiceModel;

namespace ProgrammingIndigo.UntypedSample
{
    //Client implementation code.

    class Client
    {
        static void Main(string[] args)
        {
            ISampleContract proxy = null;
            try
            {
                // Create a proxy.
                proxy = ChannelFactory.CreateChannel<ISampleContract>("SampleEndpoint");

                // Create an order item and call service operation.

                OrderItem orderItem = new OrderItem();
                orderItem.PartNo = "0001-002";
                orderItem.Description = "No. 2 Pencil";
                orderItem.Qty = 1;
                orderItem.Price = 0.25D;

                Console.WriteLine("Request:  ProcessMessage(OrderItem)");
                ShowOrderItem(orderItem);
                Message message = Message.CreateMessage("http://tempuri.org/ISampleContract/
                    ProcessMessage", orderItem);
                proxy.ProcessMessage(message);
                Console.WriteLine();

                //Create a second order item and call service operation again.

                orderItem = new OrderItem();
                orderItem.PartNo = "0034-009";
                orderItem.Description = "Eraser";
                orderItem.Qty = 20;
                orderItem.Price = 0.11D;

                Console.WriteLine("Request:  ProcessMessage(OrderItem)");
                ShowOrderItem(orderItem);
                message = Message.CreateMessage("http://tempuri.org/ISampleContract/
                    ProcessMessage", orderItem);
                proxy.ProcessMessage(message);
                Console.WriteLine();

                ((IChannel)proxy).Close();
            }
            finally
            {
                // Dispose of the proxy.
                ((IChannel)proxy).Dispose();
            }

            Console.WriteLine();
```

```
            Console.WriteLine("Press ENTER to shut down client");
            Console.ReadLine();
        }

        static void ShowOrderItem(OrderItem orderItem)
        {
            Console.WriteLine("            PartNo:      {0}", orderItem.PartNo);
            Console.WriteLine("            Description: {0}", orderItem.Description);
            Console.WriteLine("            Qty:         {0}", orderItem.Qty);
            Console.WriteLine("            Price:       {0}", orderItem.Price.ToString("C"));
        }
    }
}
```

Invoking Service Operations for a Typed Message Service

In a typed message service, developers pass custom messages to and from service operations. The service defines custom request and response messages as classes with message contracts. Typed message services combine elements of untyped services and typed services: developers have precise control over message format but can easily get at the data in a message.

Creating a message to send is accomplished by creating a new instance of a custom message class and setting its members. The custom message is passed as the parameter to the typed message service. The following code creates and populates a custom request message and then passes it to a service operation.

```
request = new CustomRequestMessage();
request.orderNo = "1002";
request.orderItem = orderItem;
proxy.ProcessMessage(request);
```

Received messages are similarly easy to work with. A response from a typed message service is also a custom message class. Data in the custom message can be accessed through the class's members. The following code receives a response from a typed message service operation and displays.

```
CustomResponseMessage response = proxy.ProcessMessage(request);
Console.WriteLine("Order No.:   {0}", response.orderNo);
Console.WriteLine("PartNo:      {0}", response.orderItem.PartNo);
Console.WriteLine("Description: {0}", response.orderItem.Description);
Console.WriteLine("Qty:         {0}", response.orderItem.Qty);
Console.WriteLine("Price:       {0}", response.orderItem.Price);
Console.WriteLine();
```

Generating Typed Message Client Proxy Code

The Svcutil tool does not generate typed-message custom message classes by default. The /tm (typed message) command-line option includes custom message classes in the generated code, for example:

```
Svcutil http://localhost:8000/CalculatorService /tm /out:tmProxy.cs
```

Asynchronous Client Communication

Service operations can be accessed synchronously or asynchronously. A client can call a service operation asynchronously using the Microsoft .NET Framework Async Pattern. For information on how to write service operations to be asynchronous, see Chapter 7.

When accessing a service operation asynchronously, a service operation is divided into two operations, one named *Begin<operation-name>* and one named *End<operation-name>*. The client calls the *Begin* operation to trigger processing. The client is then free to do other work. When the operation completes, the client's callback function executes. The client calls the *End* operation to retrieve the results of the operation.

The *Begin* version of an operation takes two additional parameters, a callback and a state. The callback is a client-provided function that will run when the operation completes. The state parameter can be any object state you want the callback function to be able to access when the operation completes. In Indigo programming, the client proxy is typically specified for the state parameter. This allows the callback function to call the *End* service operation to obtain a result.

The following code shows a *BeginAdd* operation being called for a calculator service. The client specifies the parameters needed by the *Add* service operation, plus a callback function named *AddCallback* and the client proxy as the state object.

```
static void Main()
{
    using (CalculatorProxy proxy = new CalculatorProxy("CalcEndpoint"))
    {
        double value1 = 100.00D;
        double value2 = 15.99D;
        Console.WriteLine("Calling BeginAdd({0},{1})", value1, value2);
        IAsyncResult arAdd = proxy.BeginAdd(value1, value2, AddCallback, proxy);
        Console.WriteLine("Press <ENTER> to terminate client.");
        Console.ReadLine();
        // Close the proxy.
        proxy.Close();
    }
}
```

The callback function is a static method that accepts an *IAsyncResult* parameter. It runs when the service operation finishes and is obligated to call the *End* version of the service operation to complete the asynchronous communication. The callback function can obtain the client proxy that was passed as a state object by using the *IAsyncResult* parameter's *AsyncProperty*, which must be cast to its original type. With the proxy obtained, the callback function can call the *End* version of the service operation and receive the service operation results. The following code shows the callback function for the calculator service example.

```
// Asynchronous callback for obtaining result.
static void AddCallback(IAsyncResult ar)
{
```

```
    double result = ((CalculatorProxy)ar.AsyncState).EndAdd(ar);
    Console.WriteLine("EndAdd result: {0}", result);
}
```

For more information on working with the Async Pattern, refer to the .NET Framework documentation.

Generating Asynchronous Client Proxy Code

The Svcutil tool can generate client proxy code for clients that desire to access services asynchronously. The */a* command-line option generates an asynchronous version of the service operations with *Begin-End* pairs of service operations, for example:

```
Svcutil http://localhost:8000/CalculatorService /a /out:async.cs
```

Programming Clients for Reliable Messaging

Reliable messaging is one benefit of the Reliable Sessions feature that is available in some bindings. Reliable messaging can implement retries in the face of disrupted communication and can provide delivery assurances such as exactly-once, in-order delivery of messages. To get the benefits of reliable messaging, you don't have to program your client any differently than usual. You simply use a binding with reliable sessions enabled.

Enabling Reliable Sessions

Reliable sessions are enabled through the *ReliableSessionEnabled* property of a binding. When you define an endpoint in code or in a configuration file, the binding used by the client and by the service must support reliable sessions and have the feature enabled. Not all bindings support reliable sessions, and those that do might have the feature enabled or disabled by default. For more information about binding properties and defaults, see Chapter 4.

The following client configuration file shows a binding configuration that enables reliable sessions and specifies exactly-once, in-order delivery.

```
<?xml version="1.0" encoding="utf-8" ?>
<configuration xmlns="http://schemas.microsoft.com/.NetConfiguration/v2.0">
    <system.serviceModel>
        <client>
            <endpoint
                configurationName="MyEndpoint"
                address="http://localhost:8000/Weather/"
                bindingSectionName="wsProfileBinding"
                bindingConfiguration="MyBinding"
                contractType="IWeather" />
        </client>

        <bindings>
            <wsProfileBinding>
```

```
        <binding
            configurationName="MyBinding"
            reliableSessionEnabled="true"
            orderedSession="true" />
        </wsProfileBinding>
    </bindings>
  </system.serviceModel>
</configuration>
```

For more information on reliable sessions binding properties, see Chapter 4.

Requiring Reliable Sessions

A service contract can specify that the session support be required. The *[ServiceContract]* attribute contains a *Session* parameter. If this parameter is set to *true*, an error will occur if there is an attempt to use a binding that does not support sessions.

```
[ServiceContract(Session=true)]
```

Programming Clients for Transactions

A transaction treats a group of operations as a single atomic unit: they either all succeed or all fail, leaving a consistent state. Most developers are familiar with transactions in connection with database programming, but any work controlled by a resource manager can be transactional. There are two interesting transaction behaviors to consider: flowed transactions and transacted communication.

Indigo and the Web Services Architecture support the concept of **flowed transactions** across services. This means a client can create a transaction and call on one or more services to do work as part of that transaction. A failure in a service operation can cause the client's transaction to fail. Flowed transactions require two-way communication.

The ability to flow transactions across services, even if their platforms differ, is a powerful tool for getting disparate systems to work together as a functional unit. Although you probably wouldn't want to do this across organizational boundaries (putting your data center at the mercy of someone else's), this approach makes a lot of sense within an enterprise in which integration of systems is an ongoing concern.

When you are using the MSMQ transport, you can use **transacted communication**. In transacted communication, a client sends a related group of queued messages within a transaction scope. The service must receive all of the messages or it will not see any of them. Transacted communication requires only one-way communication.

Creating a Transaction

A client starts a transaction by creating a *TransactionScope*. It's convenient to control the lifetime of a *TransactionScope* by using a *using* statement. The client calls the *Complete* method of the transaction scope to commit the transaction. Failing to call *Complete* or throwing an exception causes the transaction to abort and roll back its work.

```
using (TransactionScope tx = new TransactionScope(TransactionScopeOption.RequiresNew))
{
    ...do work...
    tx.Complete();
}
```

If the client accesses services within the transaction scope, those services can participate in the transaction. In the following code, two services are accessed to debit one account and credit another, respectively, within the scope of a client transaction.

```
using (TransactionScope tx = new TransactionScope(TransactionScopeOption.RequiresNew))
{
    Account1Proxy.Debit(accountNo, amount);
    Account2Proxy.Credit(accountNo, amount);
    tx.Complete();
}
```

Transactions don't flow from client to services automatically; they have to be explicitly enabled. Both the client and the service have to enable transaction flow (as explained in the next section). In addition, service operations have to enlist in a transaction to participate in it. (For more information, see Chapter 7.)

Enabling Transaction Flow

Transaction flow is enabled through the *FlowTransactions* property of a binding. When you define an endpoint in code or in a configuration file, the binding used by the client and by the service must enable transaction flow. The *FlowTransactions* property can be set to *NotAllowed*, *Allowed*, or *Required*.

- *NotAllowed*, the default, prevents transaction flow.

- *Allowed* permits transaction flow but does not require it.

- *Required* requires transaction flow.

The following client configuration file shows transaction flow being enabled by setting the *FlowTransactions* property to *Required*.

```
<?xml version="1.0" encoding="utf-8" ?>
<configuration xmlns="http://schemas.microsoft.com/.NetConfiguration/v2.0">
    <system.serviceModel>

        <client>
            <endpoint
                configurationName="MyEndpoint"
                address="http://localhost/MyService/"
                bindingSectionName="wsProfileBinding"
                bindingConfiguration="MyBinding"
```

```
                contractType="IMyService" />
        </client>

        <bindings>
            <wsProfileBinding>
                <binding configurationName="MyBinding" flowTransactions="Required" />
            </wsProfileBinding>
        </bindings>

    </system.serviceModel>
</configuration>
```

Transacted Communication

Transacted communication treats a batch of queued messages as a unit. When you send messages over a queued transport from within a transaction scope, the messages must all be received by the service or none of them will be seen.

To use transacted communication, do the following:

1.   Use the MSMQ transport (for example, via the *NetProfileMsmq* binding).

2.   In the client, perform messaging within a transaction scope and complete the transaction.

3.   In the service, specify transaction enlistment in *OperationBehavior* attributes.

The following client code shows a client sending queued messages in a transaction. A *TransactionScope* object demarcates the lifetime of the transaction. The *Complete* method of the transaction scope is called to commit the transaction.

```
using (CalculatorProxy proxy = new CalculatorProxy("CalculatorEndpoint"))
{
  //Create a transaction scope.
   using (TransactionScope scope = new TransactionScope(TransactionScopeOption.Required))
   {
        // Call the Add service operation.
        double value1 = 100.00D;
        double value2 = 15.99D;
        proxy.Add(value1, value2);
        Console.WriteLine("Add({0},{1})", value1, value2);

        // Call the Subtract service operation.
        value1 = 145.00D;
        value2 = 76.54D;
        proxy.Subtract(value1, value2);
        Console.WriteLine("Subtract({0},{1})", value1, value2);

        // Call the Multiply service operation.
        value1 = 9.00D;
        value2 = 81.25D;
```

```
        proxy.Multiply(value1, value2);
        Console.WriteLine("Multiply({0},{1})", value1, value2);

        // Call the Divide service operation.
        value1 = 22.00D;
        value2 = 7.00D;
        proxy.Divide(value1, value2);
        Console.WriteLine("Divide({0},{1})", value1, value2);

        // Complete the transaction.
        scope.Complete();
    }

    // Close the proxy.
    proxy.Close();
}
```

Programming Exercise: Duplex Client

In this programming exercise, we will create a service and a client to access it by using the duplex messaging pattern. The application controls a simulated remote-control vehicle. A client sends commands to a vehicle service, which sends the client its position as it changes. The service is hosted in Microsoft Internet Information Services (IIS). The client is a console application.

This exercise has 10 development steps:

1. Create the service program.

2. Create an .svc file.

3. Create a configuration file for the service.

4. Build the service.

5. Create a virtual directory and deploy the service.

6. Test the service with a browser.

7. Create the client.

8. Generate proxy code for the client.

9. Create a configuration file for the client.

10. Build the client.

Step 1: Create the Service Program

We'll now create the service program, which will compile to a DLL library assembly. Launch your development environment and create a new C# console application project named *service*. Enter the code in Listing 6-1.

To perform these tasks using Microsoft Visual Studio:

1. Select New, Project from the File menu.

2. Under Project Type, select Windows under Visual C#. Under Templates, select Console Application. In the Name box, type **service**, in the Location box, type any path you want, and in the Solution Name box, type **duplex**. Click OK to generate and open the new project.

3. Replace the generated code in Program.cs with the code shown in Listing 6-1.

Your service project will need to reference System.ServiceModel.dll. In Visual Studio, right-click References in the Solution Explorer window, and then select Add Reference. An Add Reference dialog box appears. On the .NET tab, select System.ServiceModel.dll, and then click OK.

Listing 6-1 Duplex Service: Program.cs

```
using System;
using System.ServiceModel;
using System.Diagnostics;

namespace ProgrammingIndigo
{
    [ServiceContract(CallbackContract=typeof(ISampleClientContract))]
    public interface ISampleContract
    {
        [OperationContract(IsOneWay=false)]
        void MoveForward(int units);
        [OperationContract(IsOneWay=false)]
        void MoveBackward(int units);
        [OperationContract(IsOneWay=false)]
        void TurnLeft();
        [OperationContract(IsOneWay=false)]
        void TurnRight();
    }

    public interface ISampleClientContract
    {
        [OperationContract(IsOneWay=false)]
        void Position(int x, int y, string direction);
    }

    [ServiceBehavior(InstanceMode=InstanceMode.PrivateSession)]
    public class SampleService : ISampleContract
    {
        enum Direction { North, South, East, West }

        Direction direction = Direction.North;

        ISampleClientContract callback = null;

        int x = 100, y = 100;
```

```
public SampleService()
{
    callback = OperationContext.Current.GetCallbackChannel
        <ISampleClientContract>();
}

public void MoveForward(int units)
{
    for (int i = 0; i < units; i++)
    {
        switch (direction)
        {
            case Direction.North:
                y--;
                break;
            case Direction.South:
                y++;
                break;
            case Direction.West:
                x--;
                break;
            case Direction.East:
                x++;
                break;
        }
        callback.Position(x, y, direction.ToString());
    }
}

public void MoveBackward(int units)
{
    for (int i = 0; i < units; i++)
    {
        switch (direction)
        {
            case Direction.North:
                y++;
                break;
            case Direction.South:
                y--;
                break;
            case Direction.West:
                x++;
                break;
            case Direction.East:
                x--;
                break;
        }
        callback.Position(x, y, direction.ToString());
    }
}

public void TurnLeft()
{
    switch (direction)
```

```
        {
            case Direction.South:
                direction = Direction.East;
                break;
            case Direction.North:
                direction = Direction.West;
                break;
            case Direction.East:
                direction = Direction.North;
                break;
            case Direction.West:
                direction = Direction.South;
                break;
        }
        callback.Position(x, y, direction.ToString());
    }

    public void TurnRight()
    {
        switch (direction)
        {
            case Direction.North:
                direction = Direction.East;
                break;
            case Direction.South:
                direction = Direction.West;
                break;
            case Direction.West:
                direction = Direction.North;
                break;
            case Direction.East:
                direction = Direction.South;
                break;
        }
        callback.Position(x, y, direction.ToString());
    }
    }

}
```

Step 2: Create an .svc File

An .svc file is needed to identify the Indigo service to IIS. Using an editor or development environment, create a text file named Service.svc. Enter the code shown in Listing 6-2.

In Visual Studio, right-click the service project, and then select Add, New Item. Select Text File, and then click Add. Rename the text file Service.svc. Enter the code in Listing 6-2 into Service.svc.

Listing 6-2   Duplex Service: Service.svc

```
<%@Service language=c# Debug="true" class="ProgrammingIndigo.SampleService" %>
<%@Assembly Name="service" %>
```

Step 3: Create a Configuration File for the Service

A Web.config file is needed to specify endpoints and bindings for the service. Using an editor or development environment, create a text file with the code shown in Listing 6-3. Save the code under the name Web.config in the same folder in which the service program and .svc file are located.

In Visual Studio, right-click the service project, and then select Add, New Item. Select Application Configuration File, and then click Add. Name the file Web.config. Enter the code in Listing 6-3 into Web.config.

Listing 6-3   Duplex Service: Web.config

```xml
<?xml version="1.0" encoding="utf-8" ?>
<configuration xmlns="http://schemas.microsoft.com/.NetConfiguration/v2.0">
    <system.serviceModel>
        <services>
            <service
                serviceType="ProgrammingIndigo.SampleService">
                <endpoint
                    address=""
                    bindingConfiguration="SampleBinding"
                    bindingSectionName="wsDualHttpBinding"
                    contractType="ProgrammingIndigo.ISampleContract" />
            </service>
        </services>
        <bindings>
            <wsDualHttpBinding>
                <binding configurationName="SampleBinding" >
                </binding>
            </wsDualHttpBinding>
        </bindings>
    </system.serviceModel>
    <system.web>
        <compilation debug="true" />
    </system.web>
</configuration>
```

Step 4: Build the Service

Build the service program to make Service.dll. Resolve any typographical errors.

In Visual Studio, select Build Solution from the Build menu to generate Service.dll.

Step 5: Create a Virtual Directory for the Service

Like ASP.NET applications, services hosted in IIS reside in virtual directories. Follow this procedure to set up a virtual directory for the service.

1. **Create a directory.** Create a folder on your computer named duplex.

2. **Create a virtual directory**. From the Start menu, launch Control Panel. Select Adminis-trative Tools, Internet Information Services to open IIS Manager. Navigate to Web Sites, Default Web Sites. Right-click and select New, Virtual Directory. Specify the name **duplex** and then associate it with the duplex folder created in step 1. Before exiting IIS Manager, check step 3.

3. **Enable anonymous access**. While in IIS, navigate to Web Sites, Default Web Sites. Duplex should be listed. Right-click duplex, and then select Properties. On the Direc-tory Security tab, click Edit. An Authentication Methods dialog box appears. In this dia-log box, Anonymous Access should be selected; if it isn't, select it. Close all dialog boxes by clicking OK. Close IIS.

4. **Deploy the service.** Copy the Service.svc file to the duplex folder. Underneath duplex, create a bin subdirectory, and then copy Service.dll into it. You should have the follow-ing directory/file structure.

```
\duplex
    service.svc
    \bin
        service.dll
```

Step 6: Test the Service with a Browser

Before going on to the client, we want to test that the service can be accessed. Launch Microsoft Internet Explorer. On the address bar, specify the URL *http://localhost/duplex/service.svc*, and then press ENTER. If the resulting page does not list any errors, proceed to step 7. If there are problems, check the following:

- If the page returned by the browser describes compilation errors, check the code entered in the preceding steps. The compilation error display should highlight the offending code.

- If the resulting page describes HTTP errors, make sure your system has IIS enabled. You should be able to access *http://localhost* in a browser without receiving an error. If IIS seems to be properly enabled, review the virtual directory setup in the prior steps. If this also fails, look for clues in Control Panel, Administrative Tools, Event Log, or try an *IIS-RESET*.

The service is now ready. Next we need a client program to access it.

Step 7: Create the Client

Create the client program. Launch your development environment and create a new C# con-sole application project named *client*. Enter the code in Listing 6-4.

To perform these tasks using Visual Studio:

1. Select New, Project from the File menu.

2. Under Project Type, select Windows under Visual C#. Under Templates, select Console Application. In the Name box, type **service**, in the Location box, type any path you want, and in the Solution Name box, type **duplex**. Click OK to generate and open the new project.

3. Replace the generated code in Program.cs with the code shown in Listing 6-4.

Your client project will need to reference System.ServiceModel.dll.

In Visual Studio, right-click References in the Solution Explorer window, and then select Add Reference. An Add Reference dialog box appears. On the .NET tab, select System.Service-Model.dll, and then click OK.

Build the client, which will create Client.exe.

Listing 6-4   Duplex Client: Program.cs

```csharp
using System;
using System.ServiceModel;

namespace ProgrammingIndigo
{

    class Client : ISampleContractCallback
    {
        static void Main(string[] args)
        {
            // Create a proxy.
            ServiceSite clientSite = new ServiceSite(null, new Client());
            using (SampleContractProxy proxy = new SampleContractProxy(clientSite,
                "SampleEndpoint"))
            {
                // Call a service operation.
                Console.WriteLine("Sending command: MoveForward(3)");
                proxy.MoveForward(3);

                // Call a service operation.
                Console.WriteLine("Sending command: TurnRight()");
                proxy.TurnRight();

                // Call a service operation.
                Console.WriteLine("Sending command: MoveForward(5)");
                proxy.MoveForward(5);

                // Call a service operation.
                Console.WriteLine("Sending command: TurnLeft()");
                proxy.TurnLeft();
```

```
            // Call a service operation.
            Console.WriteLine("Sending command: MoveBackward(2)");
            proxy.MoveBackward(2);

            Console.WriteLine();
            Console.WriteLine("Press ENTER to shut down client");
            Console.ReadLine();

            proxy.Close();
        }
    }

    public void Position(int x, int y, string direction)
    {
        Console.WriteLine("Received notification: Position(" + x + "," + y + "," +
            direction + ")");
    }

    }
}
```

Step 8: Generate Proxy Code

We will now generate client proxy code by accessing the service's MEX endpoint with the Svcutil tool. From a command window, change the directory to the location where your client project and source files reside. Run the following Svcutil command:

```
svcutil http://localhost/duplex/service.svc/ /out:proxy.cs
```

The file Proxy.cs is generated, containing the service contract and a proxy class for accessing the service. It should match the code that's downloadable from the Web.

Add Out.cs to your client project. In Visual Studio, right-click the project in the Solution Explorer window, and then select Add, Existing Item. Select Proxy.cs in the File, Open dialog box, and click OK. Out.cs is added to the client project.

Step 9: Create a Configuration File for the Client

A Client.exe.config file is needed to specify the service endpoint and binding to use. Using an editor or development environment, create a text file with the code shown in Listing 6-5. Save the code under the name Client.exe.config.

To perform these tasks using Visual Studio:

1. Right-click the service project, and then select Add, New Item.

2. Select Application Configuration File, and then click Add.

3. Name the file App.config. (It will be copied to Client.exe.config at build time.)

4. Enter the code in Listing 6-5 into App.config.

Listing 6-5   Duplex Client: App.config

```xml
<?xml version="1.0" encoding="utf-8" ?>
<configuration xmlns="http://schemas.microsoft.com/.NetConfiguration/v2.0">
    <system.serviceModel>
        <client>
            <endpoint
                configurationName="SampleEndpoint"
                address="http://localhost/Duplex/service.svc"
                bindingConfiguration="SampleBinding"
                bindingSectionName="wsDualHttpBinding"
                contractType="ISampleContract" />
        </client>
        <bindings>
            <wsDualHttpBinding>
                <binding configurationName="SampleBinding" />
            </wsDualHttpBinding>
        </bindings>
    </system.serviceModel>
</configuration>
```

Step 10: Build the Client

Build the client program to make Client.exe. Resolve any typographical errors.

In Visual Studio, select Build Solution from the Build menu to generate Client.exe.

Deployment

We're now ready to try things out. Run the client from your development environment or from a command line. You should see output like that shown in Figure 6-5. There's no need to launch the service; services hosted in IIS are activated when they are accessed. If the program fails, double-check that you've properly carried out each of the preceding steps.

Figure 6-5   Duplex client

Press ENTER on the client to shut it down. Congratulations on successfully completing a duplex service and client!

Understanding the Service Code

The service is hosted in IIS. There is no hosting code in the service program. The service is defined by the file Service.svc in the virtual directory. The directives in Service.svc indicate that the service class is *ProgrammingIndigo.SampleService*, found in the assembly named *service* (Service.dll, which resides in the bin directory underneath the virtual directory).

```
<%@Service language=c# Debug="true" class="ProgrammingIndigo.SampleService" %>
<%@Assembly Name="service" %>
```

The service code contains the service contract and implementation code. The service contract is a duplex contract. The service implements the contract *ISampleContract*; the client implements the callback contract *ISampleClientContract*.

```
[ServiceContract(CallbackContract=typeof(ISampleClientContract))]
public interface ISampleContract
{
    [OperationContract(IsOneWay=false)]
    void MoveForward(int units);
    [OperationContract(IsOneWay=false)]
    void MoveBackward(int units);
    [OperationContract(IsOneWay=false)]
    void TurnLeft();
    [OperationContract(IsOneWay=false)]
    void TurnRight();
}

public interface ISampleClientContract
{
    [OperationContract(IsOneWay=false)]
    void Position(int x, int y, string direction);
}
```

The *SampleService* class implements the service, which simulates a remote-control vehicle. *PrivateSession* instancing is specified, which means there will be a unique instance of the *SampleService* class for each client. The class defines an enumeration for four directions and declares variables to hold the current direction and current position. The service class also maintains a way to communicate back to the client through the *ISampleClientContract* variable callback. When a client connects to the service and begins a session, the constructor for *SampleService* sets *callback* to the callback channel to the client. The callback is thus a proxy that the service can use to talk to the client.

```
[ServiceBehavior(InstanceMode=InstanceMode.PrivateSession)]
public class SampleService : ISampleContract
{
    enum Direction { North, South, East, West }

    Direction direction = Direction.North;

    ISampleClientContract callback = null;
```

```
    int x = 100, y = 100;

    public SampleService()
    {
        callback = OperationContext.Current.GetCallbackChannel<ISampleClientContract>();
    }

    public void MoveForward(int units)
    {
        ...
    }
    ...
}
```

As the service performs its service operations, which move the vehicle, the client is notified of changes in position. This is done by calling the client's service operation *Position* using the callback variable as a proxy.

```
public void MoveForward(int units)
{
    for (int i = 0; i < units; i++)
    {
        switch (direction)
        {
            case Direction.North:
                y--;
                break;
            case Direction.South:
                y++;
                break;
            case Direction.West:
                x--;
                break;
            case Direction.East:
                x++;
                break;
        }
        callback.Position(x, y, direction.ToString());
    }
}
```

The endpoint for the service and the binding that it uses are defined in the .config file. The service endpoint specifies a default address, a *WSProfileDualHttpBinding* standard binding that supports duplex communication, and the contract *ISampleContract*. The endpoint address for this service reflects hosting by IIS: the virtual directory (duplex) and .svc filename (Service.svc) form part of the address. The actual endpoint address is *http://localhost/duplex/service.svc*.

```
<service
    serviceType="ProgrammingIndigo.SampleService"
    serviceBehaviorName="SampleServiceBehavior">
    <endpoint
        address=""
```

```
        bindingConfiguration="SampleBinding" bindingSectionName="wsDualHttpBinding"
        contractType="ProgrammingIndigo.ISampleContract" />
</service>
```

Understanding the Client Code

The client must agree with the service about address, binding, and contract; otherwise communication is not possible. Because we are using contract-first development for this client, we generated client proxy code from the service by using the Svcutil tool. The code includes both the service contract, *ISampleContract*, and a class for accessing the service, *SampleContractProxy*. The client callback contract is named *ISampleContractCallback* in the generated code, which originally had the name *ISampleClientContract* in the service.

Because a duplex contract is in use, the client is responsible for implementing the callback contract. This particular contract has just one service operation to implement, named *Position*.

```
class Client : ISampleContractCallback
{
    static void Main(string[] args)
    {
        ...
    }

    public void Position(int x, int y, string direction)
    {
        Console.WriteLine("Received notification: Position(" + x + "," + y + "," +
            direction + ")");
    }

}
```

The client first creates an instance of itself to handle callback requests and creates a *ServiceSite* instance. Next it makes a proxy to the service by creating a new instance of the generated *SampleContractProxy* class, specifying the client's *ServiceSite*. The string specified in the constructor, *SampleEndpoint*, specifies a configuration section in which the endpoint for the service is defined. The proxy is created in a *using* statement; when the *using* statement block exits, the proxy is disposed.

```
ServiceSite clientSite = new ServiceSite(null, new Client());
using (SampleContractProxy proxy = new SampleContractProxy(clientSite, "SampleEndpoint"))
{
    ...
}
```

The client's access to the service is straightforward. The service's operations can be called using the proxy channel. When the client is finished communicating with the service, the proxy is closed.

```csharp
// Create a proxy.
ServiceSite clientSite = new ServiceSite(null, new Client());
using (SampleContractProxy proxy = new SampleContractProxy(clientSite, "SampleEndpoint"))
{
    // Call a service operation.
    Console.WriteLine("Sending command: MoveForward(3)");
    proxy.MoveForward(3);

    // Call a service operation.
    Console.WriteLine("Sending command: TurnRight()");
    proxy.TurnRight();

    // Call a service operation.
    Console.WriteLine("Sending command: MoveForward(5)");
    proxy.MoveForward(5);

    // Call a service operation.
    Console.WriteLine("Sending command: TurnLeft()");
    proxy.TurnLeft();

    // Call a service operation.
    Console.WriteLine("Sending command: MoveBackward(2)");
    proxy.MoveBackward(2);

    Console.WriteLine();
    Console.WriteLine("Press ENTER to shut down client");
    Console.ReadLine();

    proxy.Close();
}
```

As the client runs, the code in the *Main* function creates a proxy and accesses the service. When the service calls back to the client, the *Position* method runs.

Summary

This chapter covered how to create clients. With code generated by the Svcutil tool, creating a proxy is simply a matter of creating a new instance of a proxy class. Alternatively, you can create a proxy channel by using the *ChannelFactory* class's *CreateChannel* method.

For duplex clients, a pair of contracts is used, one for the service and one for callbacks to the client. Generated proxy code for a duplex contract takes an additional parameter, a *ServiceSite* that implements the client's callback contract. To create a duplex channel using *ChannelFactory*, we use the *CreateDuplexChannel* method, which also requires a *ServiceSite*.

Endpoints for proxies can be specified in code or in a configuration file. Bindings can also be specified in code or in a configuration file. Standard bindings provide convenient predefined ways to access services in common scenarios. Custom bindings allow you to build just what you need when a standard binding doesn't fit the bill.

In the next chapter, we'll travel to the other end of the channel: services.

Chapter 7
Services

Great services are not canceled by one act or by one single error.

—Benjamin Disraeli

Previous chapters have described the fundamental concepts behind services, the contracts found in services, and how to write clients that access services. In this chapter, you will learn how to write service programs themselves.

After completing this chapter, you will:

- Know how to create service programs.
- Know how to create typed services, untyped services, and typed message services.
- Understand how to define service endpoints and bindings.
- Know how to specify binding requirements.
- Know how to use transactions.

Understanding Services

Service programs define and implement one or more service contracts. They can also contain data and message contracts.

Service Program Structure

From the developer's perspective, an Indigo service program has four distinct parts:

- **Service contract**   Service, data, and message contract definitions
- **Service type**   A class that implements a service contract
- **Hosting code**   Code that controls the lifetime of a service
- **Endpoint definition**   An address, a binding, and a service contract

Listings 7-1 and 7-2 show a complete sample service that is self-hosted. The program code in Listing 7-1 contains the service contract, service type, and hosting code. The configuration file in Listing 7-2 contains the endpoint definitions.

Listing 7-1   Sample Service Program Code

```
using System;
using System.ServiceModel;

namespace ProgrammingIndigo
{
    // Service contract.
    [ServiceContract]
    public interface ISampleService
    {
        // Look up the sales tax rate for a region.
        [OperationContract]
        decimal LookupSalesTaxRate(string region);

        // Compute the sales tax on an order subtotal.
        [OperationContract]
        decimal ComputeSalesTax(decimal subtotal, decimal taxRate);
    }

    // Service implementation.
    public class SampleService : ISampleService
    {
        // Host the service.
        static void Main(string[] args)
        {
            using (ServiceHost<SampleService> serviceHost = new
                ServiceHost<SampleService>())
            {
                serviceHost.Open();
                Console.WriteLine("Press ENTER to shut down the service");
                Console.ReadLine();
                serviceHost.Close();
            }
        }

        // Implement the LookupSalesTaxRate service operation.
        // Look up the sales tax rate for a region.
        public decimal LookupSalesTaxRate(string region)
        {
            decimal taxRate = 0.000M;
            switch (region)
            {
                case "A":
                    taxRate = 0.070M;
                    break;
                case "B":
                    taxRate = 0.072M;
                    break;
```

```
            case "C":
                taxRate = 0.075M;
                break;
            case "D":
                taxRate = 0.090M;
                break;
            case "E":
                taxRate = 0.092M;
                break;
        }
        return taxRate;
    }


    // Implement the ComputeSalesTax service operation.
    // Compute the sales tax on an order subtotal.
    public decimal ComputeSalesTax(decimal subtotal, decimal taxRate)
    {
        decimal taxAmount = subtotal * taxRate;
        return taxAmount;
    }
    }
}
```

Listing 7-2   Sample Service Configuration File

```
<?xml version="1.0" encoding="utf-8" ?>
<configuration xmlns="http://schemas.microsoft.com/.NetConfiguration/v2.0">
    <system.serviceModel>
        <services>
            <service
                serviceType="ProgrammingIndigo.SampleService">
                <endpoint
                    address="http://localhost:8000/SampleService/"
                    bindingSectionName="basicProfileBinding"
                    contractType="ProgrammingIndigo.ISampleService" />
            </service>
        </services>
    </system.serviceModel>
</configuration>
```

Service Contracts

A service must define and implement at least one service contract. However, a service can contain multiple service contracts as well as data and message contracts.

Service contracts and the classes that implement them can be defined separately or together. When they are defined separately, service contract attributes are applied to an interface, and a class implements the interface. When they are defined together, a single class both defines the service contract and implements it.

A service might have to call upon another service as part of its processing. In this situation, the service is really acting as a client of the dependent service. To access the dependent service, its service contract must be defined. The contract definition is usually generated with the Svcutil tool.

For detailed information about contracts, see Chapter 5.

Service Types

A class that implements a service contract is called a **service type**, or a **service implementation class**. A service type can implement one service contract or several. For each operation defined in the service contract, the service type must provide a method that implements the operation.

You can specify behaviors for a service type and its methods. At the class level, the *[Service-Behavior]* attribute defines service behaviors. At the method level, the *[OperationBehavior]* attribute defines service operation behaviors.

Hosting Code

A service isn't available to the outside world until it is created, associated with one or more endpoints, and opened. Hosting code controls the lifetime of the service with a *ServiceHost* object. The lifecycle of a service consists of creation of a *ServiceHost*, opening of the service, closing of the service, and disposing of the service.

If services are hosted by Microsoft Internet Information Services (IIS), IIS takes care of these tasks and you do not have to write any hosting code. You simply create an.svc file in a virtual directory that defines the service.

For more information on hosting, see Chapter 10.

Endpoint Definitions

A service can't be accessed without endpoints. Endpoints can be defined in configuration file settings or in code. An endpoint definition specifies an address, a binding, and a service contract. The binding can be a standard binding or a custom binding. Custom bindings require additional information—a binding configuration that provides binding details. Binding configurations can also be specified for standard bindings for the purpose of fine-tuning their properties.

Service endpoint addresses can be absolute, or they can be relative to a base address. You can specify one or more base addresses for a service (but no more than one per transport type). Then you can specify a relative endpoint address according to standard URI composition rules. An endpoint address can be as simple as an empty string (" "), which means it has the same address as the base address, or it can be a path, such as "*PremiumService*", which is appended to the base address. Paths beginning with /, such as "/*PremiumService* ", replace the previous path. Table 7-1 shows examples of base addresses and endpoint addresses.

Table 7-1 Base Address and Endpoint Address Examples

Base Address	Specified Endpoint Address	Actual Endpoint Address
None	*http://www.contoso.com*	*http://www.contoso.com*
http://www.contoso.com	none	*http://www.contoso.com*
http://www.contoso.com	*MyService*	*http://www.contoso.com/ MyService*
http://www.contoso.com/Service	*Test*	*http://www.contoso.com/Service/ Test*
http://www.contoso.com/Service	*/Test*	*http://www.contoso.com/Test*
http://www.contoso.com/Service/ service.svc	*Test*	*http://www.contoso.com/Service/ service.svc/Test*

For more information about endpoint definitions, bindings, and base addresses, see Chapter 4.

Services at Runtime

At runtime, services are represented in a series of objects containing the service's description, program code, and runtime information. Figure 7-1 shows the runtime representation of a service. The service description includes the service's contracts, behaviors, and endpoints. The program code for the service is the service type. The runtime information includes channels, instances of the service type, and extensions to the service.

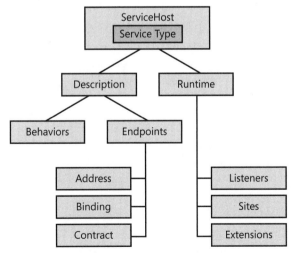

Figure 7-1   Runtime representation of a service

ServiceHost

The master class that represents a service at runtime is *ServiceHost<T>*. The *ServiceHost* object contains the service type. When a *ServiceHost* object is created, the service type for the service is specified as a generic.

ServiceDescription

A *ServiceHost* contains a service description that uses the *ServiceDescription* class. A service description contains the information about a service that can be exposed as metadata. This includes its contracts, schema, and endpoint definitions.

ServiceSite

As a service runs, it can create multiple instances of a service type in response to client activity. A **service site** links a channel to an instance of the service type. Service sites make it possible for channels and service instances to have different lifetimes. The *ServiceHost* maintains a collection of service sites using the *ServiceSite* class.

OperationContext

The code in a service operation might need to find out something about the context it is running in. An operation context is maintained for the service operation that can be used to locate the service host, service site, incoming message information, and security context. The operation context is accessed through the *OperationContext* class.

ServiceSecurityContext

The code in a service operation might also need to find out something about the security environment it is running in. A security context is maintained for the service operation. Service operations can use the security context to determine information such as the caller's identity. The security context is accessed through the *ServiceSecurityContext* class.

Messages and Service Operations

When a valid request message is received for a service, it is dispatched to a method implementing the requested service operation. The method can access data from the request message through its input parameters. If the service operation is two-way, there will be a response message. The method can specify data for the response message through the method's result or through output parameters. To understand how this works, let's consider what happens when the following service operation is accessed.

```
[OperationContract]
double Add(double n1, double n2);
```

If a client calls this service operation, a message such as the one in Listing 7-3 is sent to the service. The message identifies the target operation, *Add*, and contains data for the operation. In this case, the operands for *<Add>* are *n1* with a value of 100 and *n2* with a value of 15.99.

Listing 7-3   Request Message

```
<s:Envelope xmlns:s="http://schemas.xmlsoap.org/soap/envelope/">
  <s:Header />
  <s:Body>
    <Add xmlns="http://tempuri.org/">
      <n1>100</n1>
      <n2>15.99</n2>
    </Add>
  </s:Body>
</s:Envelope>
```

The method implementing *Add* is invoked. The *n1* and *n2* parameters contain the values 100 and 15.99 from the message.

```
public double Add(double n1, double n2)
{
    return n1 + n2;
}
```

When the *Add* method completes, its result value, 115.99, is part of the response message. Listing 7-4 shows the response message.

Listing 7-4   Response Message

```
<s:Envelope xmlns:s="http://schemas.xmlsoap.org/soap/envelope/">
  <s:Header />
  <s:Body>
    <AddResponse xmlns="http://tempuri.org/">
      <AddResult>115.99</AddResult>
    </AddResponse>
  </s:Body>
</s:Envelope>
```

If a service operation needs to return more than one result value, you can use *out* or *ref* parameters.

Types of Services

You can develop three types of services. The service contract determines which type of service you are dealing with.

- **Typed services**   Service operations resemble methods.
- **Untyped services**   Messages are sent or received.
- **Typed message services**   Custom messages are sent or received.

The primary difference between the three types of services is in what your service operations can accept as parameters or return as results. Typed services are the simplest to use. Untyped services and typed message services are more complex to implement but allow developers to work at the message level.

Typed services have service operations that act just like functions or methods. They can accept any number of parameters and can return a result. Parameters and results can be simple types, such as *int* and *string*, or complex types, such as *Order* and *Customer*. A data contract must be defined for each complex type. Indigo takes care of turning method calls into request and response messages. The developer doesn't have to work directly with messages at all.

Untyped services pass *Message* objects to and from service operations. Service operations accept a parameter that is a *Message* object. If a service operation is two-way, it returns a *Message* object as well. Developers work directly with messages, creating *Message* objects to send and interpreting received *Message* objects.

Typed message services send custom messages to and from service operations. Typed messages combine elements of typed services and untyped services. Message contracts are used to define typed message classes. Typed messages can be treated as messages and as objects containing structured data. Developers can exercise control over the structure of messages while retaining ease of access to the data in a message.

Important   Don't confuse a typed service with a service type. A typed service is a service that acts like the methods of a class. A service type is a class that implements a service contract.

Service Behaviors

You can specify behaviors for services and service operations. At the service level, behaviors include instancing, concurrency, throttling, and error handling. At the service operation level, behaviors include transaction control, instance recycling, and identity impersonation. Design-time behaviors are specified with attributes. Deployment-time service behaviors are specified in configuration file settings.

Service behaviors are purely local. They have no effect on service descriptions, message content, or client behavior.

Instancing Behavior

As a service executes, one or more instances of its implementation class are created in response to request messages. The implementation class specifies an **instance mode,** which determines when instances are created and destroyed. There are four instance modes:

- **Per call** An instance of the class is created for every request and is then destroyed.

- **Singleton** A single instance of the class handles every request.

- **Private session** An instance of the class is created for each client connection.

- **Shared session** An instance of the class is created for each client connection, but it is possible for multiple clients to share access to the same instance.

Per call is the default instance mode. Select an instance mode that suits your requirements for state management.

- Per-call instancing is appropriate when service operations require no state at all to be saved between calls. Per-call instancing would be a good choice for a mathematics service whose service operations perform independent calculations.

- Singleton instancing is appropriate when service operations need to maintain state across all activity. Singleton instancing would be a good choice for a voting service that tallies votes from clients.

- Private-session instancing is appropriate when service operations need to maintain separate state for each client. Private-session instancing would be a good choice for an e-commerce service in which each user has a shopping cart.

- Shared-session instancing is appropriate when service operations need to maintain separate state for groups of clients rather than individual clients. Shared-session instancing would be a good choice for a multiplayer game service in which each group of players shares an instance representing their game state.

When private-session or shared-session instancing is in use, the service contract definition can specify which service operations are initiating and which are terminating. Initiating service operations causes a new instance to be created. Terminating service operations releases an instance.

To understand instancing, let's consider what happens under each instancing scheme when the following sequence of activities occurs:

1. Client A accesses the service.

2. Client B accesses the service.

3. Client A accesses the service a second time.

4. Client C accesses the service.

Figure 7-2 shows the per-call instancing case. Each client accesses results in a new instance of the service class. The second call by Client A does not reuse the instance from the first call. Each instance is released right after the service operation completes.

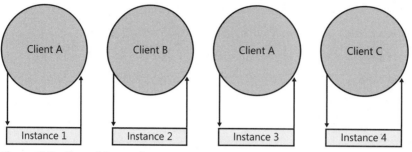

Figure 7-2 Per-call instancing

Figure 7-3 shows the singleton instancing case. All clients access the same instance.

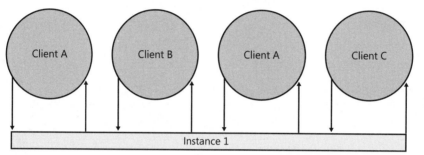

Figure 7-3 Singleton instancing

Figure 7-4 shows the private-session instancing case. Client state is maintained between calls over the same client connection. The second call by Client A uses the same instance from the first call. The instance for each client goes away when the connection is closed or when the client accesses a terminating service operation.

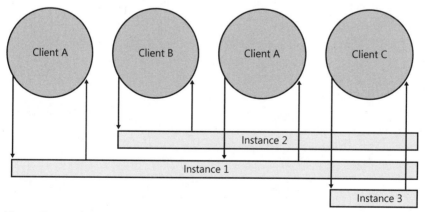

Figure 7-4 Private-session instancing

Figure 7-5 shows the shared-session instancing case. Here Client B and Client C share the same session instance. Client B obtains a unique instance address for its instance and shares the address with Client C. As with private-session instancing, client state is maintained between calls over the same client connection. The second call by Client A uses the same instance from the first call. Client B and Client C share the same instance.

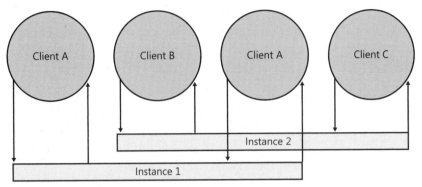

Figure 7-5   Shared-session instancing

Concurrency Behavior

A service can specify how each service instance is to be handled with regard to threads. The implementation class specifies a **concurrency mode**, which determines how many threads are permitted to simultaneously access a service instance. There are three concurrency modes:

- **Single**   Only one thread at a time accesses a service instance.

- **Reentrant**   Only one thread at a time accesses a service instance, and reentrant calls back into the service instance are permitted.

- **Multiple**   More than one thread can concurrently access a service instance.

> **Tip**   The concurrency setting has no meaning if the instance mode is set to *PerCall*.

You should use the single concurrency mode when a service class is not thread-safe. If multiple threads need to access the same service instance, they are synchronized so that only one thread at a time accesses the service instance. Single is the default concurrency behavior.

The reentrant concurrency mode is similar to the single concurrency mode but supports reentrancy. It should be used when a service class is not thread-safe and will call software that calls back into the same service instance. For example, a non-thread-safe service might call a helper object that calls it back. The reentrant concurrency mode adds an identifier to calls made and allows only calls with the identifier to reenter.

The multiple concurrency mode allows multiple threads to access the service instance at the same time. This concurrency mode should be used only with thread-safe code.

If a message arrives that would conflict with the concurrency mode, it waits until the service instance becomes available.

Throttling

Throttling behavior allows control over the amount of work a service takes on. This feature allows you to set limits to avoid overconsumption of server resources. Throttling provides control in four areas:

- Number of calls to the service
- Number of connections to the service
- Number of service instances
- Number of pending calls for the service

You should apply throttling when a service is overwhelming a resource. Consider a service that is becoming so popular that memory consumption is reaching critical levels. You can limit the number of service instances to reduce the memory required by the service.

Messaging Patterns

Services can communicate in datagram, request-reply, or duplex messaging patterns. The binding in use by a service might limit which messaging patterns are available. For more information on message patterns supported by the standard bindings, see Chapter 4.

For datagram communication, a service provides one-way service operations. The client does not wait for completion, and no results are returned by the service operation. The service contract specifies an *[OperationContract(IsOneWay=true)]* parameter.

For request-reply communication, a service provides two-way service operations. The client waits for a response, and the service operation can return results. The service contract specifies an *[OperationContract (IsOneWay=false)]* parameter.

For duplex communication, a service provides a duplex pair of contracts. One service contract is implemented by the service, and a callback contract is implemented by the client. The client and the service can communicate with each other asynchronously. The service contract specifies a *[ServiceContract(typeof(CallbackContract))]* parameter to pair itself with a client callback contract.

For more information on how clients access services in each messaging pattern, see Chapter 6.

Error Handling

Indigo services have to bridge two error-reporting systems, the system used by the Microsoft .NET Framework and the system used in SOAP applications. Errors in managed code are reported as exceptions, which are common language runtime (CLR) types. Errors in SOAP applications are reported as SOAP fault messages.

A service reports an error to a client by throwing a fault. A fault is created using the *Fault<T>* class from an object containing details about the error. Fault types generated by service operations must be explicitly specified using a *[FaultContract]* attribute in the service contract. If a fault is thrown but the generated fault is not specified in a fault contract, the error is reported to the client as an unknown fault.

A service type can be involved in what happens when a fault is thrown. Developers can implement the *IErrorHandler* interface to exercise control of the fault that is generated and whether it is sent to the client.

Exceptions that occur in a service are usually handled locally. To automatically pass unhandled exceptions to a client as faults, you can use the *ReturnUnknownExceptionsAsFaults* service behavior. This feature is valuable primarily when you are debugging a service; it is not recommended for production systems. You can specify *ReturnUnknownExceptionsAsFaults* in code or in configuration file settings.

Programming Services

The principal activities in creating a service are defining its contracts and writing code to implement its service operations. Other activities include specifying behaviors.

Defining Service Contracts and Implementation Code

You define service contracts by annotating interfaces or classes with attributes. (For detailed information on how to define service contracts, see Chapter 5.) A service contract and its implementation can be defined separately or together.

Defining Service Contracts and Implementation Code Separately

When a contract and implementation are defined separately, an interface defines the service contract and a class implements the contract. The interface contains *[ServiceContract]* and *[OperationContract]* attributes. The class implements the interface and can contain the optional *[ServiceBehavior]* and *[OperationBehavior]* attributes. Each service operation defined in the interface must be implemented in the class as a method. The following code shows a simple service contract and service class.

```
[ServiceContract]
public interface IEventRegistration
{
    [OperationContract]
    string RegisterForEvent(string eventCode);
    [OperationContract]
    void SelectTalk(string eventCode, string classCode);
```

```
    [OperationContract]
    string[] GetItinerary(string eventCode);
}


[ServiceBehavior(InstanceMode=InstanceMode.PerCall)]
public class EventRegistrationService : IEventRegistration
{
    public string RegisterForEvent(string eventCode)
    {
        ...
    }
    public void SelectTalk(string eventCode, string classCode)
    {
        ...
    }
    public string[] GetItinerary(string eventCode)
    {
        ...
    }
}
```

Defining Service Contracts and Implementation Code Together

When a contract and implementation are defined together, the class implementing the service also defines the contract. The *[ServiceContract]* and *[OperationContract]* attributes are applied directly to the class and methods. The following code shows a class that defines and implements a service contract.

```
[ServiceContract]
[ServiceBehavior(InstanceMode=InstanceMode.PerCall)]
public class EventRegistrationService : IEventRegistration
{
    [OperationContract]
    public string RegisterForEvent(string eventCode)
    {
        ...
    }
    [OperationContract]
    public void SelectTalk(string eventCode, string classCode)
    {
        ...
    }
    [OperationContract]
    public string[] GetItinerary(string eventCode)
    {
        ...
    }
}
```

Defining Endpoints

Endpoints provide the means of access to a service. They have three parts: address, binding, and service contract. Endpoints can be defined in code or a .config file. You can define multiple endpoints for a service. (For information about addresses and bindings, see Chapter 4.)

Defining an Endpoint in Code

An endpoint can be added to a service through its *ServiceHost* instance before the *ServiceHost* object is opened. To add an endpoint, call the *AddEndpoint* method of the *ServiceHost* instance, specifying the contract type, binding, and address. The following code creates a *ServiceHost*, adds an endpoint, and opens the service.

```
// Create a ServiceHost.
ServiceHost<HelloService> serviceHost = new ServiceHost<HelloService>();

// Add an endpoint.
BasicProfileBinding binding = new BasicProfileBinding();
Uri uri = new Uri("http://localhost:8000/SampleService/");
serviceHost.AddEndpoint(typeof(IHello), binding, uri);

// Open the service.
serviceHost.Open();
```

Defining a Binding in Code

Each standard binding has a class associated with it. To create a standard binding, you create an instance of the appropriate class:

```
BasicProfileBinding binding = new BasicProfileBinding();
```

Once the binding is created, you can tune it by modifying its properties. The following code creates a standard binding and then modifies it to disable security and enable reliable sessions.

```
WSProfileBinding currentBinding = new WSProfileBinding();
currentBinding.SecurityMode = WSProfileSecurityMode.None;
currentBinding.ReliableSessionEnabled = true;
```

For more information about bindings, see Chapter 4.

Defining an Endpoint in Configuration File Settings

Defining an endpoint in a .config file gives you the freedom of making deployment-time decisions about addressing and binding. When you create a *ServiceHost* object, the service program's application configuration file is scanned for endpoint definitions.

A service endpoint is defined with an *<endpoint>* element in the application .config file. The endpoint's address, binding, and service contract are specified in attributes.

```
<endpoint
    address="http://localhost:8000/weather/"
    bindingSectionName="wsProfileBinding"
    contractType="ProgrammingIndigo.IWeather" />
```

The *<endpoint>* elements are contained in a *<service>* section for the service. The *<service>* element specifies the service implementation class in a *serviceType* parameter. The *<service>* section appears under *<configuration><system.serviceModel><services>* in the configuration file. The following configuration settings show the previous endpoint definition in context.

```
<?xml version="1.0" encoding="utf-8" ?>
<configuration xmlns="http://schemas.microsoft.com/.NetConfiguration/v2.0">
    <system.serviceModel>
        <services>
            <service
                serviceType="ProgrammingIndigo.WeatherService">
                <endpoint
                    address="http://localhost:8000/weather/"
                    bindingSectionName="wsProfileBinding"
                    contractType="ProgrammingIndigo.IWeather" />
            </service>
        </services>
    </system.serviceModel>
</configuration>
```

A service endpoint definition has three key attributes: *address*, *bindingSectionName*, and *contractType*.

- *Address*: The address of the service endpoint.

- *bindingSectionName*: The name of a standard binding, or "*customBinding*". This can be accompanied by a *bindingConfiguration* parameter for a detailed binding definition.

- *contractType*: The service contract's type.

Defining a Binding Configuration in a Configuration File

When you want to fine-tune a binding by changing some of its settings, or if you want to create your own custom binding, you can define a binding configuration. You can link an endpoint definition to a binding configuration with a *bindingConfiguration* attribute. In the following endpoint definition, the endpoint specifies a *WSProfile* standard binding but indicates that there is a binding configuration to use named *SampleBinding*.

```
<?xml version="1.0" encoding="utf-8" ?>
<configuration xmlns="http://schemas.microsoft.com/.NetConfiguration/v2.0">
    <system.serviceModel>
        <services>
            <service
                serviceType="ProgrammingIndigo.WeatherService">
                <endpoint
                    address="http://localhost:8000/weather/"
                    bindingSectionName="wsProfileBinding"
```

```
                    bindingConfiguration="SampleBinding"
                    contractType="ProgrammingIndigo.IWeather" />
            </service>
        </services>
        ...binding configuration must be defined here...
    </system.serviceModel>
</configuration>
```

A binding configuration is defined in an element named after the binding type (such as
<wsProfileBinding>); this element appears in the application configuration file under the
<configuration><system.serviceModel><bindings> section. A .config file with a binding configuration is shown here. In this case, a standard *WSProfile* binding has been configured to enable
the flow of transactions from client to service.

```
<?xml version="1.0" encoding="utf-8" ?>
<configuration xmlns="http://schemas.microsoft.com/.NetConfiguration/v2.0">
    <system.serviceModel>
        <services>
            <service
                serviceType="ProgrammingIndigo.WeatherService">
                <endpoint
                    address="http://localhost:8000/Weather/"
                    bindingSectionName="wsProfileBinding"
                    bindingConfiguration="SampleBinding"
                    contractType="ProgrammingIndigo.IWeather" />
            </service>
        </services>
        <bindings>
            <wsProfileBinding>
                <binding configurationName="SampleBinding">
                    <contextFlow transactions="Allowed" />
                </binding>
            </wsProfileBinding>
        </bindings>
    </system.serviceModel>
</configuration>
```

For more about the features and configuration of bindings, see Chapter 4.

> **Tip**   The *endpoint* element used to define endpoints in configuration files is nearly identical
> for clients and services. One important difference is that client endpoint definitions specify a
> *configurationName* attribute and service endpoint definitions do not.

Implementing Service Operations

Service operations are implemented as methods. An incoming message is mapped to a service
operation's input parameters. A service operation's results are mapped to an outgoing message. The kinds of parameters and results that may be used with service operations differ for
the three types of services described earlier in the chapter.

Implementing Service Operations for a Typed Service

In a typed service, service operations are just like methods of a class. They can accept zero or more parameters and can return a result. Parameters and return types can be simple types such as *int* and *string* or complex types such as *Customer* and *Order*. The following code shows several examples of service operations for typed services.

```
public void Notify(string message)
{
    ...
}

public double Add(double n1, double n2)
{
    return n1 + n2;
}

public string AddCustomer(Customer customer)
{
    ...
    return custId;
}
```

Like object-oriented methods, service operations support the use of *ref* and *out* parameters. This permits a service operation to return multiple results. When you use the *ref* parameter, keep in mind that all information is passed by value, unlike in the .NET CLR. The following code shows examples of service operations that use *ref* and *out*.

```
public void Sort(ref int[] values)
{
    ...
}

public void GetStockQuote(string symbol, out decimal highPrice, out decimal lowPrice,
    out decimal currentPrice, out int volume)
{
    ...
}
```

Implementing Service Operations for an Untyped Service

In an untyped service, developers work at the message level. A message object is passed to the service operation. If the service operation returns a result, it also returns a *Message* object. The *Message* class's methods allow a message body to be accessed or created using serialization or an *XmlReader*.

You can deserialize the body of a request message to an object by calling the message object's *GetBody* method. You specify the type to deserialize to as a generic argument to the method. The following service operation retrieves an *OrderItem* object from the body of a received message.

```
public void ProcessMessage(Message message)
{
    OrderItem orderItem = message.GetBody<OrderItem>();
    Console.WriteLine("Request:  ProcessMessage(OrderItem)");
    Console.WriteLine("               PartNo:     {0}", orderItem.PartNo);
    Console.WriteLine("               Description: {0}", orderItem.Description);
    Console.WriteLine("               Qty:        {0}", orderItem.Qty);
    Console.WriteLine("               Price:      {0}", orderItem.Price);
    Console.WriteLine("Response: (string) processing done");
    Console.WriteLine();
}
```

You create a response message by calling the static *CreateMessage* method of the *Message* class. Several editions of *CreateMessage* are described in the Indigo documentation. The following service operation uses a form of *CreateMessage* to create a response message from an object. The object is serialized into the body of the message.

```
public Message ProcessMessage(Message message)
{
    ...
    OrderItem orderItem = new OrderItem();
    orderItem.PartNo = "0001-002";
    orderItem.Description = "No. 2 Pencil";
    orderItem.Qty = 1;
    orderItem.Price = 0.25D;
    Message reply = Message.CreateMessage("http://tempuri.org/ISampleContract/
        ProcessMessageResponse", orderItem);
    return reply;
}
```

Implementing Service Operations for a Typed Message Service

In a typed message service, developers pass custom messages to and from service operations. The service defines custom request and response messages as classes with message contracts. Typed message services combine elements of untyped services and typed services: developers have precise control over message format but can easily get at the data in a message.

Incoming messages are easy to work with. A request to a typed message service operation is a custom message class defined with a message contract. Data in the custom message can be accessed through the class's members. The following code receives a request from a client and displays data from the request message.

```
void ProcessMessage(CustomRequestMessage request)
{
    Console.WriteLine("Order No.:   {0}", request.orderNo);
    Console.WriteLine("PartNo:      {0}", request.orderItem.PartNo);
    Console.WriteLine("Description: {0}", request.orderItem.Description);
    Console.WriteLine("Qty:         {0}", request.orderItem.Qty);
    Console.WriteLine("Price:       {0}", request.orderItem.Price);
}
```

You create a response message by creating a new instance of a custom message class and setting its members. The custom message is returned as the service operation result. The following code creates and populates a custom response message and then returns it as the result of a service operation.

```
CustomResponseMessage ProcessMessage(CustomRequestMessage request)
{
    ...
    reply = new CustomResponseMessage();
    reply.orderNo = "1002";
    reply.orderItem = orderItem;
    return reply;
}
```

For information about defining message contracts, see Chapter 5.

The *[ServiceBehavior]* Attribute

The *[ServiceBehavior]* attribute specifies behaviors that apply to the entire service. It is applied to a service implementation class. The attribute is optional and does not need to be specified when using default behaviors.

```
[ServiceBehavior(InstanceMode=InstanceMode.PrivateSession)]
public class PortfolioService: IPortfolioService
{
    ...
}
```

The following parameters can be specified for the *[ServiceBehavior]* attribute:

- *AllowConcurrentTransactions (bool)*   Controls whether multiple transactions can occur concurrently. A value of *true* allows concurrent transactions. The default is *false*.

- *ConcurrencyMode (ConcurrencyMode)*   Controls the concurrency of threads per service instance. Possible values are *Single*, *Multiple*, and *Reentrant*. *Single* permits only one thread at a time to access an instance. *Reentrant* likewise limits access to one thread at a time but also allows reentrant calls back into the service instance. *Multiple* permits more than one thread to access an instance concurrently. The default is *Single*.

- *InstanceMode (InstanceMode)*   Sets the instance mode. Possible values are *PerCall*, *PrivateSession*, *SharedSession*, and *Singleton*. *PerCall* creates a new instance for each call. *PrivateSession* and *SharedSession* create an instance for each client connection. *SharedSession* allows clients to share instances with other clients. *Singleton* sends all client activity to a single instance. The default is *PerCall*.

- *ReturnUnknownExceptionsAsFaults (bool)*   Controls whether unhandled exceptions in a service are reported back to the client. A value of *true* reports unhandled exceptions back to the client as faults. The default is *false*.

- *RunOnUIThread (bool)*   Used to synchronize service operation calls with the user inter-face thread of a Microsoft Windows Forms application. The default is *true*.

- *TransactionIsolationLevel (IsolationLevel)*   Sets the isolation level for transactions. Possi-ble values are *Chaos*, *ReadCommitted*, *ReadUncommitted*, *RepeatableRead*, *Serializable*, *Snapshot*, and *Unspecified*. The default is *Unspecified*.

- *ValidateMustUnderstand (bool)*   Used to disable validation that received message head-ers are understood. A value of *false* disables validation. The default is *true*.

AllowConcurrentTransactions: Controlling Transaction Concurrency

When a service operation that participates in a transaction is called, it might already be exe-cuting in a transaction on another thread. If that's an unsafe condition for your code, you can disallow concurrent transactions. If concurrent transactions are disallowed, the following occurs if a service operation is called and it is already in a transaction:

- If the transaction that the service method is executing has already passed transaction phase 0, the request is placed in a queue until the transaction completes.

- Otherwise, an exception is thrown.

To disallow concurrent transactions, set the *AllowConcurrentTransactions* property to *false*. The following code disallows concurrent transactions.

```
[ServiceBehavior(AllowConcurrentTransactions=false)]
public class TicketService
{
    [OperationBehavior(AutoEnlistTransaction=true)]
    public PlaceOrder()
    {
        ...
    }
}
```

ConcurrencyMode: Controlling Thread Concurrency

You can control what happens when multiple threads access a service instance. The three con-currency modes are single, reentrant, and multiple, as described earlier in the chapter. If you're unfamiliar with multithreaded programming or are unsure whether your service class is thread-safe, use the default *Single* concurrency mode.

To set the concurrency mode, specify the *ConcurrencyMode* parameter in a *[ServiceBehavior]* attribute. Specify a *ConcurrencyMode* value of *Single*, *Reentrant*, or *Multiple*. The following code specifies reentrant concurrency.

```
[ServiceBehavior(ConcurrencyMode=ConcurrencyMode.Reentrant)]
public class MyService : IMyService
{
    ...
}
```

InstanceMode: Controlling Instancing

You can control how service instances are created. The four instance modes are per call, private session, shared session, and singleton, as described earlier in the chapter.

To set the instance mode, specify the *InstanceMode* parameter in a *[ServiceBehavior]* attribute. Specify an *InstanceMode* value of *PerCall*, *PrivateSession*, *SharedSession*, or *Singleton*. The following code specifies private session instancing:

```
[ServiceBehavior(InstanceMode=InstanceMode.PrivateSession)]
public class MyService : IMyService
{
    ...
}
```

When *PrivateSession* or *SharedSession* instancing is in effect, programs can save client state between calls by using members of the service implementation class. The following class remembers a client's name between calls to *Hello* and *Goodbye*. A member variable of the class preserves the name between calls. Because there is a separate instance of the class for each client connection, each client's name is correctly stored and retrieved even when multiple clients are accessing the service.

```
[ServiceBehavior(InstanceMode=InstanceMode.PrivateSession)]
public class MyService : IMyService
{
    string Name = "";

    public string Hello(string name)
    {
        Name = name;
        return "Hello, " + name;
    }

    public string Goodbye()
    {
        return "Goodbye, " + Name;
    }
}
```

Similarly, global state can be stored and retrieved using static members of the class. You can do this with any of the four instance modes. You should use safe synchronization practices, such as the *lock* statement or *Interlocked* class, to access static members. The following code uses global state to count the number of calls made.

```
[ServiceBehavior(InstanceMode=InstanceMode.PerCall)]
public class MyService : IMyService
{
    static int visitors = 0;

    public string Hello()
    {
        Interlocked.Increment(ref visitors);
```

```
        return "Hello, you are visitor number " + visitors;
    }
}
```

With *SharedSession* instancing, the nominal behavior is like *PrivateSession*, but clients can obtain a unique address that other clients can specify to share the same instance. To obtain the unique address, a proxy's inner channel *ResolveInstance* method is called.

```
SampleServiceProxy proxy = new SampleServiceProxy("DefaultEndpoint");
    ...
EndpointAddress address = proxy.InnerChannel.ResolveInstance();
```

A client can join a shared instance by specifying the unique address when creating a channel. The following code creates two client channels that share an instance. The second client specifies the unique address of the first client.

```
// Not shown: define binding and address.

ChannelFactory<IGame> channelFactory1 = new ChannelFactory<IGame>(address, binding);
IGame client1 = channelFactory1.CreateChannel();

ChannelFactory<IGame> channelFactory2 = new ChannelFactory<IGame>
    (((IProxyChannel)client1).ResolveInstance(), binding);
IGame client2 = channelFactory2.CreateChannel();
```

ReturnUnknownExceptionsAsFaults: Reporting Errors Back to the Client

Indigo services must bridge two error-reporting systems—the system used by the.NET Framework and the system used in SOAP applications. Errors in managed code are reported as exceptions. Exceptions are CLR types. Errors in SOAP applications are reported as fault messages.

When an error occurs in a service operation, an exception is raised. You can use the usual .NET programming techniques to intercept and handle the exception: *try*, *catch*, and *finally* blocks. Reporting the error to the client requires converting the exception to a fault.

To have unhandled exceptions automatically converted to faults and reported back to clients, specify *ReturnUnknownExceptionsAsFaults=true* in a *[ServiceBehavior]* attribute. The following class enables this behavior.

```
[ServiceBehavior(ReturnUnknownExceptionsAsFaults=true)]
public class MyService : IMyService
{
    ...
}
```

A client can intercept an unknown fault by catching *UnknownFault*.

Sending unhandled exceptions back to the client is useful primarily in debugging. It is often considered an unwanted behavior in a production system because it might expose internal details of your service.

RunOnUIThread: Synchronizing with User Interface Threads

A service hosted in an application might be required to run on the application's user interface (UI) thread. For example, this behavior might be desirable in a Windows Forms application that hosts a service. The default behavior is to provide this synchronization.

To disable UI thread synchronization, specify *RunOnUIThread=false* in a *[ServiceBehavior]* attribute. The following code sets *RunOnUIThread* to *false* for a class.

```
[ServiceBehavior(RunOnUIThread=false)]
public class MyService : IMyService
{
    ...
}
```

TransactionIsolationLevel: Setting Transaction Isolation Level

Ideally, transactions exhibit four key properties: atomic, consistent, isolated, and durable (ACID). In practice, keeping transactions fully isolated from each other can mean holding locks longer than necessary. Transaction isolation levels allow developers to choose the degree of isolation to match their application's sensitivity to changes made by other transactions.

To set the isolation level for a service that participates in transactions, specify the *Transaction-IsolationLevel* parameter in a *[ServiceBehavior]* attribute. The following code sets the transaction isolation level to *ReadCommitted*.

```
[ServiceBehavior(TransactionIsolationLevel=IsolationLevel.ReadCommitted)]
public class BankingService: IBankingService
{
    [OperationBehavior(AutoEnlistTransaction=true, AutoCompleteTransaction=true)]
    bool DebitAccount(string account, decimal amount)
    {
        ...
    }
}
```

ValidateMustUnderstand: Validating Message Headers

Incoming request messages might contain headers that are not understood. By default, headers are validated and an error occurs if non-understood headers are found.

To disable message header validation, specify *ValidateMustUnderstand=false* in a *[ServiceBehavior]* attribute. The following code disables message header validation.

```
[ServiceBehavior(ValidateMustUnderstand=false)]
public class MyService: IMyService
{
    ...
}
```

The *[OperationBehavior]* Attribute

The *[OperationBehavior]* attribute specifies behaviors for a service operation. It is applied to the methods of a service implementation class. The attribute is optional and does not need to be specified when you are using default behaviors.

```
[ServiceBehavior(TransactionIsolationLevel=IsolationLevel.ReadCommitted)]
public class BankingService: IBankingService
{
    [OperationBehavior(AutoEnlistTransaction=true, AutoCompleteTransaction=true)]
    bool DebitAccount(string account, decimal amount)
    {
        ...
    }
    ...
}
```

The following parameters can be specified for the *[OperationBehavior]* attribute:

- *AutoEnlistTransaction (bool)*   Controls whether the service operation must run within a transaction. A value of *true* means a transaction is required. The default is *true*.

- *AutoCompleteTransaction (bool)*   Controls whether the transaction is completed automatically when the service operation finishes executing if the service operation is participating in a transaction. A value of *true* means the transaction is completed unless an unhandled exception occurs. The default is *false*.

- *Impersonate (bool)*   Controls whether identity impersonation takes place. The default is *false*. For more information about this parameter, see Chapter 8.

- *ReleaseInstance (ReleaseInstanceMode)*   Can be used to recycle a service instance before and/or after the service operation executes. Possible values are *None, BeforeCall, After-Call,* and *BeforeAndAfterCall.* The default is *None,* which lets the service's instance mode determine when instances are created or destroyed.

- *RoleProviderName (string)*   Specifies a Microsoft ASP.NET role provider. It is used to map users to roles in a custom implementation of security roles. For more information about this parameter, see Chapter 8.

- *SetThreadPrincipal (bool)*   Controls whether the *Thread.CurrentPrincipal* property is set to reflect the current caller before the service operation executes. The default is *true,* which permits authorization using the .NET Framework's *[PrincipalPermission]* attribute. For more information about this parameter, see Chapter 8.

AutoEnlistTransaction and *AutoCompleteTransaction*: Working with Transactions

The *AutoEnlistTransaction* parameter, when set to *true,* ensures that the service operation runs in the context of a transaction. If a transaction is flowed from the client, the service operation participates in that transaction. If the client does not flow a transaction, a new transaction is created for the service operation.

A client can flow a transaction to a service only if the binding in use permits transaction flow. For information on how to enable transaction flow, see Chapter 4.

The *AutoCompleteTransaction* parameter, when set to *true*, commits the transaction when the service operation finishes executing. If an unhandled exception occurs, the transaction is aborted.

The following code shows a service operation method performing work in the scope of a transaction.

```
[OperationBehavior(AutoEnlistTransaction=true,AutoCompleteTransaction=true)]
public void Debit(string accountNo, decimal amount)
{
    SqlConnection conn = new SqlConnection(ConnectionString);
    conn.Open();
    SqlCommand command = conn.CreateCommand();
    command.CommandText = "INSERT INTO Account " +
        "(TransactionID,TransactionType,Account,Amount) VALUES
        ('" + transactionId + "','DEBIT','" + accountNo + "'," + amount + ");";
    command.ExecuteNonQuery();
    conn.Close();
}
```

ReleaseInstance: Recycling Instances

Developers control the lifetime of service type instances primarily by using the *[Service-Behavior]* attribute's *InstanceMode* parameter and the *[OperationContract]* attribute's *IsInitiating* and *IsTerminating* parameters. When you're working with transactions, you might want a finer degree of control. The *ReleaseInstance* property allows a service operation to force recycling of the service instance. This can be useful to force cleanup of data in the service instance from previous calls.

The *ReleaseBeforeCall* value for *ReleaseInstance* recycles the service instance before the service operation executes. The *ReleaseAfterCall* value recycles the service instance after the service operation executes. The *ReleaseBeforeAndAfterCall* combines both behaviors. The following service operation recycles its service instance before and after each call.

```
[OperationBehavior(
    AutoEnlistTransaction=true,
    AutoCompleteTransaction=true,
    ReleaseInstance=ReleaseInstanceMode.BeforeAndAfterCall)]
Customer MergeCustomerRecords(Customer customer1, Customer customer2)
{
    ...
}
```

Error Handling in Service Operations

As in any managed code, errors can cause exceptions to be raised. A service operation can catch exceptions with *try-catch* blocks. In a *catch* handler, the code can handle the exception or elect to report it to the client. An exception must be converted to a SOAP fault to be sent to the client.

Reporting Errors with Faults and Fault Contracts

Faults are created with the *Fault<T>* class. An object containing information about the error is specified as a generic argument to the *Fault* class. The object can be as simple as a string or as elaborate as a custom class, as long as it is serializable. The object can also be an exception class. The following code shows a service operation catching a *DivideByZeroException* and creating a fault from the exception.

```
public int Divide(int n1, int n2)
{
    try
    {
        return n1 / n2;
    }
    catch (DivideByZeroException e)
    {
        throw new Fault<DivideByZeroException>(e);
    }
}
```

The constructor to *Fault<T>* has variations that accept a reason and an error code, allowing additional information to be specified beyond what is in the fault type object. The following code creates a fault from a *Customer* object and adds a reason for the error.

```
throw new Fault<Customer>(customer, "This customer is on hold.");
```

A client can't determine a fault's type unless it is defined in a **fault contract**. A fault contract is part of the service contract. The *[FaultContract]* attribute specifies a fault type that can be reported by a service operation. The following service contract defines several types of faults for a service operation.

```
[ServiceContract]
public interface MyService
{
    [OperationContract]
    [FaultContract(typeof(Order))]
    [FaultContract(typeof(Customer))]
    void SubmitOrder(Customer, Order);
}
```

If a fault is thrown that is not covered by a fault contract, the client receives the fault as an *UnknownFault*.

Providing a Custom Error Handler with *IErrorHandler*

A service can be involved in deciding how a fault is generated and whether it is reported back to the client through a custom error handler. To provide a custom error handler, the service type must implement the *IErrorHandler* interface and implement the *ProvideFault* and *Handle-Error* methods.

The *ProvideFault* method can specify the fault message sent in the event of an error. The arguments are an exception, a fault, and an action string. The *ProvideFault* method can set the *fault* parameter to a custom fault to control how the error is reported. If the *fault* parameter is set to *null*, no error is reported. The following code creates a custom fault using the *ProvideFault* method.

```
public void ProvideFault(Exception error, ref MessageFault fault, ref string faultAction)
{
    FaultCode code = new FaultCode("TravelServiceError", "uuid://www.adventureworks.com/
        TravelServiceError");
    FaultReason reason = new FaultReason(new FaultReasonText(
        "We're sorry. An error has occurred processing your reservation."));
    fault = MessageFault.CreateFault(code, reason, "WCQ735");
}
```

When an error occurs, the *HandleError* method allows custom behavior, such as logging the error or shutting down the affected application. *HandleError* returns *true* if other implementations of *IErrorHandler* should not be called, or *false* to permit further processing. The following code logs an error to the event log using a *HandleError* method.

```
public bool HandleError(Exception error, MessageFault fault)
{
    EventLog eventLog = new EventLog("Application");
    eventLog.Source = "TravelService";
    eventLog.WriteEntry("A reservation could not processed", EventLogEntryType.Error);
    eventLog.Close();
    return true;
}
```

Specifying Behaviors in Configuration File Settings

You can specify the throttling and error-reporting service behaviors in configuration file settings. Service behaviors are specified in a *<behavior>* element of a service configuration file, and *<behavior>* elements are contained in a *<behaviors>* element.

```
<behaviors>
    <behavior configurationName="NormalLoad" >
        <throttling maxConnections="10" />
    </behavior>
</behaviors>
```

You give a name to a *<behavior>* element by using a *configurationName* attribute. The *<service>* element that defines a service and its endpoints can reference a behavior by specifying its configuration name in a *behaviorConfiguration* attribute. In the following configuration file, the service definition for *LibraryService* references a behavior named *LibraryServiceBehavior*, which specifies error-handling behavior.

```xml
<?xml version="1.0" encoding="utf-8" ?>
<configuration xmlns="http://schemas.microsoft.com/.NetConfiguration/v2.0">
   <system.serviceModel>
      <services>
         <service
             serviceType="ProgrammingIndigo.LibraryService"
             behaviorConfiguration="LibraryServiceBehavior">
            <endpoint address=""
                      bindingSectionName="wsProfileBinding"
                      bindingConfiguration="Binding1"
                      contractType="Microsoft.ServiceModel.Samples.ILibrary " />
         </service>
      </services>

      <bindings>
         <wsProfileBinding>
            <binding configurationName="Binding1" />
         </wsProfileBinding>
      </bindings>

      <behaviors>
         <behavior
             configurationName="LibraryServiceBehavior"
             returnUnknownExceptionsAsFaults="True" >
         </behavior>
      </behaviors>

   </system.serviceModel>

   <system.web>
      <compilation debug="true" />
   </system.web>

</configuration>
```

Specifying Throttling Behavior in Configuration Files

Throttling sets limits on the amount of work a service can accept. Limits can be set on the number of concurrent calls, connections, instances, and pending operations.

To specify throttling controls, you include a *<throttling>* element, which is contained within a *<behavior>* element. Specify one or more of the following attributes in the *<throttling>* element:

- To set the maximum number of concurrent calls, specify the *maxConcurrentCalls* attribute.

- To set the maximum number of connections, specify the *maxConnections* attribute.

■ To set the maximum number of instances, specify the *maxInstances* attribute.

■ To set the maximum number of pending operations, specify the *maxPendingOperations* attribute.

The following behavior uses throttling to limit concurrent calls, connections, instances, and pending operations.

```
<behavior configurationName="NormalLoad">
    <throttling maxConcurrentCalls="10"
                maxConnections="3"
                maxInstances="3"
                maxPendingOperations="100" />
</behavior>
```

Specifying Exception-Handling Behavior in Configuration Files

To automatically pass unhandled exceptions to a client as faults, you can use the *return-UnknownExceptionsAsFaults* service behavior. To enable returning unknown exceptions as faults, include a *returnUnknownExceptionsAsFaults* attribute, which is contained within a *<behavior>* element. Set the attribute to *true* to enable automatic reporting of exceptions as faults.

```
<behaviors>
    <behavior
        configurationName="MyBehavior"
        returnUnknownExceptionsAsFaults="True" >
    </behavior>
</behaviors>
```

Controlling Metadata-Publishing Behavior in Configuration Files

By default, metadata-publishing features are enabled for any IIS-hosted service and for any self-hosted service with an HTTP base address. To control metadata publishing, include a *<metadataPublishing>* element within a *<behavior>* element. There are three metadata-publishing properties you can enable or disable through attributes:

■ *enableGetWsdl*: If *true*, this property causes a service to respond to an HTTP *GET* request for the service address with av*?wsdl* suffix.

■ *enableHelpPage*: If *true*, this property causes a help page to be displayed when the service is accessed by a browser.

■ *enableMetadataExchange*: If *true*, this property exposes a Metadata Exchange (MEX) endpoint for the service.

The following behavior settings disable all three properties.

```
<behaviors>
    <behavior
        configurationName="CalculatorServiceBehavior">
```

```
        <metadataPublishing enableGetWsdl="false"
            enableHelpPage="false"
            enableMetadataExchange="false" />
    </behavior>
</behaviors>
```

Streaming Content

Services can stream data to or from clients. Normally, messages are buffered, which means they have to fully arrive before they can be accessed. With streaming, the data in a message can be accessed while it is still being delivered. A service operation can accept a *Stream* object as a parameter or return a *Stream* object as a result.

The following service operation returns a series of Fibonacci numbers as a stream.

```
public Stream Fibonacci(int iterations)
{
    Console.Write("Fibonacci(" + iterations + "): ");
    double n1 = 1;
    double n2 = 1;
    MemoryStream stream = new MemoryStream();
    double[] sequence = new double[iterations];
    XmlFormatter formatter = new XmlFormatter();

    for (int i = 0; i < iterations; i++)
    {
        Console.Write(n1 + "  ");
        sequence[i] = n1;
        double next = n1 + n2;
        n1 = n2;
        n2 = next;
    }
    formatter.Serialize(stream, sequence);
    Console.WriteLine("Returning stream");
    stream.Seek(0, SeekOrigin.Begin);
    return stream;
}
```

To perform streaming, you must use a binding that supports streaming. The binding's configuration must set the *TransferMode* property to *Streaming* to enable streaming. For information on standard bindings that support streaming, see Chapter 4.

Obtaining Runtime Information

A service operation can retrieve a great deal of information about the service and its operating environment at runtime. The first step in getting at this information is to obtain an operation context by using the *OperationContext* class.

Obtaining a Duplex Callback

In a duplex contract, a service must be able to communicate back to the client. The operation context contains a *GetCallbackChannel<T>* method for this purpose. The callback returned is a proxy object that allows the service to invoke operations on the client. The following service operation code obtains a client callback and invokes an operation on the client.

```
public void MyServiceOperation()
{
    ISampleClientContract callback = OperationContext.Current.GetCallbackChannel
        <ISampleClientContract>();
    callback.Say("Hello, client!");
}
```

For examples of duplex communication, see Chapters 6, 14, and 15.

Obtaining an Operation Context

To obtain an operation context, use the static *Current* method of the *OperationContext* class. Using an operation context, you can access information about the service host, service description, and security context. The following service operation obtains its operation context.

```
public void MyServiceOperation()
{
    OperationContext operationContext = OperationContext.Current;
    ...
}
```

Accessing Your Service Description

You can get to the service description for your service using the *Description* property of an *OperationContext*. The description is a *ServiceDescription* object. The following service operation obtains its service description.

```
public void MyServiceOperation()
{
    OperationContext operationContext = OperationContext.Current;
    ServiceDescription serviceDescription = operationContext.Description;
    ...
}
```

Enumerating Service Endpoints

A service can discover its endpoints using its service description. To enumerate endpoints, access the *Endpoints* property of a *ServiceDescription*, which is a collection of *ServiceEndpoint* objects. *ServiceEndpoint* has *Address*, *Binding*, and *Contract* properties for accessing each area of the endpoint. The following code obtains and displays the address, binding name, and contract name of the service's endpoints.

```
ServiceHost<SampleService> host = (ServiceHost<SampleService>)OperationContext.Current.Host;
ServiceDescription desc = host.Description;
foreach (ServiceEndpoint endpoint in desc.Endpoints)
{
    Console.WriteLine(endpoint.Address);
    Console.WriteLine(endpoint.Binding.Name);
    Console.WriteLine(endpoint.Contract.Name);
}
```

Accessing Your Security Context

You can obtain a service operation's security context from its operation context. The *ServiceSecurityContext* property of *OperationContext* is a *ServiceSecurityContext* object. The following service operation obtains its security context and displays the current Windows identity name.

```
public void MyServiceOperation()
{
    ServiceSecurityContext securityContext =
        OperationContext.Current.ServiceSecurityContext;
    Console.WriteLine(securityContext.WindowsIdentity.Name);
    ...
}
```

Programming Exercise: Travel Service

In this programming exercise, we will create a service and client for a travel service. The service will accept multiple flight, car rental, and hotel reservations from a client and then return an ordered itinerary. The service will be hosted in IIS, which eliminates the need to write hosting code. The client will be a console application.

The service must maintain a session for each client to remember reservation information between calls to service operations. *PrivateSession* instancing will provide the session capability. The *WSProfile* binding will be used. *WSProfile* supports sessions, but it is necessary to explicitly enable reliable sessions in the binding configuration.

This exercise has 10 development steps:

1. Create the service program.

2. Create the .svc file.

3. Create a configuration file for the service.

4. Build the service.

5. Create a virtual directory for the service.

6. Test the service with a browser.

7. Create the client.

8.   Generate proxy code for the client.

9.   Create a configuration file for the client.

10.   Build the client.

Step 1: Create the Service Program

We'll now create the service program. This will compile to a DLL library assembly. Launch your development environment and create a new C# console application project named *service*. Enter the code in Listing 7-5.

To perform these tasks using Microsoft Visual Studio:

1.   Select New, Project from the File menu. Under Project Type, select Windows under Visual C#. Under Templates, select Class Library. In the Name box, type **service**, in the Location box, type any path you want, and in the Solution Name box, type **travel**. Click OK to generate and open the new project.

2.   Replace the generated code in Program.cs with the code shown in Listing 7-5.

Your service project will need to reference System.ServiceModel.dll and System.Runtime.Serialization.dll.

To perform these tasks using Visual Studio:

1.   Right-click References in the Solution Explorer window, and then select Add Reference.

2.   In the Add Reference dialog box, on the .NET tab, select System.ServiceModel.dll. Click OK. Repeat the procedure for System.Runtime.Serialization.dll.

Listing 7-5   Travel Service: Program.cs

```
using System;
using System.Collections;
using System.ServiceModel;
using System.Runtime.Serialization;

namespace ProgrammingIndigo
{
    [ServiceContract]
    public interface ITravel
    {
        [OperationContract]
        void ReserveFlight(string date, int flightNumber, string origin, string
            destination);
        [OperationContract]
        void ReserveCar(string date, string location, string vehicle, int days);
        [OperationContract]
        void ReserveHotel(string date, string location, int days);
        [OperationContract]
        string GetItinerary();
```

```
}

public class Flight
{
    public string Date;
    public long JulianDate;
    public int FlightNumber;
    public string Origin;
    public string Destination;
}

public class Car
{
    public string Date;
    public long JulianDate;
    public string Location;
    public string Vehicle;
    public int Days;
}

public class Hotel
{
    public string Date;
    public long JulianDate;
    public string Location;
    public int Days;
}

[ServiceBehavior(InstanceMode=InstanceMode.PrivateSession)]
public class TravelService : ITravel
{
    long startDate = 0;
    long endDate = 0;

    ArrayList flights = new ArrayList();
    ArrayList cars = new ArrayList();
    ArrayList hotels = new ArrayList();

    // Convert a Gregorian date to a Julian-style numbered date.

    public long DateToJulian(string gregorianDate)
    {
        DateTime dt = DateTime.Parse(gregorianDate);
        DateTime originOfTime = new DateTime(2000, 1, 1);
        return dt.Subtract(originOfTime).Days;
    }

    // Make a flight reservation.

    public void ReserveFlight(string date, int flightNumber, string origin,
        string destination)
    {
        Flight flight = new Flight();
        flight.Date = date;
        flight.JulianDate = DateToJulian(date);
        if (startDate == 0 || flight.JulianDate < startDate)
```

```
            startDate = flight.JulianDate;
        if (endDate == 0 || flight.JulianDate > endDate)
            endDate = flight.JulianDate;
        flight.FlightNumber = flightNumber;
        flight.Origin = origin;
        flight.Destination = destination;
        flights.Add(flight);
    }

    // Make a car rental reservation.

    public void ReserveCar(string date, string location, string vehicle, int days)
    {
        Car car = new Car();
        car.Date = date;
        car.JulianDate = DateToJulian(date);
        if (startDate == 0 || car.JulianDate < startDate)
            startDate = car.JulianDate;
        if (endDate == 0 || car.JulianDate > endDate)
            endDate = car.JulianDate;
        car.Location = location;
        car.Vehicle = vehicle;
        car.Days = days;
        cars.Add(car);
    }

    // Make a hotel reservation.

    public void ReserveHotel(string date, string location, int days)
    {
        Hotel hotel = new Hotel();
        hotel.Date = date;
        hotel.JulianDate = DateToJulian(date);
        if (startDate == 0 || hotel.JulianDate < startDate)
            startDate = hotel.JulianDate;
        if (endDate == 0 || hotel.JulianDate > endDate)
            endDate = hotel.JulianDate;
        hotel.Location = location;
        hotel.Days = days;
        hotels.Add(hotel);
    }

    // Return a travel itinerary (multi-line string).

    public string GetItinerary()
    {
        string itinerary = "Itinerary\n---------\n";
        for (long travelDate = startDate; travelDate <= endDate; travelDate++)
        {
            bool firstItem = true;

            //List flights for travel date.
            foreach (Flight flight in flights)
            {
                if (flight.JulianDate == travelDate)
```

```
            {
                if (firstItem)
                    itinerary += "TRAVEL DATE: " + flight.Date + "\n\n";
                firstItem = false;
                itinerary += "AIR TRAVEL\n";
                itinerary += "    Jul Date " + flight.JulianDate + "\n";
                itinerary += "    Flight " + flight.FlightNumber + "\n";
                itinerary += "    Origin " + flight.Origin + "\n";
                itinerary += "    Dest   " + flight.Destination + "\n";
                itinerary += "\n";
            }
        }


        //List car rentals for travel date.
        foreach (Car car in cars)
        {
            if (car.JulianDate == travelDate)
            {
                if (firstItem)
                    itinerary += "TRAVEL DATE: " + car.Date + "\n\n";
                firstItem = false;
                itinerary += "CAR RENTAL\n";
                itinerary += "    Jul Date " + car.JulianDate + "\n";
                itinerary += "    Location " + car.Location + "\n";
                itinerary += "    Vehicle  " + car.Vehicle + "\n";
                itinerary += "    Days     " + car.Days + "\n";
                itinerary += "\n";
            }
        }


        //List hotel stays for travel date.
        foreach (Hotel hotel in hotels)
        {
            if (hotel.JulianDate == travelDate)
            {
                if (firstItem)
                    itinerary += "TRAVEL DATE: " + hotel.Date + "\n\n";
                firstItem = false;
                itinerary += "HOTEL STAY\n";
                itinerary += "    Jul Date " + hotel.JulianDate + "\n";
                itinerary += "    Location " + hotel.Location + "\n";
                itinerary += "    Days     " + hotel.Days + "\n";
                itinerary += "\n";
            }
        }
    }
    return itinerary;
    }

    }
}
```

Step 2: Create the .svc File

An .svc file is needed to identify the Indigo service to IIS. Using an editor or development environment, create a text file named Service.svc. Enter the code shown in Listing 7-6.

To perform these tasks using Visual Studio:

1. Right-click the service project and select Add, New Item.

2. Select Text File, and then click Add. Rename the text file Service.svc. Enter the code in Listing 7-6 into Service.svc.

Listing 7-6   Travel Service: Service.svc

```
<%@Service language=c# Debug="true" class="ProgrammingIndigo.TravelService" %>
<%@Assembly Name="service" %>
```

Step 3: Create a Configuration File for the Service

A Web.config file is needed to specify endpoints and bindings for the service. Using an editor or development environment, create a text file with the code shown in Listing 7-7. Save the code under the name Web.config in the same folder where the service program and .svc file are located.

To perform these tasks using Visual Studio:

1. Right-click the service project, and then select Add, New Item. Select Application Configuration File, and then click Add. Name the file Web.config.

2. Enter the code in Listing 7-7 into Web.config.

Listing 7-7   Travel Service: Web.config

```
<?xml version="1.0" encoding="utf-8" ?>
<configuration xmlns="http://schemas.microsoft.com/.NetConfiguration/v2.0">
    <system.serviceModel>
        <services>
            <service
                serviceType="ProgrammingIndigo.TravelService">
                <endpoint
                    address=""
                    bindingSectionName="wsProfileBinding"
                    bindingConfiguration="SessionBinding"
                    contractType="ProgrammingIndigo.ITravel" />
            </service>
        </services>

        <bindings>
            <wsProfileBinding>
                <binding
                    configurationName="SessionBinding"
```

```
                        reliableSessionEnabled="true" />
            </wsProfileBinding>
        </bindings>

    </system.serviceModel>
    <system.web>
        <compilation debug="true" />
    </system.web>
</configuration>
```

Step 4: Build the Service

Build the service program to create Service.dll. Resolve any typographical errors.

In Visual Studio, select Build Solution from the Build menu to generate Service.dll.

Step 5: Create a Virtual Directory for the Service

Like ASP.NET applications, services hosted in IIS reside in virtual directories. Follow this procedure to set up a virtual directory for the service:

1. Create a folder on your computer named travel.

2. From the Start menu, launch Control Panel. Select Administrative Tools, Internet Information Services. Navigate to Web Sites, Default Web Sites. Right-click and select New, Virtual Directory. Specify the name **travel**, and then associate it with the travel folder created in step 1. Before exiting IIS Manager, check step 3.

3. While in IIS, navigate to Web Sites, Default Web Sites. The travel folder should be listed. Right-click it, and then select Properties.

4. On the Directory Security tab, click Edit to open the Authentication Methods dialog box. Anonymous Access should be selected; if it is not, select it. Close all dialog boxes by clicking OK, and then close IIS.

5. Copy the Service.svc and Web.config files to the travel folder. Underneath travel, create a bin subdirectory, and then copy Service.dll into it. You should have the following directory-file structure:

```
\travel
    service.svc
    web.config
    \bin
        service.dll
```

Step 6: Test the Service with a Browser

Before going on to the client, we want to test that the service can be accessed. Launch Internet Explorer. On the address bar, specify the URL *http://localhost/travel/service.svc*, and then press ENTER. If the resulting page does not list any errors, proceed to step 7. If there are problems, check the following:

- If the page returned by the browser describes compilation errors, check the code entered in the preceding steps. The compilation error display should highlight the offending code.

- If the resulting page describes HTTP errors, make sure your system has IIS enabled. You should be able to access *http://localhost* in a browser without receiving an error. If IIS seems to be properly enabled, review the virtual directory setup in the prior steps. If this also fails, look for clues under Control Panel, Administrative Tools; check the event log; or try an IISRESET.

The service is now ready. Next we need a client program to access it.

Step 7: Create the Client

Create the client program. Launch your development environment, and then create a new C# console application project named *client*. Enter the code in Listing 7-8.

To perform these tasks using Visual Studio:

1. Select New, Project from the File menu. Under Project Type, select Windows under Visual C#. Under Templates, select Console Application. In the Name box, type **client**, in the Location box, type any path you want, and in the Solution Name box, type **travel**. Click OK to generate and open the new project.

2. Replace the generated code in Program.cs with the code shown in Listing 7-8.

Your client project will need to reference System.ServiceModel.dll.

In Visual Studio, right-click References in the Solution Explorer window, and then select Add Reference. In the Add Reference dialog box, on the .NET tab, select System.ServiceModel.dll, and then click OK.

Build the client to create Client.exe.

Listing 7-8   Travel Client: Program.cs

```csharp
using System;
using System.ServiceModel;

namespace ProgrammingIndigo
{
    class Client
    {
        static void Main(string[] args)
        {
            // Create a proxy.
            Console.WriteLine("Creating proxy to service");
            using (TravelProxy proxy = new TravelProxy("TravelEndpoint"))
```

```
        {
            Console.WriteLine("Reserving flights");
            proxy.ReserveFlight("12/15/2005", 106, "JFK", "LAX");
            proxy.ReserveFlight("12/18/2005", 107, "LAX", "JFK");

            Console.WriteLine("Reserving car");
            proxy.ReserveCar("12/15/2005", "LAX", "compact", 4);

            Console.WriteLine("Reserving hotel stays");
            proxy.ReserveHotel("12/16/2005", "SAN", 1);
            proxy.ReserveHotel("12/15/2005", "LAX", 2);

            Console.WriteLine("Retrieving itinerary");
            Console.WriteLine(proxy.GetItinerary());
            proxy.Close();
        }

        Console.WriteLine();
        Console.WriteLine("Press ENTER to end");
        Console.ReadLine();
    }
  }
}
```

Step 8: Generate Proxy Code for the Client

We will now generate client proxy code by accessing the service's MEX endpoint with the Svcutil tool. From a command window, change the directory to the location where your client project and source files reside. Run the following Svcutil command:

```
svcutil http://localhost/travel/service.svc /out:proxy.cs
```

The file Proxy.cs is generated, containing the service contract and a proxy class for accessing the service. It should match the code that is downloadable from the Web.

Add Proxy.cs to your client project. In Visual Studio, right-click the project in the Solution Explorer window, and then select Add, Existing Item. Select Proxy.cs from the File Open dialog box, and then click OK. Proxy.cs is added to the client project.

Step 9: Create a Configuration File for the Client

A Client.exe.config file is needed to specify the service endpoint and binding to use. Using an editor or development environment, create a text file with the code shown in Listing 7-9. Save the code under the name Client.exe.config.

To perform these tasks using Visual Studio:

1. Right-click the service project, and then select Add, New Item. Select Application Configuration File, and then click Add. Name the file App.config. (It will be copied to client.exe.config at build time.)

2. Enter the code in Listing 7-9 into App.config.

Listing 7-9   Travel Client: App.config

```xml
<?xml version="1.0" encoding="utf-8" ?>
<configuration xmlns="http://schemas.microsoft.com/.NetConfiguration/v2.0">
    <system.serviceModel>
        <client>
            <endpoint
                configurationName="TravelEndpoint"
                address="http://localhost/travel/service.svc"
                bindingSectionName="wsProfileBinding"
                bindingConfiguration="SessionBinding"
                contractType="ITravel" />
        </client>

        <bindings>
            <wsProfileBinding>
                <binding
                    configurationName="SessionBinding"
                    reliableSessionEnabled="true" />
            </wsProfileBinding>
        </bindings>
    </system.serviceModel>
</configuration>
```

Step 10: Build the Client

Build the client program to make Client.exe. Resolve any typographical errors.

In Visual Studio, select Build Solution from the Build menu to generate Client.exe.

Deployment

We're now ready to try things out. Run the client from your development environment or from a command line. You should see output like that shown in Figure 7-6. There's no need to launch the service; services hosted in IIS activate when they are accessed. If the program fails, make sure you've properly carried out each of the preceding steps.

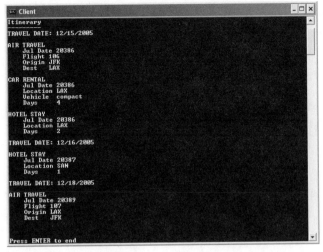

Figure 7-6   Travel client

Press ENTER on the client to shut it down. Congratulations on successfully completing the travel service and client!

Understanding the Service Code

The service is hosted in IIS. There is no hosting code in the service program. The service is defined by the file Service.svc in the virtual directory, shown earlier in Listing 7-6. The directives in Service.svc indicate that the service class is *ProgrammingIndigo.TravelService*, found in the assembly named service (Service.dll, which resides in the bin directory underneath the virtual directory).

```
<%@Service language=c# Debug="true" class="ProgrammingIndigo.TravelService" %>
<%@Assembly Name="service" %>
```

The service code, shown in Listing 7-5, contains the service contract and implementation code. The service contract is defined in the interface *ITravel* and contains two-way (request-reply) service operations.

```
[ServiceContract]
public interface ITravel
{
    [OperationContract]
    void ReserveFlight(string date, int flightNumber, string origin, string destination);
    [OperationContract]
    void ReserveCar(string date, string location, string vehicle, int days);
    [OperationContract]
    void ReserveHotel(string date, string location, int days);
    [OperationContract]
    string GetItinerary();
}
```

The service code also defines *Flight*, *Car*, and *Hotel* classes. These classes will hold reservation information during a client session.

```
public class Flight
{
    public string Date;
    public long JulianDate;
    public int FlightNumber;
    public string Origin;
    public string Destination;
}
```

The *TravelService* class, shown in Listing 7-5, implements the service. The service accepts and stores individual flight, car rental, and hotel reservations in any order and can then generate an ordered travel itinerary. A *[ServiceBehavior]* attribute specifies *PrivateSession* instancing so there will be a unique instance of the *TravelService* class for each client connection. The class contains several *ArrayList* variables for storing flight, car rental, and hotel reservations. There are also two *long* variables, which will be used to track the starting and ending dates of a travel reservation. Dates will be represented internally as the number of days since January 1, 2000, so that they can be easily sorted. They are called Julian dates in the code. A *DateToJulian* function will be used to convert a Gregorian calendar date string to a numbered date that can be represented as a *long* integer.

```
[ServiceBehavior(InstanceMode=InstanceMode.PrivateSession)]
public class TravelService : ITravel
{
    long startDate = 0;
    long endDate = 0;

    ArrayList flights = new ArrayList();
    ArrayList cars = new ArrayList();
    ArrayList hotels = new ArrayList();

    // Convert a Gregorian date to a Julian date.

    public long DateToJulian(string gregorianDate)
    {
        DateTime dt = DateTime.Parse(gregorianDate);
        DateTime originOfTime = new DateTime(2000, 1, 1);
        return dt.Subtract(originOfTime).Days;
    }

    // Make a flight reservation.

    public void ReserveFlight(string date, int flightNumber, string origin, string
        destination)
    {
        ...
    }

    // Make a car rental reservation.
```

```
    public void ReserveCar(string date, string location, string vehicle, int days)
    {
        ...
    }

    // Make a hotel reservation.

    public void ReserveHotel(string date, string location, int days)
    {
        ...
    }

    // Return a travel itinerary (multi-line string).

    public string GetItinerary()
    {
        ...
    }
}
```

The implementation of each of the service operations for reserving flights, car rentals, and hotel stays is similar. A *Flight*, *Car*, or *Hotel* object is created and populated with the reservation information. The travel date is converted to a numbered date. The *startDate* and *endDate* variables are set to the earliest and latest dates encountered. The *Flight*, *Car*, or *Hotel* object is then added to the *flights*, *cars*, or *hotels* collection.

```
// Make a flight reservation.

public void ReserveFlight(string date, int flightNumber, string origin, string destination)
{
    Flight flight = new Flight();
    flight.Date = date;
    flight.JulianDate = DateToJulian(date);
    if (startDate == 0 || flight.JulianDate < startDate)
        startDate = flight.JulianDate;
    if (endDate == 0 || flight.JulianDate > endDate)
        endDate = flight.JulianDate;
    flight.FlightNumber = flightNumber;
    flight.Origin = origin;
    flight.Destination = destination;
    flights.Add(flight);
}
```

Once a client is finished making flight, car, and hotel reservations, it can request an ordered travel itinerary by calling the *GetItinerary* service operation. The itinerary is built in steps and returned as a multi-line string. To return the itinerary in date order, the service operation iterates through all travel dates from *startDate* to *endDate* in an outer loop. The reservations in the *flights*, *cars*, and *hotels* arrays are scanned using inner loops. Any matching reservations for the current travel date in the outer loop are added to the itinerary string. When the outer loop completes, the itinerary string is returned to the client.

```csharp
// Return a travel itinerary (multi-line string).

public string GetItinerary()
{
    string itinerary = "Itinerary\n---------\n";
    for (long travelDate = startDate; travelDate <= endDate; travelDate++)
    {
        bool firstItem = true;

        // List flights for travel date.
        foreach (Flight flight in flights)
        {
                if (flight.JulianDate == travelDate)
                {
                    if (firstItem)
                        itinerary += "TRAVEL DATE: " + flight.Date + "\n\n";
                    firstItem = false;
                    itinerary += "AIR TRAVEL\n";
                    itinerary += "    Jul Date " + flight.JulianDate + "\n";
                    itinerary += "    Flight " + flight.FlightNumber + "\n";
                    itinerary += "    Origin " + flight.Origin + "\n";
                    itinerary += "    Dest   " + flight.Destination + "\n";
                    itinerary += "\n";
                }
        }

        // List car rentals for travel date.
        foreach (Car car in cars)
        {
            if (car.JulianDate == travelDate)
            {
                if (firstItem)
                    itinerary += "TRAVEL DATE: " + car.Date + "\n\n";
                firstItem = false;
                itinerary += "CAR RENTAL\n";
                itinerary += "    Jul Date " + car.JulianDate + "\n";
                itinerary += "    Location " + car.Location + "\n";
                itinerary += "    Vehicle  " + car.Vehicle + "\n";
                itinerary += "    Days     " + car.Days + "\n";
                itinerary += "\n";
            }
        }

        // List hotel stays for travel date.
        foreach (Hotel hotel in hotels)
        {
            if (hotel.JulianDate == travelDate)
            {
                if (firstItem)
                    itinerary += "TRAVEL DATE: " + hotel.Date + "\n\n";
                firstItem = false;
                itinerary += "HOTEL STAY\n";
                itinerary += "    Jul Date " + hotel.JulianDate + "\n";
                itinerary += "    Location " + hotel.Location + "\n";
                itinerary += "    Days     " + hotel.Days + "\n";
```

```
                    itinerary += "\n";
                }
            }
        }
        return itinerary;
    }
}
```

The endpoint for the service and the binding it uses is defined in the service's configuration file, shown in Listing 7-7. The configuration file is named Web.config because the service is hosted in IIS. The endpoint definition specifies an empty address that will default to the IIS-hosted address. The actual endpoint address is *http://localhost/travel/service.svc* and is determined by the name of the machine, virtual directory, and .svc file. The endpoint definition specifies a *WSProfileBinding* standard binding and contract *ITravel*.

```
<services>
    <service
        serviceType="ProgrammingIndigo.TravelService">
        <endpoint
            address=""
            bindingSectionName="wsProfileBinding"
            bindingConfiguration="SessionBinding"
            contractType="ProgrammingIndigo.ITravel" />
    </service>
</services>
```

The *WSProfile* binding does not enable reliable sessions by default, so you must include a binding configuration to enable the feature. The binding configuration, named *SessionBinding*, enables reliable sessions.

```
<bindings>
    <wsProfileBinding>
        <binding
            configurationName="SessionBinding"
            reliableSessionEnabled="true" />
    </wsProfileBinding>
</bindings>
```

Understanding the Client Code

The client must agree with the service about address, binding, and contract; otherwise, communication will not be possible. Client proxy code was generated from the service using the Svcutil tool. The code generated includes both the service contract, *ITravel*, and a class for accessing the service, *TravelProxy*.

The client creates a proxy for the travel service by creating an instance of the generated *Travel-Proxy* class. The proxy is created in a *using* statement; when the *using* statement block exits, the proxy will be disposed.

```
using (TravelProxy proxy = new TravelProxy("TravelEndpoint"))
{
    ...
}
```

The client makes flight, car, and hotel reservations by calling service operations using the proxy.

```
Console.WriteLine("Reserving flights");
proxy.ReserveFlight("12/15/2005", 106, "JFK", "LAX");
proxy.ReserveFlight("12/18/2005", 107, "LAX", "JFK");

Console.WriteLine("Reserving car");
proxy.ReserveCar("12/15/2005", "LAX", "compact", 4);

Console.WriteLine("Reserving hotel stays");
proxy.ReserveHotel("12/16/2005", "SAN", 1);
proxy.ReserveHotel("12/15/2005", "LAX", 2);
```

After making reservations, the client retrieves a travel itinerary and closes the proxy.

```
Console.WriteLine("Retrieving itinerary");
Console.WriteLine(proxy.GetItinerary());
proxy.Close();
```

Summary

This chapter covered how to create services. Services contain contracts, service types, hosting code, and endpoint definitions. If the service is hosted by IIS, you do not have to write hosting code.

At runtime, services are represented by a *ServiceHost* object, which contains the service type. *ServiceHost* contains a collection of *ServiceSite* objects that associate a channel with an instance of the service type. An *OperationContext* object allows the code in a service operation to access its *ServiceHost*, *ServiceSite*, and other information, including a security context.

There are three types of services. Typed services have service operations that are similar to class methods. Untyped services only send or receive *Message* objects. Typed message services only send or receive custom messages.

Behaviors can be specified for service types. Behaviors include instancing, concurrency, throttling, error handling, transaction control, instance recycling, and identity impersonation.

Errors can be reported to clients as faults. Faults are created from serializable objects. Fault contracts specify the reportable fault types. A service can take control of error handling and reporting by implementing the *IErrorHandling* interface.

Chapter 8
Security

Love all, trust a few, do wrong to none.

—William Shakespeare

Distributed systems require extensive security. Parties must be able to identify each other and place limits on what others can do. Communication between parties should be protected against eavesdropping or tampering.

After completing this chapter, you will:

- Be familiar with the security features Indigo provides.
- Understand authentication, authorization, message confidentiality, and message integrity.

Understanding Security

Indigo provides a comprehensive set of features that secure the transfer of messages and secure access to resources. You can secure the transfer of messages using **transport security** or **SOAP security**. Transport security is provided by your choice of communication transport, such as HTTPS. SOAP security is provided at the SOAP message level and is independent of transport. Securing access to resources is achieved through a claims-based approach.

Indigo is secure by default. With the exception of the *BasicProfile* binding, the standard bindings have Microsoft Windows security enabled.

To talk meaningfully about security, we must define some key security terms.

- **Credential**   Information that provides proof of identity, such as a birth certificate or business license
- **Entity**   Something that possesses credentials, such as a person, an organization, or a machine
- **Resource**   Something an entity might want to access, such as a file, a database, a service, or an operation
- **Security token**   A representation of a credential that can be passed as part of a message

Indigo's security features include authentication, authorization, message confidentiality, and message integrity.

- **Authentication**   Requires an entity to present proof of identity
- **Authorization**   Confirms that an entity is entitled to access a resource
- **Message confidentiality**   Ensures that only the intended recipient of a message can see the message in its original form
- **Message integrity**   Ensures that a message is not tampered with in transit

> **Caution**   Indigo Beta 1 does not fully implement all of the security features planned for version 1. The object model for security presented in this chapter might change by version 1 in response to customer feedback.

Credentials and Identity

A credential provides proof of identity for an entity. An example of a credential held by a person is a driver's license. An example of a credential held by a company is a business license. A common credential in software is an account name and password.

Credentials contain **claims**. A claim is information about an entity, such as an account name or an e-mail address. Claims are certified by a trusted party called an **issuer**. An entity can present **proof of possession** to show that it is the party that supplied the claims.

There are many kinds of credentials, including username/password, X.509 certificates with private keys, Kerberos credentials, and Security Access Markup Language (SAML) tokens. Table 8-1 shows the credential types built into Indigo. When security information is communicated, credentials are represented as **security tokens**.

Table 8-1   Built-In Credential Types

Client	Service
None	None
Windows	Windows
X.509 certificates	X.509 certificates
Username/password	N/A

Authentication

Authentication allows a client or service to confirm whether the other party is who it claims to be. Authentication seeks to answer the question, "Are you who you say you are?"

Figure 8-1 illustrates authentication in the setting of an online banking service. Jay Adams attempts to access the service and is recognized as a bank customer. Mary Baker attempts to access the service and is also recognized as a bank customer. Scott Cooper is not recognized as a bank customer and is not permitted to access the service.

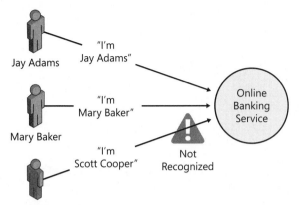

Figure 8-1   Authentication

The four types of authentication built into Indigo are:

- *Anonymous*   Performs no identification of the client and identifies the service using an X.509 certificate. All application messages between the client and the service are signed and encrypted by default.

- *Certificate*   Identifies the client and the service using X.509 certificates. All application messages between the client and the service are signed and encrypted by default.

- *Username*   Identifies the client using a username and password and identifies the service using an X.509 certificate. All application messages between the client and the service are signed and encrypted by default.

- *Windows*   Identifies the client and service using NTLM/Kerberos. All application messages between the client and the service are signed and encrypted by default.

Authorization

Authorization allows a service to determine whether an authenticated client should be allowed to access a service operation or resource. The purpose of authorization is to answer the question, "What are you allowed to do?"

It's important to understand the distinction between authentication and authorization because they are often confused. Authentication identifies a client but draws no conclusions about what the client is allowed to do. In contrast, authorization is concerned with allowing or withholding access to operations and resources based on what a client's claims entitle it to.

Figure 8-2 illustrates authorization in the setting of an online banking service. Jay Adams and Mary Baker are both recognized as bank customers and are authenticated, but only Jay Adams is authorized to access Jay Adams's bank account. If Mary Baker attempts to access Jay Adams's account, she is denied access to the resource. Jay Adams can access the account because he has been given permission to do so.

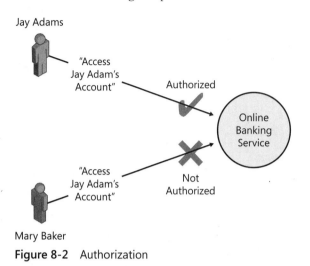

Figure 8-2 Authorization

Authorization can be user-based or role-based. In user-based authorization, a client is granted or denied access to a resource based on his identity. In role-based authorization, a client is granted or denied access to a resource based on what groups he belongs to. An example of user-based authorization is an airline allowing the use of an airline ticket only by the person it was issued for. An example of role-based authorization is a health club allowing any person who is a member to gain access to the facilities.

Message Integrity and Confidentiality

Message integrity prevents message tampering. When messages are sent, they are signed and encrypted using the sender's credential. The recipient can be satisfied about the fidelity of messages received because a tampered message will not be verified.

Message confidentiality prevents message contents from being visible to anyone but the intended recipient. Message bodies are encrypted with the recipient's credential when sent and decrypted when received. If messages pass through intermediaries, the intermediaries are blind to the message contents because the messages are still encrypted at that point.

Message integrity and confidentiality are automatic features. They are enabled by default on most of the standard bindings.

Secure Bindings

Bindings play a major role in enabling security features and specifying which security modes to use. With the exception of the *BasicProfile* binding, all of the standard bindings are secure.

Security is on by default, and Windows security is the default authentication mode. You can change or disable the authentication mode by configuring the binding. For more information on configuring bindings, see Chapter 4.

Programming Security

Security development tasks include specifying a security mode, protection level, authentication mode, and credentials; obtaining identity information; and specifying authorization controls.

Specifying a Security Mode

SecurityMode is the property that determines the type of security to apply. At the highest level, the type is either transport or WS-Security. To enable security features, you choose an appropriate binding and configure its security properties. Many of the standard bindings have a *SecurityMode* property, which determines the type of security to apply. The *BasicProfile* binding has no security in effect by default. All of the other standard bindings default to Windows authentication. The available security modes vary from one binding to another and are described in Chapter 4. Table 8-2 shows the default security mode for each of the standard bindings.

Table 8-2   Standard Binding Security Modes

Binding	Default Security Mode
BasicProfile	None
Integration	N/A
MsmqIntegration	N/A
NetProfileMsmq	N/A
NetProfileNamedPipe	*NamedPipeWithWindowsSecurity*
NetProfileTcp	*TcpWithWindowsSecurity*
NetProfileDualTcp	*WSSecurityOverTcp*
WSProfile	*WSSecurityOverHttp*
WSProfileDualHttp	*WSSecurityOverHttp*

The *SecurityMode* property can be set to any of the following values, if supported by the binding in use:

- *None*   Security is disabled.

- *HttpAuthentication*   HTTP authentication transport security. The specific authentication scheme is controlled by *HttpAuthentication.Scheme*.

- *BasicSecurityProfileMutualCertificate*   Basic Security Profile SOAP security with certificates used to authenticate both the client and the server.

- *Https*   HTTPS transport security. This security mode provides message integrity, confidentiality, and server authentication. There is no client authentication.

- *HttpsWithClientCertificate*   HTTPS transport security with an X.509 certificate on the client side. This security mode provides message integrity, confidentiality, and mutual authentication.

- *HttpAuthenticationOverHttps*   HTTP authentication over HTTPS transport security. This security mode provides message integrity, confidentiality, and server authentication. The exact authentication scheme is controlled by *HttpAuthentication.Scheme.*

- *BasicSecurityProfileCertificateOverHttps*   Basic Security Profile SOAP security with certificate over HTTPS transport security.

- *BasicSecurityProfileUsernameOverHttps*   Basic Security Profile SOAP security with Username authentication over HTTPS transport security.

- *WSSecurityOverHttp*   WS-Security SOAP security over HTTP. This security mode provides message integrity, confidentiality, and authentication. The exact authentication mode is controlled by *WSSecurity.AuthenticationMode.*

- *TcpWithWindowsSecurity*   Windows security over TCP. This security mode provides message integrity, confidentiality, and mutual authentication.

- *TcpWithSsl*   SSL security over TCP. This security mode provides message integrity, confidentiality, and server authentication. There is no client authentication.

- *WSSecurityOverTcp*   WS-Security SOAP security over TCP. This security mode provides message integrity, confidentiality, and authentication. The exact authentication mode is controlled by *WSSecurity.AuthenticationMode.*

Specifying a Security Mode in Code

When you create a binding in code using one of the standard binding classes, you specify a security mode by setting the *SecurityMode* property of the binding. Because the allowable security modes vary between bindings, each binding has a separate enumeration of the security modes. For example, the allowable security modes for the *BasicProfile* binding are contained in the *BasicProfileSecurityMode* enumeration. The following code shows a *BasicProfile* binding set to the Https security mode in the creation of an endpoint for service.

```
ServiceHost<IMyService> service = new ServiceHost<IMyService>();
Uri address = new Uri("http://localhost:8000/MyService/");
BasicProfileBinding binding = new BasicProfileBinding();
binding.SecurityMode = BasicProfileSecurityMode.Https;
service.AddEndpoint(typeof(IMyService), binding, address);
service.Open();
```

Specifying a Security Mode in Configuration File Settings

When you specify a binding in configuration file settings using one of the standard bindings, you specify a security mode by setting the *securityMode* attribute of the *<binding>* element in a binding configuration. The following code shows a binding configuration for a *WSProfile* binding, where the security mode is set to *WSSecurityOverHttp*.

```
<bindings>
    <wsProfileBinding>
        <binding configurationName="MyBinding"
                 securityMode="WSSecurityOverHttp">
            <wsSecurity authenticationMode="Certificate" />
        </binding>
    </wsProfileBinding>
</bindings>
```

Programming the Protection Level

The protection level determines the degree to which messages are protected during transfer. Bindings contain a *protectionLevel* property, which you can set to any of the following values. The default protection level is *EncryptAndSign*.

- *None* Messages are neither signed nor encrypted.
- *Sign* Messages are signed for integrity.
- *EncryptAndSign* Messages are encrypted for confidentiality and signed for integrity.

The following code shows a binding configuration that specifies a protection level.

```
<binding configurationName="Binding1"
         useSystemWebProxy="true"
         bypassProxyOnLocal="false"
         securityMode="WSSecurityOverHttp">
    <wsSecurity authenticationMode="Windows"
                protectionLevel="EncryptAndSign"
                useNegotiation="true"
                algorithmSuite="Default" />
</binding>
```

Programming Authentication

Many of the standard bindings support more than one authentication mode. When you use SOAP security, you specify the authentication mode by using the *WSSecurity.Authentication-Mode* property.

Specifying Anonymous Authentication

In Anonymous authentication, the server is authenticated using an X.509 certificate. The client is not authenticated, and no client-side certificate is required. The following client configuration code specifies Anonymous authentication for the *WSProfile* binding.

```
<bindings>
    <wsProfileBinding>
        <binding configurationName="MyBinding"
                securityMode="WSSecurityOverHttp">
            <wsSecurity authenticationMode="Anonymous" />
        </binding>
    </wsProfileBinding>
</bindings>
```

Specifying Certificate Authentication

In Certificate authentication, the client and server are both authenticated using X.509 certificates, and both require certificates. The following client configuration code specifies Certificate authentication for the *WSProfile* binding.

```
<bindings>
    <wsProfileBinding>
        <binding configurationName="MyBinding"
                securityMode="WSSecurityOverHttp">
            <wsSecurity authenticationMode="Certificate" />
        </binding>
    </wsProfileBinding>
</bindings>
```

Specifying Username Authentication

In Username authentication, clients are authenticated by username and password, and servers are authenticated using an X.509 certificate. All application messages between the client and the server are signed and encrypted. By default, the username and password are used to log on to a Microsoft Windows NT account. The following client configuration code specifies Username authentication for the *WSProfile* binding.

```
<bindings>
    <wsProfileBinding>
        <binding configurationName="MyBinding"
                securityMode="WSSecurityOverHttp">
            <wsSecurity authenticationMode="Username" />
        </binding>
    </wsProfileBinding>
</bindings>
```

In Username authentication, the client must specify a username and password for authentication. For details and an example, see the section titled "Specifying Client Username and Password Credentials" later in this chapter.

By default, Username authentication treats the username and password as a Windows account. You can also use another source for usernames and passwords, called a **membership provider**, as described in the next section.

Using the ASP.NET Membership Provider for Username Authentication

You can configure Username authentication to use the ASP.NET membership provider for verifying usernames and passwords. To select the ASP.NET membership provider, you must specify both ASP.NET configuration settings and Indigo configuration settings in the service's configuration file.

In the ASP.NET part of the service configuration file, you include a *<membership>* section and define a provider in the *<providers>* group with the name *AspNetSqlMembershipProvider* and the type *System.Web.Security.SqlMembershipProvider*, as shown here.

```
<!-- ASP.NET configuration settings -->
  <membership>
    <providers>
      <add name = "AspNetSqlMembershipProvider"
        type="System.Web.Security.SqlMembershipProvider..." .../>
    </providers>
  </membership>
```

In the Indigo part of the service configuration file, you include a *<serviceBehaviors>* section and specify a *<securityCredentials>* element that sets *userNameAuthenticationProviderName* to *AspNetSqlMembershipProvider*, as shown here.

```
<!-- Indigo configuration settings -->
<serviceBehaviors>
    <securityCredentials
        userNameAuthenticationProviderName="AspNetSqlMembershipProvider" />
</serviceBehaviors>
```

The ASP.NET membership provider contains two parts: a membership provider and a role provider. The membership provider is where usernames and passwords are stored, and the role provider is where roles for users are stored. To populate members and roles in the ASP.NET membership provider, follow these steps:

1. Create a virtual directory for an Indigo service using the Internet Information Services applet in Control Panel.

2. Access the ASP.NET Web administration tool by launching Microsoft Visual Studio and selecting ASP.NET Configuration from the Website Menu.

3. On the home page, click the Security link. The Security tab page loads.

4. Click the Use The Security Setup Wizard To Configure Security Step By Step link to start the Security Setup Wizard. Click Next.

5. On the Select Access Method page, select From The Internet to indicate Internet authentication. Click Next.

6. The next page should confirm that the access provider is *AspNetAccessProvider*. Click Next.

7. On the Define Roles page, select the Enable Roles For This Web Site option. Click Next.

8. On the Create New Role page, add an Administrator role. Click Next.

9. On the Create User page, add one or more users for the service. Click Next.

10. On the Add New Access Rules page, add an access rule to grant access to the administrator and a second access rule denying access to all users. Complete the wizard and return to the Security tab.

11. Select the Create Or Manage Roles link to assign roles to users.

12. A Web.config file is generated. If a Web.config file already exists, prior settings are merged with the new configuration settings.

Specifying Windows Authentication

In Windows authentication, the client and service use NTLM and Kerberos to pass credentials. The following client configuration code specifies Windows authentication for the *WSProfile* binding.

```
<bindings>
    <wsProfileBinding>
        <binding configurationName="MyBinding"
                securityMode="WSSecurityOverHttp">
            <wsSecurity authenticationMode="Windows" />
        </binding>
    </wsProfileBinding>
</bindings>
```

Specifying an Authentication Mode for Transport Security

When transport security is in use, you specify an authentication mode by using a binding's *HttpAuthentication.Scheme* property. The possible values for the authentication mode are:

■ *Anonymous*   Anonymous authentication. Clients are not required to identify themselves and are assigned to the Windows user account IUSR_*computername*.

■ *Basic*   Basic authentication. The client identifies itself with a Base64-encoded username and password.

■ *Digest*   Digest authentication. The client identifies itself with a username and password that have been hashed into a message digest. Digest authentication is resistant to interception and unauthorized use and can be used across firewalls and proxy servers.

- *IntegratedWindowsAuthentication* Integrated Windows authentication, which uses NTLM and Kerberos.

- *Negotiate* The service and client negotiate to determine the authentication scheme (Kerberos or NTLM).

- *None* No authentication.

- *Ntlm* NTLM authentication, also called Windows NT Challenge/Response.

Programming Impersonation

Impersonation allows a service to access resources on behalf of the caller. By default, clients are authenticated when they access a service, but the service does not take on the caller's identity. Impersonation allows the service to act as the caller.

Declarative Service Method Impersonation

To enable impersonation for a service method, you specify an *[OperationBehavior]* attribute for a method implementation of a service operation and set the *Impersonate* parameter to *true*, as shown here. This causes the service thread responding to the client's request to impersonate the caller while the method executes.

```
[OperationBehavior(Impersonate=true)]
public double Add(double n1, double n2)
{
    double result = n1 + n2;
    Console.WriteLine("Received Add({0},{1})", n1, n2);
    Console.WriteLine("Return: {0}", result);
    // The DisplayIdentityInformation is a utility function that
    // displays the caller's identity. You could make a system call
    // in the caller's context and ACLs are enforced
    // in the caller's context.
    DisplayIdentityInformation();
    return result;
}
```

Imperative Service Method Impersonation

You can enable impersonation for a service method in another way, by using code. You call *ServiceSecurityContext.Current.WindowsIdentity.Impersonate()* to make the service impersonate the caller. Enabling impersonation in code allows you to precisely control the scope of the impersonation. The following code controls the scope of impersonation with a *using* block.

```
public double Add(double n1, double n2)
{
    double result = n1 + n2;
    Console.WriteLine("No impersonation");
    DisplayIdentityInformation();
    using (ServiceSecurityContext.Current.WindowsIdentity.Impersonate())
    {
```

```
        Console.WriteLine("The caller is now being impersonated");
        DisplayIdentityInformation();
    }
    Console.WriteLine("The caller is no longer being impersonated");
    DisplayIdentityInformation();
    return result;
}

static void DisplayIdentityInformation()
{
    Console.WriteLine("Thread Identity: {0}", WindowsIdentity.GetCurrent().Name);
    Console.WriteLine("Thread Identity level: {0}",
        WindowsIdentity.GetCurrent().ImpersonationLevel);
    return;
}
```

Specifying the Client Impersonation Level

Clients control the degree to which a service can impersonate them by specifying an **impersonation level**. There are five impersonation levels a client can specify. The default is Identification. The *TokenImpersonationLevel* enumeration defines the impersonation levels.

- *None*   No authentication

- *Anonymous*   Anonymous authentication

- *Identification*   Identification only

- *Impersonation*   Identification and impersonation; can access resources on a local machine only

- *Delegation*   Identification and impersonation; can access resources on remote machines

> **Note**   Delegation is not available in the Indigo Beta 1 release.

To specify an impersonation level for a proxy, you call the *SetSspiSettings* method of the proxy's *ChannelFactory.Security* property (as shown here), specifying one of the five impersonation levels.

```
using (MyServiceProxy proxy = new MyServiceProxy("MyEndpoint"))
{
    proxy.ChannelFactory.Security.SetSspiSettings
        (TokenImpersonationLevel.Delegation);
    ...
}
```

Programming Authorization

You can control authorization by using Microsoft .NET permission facilities, which allow you to require a specific role or user for a service method.

Controlling Access Using the *[PrincipalPermission]* Attribute

You can use the *[PrincipalPermission]* attribute to authorize access to service operations. The parameters in this attribute specify the following:

■ *SecurityAction (SecurityAction)*   Specifies the security requirement. Possible values are *Assert, Demand, Deny, InheritanceDemand, LinkDemand, PermitOnly, RequestMinimum,* and *RequestOptional. SecurityAction.Demand* is a commonly specified value.

■ *Authenticated (boolean)*   A value of *true* requires that the client has been authenticated.

■ *Name (string)*   The account name. If *null* is specified, any account name is considered a match.

■ *Role (string)*   The account role, such as a Windows group name.

To require the client to be authenticated without regard to name or role, you specify *Authenticated=true*. The following service operation allows access from any client that has been authenticated.

```
[PrincipalPermissionAttribute(SecurityAction.Demand, Authenticated=true)]
public void SubmitExpenseReport(ExpenseReport report)
{
    ...
}
```

To limit access to a specific user, you specify the *Name* parameter and an account name as a value. For Windows authentication, you specify the account name in the form *domain\username*. The following service operation can be accessed only by a client who authenticates as user contoso\jeffsmith.

```
[PrincipalPermissionAttribute(SecurityAction.Demand, Name="contoso\\jeffsmith")]
public void SubmitExpenseReport(ExpenseReport report)
{
    ...
}
```

To limit access to a specific role, you specify the *Role* parameter and a role name as a value. For Windows authentication, you specify a group name, such as *"Administrators"*. The following service operation can be accessed only by clients who are Windows administrators.

```
[PrincipalPermission(SecurityAction.Demand, Role="Builtin\\Administrators")]
public void SubmitExpenseReport(ExpenseReport report)
{
    ...
}
```

For more information, see the documentation for the *PrincipalPermissionAttribute* class in the Microsoft .NET Framework documentation.

Specifying Credentials

Depending on the security mode in use, clients and/or servers might have to provide credentials identifying themselves or the systems they are accessing.

Specifying Client Username and Password Credentials

In Username authentication, a client must specify a username and password. A client proxy provides a *SetUserNamePassword* method for this purpose; it is accessible through its *ChannelFactory.Security* property. The following client code sets a username and password for Username authentication.

```
string username = "mydomain\\myuser";
string password = "My!Password";
using (CalculatorProxy proxy = new CalculatorProxy("CalculatorEndpoint"))
{
    proxy.ChannelFactory.Security.SetUserNamePassword(username, password);
    double value1 = 100.00D;
    double value2 = 15.99D;
    double result = proxy.Add(value1, value2);
    Console.WriteLine("Add({0},{1}) = {2}", value1, value2, result);
        ...
    proxy.Close();
}
```

The username and password should conform to the *username/password* scheme used by the service. By default, Username authentication maps to a Windows NT account on the service where a user account or machine account can be specified by the client.

Specifying Client X.509 Certificate Credentials

A client specifies its security credentials using a *<channelSecurityCredentials>* element in a *<behavior>* section of its configuration file. The *clientX509Certificate* element specifies a client-side X.509 certificate. This element specifies *storeLocation* and *storeName* attributes to indicate the store for the certificate and *x509FindType* and *findValue* attributes to indicate how to locate the certificate in the store. The following code specifies a certificate security credential.

```
<behaviors>
    <behavior configurationName="MyClientBehavior">
        <channelSecurityCredentials x509AuthenticationRevocationMode="NoCheck">
            <clientX509Certificate findValue="client.com" storeLocation="CurrentUser"
                storeName="My" x509FindType="FindBySubjectName" />
        </channelSecurityCredentials>
    </behavior>
</behaviors>
```

Specifying Service X.509 Certificate Credentials

A service specifies its security credentials using a *<serviceSecurityCredentials>* element in a *<behavior>* section of its configuration file. The *serviceX509Certificate* element specifies a server-side X.509 certificate. This element specifies *storeLocation* and *storeName* attributes to indicate the store for the certificate and *x509FindType* and *findValue* attributes to indicate how to locate the certificate in the store. The following code specifies a certificate security credential.

```
<behaviors>
    <behavior
        configurationName="MyServiceBehavior"
        returnUnknownExceptionsAsFaults="true" >
        <serviceSecurityCredentials x509AuthenticationMapToWindows="false">
            <serviceX509Certificate findValue="localhost" storeLocation=
                "LocalMachine" storeName="My" x509FindType="FindBySubjectName" />
        </serviceSecurityCredentials>
    </behavior>
</behaviors>
```

Declaring the Service Identity with a Username Principal

A client can declare the identity of a service it is accessing by specifying a user principal name. An endpoint definition includes an *AddressProperties* property. *AddressProperties* contains *identityType* and *identityData* properties. To declare a user principal name, set *identityType* to *Upn* and the *identityData* property to the user's identity in *domain\account* form. The following code from a client configuration file specifies a user principal name of "mydomain\jeff-smith".

```
<client>
    <endpoint
        configurationName="DefaultEndpoint"
        address="http://localhost:8000/MyService/"
        bindingSectionName="wsProfileBinding"
        bindingConfiguration="MyBinding"
        contractType="ISampleService" >
        <addressProperties identityData="mydomain\\jeffsmith"
            identityType="Upn"/>
    </endpoint>
</client>
```

Declaring the Service Identity with a System Name Principal

A client can declare the identity of a service it is accessing by specifying a system principal name. Like a user principal name, a system principal name is specified in the *AddressProperties* property of an endpoint definition. *AddressProperties* contains *identityType* and *identityData* properties. To declare a system principal name, you set *identityType* to *Spn* and the *identityData* property to the user's identity in *domain\account* form. The following code from a client configuration file specifies a system principal name of "mycomputer\network service".

```
<client>
    <endpoint
        configurationName="DefaultEndpoint"
        address="http://localhost:8000/MyService/"
        bindingSectionName="wsProfileBinding"
        bindingConfiguration="MyBinding"
        contractType="ISampleService" >
        <addressProperties identityData="mycomputer\\network service"
            identityType="Spn"/>
    </endpoint>
</client>
```

Determining Client Identity in a Service

A service can determine the identity of a client using the Thread class's *CurrentPrincipal* property. *Thread.CurrentPrincipal.Identity.Name* contains the name of the caller. You must specify the *System.Security.Permissions* and *System.Threading* namespaces to access *CurrentPrincipal*. The following code shows a service operation obtaining the identity of its caller.

```
using System.Security.Permissions;
using System.Threading;
    ...
public string WhoAmI()
{
        string identity = Thread.CurrentPrincipal.Identity.Name;
        return identity;
}
```

Determining Whether a Client Is Anonymous

An anonymous client presents no identity for authorization. A service operation can check whether it is being called by an anonymous client by testing the Boolean *IsAnonymous* property of the service operation's *ServiceSecurityContext* object. A service operation can obtain its security context from *ServiceSecurityContext.Current* or *OperationContext.Current.ServiceSecurityContext*. The following code shows a service operation checking for an anonymous client.

```
bool isAnonymous = ServiceSecurityContext.Current.IsAnonymous
public double Add(double n1, double n2)
{
    // Incoming claims can be accessed on the SecurityContext.
    bool isAnonymous = ServiceSecurityContext.Current.IsAnonymous;
    if (isAnonymous)
        throw new Fault<string>("Sorry, anonymous users may not perform this operation");
    double result = n1 + n2;
    return result;
}
```

Programming Exercise: Voting Service

In this programming exercise, we will create a service and client for a voting service. Clients can connect to the service and vote, but they must be authenticated and cannot vote more than once. The service provides two endpoints and two service contracts, one for voters and one for administrators. Administrators can reset the voting and tally the voting results.

The service defines endpoints that specify the *WSSecurtityOverHttp* security mode. A client must provide a *username/password* combination recognized by the service. The service must authenticate using an X.509 certificate.

To vote, a voter client connects to the service on its primary endpoint and calls *StartVoting*, which creates a new service instance for the voter. The voter can then call *Vote* repeatedly to place a vote for President, Vice President, Treasurer, and Secretary. When finished casting votes, the client calls *FinishVoting* and closes its proxy.

To reset the vote count or retrieve a list of voting totals, a client connects to the service on its administrative endpoint and calls *ResetVoting* to reset the vote counts or *TallyVotes* to retrieve the current candidates and numbers of votes received.

This programming exercise uses security in four ways:

- The service authenticates itself to clients using an X.509 certificate.
- Clients authenticate themselves to the service using username/password authentication.
- The service obtains the identity of clients to prevent anyone from voting more than once.
- The service allows clients to perform administrative functions only if they are members of the Administrators group on the service machine.

This exercise has 12 development steps:

1. Create the service program.
2. Create the .svc file.
3. Create a configuration file for the service.
4. Build the service.
5. Create a certificate for the service.
6. Create a virtual directory and deploy the service.
7. Test the service with a browser.
8. Create the client.
9. Generate proxy code for the client.
10. Create a configuration file for the client.

11. Change usernames and passwords for your domain.

12. Build the client.

Step 1: Create the Service Program

We'll now create the service program, which will compile to a DLL library assembly. Launch your development environment and create a new C# console application project named *service*. Enter the code in Listing 8-1 that follows.

To perform these tasks using Visual Studio:

1. Select New, Project from the File menu. Under Project Type, select Windows under Microsoft Visual C#. Under Templates, select Class Library. In the Name box, type **service**, in the Location box, type any path you want, and in the Solution Name box, type **voting**.

2. Click OK to generate and open the new project.

Replace the generated code in Program.cs with the code shown in Listing 8-1.

Your service project will need to reference System.ServiceModel.dll, System.Runtime.Serialization.dll, and System.Security.Authorization.dll.

To perform these tasks using Visual Studio:

1. Right-click References in the Solution Explorer window and select Add Reference.

2. In the Add Reference dialog box, on the .NET tab, select System.ServiceModel.dll and click OK.

3. Repeat the procedure for System.Runtime.Serialization.dll and System.Security.Authorization.dll.

Listing 8-1   Voting Service: Program.cs

```
using System;
using System.Collections;
using System.Collections.Generic;
using System.ServiceModel;
using System.Security.Permissions;
using System.Runtime.Serialization;
using System.Threading;

namespace ProgrammingIndigo
{
    // Service contract for voters.

    [ServiceContract(Session=true)]
    public interface IVote
    {
        [OperationContract(IsInitiating=true, IsTerminating=false)]
        [FaultContract(typeof(UnauthorizedAccessException))]
```

```
        void StartVoting();
        [OperationContract(IsInitiating=false, IsTerminating=false)]
        [FaultContract(typeof(UnauthorizedAccessException))]
        void Vote(string office, string candidate);
        [OperationContract(IsInitiating = false, IsTerminating=true)]
        void FinishVoting();
        [OperationContract(IsInitiating = true, IsTerminating = true)]
        string TallyVotes();
    }

    // Service contract for administrators.

    [ServiceContract(Session = true)]
    public interface IVoteAdministrator
    {
        [OperationContract]
        void ResetVoting();
        [OperationContract]
        string TallyVotes();
    }

    // Class for storing a set of votes by one voter.

    public class Vote
    {
        public string Voter;
        public string PresidentVote = null;
        public string VicePresidentVote = null;
        public string TreasurerVote = null;
        public string SecretaryVote = null;
    }

    // Class for tracking candidates that have been voted for and their vote count.

    public class CandidateVote
    {
        public string Office;
        public string Candidate;
        public int Votes;
    }

    // Service implementation class.
    // This class implements both the IVote and IVoteAdministrator service contracts.

    [ServiceBehavior(InstanceMode=InstanceMode.PrivateSession)]
    public class VotingService : IVote, IVoteAdministrator
    {
        // List of votes cast.
        static List<Vote> votes = new List<Vote>();

        // List of candidate vote counts.
        static List<CandidateVote> candidateVotes = new List<CandidateVote>();

        // Current vote.
        Vote vote;
```

```
// Current identity.
string identity;

// StartVoting - begin a voter client session.

[PrincipalPermissionAttribute(SecurityAction.Demand, Authenticated = true)]
public void StartVoting()
{
    // Check that this user has not already cast a vote.

    identity = Thread.CurrentPrincipal.Identity.Name;

    foreach(Vote castVote in votes)
    {
        if (castVote.Voter==identity)
        {
            throw new Fault<UnauthorizedAccessException>(
                new UnauthorizedAccessException("Voter '" + identity
                + "' has already voted and may not vote again"));
        }
    }

    // Create a new Vote object for the user.

    vote = new Vote();
    vote.Voter = identity;
}


// Vote - cast a vote for an office.

public void Vote(string office, string candidate)
{
    switch (office)
    {
        case "president":
            if (vote.PresidentVote != null)
                throw new Fault<InvalidOperationException>
                (new InvalidOperationException(
                    "Can't vote more than once for the same office"));
            vote.PresidentVote = candidate;
            break;
        case "vice president":
            if (vote.VicePresidentVote != null)
                throw new Fault<InvalidOperationException>
                (new InvalidOperationException(
                    "Can't vote more than once for the same office"));
            vote.VicePresidentVote = candidate;
            break;
        case "treasurer":
            if (vote.TreasurerVote != null)
                throw new Fault<InvalidOperationException>
                (new InvalidOperationException(
                    "Can't vote more than once for the same office"));
            vote.TreasurerVote = candidate;
```

```
                break;
        case "secretary":
            if (vote.SecretaryVote != null)
                throw new Fault<InvalidOperationException>
                (new InvalidOperationException(
                    "Can't vote more than once for the same office"));
            vote.SecretaryVote = candidate;
            break;
    }

    // Update candidate vote count.

    foreach (CandidateVote candidateVote in candidateVotes)
    {
        if (candidateVote.Office == office && candidateVote.Candidate ==
            candidate)
        {
            candidateVote.Votes++;
            return;
        }
    }
    CandidateVote newCandidateVote = new CandidateVote();
    newCandidateVote.Office = office;
    newCandidateVote.Candidate = candidate;
    newCandidateVote.Votes = 1;
    candidateVotes.Add(newCandidateVote);
}

// Finish voting - store votes cast and terminate voter client session.

public void FinishVoting()
{
    votes.Add(vote);
}

// Reset voting - administrative function: clear out past memory of voting.

[PrincipalPermissionAttribute(SecurityAction.Demand,
    Role="Builtin\\Administrators")]
public void ResetVoting()
{
    votes.Clear();
    candidateVotes.Clear();
}

// TallyVotes - administrative function:
// reports back candidates and vote counts.

[PrincipalPermissionAttribute(SecurityAction.Demand, Role =
    "Builtin\\Administrators")]
public string TallyVotes()
{
    string results = "";
```

```
                foreach (CandidateVote candidateVote in candidateVotes)
                {
                    results += candidateVote.Candidate + " received " +
                        candidateVote.Votes + " votes for " + candidateVote.Office + "\r\n";
                }
                return results;
            }
        }
    }
```

Step 2: Create the .svc File

An .svc file is needed to identify the Indigo service to IIS. Using an editor or development environment, create a text file named Service.svc. Enter the code shown in Listing 8-2.

To perform these tasks using Visual Studio:

1. Right-click the service project and select Add, New Item. Select Text File and click Add.

2. Rename the text file Service.svc.

3. Enter the code in Listing 8-2 into Service.svc.

Listing 8-2   Voting Service: Service.svc

```
<%@Service language=c# Debug="true" class="ProgrammingIndigo.VotingService" %>
<%@Assembly Name="service" %>
```

Step 3: Create a Configuration File for the Service

A Web.config file is needed to specify endpoints and bindings for the service. Using an editor or development environment, create a text file with the code shown in Listing 8-3. Save the code under the name Web.config in the same folder in which the service program and .svc file are located.

To perform these tasks using Visual Studio:

1. Right-click the service project and select Add, New Item. Select Application Configuration File and click Add. Name the file Web.config.

2. Enter the code in Listing 8-3 into Web.config.

Listing 8-3   Voting Service: Web.config

```
<?xml version="1.0" encoding="utf-8" ?>
<configuration xmlns="http://schemas.microsoft.com/.NetConfiguration/v2.0">
    <system.serviceModel>
        <services>
            <service
                serviceType="ProgrammingIndigo.VotingService"
                behaviorConfiguration="VoteBehavior">
```

```xml
            <endpoint
                address=""
                bindingSectionName="wsProfileBinding"
                bindingConfiguration="VoteBinding"
                contractType="ProgrammingIndigo.IVote" />
            <endpoint
                address="admin"
                bindingSectionName="wsProfileBinding"
                bindingConfiguration="VoteBinding"
                contractType="ProgrammingIndigo.IVoteAdministrator" />
        </service>
    </services>

    <bindings>
        <wsProfileBinding>
        <!--
        This configuration defines the SecurityMode as WSSecurityOverHttp and
        the WSSecurity.AuthenticationMode to Username.
        By default, Username authentication will attempt to authenticate the
        provided username as a Windows machine or domain account.
        -->
            <binding configurationName="VoteBinding"
                securityMode="WSSecurityOverHttp"
                reliableSessionEnabled="true">
                <wsSecurity authenticationMode="Username" />
            </binding>
        </wsProfileBinding>
    </bindings>

    <behaviors>
        <behavior
            configurationName="VoteBehavior"
            returnUnknownExceptionsAsFaults="True" >
            <!--
            The serviceSecurityCredentials behavior allows one to define a
            service certificate.
            A service certificate is used by a client to authenticate the service
            and provide message protection.
            This configuration references the "localhost" certificate installed
            during the setup instructions.
            -->
            <serviceSecurityCredentials>
                <serviceX509Certificate findValue="localhost"
                    storeLocation="LocalMachine" storeName="My"
                    x509FindType="FindBySubjectName" />
            </serviceSecurityCredentials>
        </behavior>
    </behaviors>

</system.serviceModel>
<system.web>
    <compilation debug="true" />
</system.web>
</configuration>
```

Step 4: Build the Service

Build the service program to create Service.dll. Resolve any typographical errors.

To perform the task using Visual Studio, select Build Solution from the Build menu to generate Service.dll.

Step 5: Create a Certificate for the Service

The service needs to be set up for certificate authentication. The batch file Setup.bat, shown in Listing 8-4, creates a certificate for the service named localhost. Run the Setup.bat file. You can later reverse the effects of Setup.bat by running Cleanup.bat.

Listing 8-4   Voting Service: Setup.bat

```
echo off
set SERVER_NAME=%1
if (%SERVER_NAME%)==() set SERVER_NAME=localhost

echo ************
echo cleaning up the certificates from previous run
echo ************
certmgr -del -r CurrentUser -s TrustedPeople -c -n %SERVER_NAME%
certmgr -del -r LocalMachine -s My -c -n %SERVER_NAME%


echo ************
echo Server cert setup starting
echo %SERVER_NAME%
echo ************
echo making server cert
echo ************
makecert.exe -sr LocalMachine -ss MY -a sha1 -n CN=%SERVER_NAME% -sky exchange -pe
echo ************
echo copying server cert to client's CurrentUser store
echo ************
certmgr.exe -add -r LocalMachine -s My -c -n %SERVER_NAME%
    -r CurrentUser -s TrustedPeople


echo ************
echo setting privileges on server certificates
echo ************
for /F "delims=" %%i in ('"%WINFXSDK%\bin\FindPrivateKey.exe" My LocalMachine
    -n CN^=localhost -a') do set PRIVATE_KEY_FILE=%%i
set WP_ACCOUNT=NT AUTHORITY\NETWORK SERVICE
(ver | findstr "5.1") && set WP_ACCOUNT=%COMPUTERNAME%\ASPNET
echo Y|cacls.exe "%PRIVATE_KEY_FILE%" /E /G "%WP_ACCOUNT%":R
iisreset
```

Step 6: Create a Virtual Directory and Deploy the Service

Like ASP.NET applications, services hosted in IIS reside in virtual directories. Follow this procedure to set up a virtual directory for the service.

1. Create a folder on your computer named voting.

2. From the Start menu, launch Control Panel. Select Administrative Tools, Internet Information Services. Navigate to Web Sites, Default Web Sites. Right-click and select New, Virtual Directory. Specify the name **voting** and associate it with the voting folder you just created. Before exiting IIS Manager, check step 3.

3. Navigate to Web Sites, Default Web Sites. The voting directory should be listed. Right-click Voting and select Properties. On the Directory Security tab, click Edit.

4. In the Authentication Methods dialog box, Anonymous Access should be selected; if it is not, select it. Close all dialog boxes by clicking OK, and close IIS.

5. Copy the Service.svc and Web.config files to the voting folder. Underneath voting, create a bin subdirectory and copy Service.dll into it. You should have the following directory-file structure.

```
\voting
    service.svc
    web.config
    \bin
        service.dll
```

Step 7: Test the Service with a Browser

Before going on to the client, we want to test that the service can be accessed. Launch Internet Explorer. On the address bar, specify the URL *http://localhost/voting/service.svc* and press ENTER. If the resulting page does not list any errors, proceed to step 8. If there are problems, check the following.

- If the page returned by the browser describes compilation errors, check the code entered in the preceding steps. The compilation error display should highlight the offending code.

- If the resulting page describes HTTP errors, make sure your system has IIS and ASP.NET installed and enabled. You should be able to access *http://localhost* in a browser without receiving an error. If IIS and ASP.NET seem to be properly enabled, review the virtual directory setup in the prior steps. If this also fails, look for clues in Control Panel, Administrative Tools; check the Event Log; or try an IISRESET.

The service is now ready. Next we need a client program to access it.

Step 8: Create the Client

Create the client program. Launch your development environment, and create a new C# console application project named *client*. Enter the code in Listing 8-5.

To perform these tasks using Visual Studio:

1. Select New, Project from the File menu. Under Project Type, select Windows under Visual C#. Under Templates, select Console Application. In the Name box, type **client**, in the Location box, specify any path you want, and in the Solution Name box, type **voting**. Click OK to generate and open the new project.

2. Replace the generated code in Program.cs with the code shown in Listing 8-5.

Your client project will need to reference System.ServiceModel.dll and System.Runtime.Serialization.dll.

To perform these tasks using Visual Studio:

1. Right-click References in the Solution Explorer window and select Add Reference.

2. In the Add Reference dialog box, on the .NET tab, select System.ServiceModel.dll and click OK.

3. Repeat these steps for System.Runtime.Serialization.dll .

4. Build the client to create Client.exe.

Listing 8-5   Voting Client: Program.cs

```csharp
using System;
using System.ServiceModel;

namespace ProgrammingIndigo
{
    class Client
    {
        static void Main(string[] args)
        {
            // Admin: reset vote counts.

            VoteAdministratorProxy adminProxy =
                new VoteAdministratorProxy("VotingAdministratorEndpoint");

            string username = "MyDomain\\MyAdministrator";
            string password = "MyPassword";
            adminProxy.ChannelFactory.Security.SetUserNamePassword
                (username, password);

            Console.WriteLine("Admin: resetting voting");
            adminProxy.ResetVoting();

            // Voter #1.
```

```
Console.WriteLine("Voter 1: casting votes");
using (VoteProxy proxy = new VoteProxy("VotingEndpoint"))
{
    username = "MyDomain\\MyVoter1";
    password = "MyPassword1";
    proxy.ChannelFactory.Security.SetUserNamePassword(username, password);

    proxy.StartVoting();
    proxy.Vote("president", "Jeff Smith");
    proxy.Vote("vice president", "Mary Baker");
    proxy.Vote("treasurer", "Kim Akers");
    proxy.Vote("secretary", "Scott Cooper");
    proxy.FinishVoting();

    proxy.Close();
}

// Voter #2.

Console.WriteLine("Voter 2: casting votes");
using (VoteProxy proxy = new VoteProxy("VotingEndpoint"))
{
    username = "MyDomain\\MyVoter2";
    password = "MyPassword2";
    proxy.ChannelFactory.Security.SetUserNamePassword(username,
        password);

    proxy.StartVoting();
    proxy.Vote("president", "Jeff Smith");
    proxy.Vote("vice president", "Chris Gray");
    proxy.Vote("treasurer", "Brian Johnson");
    proxy.Vote("secretary", "Scott Cooper");
    proxy.FinishVoting();

    proxy.Close();
}

// Voter #3.

Console.WriteLine("Voter 3: casting votes");
using (VoteProxy proxy = new VoteProxy("VotingEndpoint"))
{
    username = "MyDomain\\MyVoter3";
    password = "MyPassword3";
    proxy.ChannelFactory.Security.SetUserNamePassword(username, password);

    proxy.StartVoting();
    proxy.Vote("president", "Jeff Smith");
    proxy.Vote("vice president", "Chris Gray");
    proxy.Vote("treasurer", "Katie Jordan");
    proxy.Vote("secretary", "Scott Cooper");
    proxy.FinishVoting();

    proxy.Close();
}
```

```
        // Admin: tally votes.

        Console.WriteLine("Admin: tallying votes");
        Console.WriteLine(adminProxy.TallyVotes());
        adminProxy.Close();

        Console.WriteLine();
        Console.WriteLine("Press ENTER to end");
        Console.ReadLine();
      }
    }
  }
```

Step 9: Generate Proxy Code for the Client

We will now generate client proxy code by accessing the service's MEX endpoint with the Svcutil tool. From a command window, change the directory to the location where your client project and source files reside. Run the following Svcutil command:

```
svcutil http://localhost/voting/service.svc /out:proxy.cs
```

The file Proxy.cs will be generated, containing the service contract and a proxy class for accessing the service. It should match the code that is downloadable from the Web.

Add Proxy.cs to your client project.

To perform the task using Visual Studio:

   1.   Right-click the project in the Solution Explorer window and select Add, Existing Item.

   2.   In the File Open dialog box, select Proxy.cs and click OK. Proxy.cs is added to the client project.

Step 10: Create a Configuration File for the Client

A Client.exe.config file is needed to specify the service endpoint and binding to use. Using an editor or development environment, create a text file with the code shown in Listing 8-6. Save the code under the name Client.exe.config.

To perform these tasks using Visual Studio:

   1.   Right-click the service project and select Add, New Item. Select Application Configuration File and click Add. Name the file App.config. (It will be copied to Client.exe.config at build time.)

   2.   Enter the code in Listing 8-6 into App.config.

Listing 8-6 Voting Client: App.config

```xml
<?xml version="1.0" encoding="utf-8" ?>
<configuration xmlns="http://schemas.microsoft.com/.NetConfiguration/v2.0">
    <system.serviceModel>
        <client>
            <endpoint configurationName="VotingEndpoint"
                     address="http://localhost/voting/service.svc"
                     bindingSectionName="wsProfileBinding"
                     bindingConfiguration="VoteBinding"
                     contractType="IVote" />
            <endpoint configurationName="VotingAdministratorEndpoint"
                     address="http://localhost/voting/service.svc/admin"
                     bindingSectionName="wsProfileBinding"
                     bindingConfiguration="VoteBinding"
                     contractType="IVoteAdministrator" />
        </client>

        <bindings>
            <wsProfileBinding>
            <!--
            This configuration defines the SecurityMode as WSSecurityOverHttp and
            the WSSecurity.AuthenticationMode to Username.
            By default, Username authentication will attempt to authenticate
            the provided username as a Windows machine or domain account.
            -->
                <binding configurationName="VoteBinding"
                    securityMode="WSSecurityOverHttp"
                    reliableSessionEnabled="true">
                    <wsSecurity authenticationMode="Username" />
                </binding>
            </wsProfileBinding>
        </bindings>
    </system.serviceModel>
</configuration>
```

Step 11: Change Usernames and Passwords for Your Domain

Next you modify the client code to specify usernames and passwords that will work for your network. Replace the "MyDomain\\MyUser" and "MyPassword" names and passwords with real ones. The administrator proxy's identity should reflect an Administrator. The three voter identities should each be different, and they do not have to be Administrators.

Step 12: Build the Client

Build the client program to create Client.exe. Resolve any typographical errors.

To complete the task using Visual Studio, select Build Solution from the Build menu to generate Client.exe.

Deployment

We're now ready to try things out. Run the client from your development environment or from a command line. You should see output like that shown in Figure 8-3. There's no need to launch the service; services hosted in IIS activate automatically when they are accessed. If the program fails, double-check that you've properly carried out each of the preceding steps.

Figure 8-3   Voting client

Press ENTER on the client to shut it down. Congratulations on successfully completing the voting service and client!

Understanding the Service Code

The service is hosted in IIS. There is no hosting code in the service program. The service is defined by the file Service.svc in the virtual directory, shown earlier in Listing 8-2. The directives in Service.svc indicate that the service class is *ProgrammingIndigo.VotingService*, found in the assembly named service (Service.dll, which resides in the bin directory underneath the virtual directory).

```
<%@Service language=c# Debug="true" class="ProgrammingIndigo.VotingService" %>
<%@Assembly Name="service" %>
```

The service code, shown earlier in Listing 8-1, contains the service contract and implementation code. The service contracts are defined in the interfaces *IVote* and *IVoteAdministrator*.

```
// Service contract for voters.

[ServiceContract(Session=true)]
public interface IVote
{
    [OperationContract(IsInitiating=true, IsTerminating=false)]
    [FaultContract(typeof(UnauthorizedAccessException))]
    void StartVoting();
    [OperationContract(IsInitiating=false, IsTerminating=false)]
    [FaultContract(typeof(UnauthorizedAccessException))]
    void Vote(string office, string candidate);
```

```
    [OperationContract(IsInitiating = false, IsTerminating=true)]
    void FinishVoting();
    [OperationContract(IsInitiating = true, IsTerminating = true)]
    string TallyVotes();
}

// Service contract for administrators.

[ServiceContract(Session = true)]
public interface IVoteAdministrator
{
    [OperationContract]
    void ResetVoting();
    [OperationContract]
    string TallyVotes();
}
```

The service code also defines *Vote* and *CandidateVote* classes. Each time a voter completes a voting session, a *Vote* object is created as a record of the vote. For each candidate in each position, a *CandidateVote* record is kept to count the number of votes.

```
// Class for storing a set of votes by one voter.

public class Vote
{
    public string Voter;
    public string PresidentVote = null;
    public string VicePresidentVote = null;
    public string TreasurerVote = null;
    public string SecretaryVote = null;
}

// Class for tracking candidates that have been voted for and their vote count.

public class CandidateVote
{
    public string Office;
    public string Candidate;
    public int Votes;
}
```

The *VotingService* class, shown in Listing 8-1, implements the service. The service allows voters to start a session with *StartVoting*, call *Vote* multiple times, and end the session with *Finish-Voting*. The service also provides administrative functionality. Administrators can reset the vote count or request a list of votes for each candidate.

The service uses the *[PrincipalPermissionAttribute]* attribute to limit access to some service operations. The service obtains the caller's identity using *Thread.CurrentPrincipal.Identity.Name*.

```
[PrincipalPermissionAttribute(SecurityAction.Demand, Authenticated = true)]
public void StartVoting()
{
```

```
// Check that this user has not already cast a vote.

identity = Thread.CurrentPrincipal.Identity.Name;
```

The endpoints for the service and their bindings are defined in the service's configuration file, shown earlier in Listing 8-3. The configuration file is named Web.config because the service is hosted in IIS. The first endpoint definition for the *IVote* contract specifies an empty address, which will default to the IIS-hosted address, *http://<machine-name>/voting/service.svc.* The second endpoint definition for the *IVoteAdministrator* contract specifies an address of "admin," which makes its address *http://<machine-name>/voting/service.svc/admin.* Both endpoint definitions specify a *WSProfile* standard binding.

```
<services>
    <service
        serviceType="ProgrammingIndigo.VotingService"
        behaviorConfiguration="VoteBehavior">
        <endpoint
            address=""
            bindingSectionName="wsProfileBinding"
            bindingConfiguration="VoteBinding"
            contractType="ProgrammingIndigo.IVote" />
        <endpoint
            address="admin"
            bindingSectionName="wsProfileBinding"
            bindingConfiguration="VoteBinding"
            contractType="ProgrammingIndigo.IVoteAdministrator" />
    </service>
</services>
```

The *WSProfile* binding does not enable reliable sessions by default, so you must include a binding configuration to enable the feature. The binding configuration is named *VoteBinding* and enables reliable sessions. The binding configuration also specifies security details. The security mode is set to *WSSecurityOverHttp,* and the authentication mode is set to *Username.* Both endpoints use this binding configuration.

```
<bindings>
    <wsProfileBinding>
        <!--
        This configuration defines the SecurityMode as WSSecurityOverHttp and
        the WSSecurity.AuthenticationMode to Username.
        By default, Username authentication will attempt to authenticate the provided
        username as a Windows machine or domain account.
        -->
        <binding configurationName="VoteBinding"
            securityMode="WSSecurityOverHttp"
            reliableSessionEnabled="true">
            <wsSecurity authenticationMode="Username" />
        </binding>
    </wsProfileBinding>
</bindings>
```

Understanding the Client Code

The client configuration file was shown earlier in Listing 8-6. The client configuration settings define endpoints and binding configurations that match the service. Client proxy code was generated from the service using the Svcutil tool. The code generated includes both of the service contracts, *IVote* and *IVoteAdministrator*, and two classes for accessing the service, *VoteProxy* and *VoteAdministratorProxy*.

The client is written to act as an administrator and three separate voters. For brevity, the logic for these four clients has been combined into a single client program. The client opens a proxy connection to the service's administration endpoint, specifies an administrator identity, and calls *ResetVoting* to reset the vote count.

```
VoteAdministratorProxy adminProxy = new
    VoteAdministratorProxy("VotingAdministratorEndpoint");

string username = "MyDomain\\MyAdministrator";
string password = "MyPassword";
adminProxy.ChannelFactory.Security.SetUserNamePassword(username, password);
```

Next the client opens a proxy connection to the service's voting endpoint and votes, by calling *StartVoting*, making four calls to *Vote* and finally calling *FinishVoting*. This is repeated for a second and third voter, using different identities. If any attempt is made to vote twice with the same identity, the service throws a fault.

```
// Voter #1.

Console.WriteLine("Voter 1: casting votes");
using (VoteProxy proxy = new VoteProxy("VotingEndpoint"))
{
    username = "MyDomain\\MyVoter1";
    password = "MyPassword1";
    proxy.ChannelFactory.Security.SetUserNamePassword(username, password);

    proxy.StartVoting();
    proxy.Vote("president", "Jeff Smith");
    proxy.Vote("vice president", "Mary Baker");
    proxy.Vote("treasurer", "Kim Akers");
    proxy.Vote("secretary", "Scott Cooper");
    proxy.FinishVoting();

    proxy.Close();
}
```

After the voting, the administrator proxy calls *TallyVotes* to obtain the results, which are displayed to the console output.

```
// Admin: tally votes.

Console.WriteLine("Admin: tallying votes");
Console.WriteLine(adminProxy.TallyVotes());
adminProxy.Close();
```

Summary

This chapter covered security. Indigo provides features for securing messages as they are transferred and for securing access to resources. Authentication determines who a client is. Authorization determines what a client is allowed to do. Message integrity guards against tampering with messages. Message confidentiality prevents intermediaries from understanding a message's content. This chapter also explained the concepts of credentials, entities, and resources.

We covered programming tasks such as setting a binding's security mode and specifying an authentication mode. For transport security, an HTTP authentication scheme is selected. For SOAP security, the authentication types are *Anonymous*, *Certificate*, *Username*, and *Windows*.

We created a voting service in our programming exercise to illustrate security with Certificate server authentication, Username client authentication, obtaining a client's identity to restrict repeated voting attempts, and use of *PrincipalPermission* attributes to limit authorization.

Chapter 9
Interoperability and Integration

Alone we can do so little; together we can do so much.

—Helen Keller

Indigo programs can communicate with other platforms and other technologies. This chapter is about Indigo's features for interoperability and integration.

After completing this chapter, you will:

- Understand the factors affecting interoperability and how to control them.
- Know how to make Indigo interoperate with an ASMX client or ASMX service.
- Know how to use the COM+ integration feature to connect Indigo programs and COM+ components and applications.
- Know how to use the Microsoft Message Queuing (MSMQ) integration feature to connect Indigo programs and MSMQ applications.

Understanding Interoperability

Indigo offers **interoperability**—the ability to communicate with other platforms through standard protocols. For example, an Indigo client can access a first-generation Web service. Indigo also offers **integration**—the ability to interact with other technologies. For example, Indigo can add Web service functionality to a COM+ component. Integration is covered later in this chapter.

SOAP messaging offers a number of choices. For systems to interoperate, they must be in agreement about the following:

- Interoperability level
- Document style
- Message format
- Message structure

Indigo gives developers control over each of these areas, as described in the sections that follow.

Bindings and Interoperability Level

The standard bindings provide varying levels of interoperability. **BasicProfile interoperability** is provided by the *BasicProfile* binding. It allows platform-independent communication with first-generation Web services such as .NET (ASMX) Web services as well as next-generation services that support the WS-* protocols. Transport security is available. This interoperability level provides maximum platform independence, but at the expense of enterprise features such as reliable sessions, transactions, and SOAP security.

WS-* interoperability is provided by the *WSProfile* and *WSProfileDualHttp* bindings. It allows platform-independent communication with next-generation services that support the WS-* protocols. This interoperability level provides platform independence and supports reliable sessions, transactions, transport security, and SOAP security.

.NET interoperability is provided by the *NetProfileNamedPipe*, *NetProfileMsmq*, *NetProfileTcp*, and *NetProfileDualTcp* bindings. It allows .NET-to-.NET communication and supports transactions, reliable sessions, and SOAP security. This interoperability level is very efficient but requires the Microsoft .NET Platform.

Document Style

A message description can be represented in several ways in Web Services Description Language (WSDL). It can be in **document format** or **RPC format**. Document format has two varieties: **document/wrapped**, in which the content is contained in a single element, and **document/bare**, in which there is no outer container element. The three document styles supported by Indigo are described here.

- **DocumentWrapped**   The WSDL uses document format, and messages are wrapped. This is the default. Listing 9-1 shows a request message in document/wrapped style.

- **DocumentBare**   The WSDL uses document format, and message content is not wrapped. Listing 9-2 shows a request message in document/bare style.

- **RPC**   WSDL uses RPC format, and the message content follows the WS-I Basic Profile RPC rules. Listing 9-3 shows a request message in RPC style.

To set the document style to match another system's expectations, you specify a *Style* parameter in a service contract's *[ServiceContract]* or *[OperationContract]* attribute. For details on how to specify document style, see Chapter 5.

Listing 9-1   Message in Document/Wrapped Style

```
<s:Envelope xmlns:s="http://schemas.xmlsoap.org/soap/envelope/">
  <s:Body>
    <Add xmlns="http://ProgrammingIndigo">
      <n1>100</n1>
      <n2>15.99</n2>
    </Add>
  </s:Body>
<s:Envelope>
```

Listing 9-2   Message in Document/Bare Style

```
<s:Envelope xmlns:s="http://schemas.xmlsoap.org/soap/envelope/">
  <s:Body>
    <n1 xmlns="http://ProgrammingIndigo">100</n1>
    <n2 xmlns="http://ProgrammingIndigo">15.99</n2>
  </s:Body>
</s:Envelope>
```

Listing 9-3   Message in RPC Style

```
<s:Envelope xmlns:s="http://schemas.xmlsoap.org/soap/envelope/">
  <s:Body>
    <Add xmlns="http://ProgrammingIndigo">
      <n1 xmlns="">100</n1>
      <n2 xmlns="">15.99</n2>
    </Add>
  </s:Body>
</s:Envelope>
```

Message Format

Messages can be in either **literal** or **encoded** format. In literal format, the body of a message conforms to an XML schema. Encoded format uses SOAP encoding. The default format is literal. If the encoded format is used, the *XmlSerializer* must also be specified.

Listing 9-1 shown earlier shows a message in literal format. Listing 9-4 shows a message in encoded format. Notice the XSD type attributes that identify the parameters as double values.

Listing 9-4   Message in Encoded Format

```
<s:Envelope xmlns:s="http://schemas.xmlsoap.org/soap/envelope/">
  <s:Body s:encodingStyle="http://schemas.xmlsoap.org/soap/encoding/">
    <q1:Add xmlns:q1="http://ProgrammingIndigo"
        xmlns:xsi="http://www.w3.org/2001/XMLSchema-instance"
        xmlns:xsd="http://www.w3.org/2001/XMLSchema">
      <n1 xsi:type="xsd:double" xmlns="">100</n1>
      <n2 xsi:type="xsd:double" xmlns="">15.99</n2>
    </q1:Add>
  </s:Body>
</s:Envelope>
```

To set the message format to match another system's expectations, you specify a *Use* parameter in a service contract's *[ServiceContract]* or *[OperationContract]* attribute. For details on how to specify message format, see Chapter 5.

Message Structure

Because there is more than one way to store information in a SOAP message, you might need to override Indigo's default message structure to achieve interoperability. To accommodate remote systems with different expectations about message structure, you can use message contracts. Message contracts allow you to control which parts of a message are stored in headers or in the body. They also give you control over action, names, namespaces, and order of positioning. For more information on message contracts, see Chapter 5.

Listing 9-5 shows a simple message with the default message structure. The parameters for the *Add* operation are stored in the message body. Listing 9-6 shows the message when altered with a message contract such that the parameters are stored in message headers.

Listing 9-5   Default Message Structure

```
<s:Envelope xmlns:s="http://schemas.xmlsoap.org/soap/envelope/">
  <s:Body>
    <Add xmlns="http://ProgrammingIndigo">
      <n1>100</n1>
      <n2>15.99</n2>
    </Add>
  </s:Body>
</s:Envelope>
```

Listing 9-6   Message Structure Altered with Message Contract

```
<s:Envelope xmlns:s="http://schemas.xmlsoap.org/soap/envelope/">
  <s:Header>
    <h:n1 xmlns:h="http://ProgrammingIndigo">100</h:n1>
    <h:n2 xmlns:h="http://ProgrammingIndigo">15.99</h:n2>
  </s:Header>
  <s:Body>
    <Add xmlns="http://ProgrammingIndigo" />
  </s:Body>
</s:Envelope>
```

Understanding Integration

Indigo contains features for integrating with COM+ and MSMQ applications. These features allow Indigo programs to work with existing deployments of COM+ and MSMQ without the need to change them in any way.

COM+ Integration

Indigo can communicate with COM+ components through a feature called **COM+ integration**. COM+ integration allows existing COM+ applications to work with Indigo without the need to migrate the code.

With COM+ integration, the client or the service role can be replaced with a COM+ client application or COM+ component, respectively. For example, an Indigo client can access a COM+ component as if it were a Web service. COM+ integration also allows a COM+ application to access an Indigo service as if it were a component.

Exposing a Service for a COM+ Component

COM+ integration makes it possible to expose a service for a COM+ or Enterprise Services component. Once you add service functionality, the component can be accessed by an Indigo client just like any other service.

The service contract and service behaviors for the added service directly reflect the COM+ component. There is one service per COM class. The service contract comes directly from the component's interface. If you change a COM+ component's interface, its service contract is updated accordingly. The service enforces the same authentication and authorization security requirements as the COM+ component. If a component is marked as transactional, clients can flow transactions to the service, and the COM+ component will enlist in them.

You have two hosting options for the service:

- **COM+ hosting**   The service is hosted in the application's COM+ server process (Dll-host.exe). In this hosting mode, the component must already be running in an application in order to respond to requests.

- **Web hosting**   The Web service is hosted in Microsoft Internet Information Services (IIS). The COM+ component is activated as needed when a request is made of the service.

Some components aren't eligible to be exposed as a service. For instance, a component whose methods accept object references as parameters cannot be exposed as a service. See the Indigo documentation for a full list of restrictions.

Calling an Indigo Service as a COM+ Component

The other way to use COM+ integration is to reverse the roles: a traditional COM+ client application can access an Indigo service as if it were a COM+ component. This is made possible by an Indigo service moniker that COM+ applications can specify. You can thus call Indigo services from development environments such as Microsoft Visual Basic 6.0, Microsoft Windows Scripting Host, or Visual Basic for Applications in Microsoft Office.

The programming specifics for COM+ integration are covered later in the chapter in the section titled "Programming COM+ Integration."

MSMQ Integration

Indigo can communicate with MSMQ in two ways. One way is to use MSMQ as a transport between an Indigo client and Indigo service. In this mode of operation, MSMQ is simply a conduit for Indigo SOAP messages. The *NetProfileMsmq* binding provides this functionality.

The other way Indigo can communicate with MSMQ is when you connect an Indigo client or service to an existing MSMQ application using **MSMQ integration**. In this mode of operation, the messages sent to and received from a queue are not required to be in SOAP format. The *MsmqIntegration* binding provides this functionality. MSMQ integration allows existing MSMQ applications to work with Indigo without the need to migrate the code.

With MSMQ integration, the client or the service role can be replaced with a traditional MSMQ application. For example, an Indigo client can send messages directly to an MSMQ queue. A traditional MSMQ program can then read messages from the queue using *System.Messaging* or one of the other MSMQ APIs. In this mode of operation, the MSMQ program acts as a service. The Indigo client and the MSMQ receiving program don't have to be running at the same time.

The other way to use MSMQ integration is to reverse the roles: a traditional MSMQ program sends messages to a queue, and an Indigo service receives messages from the queue. In this mode of operation, the MSMQ program acts as a client. Once again, the Indigo service and the MSMQ sending program don't have to be running at the same time.

The programming specifics for MSMQ integration are covered later in the chapter in the section titled "Programming MSMQ Integration."

Programming Interoperability

Programming interoperability begins with learning the interoperability requirements of a remote system. You can then select the appropriate binding, document type, message format, and message structure.

Determining Interoperability Requirements

For some platforms, such as .NET (ASMX) Web services, the interoperability requirements are well known. In other cases, they might be a complete unknown. Because interoperability with a remote system depends on so many factors (interoperability level, document style, message format, and message structure), it might seem nearly impossible to determine the proper combination.

If a service exposes a MEX endpoint or WSDL address, the Svcutil tool can determine the service's interoperability requirements as well as generate matching code and configuration files with the necessary settings. When you run Svcutil against a remote service's MEX endpoint or WSDL address, interoperability information is gathered and stored as follows:

- The binding needed for interoperability is defined in the generated configuration file.

- The document style required is specified in the generated service contract.

- The message format required is specified in the generated service contract.

- The message structure required is specified in the generated service contract.

To run Svcutil against a service, you specify Svcutil and the address of a service's MEX endpoint or WSDL address. For example:

```
svcutil http://www.adventureworks.com/TravelService /out:proxy.cs
    /config:App.config
```

The command-line form and options for the Svcutil tool are described in Appendix D.

Specifying Interoperability Controls

The four key areas of interoperability, introduced earlier in the chapter, are:

- **Interoperability level**   Controlled by the choice of binding and how it is configured. For information about specifying bindings, see Chapter 4.

- **Document style**   Controlled by the *Style* attribute in a service contract. For information about specifying document style in service contracts, see Chapter 5.

- **Message format**   Controlled by the *Use* attribute in a service contract. For information about specifying message format in service contracts, see Chapter 5.

- **Message structure**   Controlled by the use of message contract attributes in a service contract. For information about specifying message contract attributes in service contracts, see Chapter 5.

If you use the Svcutil tool, it generates the appropriate settings for you.

Interoperating with .NET (ASMX) Web Services

Microsoft .NET Web services, also called ASMX Web services, are first-generation Web services. As long as certain requirements are met, an ASMX client can access an Indigo service and an Indigo client can access an ASMX Web service.

ASMX Client Interoperating with Indigo Services

An Indigo service can be accessed by an ASMX client if the following are true:

- The service contract specifies the *XmlSerializer* format mode.

```
[ServiceContract(FormatMode=ContractFormatMode.XmlSerializer)]
public interface IMyService
{
    ...
}
```

- The service exposes an endpoint using the *BasicProfile* binding. The *BasicProfile* binding uses SOAP 1.1 and is compliant with the WS-I BasicProfile 1.1.

```
<services>
    <service
        serviceType="MyService">
        <endpoint address=""
                    bindingSectionName="basicProfileBinding"
                    contractType="IMyService" />
    </service>
</services>
```

Listing 9-7 shows the program code for an Indigo calculator service, and Listing 9-8 shows the service's configuration file. The service contract specifies *XmlSerializer* as the format mode. The endpoint definition in the configuration file specifies the *BasicProfile* binding.

Listing 9-7   Indigo Service: Service.cs

```
using System;
using System.ServiceModel;

namespace ProgrammingIndigo
{
    // Define a service contract.
    [ServiceContract(Namespace="http://ProgrammingIndigo", FormatMode=
```

```
            ContractFormatMode.XmlSerializer)]
        public interface ICalculator
        {
            [OperationContract]
            double Add(double n1, double n2);
            [OperationContract]
            double Subtract(double n1, double n2);
            [OperationContract]
            double Multiply(double n1, double n2);
            [OperationContract]
            double Divide(double n1, double n2);
        }

        // Service class which implements the service contract.
        public class CalculatorService : ICalculator
        {
            public double Add(double n1, double n2)
            {
                return n1 + n2;
            }

            public double Subtract(double n1, double n2)
            {
                return n1 - n2;
            }

            public double Multiply(double n1, double n2)
            {
                return n1 * n2;
            }

            public double Divide(double n1, double n2)
            {
                return n1 / n2;
            }
        }

    }
```

Listing 9-8   Indigo Service: Web.config

```
<?xml version="1.0" encoding="utf-8" ?>
<configuration xmlns="http://schemas.microsoft.com/.NetConfiguration/v2.0">
    <system.serviceModel>
        <services>
            <service
                serviceType="ProgrammingIndigo.CalculatorService"
                behaviorConfiguration="CalculatorServiceBehavior">
                <!-- use base address provided by host -->
                <endpoint address=""
                          bindingSectionName="basicProfileBinding"
                          contractType="ProgrammingIndigo.ICalculator" />
            </service>
        </services>
```

```
        <behaviors>
          <behavior
              configurationName="CalculatorServiceBehavior"
              returnUnknownExceptionsAsFaults="true" >
          </behavior>
        </behaviors>

    </system.serviceModel>

    <system.web>
      <compilation debug="true" />
    </system.web>

  </configuration>
```

Listing 9-9 shows the program code for an ASMX client that can access this service. The client uses a typed proxy named *CalculatorProxy* to communicate with the service.

The typed proxy is generated using the Wsdl.exe tool. The *wsdl* command used is shown here.

```
wsdl /out:proxy.cs http://localhost/calculator/service.svc
```

Listing 9-10 shows the configuration file for the client, which defines the service endpoint address.

Listing 9-9   ASMX Client: Client.cs

```
using System;
using System.Configuration;

namespace ProgrammingIndigo
{
    // The service contract is defined in proxy.cs, generated
    // from the service by the wsdl tool.

    //Client implementation code.
    class Client
    {
        static void Main()
        {
            string address = ConfigurationSettings.AppSettings
                ["CalculatorServiceAddress"];
            // Create a proxy with given client endpoint address
            using (CalculatorService proxy = new CalculatorService(address))
            {
                // Call the Add service operation.
                double value1 = 100.00D;
                double value2 = 15.99D;
                double result = proxy.Add(value1, value2);
                Console.WriteLine("Add({0},{1}) = {2}", value1, value2, result);

                // Call the Subtract service operation.
                value1 = 145.00D;
                value2 = 76.54D;
```

```
            result = proxy.Subtract(value1, value2);
            Console.WriteLine("Subtract({0},{1}) = {2}", value1, value2, result);

            // Call the Multiply service operation.
            value1 = 9.00D;
            value2 = 81.25D;
            result = proxy.Multiply(value1, value2);
            Console.WriteLine("Multiply({0},{1}) = {2}", value1, value2, result);

            // Call the Divide service operation.
            value1 = 22.00D;
            value2 = 7.00D;
            result = proxy.Divide(value1, value2);
            Console.WriteLine("Divide({0},{1}) = {2}", value1, value2, result);

        }

        Console.WriteLine();
        Console.WriteLine("Press <ENTER> to terminate client.");
        Console.ReadLine();
      }
    }
}
```

Listing 9-10   ASMX Client: Client.exe.config

```
<?xml version="1.0" encoding="utf-8" ?>
<configuration xmlns="http://schemas.microsoft.com/.NetConfiguration/v2.0">
   <appSettings>
      <add key="CalculatorServiceAddress" value=
         "http://localhost/calculator/service.svc"/>
   </appSettings>
</configuration>
```

Indigo Client Interoperating with ASMX Web Services

An ASMX Web service can be accessed by an Indigo client if the proxy code for the client is generated by the Svcutil tool with the */uxs* (use *XmlSerializer*) command option:

```
svcutil /uxs http://localhost/MyService/service.svc /out:proxy.cs
```

Listing 9-11 shows the .asmx file for an ASMX calculator service, and Listing 9-12 shows the service's code-behind program file. The service contract specifies the *XmlSerializer*. The end-point definition in the configuration file specifies the *BasicProfile* binding.

Listing 9-11   ASMX Web Service: Service.asmx

```
<%@ WebService Language="c#" CodeBehind="Service.asmx.cs"
Class="ProgrammingIndigo.CalculatorService" %>
```

Listing 9-12   ASMX Web Service: Service.asmx.cs

```
using System;
using System.Web.Services;

namespace ProgrammingIndigo
{
    /// <summary>
    /// Simple ASMX Calculator Web Service.
    /// </summary>

    public class CalculatorService : System.Web.Services.WebService
    {
        public CalculatorService()
        {
        }

        [WebMethod]
        public double Add(double n1, double n2)
        {
            return n1 + n2;
        }
        [WebMethod]
        public double Subtract(double n1, double n2)
        {
            return n1 - n2;
        }
        [WebMethod]
        public double Multiply(double n1, double n2)
        {
            return n1 * n2;
        }
        [WebMethod]
        public double Divide(double n1, double n2)
        {
            return n1 / n2;
        }
    }

}
```

Listing 9-13 shows the program code for an Indigo client that can access this service. Typed proxy code is generated from the service by using the Svcutil tool using this command:

```
svcutil /uxs http://localhost/calculator/service.svc /out:proxy.cs
```

Listing 9-14 shows the configuration file for the client.

Listing 9-13   Indigo Client: Client.cs

```
using System;
using System.ServiceModel;

namespace ProgrammingIndigo
{
    // The service contract is defined in proxy.cs, generated from the service
    // by the svcutil tool.

    // Client implementation code.
    class Client
    {
        static void Main()
        {
            // Create a proxy with given client endpoint configuration.
            using (CalculatorServiceSoapProxy proxy =
                new CalculatorServiceSoapProxy("default"))
            {
                // Call the Add service operation.
                double value1 = 100.00D;
                double value2 = 15.99D;
                double result = proxy.Add(value1, value2);
                Console.WriteLine("Add({0},{1}) = {2}", value1, value2, result);

                // Call the Subtract service operation.
                value1 = 145.00D;
                value2 = 76.54D;
                result = proxy.Subtract(value1, value2);
                Console.WriteLine("Subtract({0},{1}) = {2}", value1, value2, result);

                // Call the Multiply service operation.
                value1 = 9.00D;
                value2 = 81.25D;
                result = proxy.Multiply(value1, value2);
                Console.WriteLine("Multiply({0},{1}) = {2}", value1, value2, result);

                // Call the Divide service operation.
                value1 = 22.00D;
                value2 = 7.00D;
                result = proxy.Divide(value1, value2);
                Console.WriteLine("Divide({0},{1}) = {2}", value1, value2, result);

                // Close the proxy.
                proxy.Close();
            }

            Console.WriteLine();
            Console.WriteLine("Press <ENTER> to terminate client.");
            Console.ReadLine();
        }
    }
}
```

Listing 9-14 Indigo Client: Client.exe.config

```
<?xml version="1.0" encoding="utf-8" ?>
<configuration xmlns="http://schemas.microsoft.com/.NetConfiguration/v2.0">
   <system.serviceModel>

      <client>
        <endpoint configurationName="default"
               address="http://localhost/calculator/service.asmx"
               bindingSectionName="basicProfileBinding"
               contractType="CalculatorServiceSoap" />
      </client>

   </system.serviceModel>
</configuration>
```

Programming Integration

This section describes how to use the MSMQ integration and COM+ integration features.

Programming COM+ Integration

Indigo can integrate directly with COM+ or Enterprise Services components. The COM+ integration feature allows Indigo to access these components without the need to change their code in any way. In COM+ integration, an Indigo client can access a COM+ component as if it were a service, or a COM+ client application can access an Indigo service as if it were a COM+ component.

Exposing a Service for a COM+ Component

COM+ integration can add Web service capabilities to a COM+ or Enterprise Services component. Once you add Web service functionality, an Indigo client can access the component just like any other service.

The service contract and service behaviors for the added service are a direct reflection of the COM+ component. There is one service per COM class. The service contract comes directly from the component's interface. If you change a COM+ component's interface, its service contract is updated accordingly. The service enforces the same authentication and authorization security requirements as the COM+ component. If a component is marked as transactional, clients can flow transactions to the service, and the COM+ component will enlist in them.

To add Web services capability to a COM+ component, follow these steps:

1. Begin with a functional COM+ or Enterprise Services component. The component should be a strong-named assembly that has been added to the global assembly cache (GAC) and registered using the COM+ Regsvcs tool.

2. Choose a Web directory for the service and make it a virtual directory.

3. Run the ComSvcConfig tool to generate a service from the component. On the command line, specify *add* mode, an application name, an interface name, a hosting model, a Web directory, and a */mex* option. This creates *CLSID*.svc in the specified Web directory. For more information about ComSvcConfig, see "Using the ComSvcConfig Tool" later in this chapter.

   ```
   ComSvcConfig add /application:CalculatorComponent
       /interface:CalculatorComponent.esCalculator,ICalculator /hosting:was
       /webDirectory:myservice /mex
   ```

4. Test that the service can be accessed in a browser at *http://localhost/*vdir*/CLSID.svc*, where *vdir* is the virtual directory name and *CLSID* is the class ID of the component. You should receive a confirmation page.

   ```
   http://localhost/myservice/BE62FF5B-8B53-476B-A385-0F66043049F6.svc
   ```

5. To generate client code, run the Svcutil tool and specify the address of the service.

   ```
   svcutil http://localhost/myservice/BE62FF5B-8B53-476B-A385-0F66043049F6.svc
       /out:proxy.cs
   ```

You're free to change the configuration of the service at this point, including its binding and address.

Let's take a look at an example. Listing 9-15 shows the code for an Enterprise Services component that performs simple calculator functions. The normal steps to deploy an Enterprise Services component are to create a strong-named assembly, add the assembly to the GAC, and register the assembly using the COM+ Regsvcs tool. This results in a component that can be accessed by COM or DCOM but does not expose any Web service functionality.

Listing 9-15   Enterprise Services Component

```
using System;
using System.EnterpriseServices;
using System.Runtime.InteropServices;

[assembly: ApplicationName("IndigoExample")]
[assembly: ApplicationID("E146E066-D3D1-4e0e-B175-30160BD368DE")]
```

```csharp
[assembly: ApplicationActivation(ActivationOption.Server)]
[assembly: ApplicationAccessControl(false, AccessChecksLevel =
    AccessChecksLevelOption.Application)]

namespace ProgrammingIndigo
{
    [Guid("C551FBA9-E3AA-4272-8C2A-84BD8D290AC7")]
    public interface ICalculator
    {
        double Add(double n1, double n2);
        double Subtract(double n1, double n2);
        double Multiply(double n1, double n2);
        double Divide(double n1, double n2);
    }

    [Guid("BE62FF5B-8B53-476b-A385-0F66043049F6")]
    [ProgId("IndigoExample.esCalculator")]
    public class esCalculator : ServicedComponent, ICalculator
    {
        public double Add(double n1, double n2)
        {
            return n1 + n2;
        }
        public double Subtract(double n1, double n2)
        {
            return n1 - n2;
        }
        public double Multiply(double n1, double n2)
        {
            return n1 * n2;
        }
        public double Divide(double n1, double n2)
        {
            return n1 / n2;
        }
    }
}
```

To add Web service capabilities to the component, run the ComSvcConfig tool with the following command line. The *add* mode is specified, and command-line options specify an application name, interface name, and hosting model.

```
ComSvcConfig add /application:MyService /interface:MyService.esCalculator,ICalculator
    /hosting:was /webDirectory:Myservice /mex
```

ComSvcConfig generates a *CLSID*.svc file in the specified Web directory. At this point, you can access the component as a service at this address:

```
http://localhost/Myservice/BE62FF5B-8B53-476B-A385-0F66043049F6.svc
```

Using Svcutil, you can now generate client proxy code from the service's MEX endpoint (not shown).

Listing 9-16 shows the program code for an Indigo client that can access the COM+ component as a Web service. Listing 9-17 shows the client's configuration file.

Listing 9-16   Indigo Client: Client.cs

```csharp
using System;
using System.ServiceModel;

namespace ProgrammingIndigo
{
    // The service contract is defined in proxy.cs, generated from the service
    // by the svcutil tool.

    //Client implementation code.

    class client
    {
        static void Main()
        {
            // Create a proxy with given client endpoint configuration
            using (CalculatorProxy proxy = new CalculatorProxy("CalculatorEndpoint"))
            {
                // Call the Add service operation.
                double value1 = 100.00D;
                double value2 = 15.99D;
                double result = proxy.Add(value1, value2);
                Console.WriteLine("Add({0},{1}) = {2}", value1, value2, result);

                // Call the Subtract service operation.
                value1 = 145.00D;
                value2 = 76.54D;
                result = proxy.Subtract(value1, value2);
                Console.WriteLine("Subtract({0},{1}) = {2}", value1, value2, result);

                // Call the Multiply service operation.
                value1 = 9.00D;
                value2 = 81.25D;
```

```
            result = proxy.Multiply(value1, value2);
            Console.WriteLine("Multiply({0},{1}) = {2}", value1, value2, result);

            // Call the Divide service operation.
            value1 = 22.00D;
            value2 = 7.00D;
            result = proxy.Divide(value1, value2);
            Console.WriteLine("Divide({0},{1}) = {2}", value1, value2, result);

            // Close the proxy.
            proxy.Close();
        }

        Console.WriteLine();
        Console.WriteLine("Press <ENTER> to terminate client.");
        Console.ReadLine();
    }
  }
}
```

Listing 9-17   Indigo Client: Client.exe.config

```
<?xml version="1.0" encoding="utf-8" ?>
<configuration xmlns="http://schemas.microsoft.com/.NetConfiguration/v2.0">
<system.serviceModel>
    <client>
        <endpoint configurationName="CalculatorEndpoint"
                address="http://localhost/Myservice/BE62FF5B-8B53-476B-A385-
                    0F66043049F6.svc/C551FBA9-E3AA-4272-8C2A-84BD8D290AC7"
                bindingSectionName="wsProfileBinding"
                bindingConfiguration="MyBinding"
                contractType="ICalculator" />
    </client>
    <bindings>
        <wsProfileBinding>
            <binding configurationName="MyBinding" reliableSessionEnabled="true" />
        </wsProfileBinding>
    </bindings>
</system.serviceModel>
</configuration>
```

Using the ComSvcConfig Tool

The ComSvcConfig tool adds or removes Web service functionality for a COM+ component. The ComSvcConfig command line begins with one of the keywords listed here and can be followed by command-line options.

- *Add*   Adds Web service functionality to a component
- *Remove*   Removes Web service functionality from a component
- *Query*   Lists components that have been given Web service functionality

Options on the command line specify details about the component and interface. Table 9-1 lists the ComSvcConfig command-line options.

Table 9-1   ComSvcConfig Command-Line Options

Short Form	Long Form	Description
/a	/application:<ApplicationID|ApplicationName>	Specifies the COM+ application to configure
/i	/interface:<ClassID|ProgID|*, InterfaceID|Interface-Name|*>	Specifies the interface to be configured
/h	/hosting:<complus|was>	Specifies the process to host *ServiceModel*
/w	/webSite:<WebsiteName>	Specifies the Web site for hosting
/d	/webDirectory:<WebDirectoryName>	Specifies the virtual directory for hosting
/x	/mex	Adds a metadata endpoint
/?	/help	Displays help information
/k	/id	Displays the application, component, and interface information as IDs
/n	/nologo	Suppresses display of the ComSvcConfig logo
/q	/quiet	Suppresses all output except errors

Accessing a Service from a COM+ Client Application

Applications that know how to call COM or COM+ components can call Indigo services. The Indigo service moniker makes this possible.

To set up an Indigo service so it can be called from a COM+ application, follow these steps:

1. Generate client proxy code from the service using the Svcutil tool.

   ```
   svcutil http://localhost/MyService/service.svc /language:vb /out:proxy.vb
   ```

2. Generate a signed assembly containing the generated code. Specify the *ComVisible* assembly attribute. In these steps, we'll assume the name Client.dll for the assembly.

   ```
   [assembly: ComVisible(true)]
   ```

3.   Run the *regasm* command to register the COM-visible types in the assembly. This creates a .tlb (type library) file.

```
regasm /tlb:MyServiceProxy.tlb client.dll
```

4.   Add the assembly to the GAC using the *gacutil* command.

```
gacutil.exe /i client.dll
```

Once a service is set up for COM, it can be accessed like a COM object using the *GetObject* function. A call to *GetObject* retrieves a proxy for the service. The argument specified to *GetObject* is an Indigo service moniker that takes the form *service:address=<address>, binding=<binding>, contract={<GUID>}*. Once the proxy is created, the methods of the service can be invoked. The following code shows a Windows Scripting Host script calling a calculator service using the Indigo service moniker.

```
Set calcProxy = GetObject("service:address=http://localhost/MyService/service.svc,
    binding=wsProfileBinding, contract={80CBEDDE-D82C-3BD2-8BE4-C2EBC48EB139}")

' Call the service operations on the proxy.
WScript.Echo "100 + 15.99 = " & calcProxy.Add(100, 15.99)
WScript.Echo "145 - 76.54 = " & calcProxy.Subtract(145, 76.54)
WScript.Echo "9 * 81.25 = " & calcProxy.Multiply(9, 81.25)
WScript.Echo "22 / 7 = " & calcProxy.Divide(22, 7)
```

The GUID specified for the contract is the interface ID from the .tlb file generated earlier, which you can view by using the OLE/COM Object Viewer (OleView.exe) or other COM inspection tools. In strongly typed environments such as Visual Basic 6.0 or Microsoft Office Visual Basic for Applications (VBA), it isn't necessary to specify the contract parameter and GUID value. Instead, you can add a reference to the type library and declare the type of the proxy object.

Programming MSMQ Integration

In MSMQ integration, an Indigo client can send to an MSMQ queue or an Indigo service can read from an MSMQ queue.

Indigo Client Sending to an MSMQ Queue

The *MsmqIntegration* binding allows an Indigo client to communicate with an MSMQ application. Use a binding configuration to specify details of MSMQ operation, such as security.

```
<system.serviceModel>
    <services>
        <service serviceType="ProgrammingIndigo.MyService">
            <endpoint address="net.msmq://localhost/private$/MyQueue"
                    bindingSectionName="msmqIntegrationBinding"
                    bindingConfiguration="MyBinding"
                    contractType="ProgrammingIndigo.IMyService">
            </endpoint>
```

```
            </service>
        </services>
        <bindings>
            <msmqIntegrationBinding>
                <binding configurationName="MyBinding"
                        msmqAuthenticationMode="None"
                        msmqProtectionLevel="None" />
            </msmqIntegrationBinding>
        </bindings>
    </system.serviceModel>
```

In the client code, a service contract is defined with a single one-way service operation that accepts a parameter of type *MsmqMessage<T>*, where *T* is the type for the message payload. The service operation should specify an action of *, as shown here.

```
[ServiceContract(Namespace="http://ProgrammingIndigo")]
public interface IRegister
{
    [OperationContract(IsOneWay=true, Action="*")]
    void Register(MsmqMessage<Contact> msg);
}
```

The class or struct for the message payload must be marked with the *[Serializable]* attribute.

```
[Serializable]
public class Contact
{
    public string LastName;
    public string FirstName;
    public string Phone;
}
```

Let's examine an Indigo client program that talks to an MSMQ receiving program. Listing 9-18 shows an MSMQ program that reads calculation jobs from a queue using the *System.Messaging* API. The queue is named .\private$\calculator, and the program creates the queue if necessary. As messages arrive in the queue, the program deduces from the message which operation to perform and carries out a calculation. This program contains no Indigo code, but it logically acts as a service.

Listing 9-18   MSMQ Receiving Program

```
using System;
using System.Collections.Generic;
using System.Text;
using System.Messaging;
using System.Configuration;

namespace ProgrammingIndigo
{
    [Serializable]
    public class Calculation
    {
```

```csharp
        public double n1;
        public double n2;
    }

class Receiver
{
    static void Main(string[] args)
    {
        // Create a transaction queue.
        string queueName = ".\\private$\\calculator";
        if (!MessageQueue.Exists(queueName))
            MessageQueue.Create(queueName, true);

        //Connect to the queue.
        MessageQueue Queue = new MessageQueue(queueName);

        Queue.ReceiveCompleted += new ReceiveCompletedEventHandler(Calculate);
        Queue.BeginReceive();
        Console.WriteLine("Calculator Service is running");
        Console.ReadLine();
    }

    public static void Calculate
        (Object source, ReceiveCompletedEventArgs asyncResult)
    {
        try
        {
            // Connect to the queue.
            MessageQueue Queue = (MessageQueue)source;

            // End the asynchronous receive operation.
            System.Messaging.Message msg =
                Queue.EndReceive(asyncResult.AsyncResult);

            msg.Formatter = new System.Messaging.XmlMessageFormatter(new Type[]
                { typeof(Calculation) });

            Calculation job = (Calculation) msg.Body;
            switch (msg.Label)
            {
                case "ADD":
                    Add(job.n1, job.n2);
                    break;
                case "SUB":
                    Subtract(job.n1, job.n2);
                    break;
                case "MUL":
                    Multiply(job.n1, job.n2);
                    break;
                case "DIV":
                    Divide(job.n1, job.n2);
                    break;
            }
            Queue.BeginReceive();
        }
        catch (System.Exception ex)
```

```
            {
                Console.WriteLine(ex.Message);
            }
        }

        private static void Add(double n1, double n2)
        {
            Console.WriteLine("Job: Add {0},{1}", n1, n2);
            Console.WriteLine("Result: {0}", n1 + n2);
        }

        private static void Subtract(double n1, double n2)
        {
            Console.WriteLine("Job: Subtract {0},{1}", n1, n2);
            Console.WriteLine("Result: {0}", n1 - n2);
        }

        private static void Multiply(double n1, double n2)
        {
            Console.WriteLine("Job: Multiply {0},{1}", n1, n2);
            Console.WriteLine("Result: {0}", n1 * n2);
        }

        private static void Divide(double n1, double n2)
        {
            Console.WriteLine("Job: Divide {0},{1}", n1, n2);
            Console.WriteLine("Result: {0}", n1 / n2);
        }
    }
}
```

The Indigo client program is shown in Listing 9-19. The proxy code for the client is shown in Listing 9-20. You cannot use the Svcutil tool because there is no actual service to access for code generation; you must create service contract and proxy code manually or repurpose it from another application.

In this client, the data to be transferred to the queue is defined in a class named *calculation*. To send a message, the client creates and populates a *Calculation* object and then creates an instance of *MsmqMessage<Calculation>*. The *MsmqMessage* object's *body* property is set to the *Calculation* object, and its *label* property is set to a string representing the operation to be performed. To send the message, you invoke the *Calculate* operation by using a proxy.

Listing 9-19   Indigo Client: Client.cs

```
using System;
using System.ServiceModel;

namespace ProgrammingIndigo
{
    //The service contract is defined in generatedProxy.cs, generated from the
    // service by the Svcutil tool.
```

```csharp
//Client implementation code.

class client
{
    static void Main()
    {
        // Create a proxy with given client endpoint configuration.
        using (CalculatorProxy proxy = new CalculatorProxy("CalculatorEndpoint"))
        {
            // Call the Add service operation.
            double value1 = 100.00D;
            double value2 = 15.99D;
            double result = proxy.Add(value1, value2);
            Console.WriteLine("Add({0},{1}) = {2}", value1, value2, result);

            // Call the Subtract service operation.
            value1 = 145.00D;
            value2 = 76.54D;
            result = proxy.Subtract(value1, value2);
            Console.WriteLine("Subtract({0},{1}) = {2}", value1, value2, result);

            // Call the Multiply service operation.
            value1 = 9.00D;
            value2 = 81.25D;
            result = proxy.Multiply(value1, value2);
            Console.WriteLine("Multiply({0},{1}) = {2}", value1, value2, result);

            // Call the Divide service operation.
            value1 = 22.00D;
            value2 = 7.00D;
            result = proxy.Divide(value1, value2);
            Console.WriteLine("Divide({0},{1}) = {2}", value1, value2, result);

            // Close the proxy.
            proxy.Close();
        }

        Console.WriteLine();
        Console.WriteLine("Press <ENTER> to terminate client.");
        Console.ReadLine();
    }
}
```

Listing 9-20   Indigo Client: Proxy.cs

```
//-----------------------------------------------------------------------------
// <auto-generated>
//      This code was generated by a tool.
//      Runtime Version:2.0.50215.35
//
//      Changes to this file may cause incorrect behavior and will be lost if
//      the code is regenerated.
// </auto-generated>
```

```
//----------------------------------------------------------------------------

using System.ServiceModel;
using System.ServiceModel.Channels;
using ProgrammingIndigo;

[System.ServiceModel.ServiceContractAttribute(Namespace = "http://ProgrammingIndigo")]
public interface ICalculator
{

    [System.ServiceModel.OperationContractAttribute(IsOneWay = true, Action = "*",
        Style = System.ServiceModel.ServiceOperationStyle.DocumentBare)]
    void Calculate(MsmqMessage<Calculation> msg);
}

public interface ICalculatorChannel : ICalculator, System.ServiceModel.IProxyChannel
{
}

public partial class CalculatorProxy : System.ServiceModel.ProxyBase<ICalculator>,
    ICalculator
{

    public CalculatorProxy()
    {
    }

    public CalculatorProxy(string configurationName)
        :
            base(configurationName)
    {
    }

    public CalculatorProxy(System.ServiceModel.Binding binding)
        :
            base(binding)
    {
    }

    public CalculatorProxy(System.ServiceModel.EndpointAddress address,
        System.ServiceModel.Binding binding)
        :
            base(address, binding)
    {
    }

    public void Calculate(MsmqMessage<Calculation> msg)
    {
        base.InnerProxy.Calculate(msg);
    }
}
```

Indigo Service Receiving from an MSMQ Client

An Indigo service program can receive messages directly from an MSMQ queue using Indigo's MSMQ integration feature. A traditional MSMQ program can send messages to the queue using the *System.Messaging* API. The Indigo service and the MSMQ sending program don't have to be running at the same time if the queue is durable.

The *MsmqIntegration* binding allows an Indigo service to receive messages from an MSMQ application. In the service code, a service contract is defined with a one-way service operation that accepts a parameter of type *MsmqMessage<T>*, where *T* is the type for the message payload. This class or struct must be marked with the *[Serializable]* attribute.

Let's examine an MSMQ sending program that talks to an Indigo service. Listing 9-21 shows an MSMQ program that sends calculation jobs to a queue using the *System.Messaging* API. The queue is named .\private$\calculator. This program contains no Indigo code, but it logically acts as a client. The program creates and populates an instance of *Calculation* and sends it to the *calculator* queue.

Listing 9-21   MSMQ Sending Program

```
using System;
using System.Collections.Generic;
using System.Text;
using System.Messaging;
using System.Configuration;
namespace ProgrammingIndigo
{
    [Serializable]
    public struct Calculation
    {
        public double n1;
        public double n2;
    }

    class Program
    {
        static void Main(string[] args)
        {
            //Connect to the queue
            string queueName = ".\\private$\\calculator";
            MessageQueue Queue = new MessageQueue(queueName);

            // Submit an addition job.
            Calculation job = new Calculation();
            job.n1 = 100.00D;
            job.n2 = 15.99D;
            Console.WriteLine("Submitting Job: Add({0},{1})", job.n1, job.n2);
            Queue.Send(job, "ADD", MessageQueueTransactionType.Single);
```

```
        // Submit a subtraction job.
        job.n1 = 145.00D;
        job.n2 = 76.54D;
        Console.WriteLine("Submitting Job: Subtract({0},{1})", job.n1, job.n2);
        Queue.Send(job, "SUB", MessageQueueTransactionType.Single);

        // Submit a multiplcation job.
        job.n1 = 9.00D;
        job.n2 = 81.25D;
        Console.WriteLine("Submitting Job: Multiply({0},{1})", job.n1, job.n2);
        Queue.Send(job, "MUL", MessageQueueTransactionType.Single);

        // Submit a division job.
        job.n1 = 22.00D;
        job.n2 = 7.00D;
        Console.WriteLine("Submitting Job: Divide({0},{1})", job.n1, job.n2);
        Queue.Send(job, "DIV", MessageQueueTransactionType.Single);

        //Disconnect from the queue.
        Queue.Close();

        Console.WriteLine();
        Console.WriteLine("Press <ENTER> to terminate client.");
        Console.ReadLine();
      }
    }
  }
```

The Indigo service program is shown in Listing 9-22. The service's configuration file is shown in Listing 9-23.

If the Indigo service is running, the *Calculate* service operation runs for each message in the queue. *Calculate* examines the message's *Label* property to determine which action to perform. *Calculate* can get at the *Calculation* structure using the message's *Body* property.

Listing 9-22   Indigo Service: Service.cs

```
using System;
using System.ServiceModel;
using System.Collections.Generic;
using System.ServiceModel.Channels;
using System.Runtime.Serialization;
using System.Messaging;
using System.Configuration;
namespace ProgrammingIndigo
{
    [Serializable]
    public struct Calculation
    {
        public double n1;
        public double n2;
    }
```

```csharp
// Define a service contract.
[ServiceContract(Namespace = "http://ProgrammingIndigo")]
[KnownType(typeof(Calculation))]
public interface ICalculator
{
    [OperationContract(IsOneWay = true, Action = "*")]
    void Calculate(MsmqMessage<Calculation> msg);
}

// Service class that implements the service contract.
[ServiceBehavior()]
public class CalculatorService : ICalculator
{
    [OperationBehavior]
    public void Calculate(MsmqMessage<Calculation> msg)
    {
        Calculation job = msg.Body;
        switch (msg.Label)
        {
            case "ADD":
                Add(job.n1, job.n2);
                break;
            case "SUB":
                Subtract(job.n1, job.n2);
                break;
            case "MUL":
                Multiply(job.n1, job.n2);
                break;
            case "DIV":
                Divide(job.n1, job.n2);
                break;
        }
    }

    private void Add(double n1, double n2)
    {
        Console.WriteLine("Job: Add {0},{1}", n1, n2);
        Console.WriteLine("Result:{0}", n1 + n2);
    }

    private void Subtract(double n1, double n2)
    {
        Console.WriteLine("Job: Subtract {0},{1}", n1, n2);
        Console.WriteLine("Result:{0}", n1 - n2);
    }

    private void Multiply(double n1, double n2)
    {
        Console.WriteLine("Job: Mulitply {0},{1}", n1, n2);
        Console.WriteLine("Result:{0}", n1 * n2);
    }

    private void Divide(double n1, double n2)
    {
```

```csharp
        Console.WriteLine("Job: Divide {0},{1}", n1, n2);
        Console.WriteLine("Result:{0}", n1 / n2);
    }

    [STAThread]
    static void Main(string[] args)
    {
        // Create a transaction1 queue.

        string queueName = ".\\private$\\calculator";
        if (!MessageQueue.Exists(queueName))
            MessageQueue.Create(queueName, true);

        // Create a ServiceHost<T> for the Calculator service that reads messages
        // from the queue and processes them.
        using (ServiceHost<CalculatorService> serviceHost = new
            ServiceHost<CalculatorService>())
        {
            // Open the service host.
            serviceHost.Open();

            // The service is now available.
            Console.WriteLine("The Calculator service is ready");
            Console.WriteLine("Press <ENTER> to terminate service");
            Console.WriteLine();
            Console.ReadLine();

            // Close the service host.
            serviceHost.Close();
        }
    }
}

}
```

Listing 9-23   Indigo Service: Service.exe.config

```xml
<?xml version="1.0" encoding="utf-8" ?>
<configuration xmlns="http://schemas.microsoft.com/.NetConfiguration/v2.0">
  <system.serviceModel>
    <services>
      <service serviceType="ProgrammingIndigo.CalculatorService"
               behaviorConfiguration="CalculatorServiceBehavior">
        <endpoint address="net.msmq://localhost/private$/calculator"
                  bindingSectionName="msmqIntegrationBinding"
                  bindingConfiguration="CalculatorBinding"
                  contractType="ProgrammingIndigo.ICalculator">
        </endpoint>
      </service>
    </services>
    <bindings>
      <msmqIntegrationBinding>
        <binding configurationName="CalculatorBinding"
                 msmqAuthenticationMode="None"
```

```
                    msmqProtectionLevel="None" />
        </msmqIntegrationBinding>
      </bindings>
      <behaviors>
        <behavior configurationName="CalculatorServiceBehavior"
                  returnUnknownExceptionsAsFaults="True" >
        </behavior>
      </behaviors>
    </system.serviceModel >
    <system.web>
      <compilation debug="true" />
    </system.web>
  </configuration>
```

Programming Exercise: Interoperable Catalog Service

In this programming exercise, you will create a service that provides catalog information about books. The service will support *BasicProfile* interoperability. You will create both an Indigo client and an ASMX client that are able to use the same Indigo service. The service will be hosted in IIS. Both clients will be console applications.

Development

There are 14 development steps in this exercise:

1. Create the service program.

2. Create an .svc file.

3. Create a configuration file for the service.

4. Build the service.

5. Create a virtual directory for the service.

6. Test the service with a browser.

7. Create the Indigo client.

8. Generate proxy code for the client.

9. Create a configuration file for the client.

10. Build and test the Indigo client.

11. Create the ASMX client.

12. Generate proxy code for the client.

13. Create a configuration file for the client.

14. Build and test the ASMX client.

Step 1: Create the Service Program

We'll now create the service program. This will compile to a DLL library assembly. Launch your development environment and create a new C# console application project named *service*. Enter the code in Listing 9-24.

To perform these tasks using Microsoft Visual Studio:

1. Select New, Project from the File menu. Under Project Type, select Windows under Visual C#. Under Templates, select Class Library. In the Name box, type **service**, in the Location box, type any path you want, and in the Solution Name box, type **catalog**. Click OK to generate and open the new project.

2. Replace the generated code in Program.cs with the code shown in listing 9-24.

Your service project will need to reference System.ServiceModel.dll and System.Runtime.Serialization.dll.

To perform these tasks using Visual Studio:

1. Right-click References in the Solution Explorer window and select Add Reference.

2. In the Add Reference dialog box, on the .NET tab, select System.ServiceModel.dll and click OK.

3. Add another reference in the same manner for System.Runtime.Serialization.dll.

Listing 9-24 Catalog Service: Program.cs

```
using System;
using System.Collections.Generic;
using System.ServiceModel;
using System.Runtime.Serialization;

namespace ProgrammingIndigo
{
    // Define service contract.

    [ServiceContract(Namespace="http://ProgrammingIndigo",
    FormatMode=ContractFormatMode.XmlSerializer)]
    public interface ICatalog
    {
        [OperationContract]
        Book[] GetCatalog();
        [OperationContract]
        Book[] SearchCatalogByAuthor(string author);
        [OperationContract]
        Book[] SearchCatalogByGenre(string genre);
```

```
    [OperationContract]
    Book[] SearchCatalogByTitle(string title);
}


// Define serializable data structure.

public class Book
{
    public string Genre;
    public string Title;
    public string Author;
    public decimal Price;
    public int Year;

    public Book()
    {
    }

    public Book(string genre, string title, string author, decimal price, int year)
    {
        Genre = genre;
        Title = title;
        Author = author;
        Price = price;
        Year = year;
    }
}


// Service implementation class.

public class CatalogService: ICatalog
{
    Book[] Books;

    public CatalogService()
    {
        Books = new Book[8];

        Books[0] = new Book("Biography",  "The Life and Times of Adam Barr",
            "Kim Akers",     32.59M, 1994);
        Books[1] = new Book("Technical",  "Practical Indigo",
            "Jane Clayton",     37.99M, 2006);
        Books[2] = new Book("Journalism",  "The Contoso Files",
            "Mark Hanson",     14.59M, 2002);
        Books[3] = new Book("Health",  "The Trey Research Diet",
            "Shaun Beasley",     19.59M, 2005);
        Books[4] = new Book("Biography",  "The Ted Bremer I knew",
            "John Kane",     11.99M, 1997);
        Books[5] = new Book("Romance",  "Summer at the Coho Vineyard",
            "Kim Akers",     14.99M, 2004);
        Books[6] = new Book("Sci-Fi",  "Brannon Jones and the Time Machine",
            "Frank Lee",     5.99M, 2005);
        Books[7] = new Book("Reference",  "Dictionary",
            "John Kane",     59.59M, 2006);
    }
```

```csharp
// Return all books.

public Book[] GetCatalog()
{
    return Books;
}

// Return books by a specified author.

public Book[] SearchCatalogByAuthor(string author)
{
    List<Book> matches = new List<Book>();
    foreach(Book book in Books)
    {
        if (book.Author==author)
            matches.Add(book);
    }
    Book[] results = new Book[matches.Count];
    int index = 0;
    foreach(Book book in matches)
        results[index++] = book;
    return results;
}

// Return books by a specified genre.

public Book[] SearchCatalogByGenre(string genre)
{
    List<Book> matches = new List<Book>();
    foreach (Book book in Books)
    {
        if (book.Genre == genre)
            matches.Add(book);
    }
    Book[] results = new Book[matches.Count];
    int index = 0;
    foreach (Book book in matches)
        results[index++] = book;
    return results;
}

// Return books matching a full or partial title.

public Book[] SearchCatalogByTitle(string title)
{
    List<Book> matches = new List<Book>();
    foreach (Book book in Books)
    {
        if (book.Title.IndexOf(title)!=-1)
            matches.Add(book);
    }
    Book[] results = new Book[matches.Count];
    int index = 0;
    foreach (Book book in matches)
        results[index++] = book;
```

```
                    return results;
            }
        }
    }
```

Step 2: Create an .SVC File

An .svc file is needed to identify the Indigo service to IIS. Using an editor or development environment, create a text file named Service.svc. Enter the code shown in Listing 9-25.

To perform these tasks using Visual Studio:

1. Right-click the service project, and then select Add, New Item. Select Text File, and then click Add. Name the text file Service.svc.

2. Enter the code in Listing 9-25 into Service.svc.

Listing 9-25 Catalog Service: Service.svc

```
<%@Service language=c# Debug="true" class="ProgrammingIndigo.CatalogService" %>
<%@Assembly Name="service" %>
```

Step 3: Create a Configuration File for the Service

A Web.config file is needed to specify endpoints and bindings for the service. Using an editor or development environment, create a text file with the code shown in Listing 9-26. Save the code under the name Web.config in the same folder where the service program and .svc file are located.

To perform these tasks using Visual Studio:

1. Right-click the service project, and then select Add, New Item. Select Application Configuration File, and then click Add. Name the file Web.config.

2. Enter the code in Listing 9-26 into Web.config.

Listing 9-26 Catalog Service: Web.config

```
<?xml version="1.0" encoding="utf-8" ?>
<configuration xmlns="http://schemas.microsoft.com/.NetConfiguration/v2.0">
    <system.serviceModel>
        <services>
            <service
                serviceType="ProgrammingIndigo.CatalogService"
                behaviorConfiguration="CatalogServiceBehavior">
                <!-- use base address provided by host -->
                <endpoint address=""
                        bindingSectionName="basicProfileBinding"
                        contractType="ProgrammingIndigo.ICatalog" />
            </service>
        </services>
```

```
            <behaviors>
                <behavior
                    configurationName="CatalogServiceBehavior"
                    returnUnknownExceptionsAsFaults="True" >
                </behavior>
            </behaviors>

        </system.serviceModel>

        <system.web>
            <compilation debug="true" />
        </system.web>

    </configuration>
```

Step 4: Build the Service

Build the service program to make Service.dll. Resolve any typographical errors.

To perform the task using Visual Studio, select Build Solution from the Build menu to generate Service.dll.

Step 5: Create a Virtual Directory for the Service

Like ASP.NET applications, services hosted in IIS reside in virtual directories. Follow this procedure to set up a virtual directory for the service.

1. **Create a Directory**. Create a folder on your computer named catalog.

2. **Create a Virtual Directory**. From the Start menu, launch Control Panel. Select Administrative Tools, Internet Information Services. Navigate to Web Sites, Default Web Sites. Right-click and select New, Virtual Directory. Specify the name **catalog** and associate it with the travel folder created in step 1. Before exiting IIS Manager, check step 3.

3. **Enable Anonymous Access**. While in Internet Information Services, navigate to Web Sites, Default Web Sites. catalog should be listed. Right-click catalog and select Properties. On the Directory Security tab, click Edit. An Authentication Methods dialog box appears. Anonymous Access should be checked on the dialog box that appears; if not, check it now. Close all dialog boxes by clicking OK and close Internet Information Services.

4. **Deploy the Service**. Copy the service.svc and Web.config files to the catalog folder. Underneath catalog, create a bin subdirectory and copy Service.dll into it. You should have the following directory-file structure.

```
\catalog
    service.svc
    Web.config
    \bin
        service.dll
```

Step 6: Test the Service with a Browser

Before going on to the client, we want to test that the service can be accessed. Launch Internet Explorer. On the address bar, specify the URL *http://localhost/catalog/service.svc* and press ENTER. If the resulting page does not list any errors, proceed to step 7. If there are problems, check the following:

- If the page returned by the browser describes compilation errors, check the code entered in the preceding steps. The compilation error display should highlight the offending code for you.

- If the resulting page describes HTTP errors, ensure your system has IIS enabled. You should be able to access *http://localhost* in a browser without receiving an error. If IIS seems to be properly enabled, review the virtual directory setup in the prior steps. If this also fails, look for clues in Control Panel, Administrative Tools, check the Event Log, or try an IISRESET.

The service is now ready. Next, we need a client program to access it.

Step 7: Create the Indigo Client

Create the Indigo client program. Launch your development environment and create a new C# console application project named *client*. Enter the code in Listing 9-27.

To perform these tasks using Visual Studio:

1. Select New, Project from the File menu. Under Project Type, select Windows under Visual C#. Under Templates, select Console Application. In the Name box, type **client**, in the Location box, type any path you want, and in the Solution Name box, type **catalog**. Click OK to generate and open the new project.

2. Replace the generated code in Program.cs with the code shown in Listing 9-27.

Your client project will need to reference System.ServiceModel.dll.

To perform the task using Visual Studio:

1. Right-click References in the Solution Explorer window, and then select Add Reference.

2. In the Add Reference dialog box, on the .NET tab, select System.ServiceModel.dll and click OK.

Listing 9-27   Indigo Client: Program.cs

```csharp
using System;
using System.ServiceModel;

namespace ProgrammingIndigo
{
    // Indigo client.

    class Client
    {
        static void Main()
        {
            // Create a proxy to the service.

            using (CatalogProxy proxy = new CatalogProxy("CatalogEndpoint"))
            {
                Book[] books;

                Console.WriteLine("All books");
                Console.WriteLine();
                books = proxy.GetCatalog();
                ListBooks(books);
                Console.WriteLine();

                Console.WriteLine("All books written by Kim Akers");
                Console.WriteLine();
                books = proxy.SearchCatalogByAuthor("Kim Akers");
                ListBooks(books);
                Console.WriteLine();

                Console.WriteLine("All biographies");
                Console.WriteLine();
                books = proxy.SearchCatalogByGenre("Biography");
                ListBooks(books);
                Console.WriteLine();

                // Close the proxy.
                proxy.Close();
            }

            Console.WriteLine();
            Console.WriteLine("Press <ENTER> to terminate client.");
            Console.ReadLine();
        }

        // List an array of books on the console.

        static void ListBooks(Book[] books)
        {
            foreach (Book book in books)
            {
```

```
                    Console.WriteLine("{0,-11} {1,-35} {2,-14} {3,5} {4,8}",
                        book.Genre, book.Title, book.Author, book.Year,
                        book.Price.ToString("c"));
                }
            }
        }
    }
```

Step 8: Generate Proxy Code for the Client

We will now generate client proxy code by accessing the service's MEX endpoint with the Svcutil tool. From a command window, change directory to the location where your client project and source files reside. Run the following Svcutil command:

```
svcutil http://localhost/catalog/service.svc /out:proxy.cs
```

The file Proxy.cs will be generated, containing the service contract and a proxy class for accessing the service. Add Proxy.cs to your client project.

To perform these tasks using Visual Studio:

1.   Right-click the project in the Solution Explorer window and select Add, Existing Item.

2.   Select Proxy.cs from the File Open dialog box and click OK. Proxy.cs is added to the client project.

Step 9: Create a Configuration File for the Client

A Client.exe.config file is needed to specify the service endpoint and binding to use. Using an editor or development environment, create a text file with the code shown in Listing 9-28. Save the code under the name Client.exe.config.

To perform these tasks using Visual Studio:

1.   Right-click the service project and select Add, New Item. Select Application Configuration File, and then click Add. Name the file App.config. (It will be copied to Client.exe.config at build time.)

2.   Enter the code in Listing 9-28 into App.config.

Listing 9-28   Indigo Client: App.config

```
<?xml version="1.0" encoding="utf-8" ?>
<configuration xmlns="http://schemas.microsoft.com/.NetConfiguration/v2.0">
   <system.serviceModel>
      <client>
         <endpoint configurationName="CatalogEndpoint"
               address="http://localhost/catalog/service.svc"
               bindingSectionName="basicProfileBinding"
               contractType="ICatalog" />
```

```
        </client>
    </system.serviceModel>
</configuration>
```

Step 10: Build and Test the Indigo Client

Build the client program to make Client.exe. Resolve any typographical errors.

To perform the task using Visual Studio, select Build Solution from the Build menu to generate Client.exe.

Step 11: Create the ASMX Client

Now we're ready to create the second client, which will be an ASMX client. Launch your development environment and create a new C# console application project named *client2*. Enter the code in Listing 9-29.

To perform these tasks using Visual Studio:

1. Select New, Project from the File menu. Under Project Type, select Windows under Visual C#. Under Templates, select Console Application. In the Name box, type **client2**, in the Location box, type any path you want, and in the Solution list, select Add to Solution. Click OK to generate and open the new project.

2. Replace the generated code in Program.cs with the code shown in Listing 9-29.

Your client project will need to reference System.Web.Services.dll. Because this is not an Indigo program, do not reference any Indigo assemblies such as System.ServiceModel.dll.

To perform the task using Visual Studio:

1. Right-click References in the Solution Explorer window, and then select Add Reference.

2. In the Add Reference dialog box, on the .NET tab, select System.Web.Services.dll, and then click OK.

Listing 9-29   ASMX Client: Program.cs

```csharp
using System;
using System.Runtime.Serialization;
using System.Web.Services;

namespace ProgrammingIndigo
{
    // ASMX Client.

    class Client
    {
        static void Main()
        {
```

```
                    // Create a proxy to the service.

                    using (CatalogService proxy = new CatalogService())
                    {
                        Book[] books;

                        Console.WriteLine("All books");
                        Console.WriteLine();
                        books = proxy.GetCatalog();
                        ListBooks(books);
                        Console.WriteLine();

                        Console.WriteLine("All books written by Kim Akers");
                        Console.WriteLine();
                        books = proxy.SearchCatalogByAuthor("Kim Akers");
                        ListBooks(books);
                        Console.WriteLine();

                        Console.WriteLine("All biographies");
                        Console.WriteLine();
                        books = proxy.SearchCatalogByGenre("Biography");
                        ListBooks(books);
                        Console.WriteLine();
                    }

                    Console.WriteLine();
                    Console.WriteLine("Press <ENTER> to terminate client.");
                    Console.ReadLine();
                }

                // List an array of books on the console.

                static void ListBooks(Book[] books)
                {
                    foreach (Book book in books)
                    {
                        Console.WriteLine("{0,-11} {1,-35} {2,-14} {3,5} {4,8}",
                            book.Genre, book.Title, book.Author, book.Year,
                            book.Price.ToString("c"));
                    }
                }
            }
        }
```

Step 12: Generate Proxy Code for the Client

We will now generate client proxy code by accessing the service's WSDL address with the Wsdl.exe tool. From a command window, change directory to the location where your Client2 project and source files reside. Run the following wsdl command:

```
wsdl http://localhost/catalog/service.svc
```

A CatalogService.cs proxy file will be generated, containing an ASMX proxy class for accessing the service.

Add CatalogService.cs to your client project.

To perform the task using Visual Studio:

1. Right-click the project in the Solution Explorer window and select Add, Existing Item.

2. Select CatalogService.cs from the File Open dialog box and click OK. CatalogService.cs is added to the client project.

Step 13: Create a Configuration File for the Client

A Client2.exe.config file is needed. Using an editor or development environment, create a text file with the code shown in Listing 9-30. Save the code under the name Client.exe.config.

To perform these tasks using Visual Studio:

1. Right-click the service project and select Add, New Item. Select Application Configuration File and click Add. Name the file App.config. (It will be copied to Client.exe.config at build time.)

2. Enter the code in Listing 9-30 into App.config.

Listing 9-30   ASMX Client: App.config

```
<?xml version="1.0" encoding="utf-8" ?>
<configuration xmlns="http://schemas.microsoft.com/.NetConfiguration/v2.0">
</configuration>
```

Step 14: Build and Test the ASMX Client

Build the client2 project to make Client2.exe. Resolve any typographical errors.

To perform the task using Visual Studio, select Build Solution from the Build menu to generate Client2.exe.

Deployment

We're now ready to try things out. Run either client from your development environment or from a command line. There's no need to launch the service; services hosted in IIS activate automatically when they are accessed. If the program fails, double check you've properly and fully carried out each of the preceding steps.

You should see output like that shown in Figure 9-1. Both the Indigo and ASMX clients should behave identically and provide the same output. The service you've created is fully interoperable with first-generation Web service clients as well as next-generation clients.

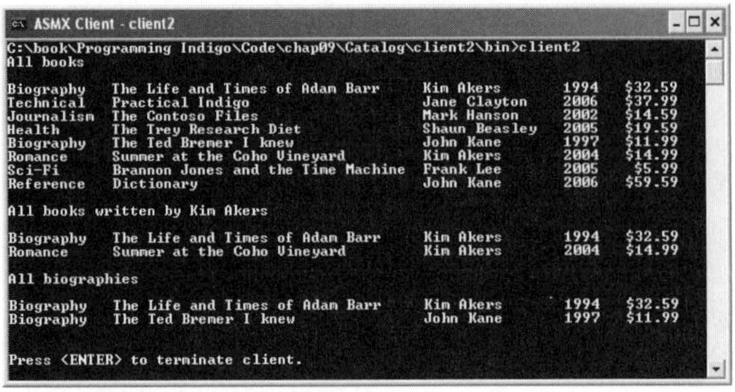

Figure 9-1 ASMX client display

Press ENTER on the clients to shut them down. Congratulations on successfully completing the catalog service and its two clients!

Understanding the Service Code

The service implements a simple service contract that returns a list of Book items in response to search criteria. The client can request all books, books from one genre, books from one author, or books with a matching title. The service contract and its implementation were shown earlier in Listing 9-24. To provide *BasicProfile* interoperability, the contract specifies the XmlSerializer.

```
[ServiceContract(Namespace="http://ProgrammingIndigo",
                 FormatMode=ContractFormatMode.XmlSerializer)]
    public interface ICatalog
    {
        [OperationContract]
        Book[] GetCatalog();
        [OperationContract]
        Book[] SearchCatalogByAuthor(string author);
        [OperationContract]
        Book[] SearchCatalogByGenre(string genre);
        [OperationContract]
        Book[] SearchCatalogByTitle(string title);
    }
```

The service code defines a *Book* class. Each of the service operations will return an array of *Book* items. No data contract is defined for this class. The XmlSerializer will serialize the public properties of the class.

```
// Define serializable data structure.

    public class Book
    {
        public string Genre;
        public string Title;
        public string Author;
```

```
    public decimal Price;
    public int Year;

    public Book()
    {
    }

    public Book(string genre, string title, string author, decimal price, int year)
    {
        Genre = genre;
        Title = title;
        Author = author;
        Price = price;
        Year = year;
    }
}
```

The endpoint for the service and the binding it uses is defined in the service's configuration file, shown earlier in Listing 9-26. The endpoint definition specifies a *BasicProfile* standard binding in order to be interoperable with first-generation Web service clients.

```
<endpoint address=""
        bindingSectionName="basicProfileBinding"
        contractType="ProgrammingIndigo.ICatalog" />
```

Understanding the Indigo Client Code

The Indigo client contains proxy code generated by the Svcutil tool. This code defines the service contract and the Book data structure for the service and also contains a CatalogProxy class for accessing the service. The client program code, shown earlier in Listing 9-27, creates an instance of the proxy and invokes the service by calling its methods.

```
using (CatalogProxy proxy = new CatalogProxy("CatalogEndpoint"))
{
    Book[] books;

    Console.WriteLine("All books");
    Console.WriteLine();
    books = proxy.GetCatalog();
    ListBooks(books);
    Console.WriteLine();

    Console.WriteLine("All books written by Kim Akers");
    Console.WriteLine();
    books = proxy.SearchCatalogByAuthor("Kim Akers");
    ListBooks(books);
    Console.WriteLine();

    Console.WriteLine("All biographies");
    Console.WriteLine();
    books = proxy.SearchCatalogByGenre("Biography");
    ListBooks(books);
    Console.WriteLine();
```

```
    // Close the proxy.
    proxy.Close();
}
```

The service endpoint is specified in the client's configuration file, shown earlier in Listing 9-28.

Understanding the ASMX Client Code

The ASMX client contains proxy code generated by the Wsdl tool. This code defines the interface and the Book data structure for the service and also contains a *CatalogService* class for accessing the service. The client program code, shown earlier in Listing 9-29, creates an instance of the proxy and invokes the service by calling its methods. The proxy knows the address of the service because it is included in the code generated by the Wsdl tool.

```
using (CatalogService proxy = new CatalogService())
{
    Book[] books;

    Console.WriteLine("All books");
    Console.WriteLine();
    books = proxy.GetCatalog();
    ListBooks(books);
    Console.WriteLine();

    Console.WriteLine("All books written by Kim Akers");
    Console.WriteLine();
    books = proxy.SearchCatalogByAuthor("Kim Akers");
    ListBooks(books);
    Console.WriteLine();

    Console.WriteLine("All biographies");
    Console.WriteLine();
    books = proxy.SearchCatalogByGenre("Biography");
    ListBooks(books);
    Console.WriteLine();
}
```

This programming exercise has demonstrated Indigo interoperability with an Indigo service that is equally accessible by first-generation and second-generation Web service clients. This was achieved by selecting a binding with *BasicProfile* interoperability and using the XmlSerializer.

Summary

This chapter covered interoperability and integration. In Indigo, interoperability refers to the ability to work with other platforms through the use of standards. Integration refers to the ability to work with non-SOAP technologies such as COM+ and MSMQ.

For an Indigo program to interoperate with other systems, there must be agreement about interoperability level, document style, message format, and message structure. These settings are controlled by the binding selected and the service contract. The Svcutil tool can determine the necessary settings for a service from its service description and generate the appropriate client proxy code and configuration settings.

COM+ integration allows the role of client or service to be replaced by a COM+ client application or a COM+ component. The ComSvcConfig tool can expose a service for a COM+ component, allowing Indigo clients to treat the component as a service. In the other direction, the Indigo service moniker allows a COM+ client application to access an Indigo service by pretending it is a component.

MSMQ integration allows the role of client or service to be replaced by a traditional program. You use the *MsmqIntegration* binding, and the service contract is required to provide a single service operation with a parameter of type *MsmqMessage<T>*.

Part III
Deploying Microsoft Code Name "Indigo" Solutions

In this part:

Chapter 10
Hosting

A word out of season may mar a whole lifetime.

—Greek proverb

Many kinds of programs can contain (or host) an Indigo service. In this chapter, the hosting choices are examined, along with their benefits and developer obligations.

After completing this chapter, you will:

- Know how to self-host services.
- Know how to host services in Microsoft Internet Information Services (IIS).
- Understand the differences between the two hosting models.
- Have created a Microsoft ASP.NET client for a service hosted in IIS.

Understanding Hosting

You can embed Indigo client or service code in just about any environment that supports managed code. For example, you can use Indigo in a console program, a Microsoft Windows Forms application, an ASP.NET Web application, a Microsoft Windows NT service, or a DLL library. The term **hosting** refers to the service-side environment that creates a service and controls its lifetime. If you do this hosting work yourself, you are **self-hosting**. An alternative to self-hosting is to host a service in IIS. IIS is a key hosting environment for Indigo services.

Self-Hosting

In general, the steps to host a service are the same for any managed environment. The lifetime of a service depends on its service host. A service comes into existence when you create an instance of the *ServiceHost* class. The service becomes available for use when you call *Open* on the *ServiceHost* object. The service stops responding to requests when you call *Close* on the *ServiceHost*. The service ceases to exist when you dispose of the *ServiceHost*.

Figure 10-1 shows a self-hosted service. An assembly creates a *ServiceHost* for its service type, which is either contained in the same assembly or a referenced assembly.

Figure 10-1   Self-hosted service

Hosting in IIS

An alternative to self-hosting is to host a service in IIS. In IIS hosting, IIS and ASP.NET collaborate with Indigo to provide a hosting environment that is Indigo-aware. Hosting in IIS provides valuable features such as compile-on-demand, automatic activation of services, health monitoring, and process recycling. Table 10-1 compares self-hosting and hosting in IIS.

> **Note**   IIS hosting is also sometimes referred to as ASP.NET hosting, Web hosting, or WAS hosting. This book uses the term *IIS hosting*.

Table 10-1   Self-Hosting vs. Hosting in IIS

Characteristic	Self-Hosting	Hosting in IIS
How a service is hosted	Write hosting code	Create an .svc file in a virtual directory
Name of service configuration file	*<exe-filename>*.config	Web.config
Address format	Follow standard addressing rules	Determined by virtual directory and .svc filename
Automatic activation of services	No	Yes
Automatic process recycling	No	Yes
Deployment options	Binary	Source or binary
Compile-on-demand	No	Yes
Health monitoring	No	Yes

Hosting a service in IIS is similar to writing an ASP.NET application. You don't have to write hosting code, but you do have to create a virtual directory and an .svc file containing directives. The .svc file indicates the service type class and language and can also contain directives to other source files or assemblies. It can also contain inline program code.

In IIS hosting, a service can be distributed in source or binary form. You can deploy a source file, which will be compiled on demand, or deploy a compiled assembly. Figure 10-2 shows three variations on hosting a service in IIS. In the first instance, the .svc file references an assembly that contains the service type. In the second instance, the .svc file contains the program code for the service type, which is compiled on demand. In the third instance, the

.svc file references an external source code file for the service type, which is compiled on demand.

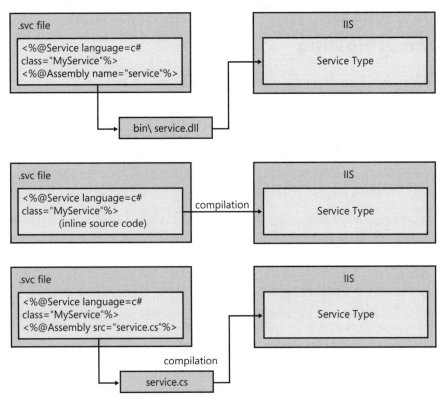

Figure 10-2 IIS-hosted services

IIS hosting provides **automatic activation** of services, which means that a service program doesn't have to be running in advance. When a message is received for a service, the service is launched if necessary. This is very different from self-hosting, in which a service has to be launched in advance of clients.

IIS monitors the health of services and performs automatic process recycling when necessary. If a service process appears to not be healthy, IIS recycles the process. IIS will also recycle an app domain after an .svc file is modified. This means all you have to do to update a service is to update the files in the virtual directory.

Hosting in IIS is not limited to HTTP communication. If Windows Activation Services (WAS) is available on your operating system, services that communicate over TCP, named pipes, or MSMQ can be hosted in the same way. This book does not cover non-HTTP hosting with WAS because the feature is not fully available at the time of this writing.

IIS and ASP.NET become Indigo-aware and recognize .svc files after Indigo is installed. If IIS and ASP.NET are installed *after* Indigo, this registration will not have taken place. You can register Indigo with IIS and ASP.NET by running the command *xws_reg −i* from a command window.

Programming Hosting

In self-hosting, developers write their own hosting code. In IIS hosting, developers create a virtual directory and define a service in an .svc file.

Self-Hosting a Service

In most environments, you must provide hosting code for your service. (It's not necessary to provide hosting code in an Indigo-aware environment such as IIS.) The lifetime of a service starts with instantiation of a *ServiceHost* object and ends with its disposal.

To self-host a service, create an instance of the *ServiceHost* class, specifying the service type as a generic.

```
ServiceHost<MyServiceClass> host = new ServiceHost<MyServiceClass>();
```

You can specify one or more base addresses for the *ServiceHost* in its constructor. You cannot specify more than one base address for the same transport scheme. The following code specifies two base addresses for a service host. If you specify an HTTP base address for a service host, a MEX endpoint will be created for the service.

```
Uri baseAddress1 = new Uri("http://localhost:8000/MyService/");
Uri baseAddress2 = new Uri("net.tcp://localhost:9000/MyService/");
ServiceHost<MyServiceClass> host = new ServiceHost<MyServiceClass>(baseAddress1,
    baseAddress2);
```

After you create a *ServiceHost*, your program's configuration file is scanned for endpoints and other configuration. The configuration file for a self-hosted service is based on its EXE name, such as service.exe.config. The following configuration settings define two endpoints for a service.

```
<system.serviceModel>
    <services>
        <service
            serviceType="ProgrammingIndigo.SampleService">
            <endpoint
                address="http://localhost:8000/MyService/"
                bindingType="wsProfileBinding"
                contractType="ProgrammingIndigo.ISampleContract" />
            <endpoint
                address="net.tcp://localhost:9000/MyService/"
                bindingType="netProfileTcpBinding"
                contractType="ProgrammingIndigo.ISampleContract" />
```

```
    </service>
  </services>
</system.serviceModel>
```

You can also add endpoints in code, as shown next. For more information on defining endpoints, see Chapter 4.

```
// Add an HTTP endpoint to the service.
EndpointAddress address = new EndpointAddress("http://localhost:8000/MyService/");
WSProfileBinding binding = new WSProfileBinding();
host.AddEndpoint(address, binding);

// Add a TCP endpoint to the service.
EndpointAddress address2 = new EndpointAddress("net.tcp://localhost:9000/MyService/");
NetProfileTcpBinding binding2 = new NetProfileTcpBinding();
host.AddEndpoint(address2, binding2);
```

> **Warning**   If you are self-hosting a service on a machine that is also running IIS 5.1, you should avoid using port 80 in service addresses because IIS 5.1 uses port 80 exclusively. That's not a concern with later versions of IIS because a module named HTTP.sys allows applications to share HTTP ports.

A service is not accessible until its *ServiceHost* is explicitly opened. This gives you an opportunity to modify the *ServiceHost* configuration before accepting client activity. Call the *Open* method of the service host to open the service. It is then "open for business" and can be accessed by clients.

```
host.Open();
```

Closing the service prevents further client requests from being accepted. Call the *Close* method of a service host to close a service.

```
host.Close();
```

Disposing of the service host ends the service altogether.

```
host.Dispose();
```

The following code shows a *ServiceHost* that is created and disposed with a *using* statement. The service host is held open until the user presses ENTER in a console window. In this example, the application's .config file defines the endpoint(s) for the service.

```
using (ServiceHost<MyService> host = new ServiceHost<MyService>)
{
    host.Open();
    Console.WriteLine("The service is open. Press ENTER to close.");
    Console.ReadLine();
```

```
        Console.WriteLine("Closing service");
        host.Close();
    }
```

Self-Hosting in a Windows Console Program

In a console program, the static *Main* function is a logical place to manage the lifetime of a service. The *Main* function can be part of the service implementation class or a different class. In the example in Listing 10-1, the static *Main* function is part of the service implementation class. The *ServiceHost* object is declared, instantiated, opened, closed, and disposed all in *Main*.

Listing 10-1   Service Hosting in a Windows Console Program

```
using System;
using System.ServiceModel;
using System.ServiceModel.Design;

namespace ProgrammingIndigo
{
    [ServiceContract]
    public interface ISampleContract
    {
        [OperationContract]
        double Add(double n1, double n2);
        [OperationContract]
        double Subtract(double n1, double n2);
        [OperationContract]
        double Multiply(double n1, double n2);
        [OperationContract]
        double Divide(double n1, double n2);
    }

    public class SampleService : ISampleContract
    {
        public double Add(double n1, double n2)
        {
            Console.WriteLine("Add called");
            return n1 + n2;
        }

        public double Subtract(double n1, double n2)
        {
            Console.WriteLine("Subtract called");
            return n1 - n2;
        }

        public double Multiply(double n1, double n2)
        {
            Console.WriteLine("Multiply called");
            return n1 * n2;
        }
```

```
    public double Divide(double n1, double n2)
    {
        Console.WriteLine("Divide called");
        return n1 / n2;
    }

    // Host the service.
    // This service is a self-hosted EXE.

    public static void Main()
    {
        using ServiceHost<SampleService> serviceHost = new
            ServiceHost<SampleService>();
        {
            serviceHost.Open();

            Console.WriteLine("The service is ready.");
            Console.WriteLine();
            Console.WriteLine("Press ENTER to shut down service.");
            Console.WriteLine();
            Console.ReadLine();

            serviceHost.Close();
        }
    }
}
```

Self-Hosting in a Windows Forms Application

In a Windows Forms program, a *ServiceHost* object can be declared as a member of the form class.

```
ServiceHost<MyService> host = null;
```

The *ServiceHost* can be instantiated and opened as the form initializes. In Listing 10-2, this is done in the Form Load function. The code in this listing creates a *ServiceHost*, adds an endpoint in code, and opens the service. Alternatively, you can define the endpoints for the service in the application configuration file.

```
private void Form1_Load(object sender, EventArgs e)
{
    host = new ServiceHost<MyService>();
    Uri address = new Uri("http://localhost:8000/MyService/");
    BasicProfileBinding binding = new BasicProfileBinding();
    host.AddEndpoint(typeof(IMyService), binding, address);
    host.Open();
}
```

The service host can be closed when the form closes. The following code closes a *ServiceHost* in a form's *FormClosing* event.

```
private void Form1_FormClosing(object sender, FormClosingEventArgs e)
{
    host.Close();
}
```

Listing 10-2 shows a Windows Forms application that hosts a service.

Listing 10-2   Service Hosting in a Windows Forms Application

```
using System;
using System.Collections.Generic;
using System.ComponentModel;
using System.Data;
using System.Drawing;
using System.Text;
using System.Windows.Forms;
using System.ServiceModel;

namespace WinForms
{
    public partial class Form1 : Form
    {
        ServiceHost<MyService> host = null;

        public Form1()
        {
            InitializeComponent();
        }

        private void Form1_Load(object sender, EventArgs e)
        {
            host = new ServiceHost<MyService>();
            Uri address = new Uri("http://localhost:8000/MyService/");
            BasicProfileBinding binding = new BasicProfileBinding();
            host.AddEndpoint(typeof(IMyService), binding, address);
            host.Open();
        }

        private void Form1_FormClosing(object sender, FormClosingEventArgs e)
        {
            host.Close();
        }
    }

    [ServiceContract]
    public interface IMyService
    {
        [OperationContract]
        decimal ComputeTax(decimal amount, decimal taxRate);
    }

    [ServiceBehavior(RunOnUIThread = true)]
    public class MyService : IMyService
    {
```

```
        public decimal ComputeTax(decimal amount, decimal taxRate)
        {
            return amount * (taxRate / 100.00M);
        }
    }
}
```

The *[ServiceBehavior]* attribute for the service implementation class specifies the *RunOn-UIThread=true* parameter. This informs Indigo that the service is hosted on a user interface thread.

```
[ServiceBehavior(RunOnUIThread=true)]
public class MyService : IMyService
{
    public decimal ComputeTax(decimal amount, decimal taxRate)
    {
        return amount * (taxRate / 100.00M);
    }
}
```

Note in this listing that the form class is defined in the source file, and then the service contract and implementation class follow. In a Windows Forms application, the first class in your form source module must be the form class, or you will not be able to use the form designer.

Self-Hosting in a Windows Service Application

A Windows service application, traditionally known as a Windows NT service, is controlled by the Services applet in Control Panel. (Choose Control Panel, Administrative Tools, Services.) NT services can be configured to start up when a system boots.

In an NT service that hosts an Indigo service, a *ServiceHost* should be instantiated and opened when the NT service is started, and it should be closed and disposed when the NT service is stopped. Listing 10-3 shows a sample NT service that hosts an Indigo service.

An NT service in managed code must implement a class based on the *ServiceBase* class. This is a logical place to declare a *ServiceHost* object.

```
public class SampleService : ServiceBase, ISampleContract
{
    public ServiceHost<SampleService> serviceHost = null;
    ...
}
```

The *OnStart* method of the class is called when the service is started. This is where the *Service-Host* should be instantiated and opened.

```
// Start the NT service.

protected override void OnStart(string[] args)
{
```

```
    if (serviceHost!=null)
    {
        serviceHost.Close();
        serviceHost.Dispose();
    }

    serviceHost = new ServiceHost<SampleService>();

    serviceHost.Open();
}
```

The *OnStop* method of the class is called when the service is stopped. This is where the *ServiceHost* should be closed and disposed.

```
// Stop the NT service.

protected override void OnStop()
{
    serviceHost.Close();
    serviceHost.Dispose();
    serviceHost = null;
}
```

You install and uninstall NT services by using the Installutil utility.

Listing 10-3   Service Hosting in an NT Service

```
using System;
using System.ComponentModel;
using System.ServiceModel;
using System.ServiceModel.Design;
using System.Configuration.Install;
using System.ServiceProcess;

namespace ProgrammingIndigo
{
    // Create a service contract and define the service operations.
    // NOTE: The service operations must be declared explicitly.
    [ServiceContract]
    public interface ISampleContract
    {
        [OperationContract]
        double Add(double n1, double n2);
        [OperationContract]
        double Subtract(double n1, double n2);
        [OperationContract]
        double Multiply(double n1, double n2);
        [OperationContract]
        double Divide(double n1, double n2);
    }

    [RunInstaller(true)]
    public class ProjectInstaller : Installer
    {
```

```
        private ServiceProcessInstaller process;
        private ServiceInstaller service;

        public ProjectInstaller()
        {
            process = new ServiceProcessInstaller();
            process.Account = ServiceAccount.LocalSystem;
            service = new ServiceInstaller();
            service.ServiceName = "IndigoNTServiceQuickstart";
            Installers.Add(process);
            Installers.Add(service);
        }
}

// The Service implementation implements your service contract.
public class SampleService : ServiceBase, ISampleContract
{
        public ServiceHost<SampleService> serviceHost = null;

        public static void Main()
        {
            ServiceBase.Run(new SampleService());
        }

        public SampleService()
        {
            ServiceName = "IndigoQuickstartNTService";
        }

        // Start the NT service.

        protected override void OnStart(string[] args)
        {
            if (serviceHost!=null)
            {
                serviceHost.Close();
                serviceHost.Dispose();
            }

            serviceHost = new ServiceHost<SampleService>();

            serviceHost.Open();
        }


        // Stop the NT service.

        protected override void OnStop()
        {
            serviceHost.Close();
            serviceHost.Dispose();
            serviceHost = null;
        }

        // Implement the service operations.
```

```
public double Add(double n1, double n2)
{
    Console.WriteLine("Add called");
    return n1 + n2;
}

public double Subtract(double n1, double n2)
{
    Console.WriteLine("Subtract called");
    return n1 - n2;
}

public double Multiply(double n1, double n2)
{
    Console.WriteLine("Multiply called");
    return n1 * n2;
}

public double Divide(double n1, double n2)
{
    Console.WriteLine("Divide called");
    return n1 / n2;
}

    }
}
```

Hosting a Service in IIS

In IIS hosting, your service is defined by an .svc file that resides in a virtual directory. The address of the service is determined by the machine name, the virtual directory name, and the .svc filename. For example, a service on the local machine defined by the file Service.svc residing in a virtual directory named MyService might have the address *http://localhost/MyService/service.svc*. You might avoid port 80 in self-hosted services on IIS 5.1, but it's fine to use port 80 in IIS-hosted services. It's also okay to put an ASP.NET application and Indigo services in the same virtual directory.

Specifying Configuration File Settings for an IIS-Hosted Service

The configuration for an IIS-hosted service is defined in a configuration file named Web.config. In addition to the usual Indigo configuration settings, the Web.config file also contains a *<system.web>* section.

```
<system.web>
    <compilation debug="true" />
</system.web>
```

Tip   In IIS hosting, the configuration file name for a service is named Web.config.

If you place multiple .svc files in the same virtual directory, those services will share a Web.config file.

Specifying Endpoints for an IIS-Hosted Service

The endpoint definitions in an IIS-hosted service are relative to the implied address from the virtual directory and .svc filename. In the following endpoint configuration, the *address* parameter is set to an empty string.

```
<system.serviceModel>
    <services>
        <service
            serviceType="ProgrammingIndigo.SampleService">
            <endpoint
                address=""
                bindingType="basicProfileBinding"
                contractType="ProgrammingIndigo.ISampleContract" />
        </service>
    </services>
</system.serviceModel>
```

If you specify a value for *address*, you can add a relative path to the base address for the service. For example, the following endpoint address yields an address like this: *http://localhost/ MyService/service.svc/test.*

```
<service serviceType="ProgrammingIndigo.SampleService">
    <endpoint
        address="test"
        bindingType="basicProfileBinding"
        contractType="ProgrammingIndigo.ISampleContract" />
</service>
```

Using .svc Files

An .svc file defines a service to IIS. An .svc file contains directives and can also program code.

All .svc files begin with a *<%@Service%>* directive (or **service directive**) that identifies the class implementing the service with a *class* parameter. The service directive also identifies the language in use with a *language* parameter. The service directive can also specify whether debug information should be reported in detail with a *debug* parameter. The following service directive identifies the service language as C#, enables the debug option, and specifies the service type class as *ProgrammingIndigo.SampleService*.

```
<%@Service language=c# debug="true" class="ProgrammingIndigo.SampleService" %>
```

Tip Be sure to include a class's namespace when you specify a service type for the *class* parameter.

An .svc file can reference a service in source form or binary form. An .svc file references a service in source form by containing direct program code, called **inline code**, or by referencing an external source module. In both cases, the source code is compiled on demand. An .svc file references a service in binary form by referencing an assembly.

An .svc file with inline code follows its directive(s) with program code in the specified language. The following .svc file contains inline code. Aside from the Web.config endpoint definitions, the .svc file fully defines the entire service and is compiled on demand.

```
<%@Service language=c# debug=true class="hello"%>

using System;
using System.ServiceModel;

[ServiceContract]
public class hello
{
    [OperationContract]
    string Hello(string name)
    {
        return "Hello, " + name + "!";
    }
}
```

A variation on the compile-on-demand technique is to reference an external source file instead of placing the program code inline in the .svc file. To reference an external source file, you use an <%@Assembly%> directive (or **assembly directive**). The assembly directive contains an *src* parameter, which specifies the name of the source file. The following .svc file indicates that the program code is located in the source file Hello.cs.

```
<%@Service language=c# debug=true class="hello"%>
<%@Assembly src="hello.cs" %>
```

An alternative to deploying source code is to deploy a compiled assembly. Any compiled assemblies must be placed in a bin directory underneath the virtual directory. The assembly directive contains a *name* parameter, which specifies the name of the assembly. The following .svc file indicates that the assembly is located in bin\hello.dll.

```
<%@Service language=c# debug=true class="hello"%>
<%@Assembly name="hello" %>
```

Testing an IIS-Hosted Service with a Browser

You can check an IIS-hosted service with a browser to verify that there are no compilation errors. Entering the address of the service in a browser returns either a successful compilation page like that shown in Figure 10-3 or a compilation error page like that shown in Figure 10-4.

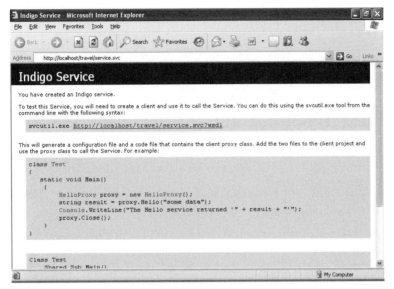

Figure 10-3   Successful compilation page

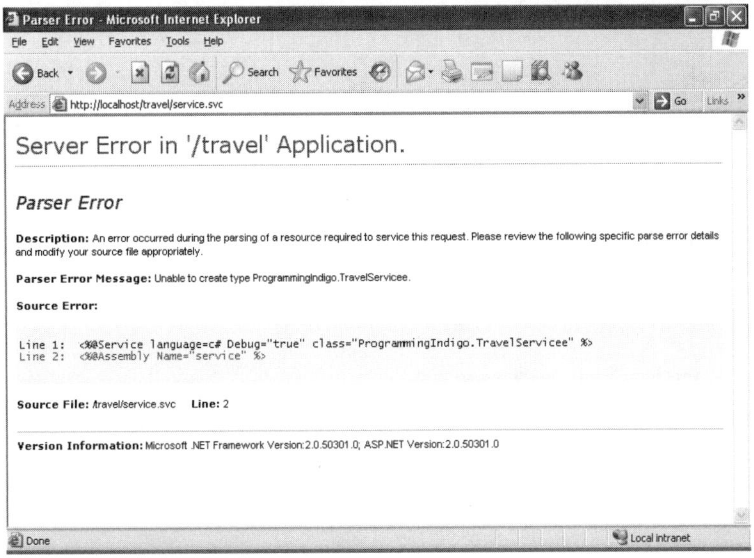

Figure 10-4   Compilation error page

Using Inline Code in an .svc File

Placing service type code directly in an .svc file compiles the service on demand. The entire service is self-contained in the .svc file and the Web.config file. The .svc file is placed in a virtual directory. For example:

```
\MyService
  MyService.svc
  web.config
```

The start of an .svc file contains a *<%@Service ... %>* directive that identifies the language, debug option, and class of the service. The remainder of the file contains the program code for the service.

```
<%@Service language=c# Debug="true" class="ProgrammingIndigo.SampleService" %>
```

Listing 10-4 shows an .svc file that contains a service.

Listing 10-4   Service Code in an .svc File

```
<%@Service language=c# Debug="true" class="ProgrammingIndigo.SampleService" %>

using System;
using System.ServiceModel;

namespace ProgrammingIndigo
{
    [ServiceContract]
    public interface ISampleContract
    {
        [OperationContract]
        double Add(double n1, double n2);
        [OperationContract]
        double Subtract(double n1, double n2);
        [OperationContract]
        double Multiply(double n1, double n2);
        [OperationContract]
        double Divide(double n1, double n2);
    }

    public class SampleService : ISampleContract
    {
        // Implement the service operations.

        public double Add(double n1, double n2)
        {
            return n1 + n2;
        }

        public double Subtract(double n1, double n2)
        {
            return n1 - n2;
        }

        public double Multiply(double n1, double n2)
        {
            return n1 * n2;
        }
```

```
        public double Divide(double n1, double n2)
        {
            return n1 / n2;
        }
    }
}
```

You might want an inline .svc file to reference source code from other files. You can use the *<%@ Assembly %>* directive to specify additional source files. The following code references the source files Service.cs and Common.cs.

```
<%@Service language=c# Debug="true" class="MyService" %>
<%@ Assembly src="service.cs" %>
<%@ Assembly src="common.cs" %>
```

In this example, the additional source files are placed in the virtual directory folder, as shown here.

```
\MyService
    service.svc
    service.cs
    common.cs
```

Using Code-Behind in an .svc File

Service type code can be placed in an assembly DLL, which the .svc file references. Underneath the virtual directory containing the .svc file is a bin directory where the service DLL resides. For example:

```
\MyService
    Web.config
    MyService.svc
      \bin
         MyService.dll
```

In the code-behind case, an .svc file contains several directives. First is a *<%@Service ... %>* directive that identifies the language, debug option, and class of the service. A *<%@Assembly %>* directive identifies an assembly in the bin directory. If additional assemblies are referenced, they should also be declared with additional *<%@Assembly %>* directives.

Listing 10-5 shows an .svc file that references an assembly, Service.dll. Listing 10-6 shows the source code to the referenced assembly.

Listing 10-5   Service Reference in an .svc File

```
<%@Service language=c# Debug="true" class="ProgrammingIndigo.SampleService" %>
<%@Assembly Name="service" %>
```

Listing 10-6 Service Code for Service.dll

```csharp
using System;
using System.ServiceModel;
using System.Diagnostics;

namespace ProgrammingIndigo
{
    [ServiceContract]
    public interface ISampleContract
    {
        [OperationContract]
        double Add(double n1, double n2);
        [OperationContract]
        double Subtract(double n1, double n2);
        [OperationContract]
        double Multiply(double n1, double n2);
        [OperationContract]
        double Divide(double n1, double n2);
    }

    public class SampleService : ISampleContract
    {
        static TraceSource ts = new TraceSource("MyTraceSource");

        public double Add(double n1, double n2)
        {
            ts.TraceInformation("Add called");
            return n1 + n2;
        }

        public double Subtract(double n1, double n2)
        {
            ts.TraceInformation("Subtract called");
            return n1 - n2;
        }

        public double Multiply(double n1, double n2)
        {
            ts.TraceInformation("Multiply called");
            return n1 * n2;
        }

        public double Divide(double n1, double n2)
        {
            ts.TraceInformation("Divide called");
            return n1 / n2;
        }
    }
}
```

Virtual Directory Sharing

You don't need to limit a virtual directory to a single service. Because services are defined with .svc files, you can place as many of them as you like in the same virtual directory. For example:

```
\MyServices
    TravelService.svc
    AirTravelService.svc
    CarRentalTravelService.svc
    HotelTravelService.svc
```

You can also place ASP.NET applications in the same virtual directory with services.

Programming Exercise: Web Calculator

In this programming exercise, we will create a calculator service and a client to access it. The service will be implemented as inline code hosted in IIS. The client will be implemented as an ASP.NET application. Both the client and the service will be compiled on demand: there will be no need to create or build a solution in Microsoft Visual Studio, and there will be no DLL or EXE files to deploy. The client and service source files will be placed in a virtual directory. Compilation will occur on demand when the client and service are first accessed.

The service contract will implement the simple calculator functions Add, Subtract, Multiply, and Divide.

There are seven development steps in this exercise:

1. Create a virtual directory for the service.
2. Create the service .svc file.
3. Create the Service.cs file.
4. Create a Web.config file for the client and service.
5. Test the service with a browser.
6. Generate proxy code for the client.
7. Create the Client.aspx file.

Step 1: Create a Virtual Directory for the Service

We will create a virtual directory that both the client and the service will share. Follow this procedure to set up a virtual directory for the service.

1. Create a folder on your computer named calculator.
2. From the Start menu, launch Control Panel. Select Administrative Tools, Internet Information Services. Navigate to Web Sites, Default Web Sites. Right-click and select New,

Virtual Directory. Specify a name of **calculator**, and then associate it with the calculator folder created in step 1. Before exiting IIS Manager, check step 3.

3. While in IIS Manager, navigate to Web Sites, Default Web Sites. The calculator folder should be listed. Right-click calculator, and then select Properties. On the Directory Security tab, click Edit.

4. In the Authentication Methods dialog box, Anonymous Access should be selected; if it isn't, select it. Close all dialog boxes by clicking OK, and then close IIS.

Step 2: Create the Service .svc File

The service definition is contained inline in an .svc file. In the calculator directory, create a file named Service.svc, and then enter the code in Listing 10-7.

Listing 10-7   Service Code for Service.svc

```
<%@Service language=c# Debug="true" class="ProgrammingIndigo.CalculatorService" %>
<%@ Assembly src="service.cs" %>
```

Step 3: Create the Service.cs File

The service implementation code is contained in Service.cs. In the calculator directory, create a file named Service.cs, and then enter the code in Listing 10-8.

Listing 10-8   Service Code for Service.svc

```csharp
using System;
using System.ServiceModel;

namespace ProgrammingIndigo
{
    // Define a service contract.
    [ServiceContract(Namespace="http://ProgrammingIndigo")]
    public interface ICalculator
    {
        [OperationContract]
        double Add(double n1, double n2);
        [OperationContract]
        double Subtract(double n1, double n2);
        [OperationContract]
        double Multiply(double n1, double n2);
        [OperationContract]
        double Divide(double n1, double n2);
    }

    // Service class, which implements the service contract.
    public class CalculatorService : ICalculator
    {
        public double Add(double n1, double n2)
        {
```

```
            return n1 + n2;
        }

        public double Subtract(double n1, double n2)
        {
            return n1 - n2;
        }

        public double Multiply(double n1, double n2)
        {
            return n1 * n2;
        }

        public double Divide(double n1, double n2)
        {
            return n1 / n2;
        }
    }

}
```

Step 4: Create a Web.config File for the Client and Service

A Web.config file is needed to specify endpoints and bindings for the service and the client. Create a text file named Web.config in the calculator folder with the code shown in Listing 10-9.

Listing 10-9   Calculator Service: Web.config

```xml
<?xml version="1.0" encoding="utf-8" ?>
<configuration xmlns="http://schemas.microsoft.com/.NetConfiguration/v2.0">
    <system.serviceModel>
        <services>
            <service
                serviceType="ProgrammingIndigo.CalculatorService"
                behaviorConfiguration="CalculatorServiceBehavior">
                <!-- use base address provided by host -->
                <endpoint address=""
                        bindingSectionName="wsProfileBinding"
                        bindingConfiguration="Binding1"
                        contractType="ProgrammingIndigo.ICalculator" />
            </service>
        </services>

        <client>
            <endpoint address="http://localhost/calculator/service.svc"
                    bindingSectionName="wsProfileBinding"
                    bindingConfiguration="Binding1"
                    contractType="ICalculator" />
        </client>

        <bindings>
          <wsProfileBinding>
            <binding configurationName="Binding1" />
```

```
        </wsProfileBinding>
      </bindings>

      <behaviors>
        <behavior
            configurationName="CalculatorServiceBehavior"
            returnUnknownExceptionsAsFaults="true" >
        </behavior>
      </behaviors>

    </system.serviceModel>

    <system.web>
      <compilation debug="true" />
    </system.web>

  </configuration>
```

Step 5: Test the Service with a Browser

Before going on to the client, we want to test that the service can be accessed. Launch Internet Explorer. On the address bar, specify the URL *http://localhost/calculator/service.svc*, and then press ENTER. If the resulting page does not list any errors, proceed to step 6. If there are problems, check the following:

- If the page returned by the browser describes compilation errors, check the code entered in the preceding steps. The compilation error display should highlight the offending code.

- If the resulting page describes HTTP errors, make sure your system has IIS enabled. You should be able to access *http://localhost* in a browser without receiving an error. If IIS seems to be properly enabled, review the virtual directory setup in the prior steps. If this also fails, look for clues in Control Panel, Administrative Tools, Event Log, or try an IIS-RESET.

The service is now ready. Next we need a client program to access it.

Step 6: Generate Proxy Code for the Client

We will now generate client proxy code by accessing the service's MEX endpoint with the Svcutil tool. From a command window, change the directory to the calculator folder where the service files reside. Run the following Svcutil command:

```
svcutil http://localhost/calculator/service.svc /out:proxy.cs
```

The file Proxy.cs is generated, containing the service contract and a proxy class for accessing the service.

Add Out.cs to your client project. In Visual Studio, right-click the project in the Solution Explorer window, and then select Add, Existing Item. Select Proxy.cs in the File Open dialog box, and then click OK. Out.cs is added to the client project.

Step 7: Create the Client.aspx File

The client ASP.NET application is contained in an .aspx file. In the calculator directory, create a file named Client.aspx, and then enter the code in Listing 10-10.

Listing 10-10   Calculator Client: Client.aspx

```
<%@ Page Language="C#" %>
<%@ Assembly src="proxy.cs" %>
<script runat="server">

    void Page_Load(object sender, EventArgs e)
    {
        Status.Text = "IndiCalc";
    }

    void Page_Unload(object sender, EventArgs e)
    {
       if (proxy != null)
          proxy.Close();
    }

    CalculatorProxy proxy;
    CalculatorProxy Proxy
    {
        get
        {
           if (proxy == null)
               proxy = new CalculatorProxy();
           return proxy;
        }
    }

    void ButtonAdd_Click(object sender, EventArgs e)
    {
        DoOperation();
        Operator.Value = "+";
    }

    void ButtonSubtract_Click(object sender, EventArgs e)
    {
        DoOperation();
        Operator.Value = "-";
    }

    void ButtonMultiple_Click(object sender, EventArgs e)
    {
        DoOperation();
        Operator.Value = "x";
```

```csharp
        }

        void ButtonDivide_Click(object sender, EventArgs e)
        {
            DoOperation();
            Operator.Value = "/";
        }

        void ButtonEquals_Click(object sender, EventArgs e)
        {
            DoOperation();
            Operator.Value = "=";
        }

        void ButtonClear_Click(object sender, EventArgs e)
        {
            Result.Text = "0";
            PreviousResult.Value = "0";
            Operator.Value = "=";
        }

        void DoOperation()
        {
            double previous = double.Parse(PreviousResult.Value);
            double current = double.Parse(Result.Text);
            switch (Operator.Value[0])
            {
                case '=' :
                    break;
                case '+' :
                    current = Proxy.Add(previous,current);
                    Result.Text = current.ToString();
                    break;
                case '-' :
                    current = Proxy.Subtract(previous,current);
                    Result.Text = current.ToString();
                    break;
                case 'x' :
                    current = Proxy.Multiply(previous,current);
                    Result.Text = current.ToString();
                    break;
                case '/' :
                    current = Proxy.Divide(previous,current);
                    Result.Text = current.ToString();
                    break;
            }
            PreviousResult.Value = Result.Text;
        }

    </script>
    <html>
    <head>
        <title>Calculator</title>
    </head>
    <body>
```

```
<form id="Form" action="Calculator.aspx" runat="server">
    <h3><asp:Label id="Label1" runat="server">Calculator</asp:Label></h3>
    <hr>
    <table cellpadding="3" cellspacing="3" style="BORDER: #0000ff 5px ridge;
        BACKGROUND-COLOR: lavender;">
        <tr>
            <td colspan="3">
                <asp:textbox id="Result" runat="server" Font-Bold="True"
                Font-Size="12pt" Width="100%" Height="35px" BorderWidth="3px"
                BackColor="#FFFFC0" BorderColor="#0000C0"></asp:textbox>
            </td>
            <td align="middle"><asp:button id="ButtonClear"
            onclick="ButtonClear_Click" runat="server" Font-Bold="True"
            Font-Size="12pt" Width="50px" Height="35px" BorderWidth="3px"
            BackColor="#FFFFC0" BorderColor="#0000C0" text="C"></asp:button>
            </td>
        </tr>
        <tr>
            <td colspan="4"><hr></td>
        </tr>
        <tr>
            <td align="middle"><input type="button" id="Button1" value="1"
            onclick="AppendToResult('1');" style="BORDER: #0000c0 3px solid;
            FONT-WEIGHT: bold; FONT-SIZE: 12pt; WIDTH: 50px; HEIGHT: 35px;
            BACKGROUND-COLOR: #c0c0ff"/>
            </td>
            <td align="middle"><input type="button" id="Button2" value="2"
            onclick="AppendToResult('2');" style="BORDER: #0000c0 3px solid;
            FONT-WEIGHT: bold; FONT-SIZE: 12pt; WIDTH: 50px; HEIGHT: 35px;
            BACKGROUND-COLOR: #c0c0ff"/>
            </td>
            <td align="middle"><input type="button" id="Button3" value="3"
            onclick="AppendToResult('3');" style="BORDER: #0000c0 3px solid;
            FONT-WEIGHT: bold; FONT-SIZE: 12pt; WIDTH: 50px; HEIGHT: 35px;
            BACKGROUND-COLOR: #c0c0ff"/>
            </td>
            <td align="middle"><asp:button id="ButtonAdd" text="+"
            onclick="ButtonAdd_Click" runat="server" Font-Bold="True"
            Font-Size="14pt" Width="50px" Height="35px" BorderWidth="3px"
            BackColor="#FFFFC0" BorderColor="#0000C0"></asp:button>
            </td>
        </tr>
        <tr>
            <td align="middle"><input type="button" id="Button4" value="4"
            onclick="AppendToResult('4');" style="BORDER: #0000c0 3px solid;
            FONT-WEIGHT: bold; FONT-SIZE: 12pt; WIDTH: 50px; HEIGHT: 35px;
            BACKGROUND-COLOR: #c0c0ff"/>
            </td>
            <td align="middle"><input type="button" id="Button5" value="5"
            onclick="AppendToResult('5');" style="BORDER: #0000c0 3px solid;
            FONT-WEIGHT: bold; FONT-SIZE: 12pt; WIDTH: 50px; HEIGHT: 35px;
            BACKGROUND-COLOR: #c0c0ff"/>
            </td>
            <td align="middle"><input type="button" id="Button6" value="6"
            onclick="AppendToResult('6');" style="BORDER: #0000c0 3px solid;
            FONT-WEIGHT: bold; FONT-SIZE: 12pt; WIDTH: 50px; HEIGHT: 35px;
```

```
                    BACKGROUND-COLOR: #c0c0ff"/>
                    </td>
                    <td align="middle"><asp:button id="ButtonSubtract" text="-"
                    onclick="ButtonSubtract_Click" runat="server" Font-Bold="True"
                    Font-Size="14pt" Width="50px" Height="35px" BorderWidth="3px"
                    BackColor="#FFFFC0" BorderColor="#0000C0"></asp:button>
                    </td>
                </tr>
                <tr>
                    <td align="middle"><input type="button" id="Button7" value="7"
                    onclick="AppendToResult('7');" style="BORDER: #0000c0 3px solid;
                    FONT-WEIGHT: bold; FONT-SIZE: 12pt; WIDTH: 50px; HEIGHT: 35px;
                    BACKGROUND-COLOR: #c0c0ff"/>
                    </td>
                    <td align="middle"><input type="button" id="Button8" value="8"
                    onclick="AppendToResult('8');" style="BORDER: #0000c0 3px solid;
                    FONT-WEIGHT: bold; FONT-SIZE: 12pt; WIDTH: 50px; HEIGHT: 35px;
                    BACKGROUND-COLOR: #c0c0ff"/>
                    </td>
                    <td align="middle"><input type="button" id="Button9" value="9"
                    onclick="AppendToResult('9');" style="BORDER: #0000c0 3px solid;
                    FONT-WEIGHT: bold; FONT-SIZE: 12pt; WIDTH: 50px; HEIGHT: 35px;
                    BACKGROUND-COLOR: #c0c0ff"/>
                    </td>
                    <td align="middle"><asp:button id="ButtonMultiple" text="x"
                    onclick="ButtonMultiple_Click" runat="server" Font-Bold="True"
                    Font-Size="12pt" Width="50px" Height="35px" BorderWidth="3px"
                    BackColor="#FFFFC0" BorderColor="#0000C0"></asp:button>
                    </td>
                </tr>
                <tr>
                    <td align="middle"><input type="button" id="ButtonDecimal" value="."
                    onclick="AppendToResult('.');" style="BORDER: #0000c0 3px solid;
                    FONT-WEIGHT: bold; FONT-SIZE: 14pt; WIDTH: 50px; HEIGHT: 35px;
                    BACKGROUND-COLOR: #c0c0ff"/>
                    </td>
                    <td align="middle"><input type="button" id="Button0" value="0"
                    onclick="AppendToResult('0');" style="BORDER: #0000c0 3px solid;
                    FONT-WEIGHT: bold; FONT-SIZE: 12pt; WIDTH: 50px; HEIGHT: 35px;
                    BACKGROUND-COLOR: #c0c0ff"/>
                    </td>
                    <td align="middle"><asp:button id="ButtonEquals"
                    onclick="ButtonEquals_Click" runat="server" Font-Bold="True"
                    Font-Size="14pt" Width="50px" Height="35px" BorderWidth="3px"
                    BackColor="#FFFFC0" BorderColor="#0000C0" text="="></asp:button>
                    </td>
                    <td align="middle"><asp:button id="ButtonDivide"
                    onclick="ButtonDivide_Click" runat="server" Font-Bold="True"
                    Font-Size="12pt" Width="50px" Height="35px" BorderWidth="3px"
                    BackColor="#FFFFC0" BorderColor="#0000C0" text="/"></asp:button>
                    </td>
                </tr>
                <tr>
                    <td colspan="4" align="right"><hr><asp:label id="Status" runat="server"
                    Text="" Font-Italic="True" Font-Size="12pt" Width="100%"
```

```
            ForeColor="#0000C0" />
          </td>
        </tr>
      </table>
      <!-- Hidden fields used to maintain PreviousResult and active Operator -->
      <input id="PreviousResult" type="hidden" value="0" runat="server" />
      <input id="Operator" type="hidden" value="=" runat="server" />
    </form>
  </body>
</html>

<script>
<!-- Client script -->
    var reset = 1;
    function AppendToResult(n)
    {
        if (reset == 1)
        {
            Form.Result.value = "";
            reset = 0;
        }
        Form.Result.value += n;
    }
</script>
```

At this point, your calculator folder should contain the following files:

- Client.aspx, containing the source code to the ASP.NET client

- Proxy.cs, containing the generated client proxy code for the service

- Service.cs, containing the service implementation code

- Service.svc, the .svc file identifying the service to IIS

- Web.config, the configuration file for the service and the client

Deployment

We're now ready to try things out. Launch a browser and enter the address *http://localhost/calculator/client.aspx*. You should see output like that shown in Figure 10-5. You are seeing an interface displayed by the ASP.NET client, which was compiled on demand. We have not yet accessed the service.

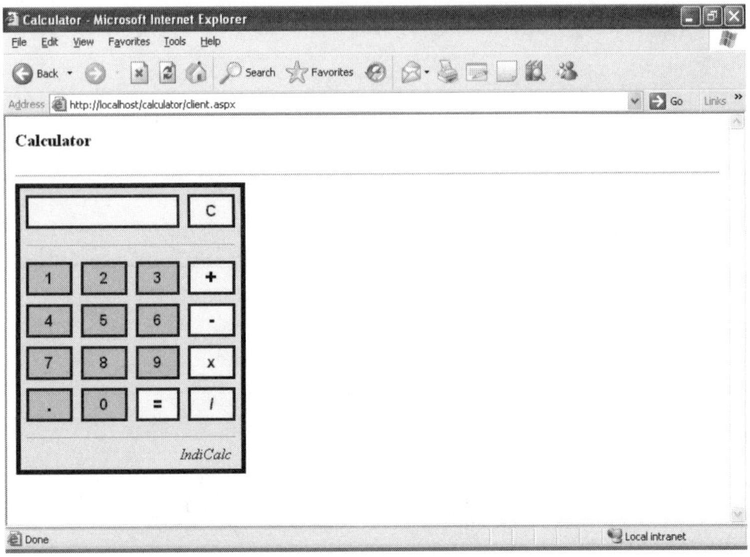

Figure 10-5   Calculator client

Perform a calculation with the calculator that involves addition, subtraction, multiplication, or division. For example, enter these keystrokes: 1 0 0 / 2 =. After you call the service's *Divide* operation, the client displays the result, 50. Like the client, the service is compiled on demand.

Understanding the Service Code

The service is hosted in IIS, so there is no hosting code in the service program. The service is defined by the file Service.svc in the calculator virtual directory, shown earlier in Listing 10-7. The *<%@Service%>* directive indicates that the service type is *ProgrammingIndigo.CalculatorService*. The *<%Assembly%>* directive indicates that source code in Service.cs should be included in the compilation.

```
<%@Service language=c# Debug="true" class="ProgrammingIndigo.CalculatorService" %>
<%@ Assembly src="service.cs" %>
```

The service implementation code in Service.cs, shown in Listing 10-8, defines and implements a service contract for a simple calculator service. The contract is shown here.

```
[ServiceContract(Namespace="http://ProgrammingIndigo")]
public interface ICalculator
{
    [OperationContract]
    double Add(double n1, double n2);
    [OperationContract]
    double Subtract(double n1, double n2);
    [OperationContract]
    double Multiply(double n1, double n2);
```

```
    [OperationContract]
    double Divide(double n1, double n2);
}
```

The configuration file for the service is Web.config, shown earlier in Listing 10-9. It is shared by both the service and the client because they are located in the same virtual directory in this exercise. If you were to separate the client and service into separate virtual directories or place them on separate machines, the client and service sections of Web.config would need to be separated. The service configuration in Web.config defines a single endpoint with the *WSProfile* binding. The address is specified as an empty string, which defaults to the base address for the service, *http://localhost/calculator/service.svc.*

```
<services>
    <service
        serviceType="ProgrammingIndigo.CalculatorService"
        behaviorConfiguration="CalculatorServiceBehavior">
        <!-- use base address provided by host -->
        <endpoint address=""
            bindingSectionName="wsProfileBinding"
            bindingConfiguration="Binding1"
            contractType="ProgrammingIndigo.ICalculator" />
    </service>
</services>
```

When the service is accessed for the first time by the client, it is automatically compiled.

Understanding the Client Code

The client is an ASP.NET application, as shown earlier in Listing 10-10. An *<%Assembly%>* directive includes the Proxy.cs source file in the compilation; Proxy.cs contains the client proxy code for the service generated by the Svcutil tool. It contains the definition of the service contract and a *CalculatorProxy* class.

```
<%@ Page Language="C#" %>
<%@ Assembly src="proxy.cs" %>
```

The client ASP.NET application defines a *CalculatorProxy* object. The *CalculatorProxy* is implemented as a property. The first time the property is accessed, the *CalculatorProxy* is created. No endpoint configuration name is specified in the proxy constructor because there is only a single unnamed client endpoint definition in the configuration file.

```
void Page_Unload(object sender, EventArgs e)
{
    if (proxy != null)
        proxy.Close();
}

CalculatorProxy proxy;
CalculatorProxy Proxy
{
```

```
get
{
    if (proxy == null)
        proxy = new CalculatorProxy();
    return proxy;
}
}
```

The Add, Subtract, Multiply, and Divide buttons call a common method named *DoOperation*. *DoOperation* invokes the appropriate service operation and updates the display with the result.

```
void ButtonAdd_Click(object sender, EventArgs e)
{
    DoOperation();
    Operator.Value = "+";
}

void ButtonSubtract_Click(object sender, EventArgs e)
{
    DoOperation();
    Operator.Value = "-";
}

void ButtonMultiple_Click(object sender, EventArgs e)
{
    DoOperation();
    Operator.Value = "x";
}

void ButtonDivide_Click(object sender, EventArgs e)
{
    DoOperation();
    Operator.Value = "/";
}

void ButtonEquals_Click(object sender, EventArgs e)
{
    DoOperation();
    Operator.Value = "=";
}

void ButtonClear_Click(object sender, EventArgs e)
{
    Result.Text = "0";
    PreviousResult.Value = "0";
    Operator.Value = "=";
}

void DoOperation()
{
    double previous = double.Parse(PreviousResult.Value);
    double current = double.Parse(Result.Text);
    switch (Operator.Value[0])
    {
```

```
        case '=' :
            break;
        case '+' :
            current = Proxy.Add(previous,current);
            Result.Text = current.ToString();
            break;
        case '-' :
            current = Proxy.Subtract(previous,current);
            Result.Text = current.ToString();
            break;
        case 'x' :
            current = Proxy.Multiply(previous,current);
            Result.Text = current.ToString();
            break;
        case '/' :
            current = Proxy.Divide(previous,current);
            Result.Text = current.ToString();
            break;
    }
    PreviousResult.Value = Result.Text;
}
```

The Web.config file, shown in Listing 10-9, contains the client endpoint definition.

```
<client>
    <endpoint address="http://localhost/calculator/service.svc"
        bindingSectionName="wsProfileBinding"
        bindingConfiguration="Binding1"
        contractType="ICalculator" />
</client>
```

The calculator example demonstrates on-demand compilation of an Indigo service hosted in
IIS and an Indigo client contained within an ASP.NET application.

Summary

This chapter covered hosting. Indigo code can be embedded in nearly any managed code environment. There are two hosting modes: self-hosting and hosting in IIS.

In self-hosting, developers are in control of the service lifetime. The life cycle of a service is
controlled by creating, opening, closing, and disposing of a *ServiceHost<T>* object.

In IIS hosting, developers don't have to write hosting code. As with ASP.NET applications,
developers place source code or binary code in a virtual directory. An .svc file contains directives and can also contain inline code. The .svc file can reference compiled assemblies or
source code files. The configuration file for an IIS-hosted service is named Web.config. IIS
hosting provides the most reliable hosting environment.

The example application showed an ASP.NET client accessing a calculator service hosted in
IIS. Both the client and the service were placed in a virtual directory and were compiled on
demand.

Chapter 11

Management

> *To manage a system effectively, you might focus on the interactions of the parts rather than their behavior taken separately.*
>
> *—Russell L. Ackoff*

Management capabilities help administrators configure, monitor, and debug software systems. Indigo provides management tools and features and integrates with Microsoft Windows management facilities.

After completing this chapter, you will:

- Know how to configure end-to-end tracing.
- Know how to configure message logging.
- Know how to enable Windows Management Instrumentation (WMI) reporting for an Indigo service.
- Understand how to use the SvcTraceViewer tool to analyze traces and logged messages.
- Be familiar with the SvcConfigEditor tool, which is used to edit configuration files.

Understanding Management

Distributed systems can be challenging to manage: activity takes place across multiple computers and potentially across multiple locations and organizations as well. In decentralized systems, no single system has a complete view of activity.

Indigo provides several features for management:

- **End-to-end tracing**   Logs the activities of Indigo programs
- **Messaging logging**   Logs messages sent and received
- **SvcTraceViewer**   A tool that provides a GUI for viewing end-to-end traces and logged messages

- **Windows Management Instrumentation** For monitoring and controlling Indigo programs at runtime

- **Windows Performance Counters** For statistically monitoring the behavior of Indigo programs

- **SvcConfigEditor** A tool that provides a GUI for editing configuration files

End-to-End Tracing

End-to-end tracing records events as an Indigo program executes. It uses these Windows tracing mechanisms: System.Diagnostics, Event Tracing for Windows (ETW), and WMI. In addition to Indigo, many other Microsoft technologies participate in end-to-end tracing, including Internet Information Services (IIS), ASP.NET, System.Net, and SQL Server 2005. Tracing can be enabled in configuration file settings or at runtime through WMI and ETW.

The events logged can include both successful operations and failures. Traces can include information ranging from "verbose" details about service behavior to critical errors. Traces are useful for verifying correct operation and for debugging problems. Looking at the events in a trace helps put errors in context. Figure 11-1 is a partial display of a trace log for a calculator service; it shows the events that occur when an *Add* operation is invoked.

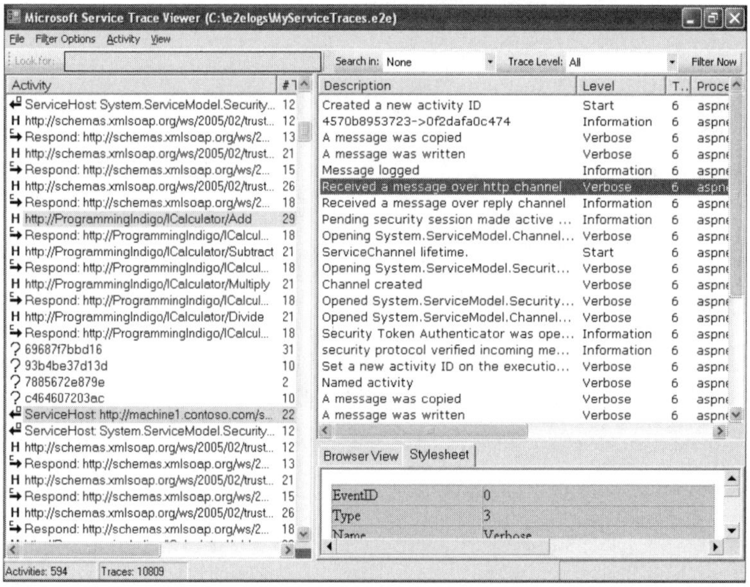

Figure 11-1 Example trace

Events are grouped into **activities**. Indigo assigns an **activity ID** to events that are logged. New activities are started when significant events occur, such as sending a request message or receiving a response message. The event sequence shown earlier in Figure 11-1 contains the events for a single activity.

End-to-end tracing is available to both clients and services. It is enabled through configuration file settings. The level of information logged can be set to None, Critical, Error, Warning, Information, or Verbose.

Traces are sent to **trace listeners**. Microsoft provides listeners for writing XML and for writing to ETW logs. You can also create new trace listeners to record traces to a remote system, a database, or whatever your solution demands.

The recommended way to view traces is through the SvcTraceViewer tool, described later in the chapter. This tool provides an integrated view of activities, traces, and logged messages.

As messages are sent from one machine to another, an activity ID is maintained. Activity IDs make it possible to analyze batches of end-to-end traces and follow the flow of messages across machines.

Message Logging

Message logging saves messages sent or received by an Indigo program. Specifically, messages are sent to a trace source named IndigoMessageLogTraceSource, and a trace listener named MessageWriterTraceListener writes these messages to disk. By using a different trace listener, you can send messages to other places, such as a database or another machine.

Message logging is useful for verifying the content of messages when you troubleshoot problems. Messages can be logged at two levels: the transport level and the service level. Messages logged at the transport level are in their sent or received state and might be encrypted. Messages logged at the service level have had their headers processed and might have been decrypted.

Messages are logged as XML files. The default location for logged messages is %Windir%\system32\LogFiles\Messages. The location can be changed in configuration file settings.

Listing 11-1 shows a logged message that was received for the activity shown earlier in Figure 11-1. The message is in its original form and has an encrypted body. There is an outer *<MessageLogTraceRecord>* element that contains the message. *<MessageLogTraceRecord>* contains a *Source* attribute that identifies the source of the message and a *Type* attribute that identifies the condition of the message when it was logged. In this case, the message source is *TransportRead* and the type is *System.ServiceModel.BufferedMessage*.

Listing 11-1 Logged Message

```
<MessageLogTraceRecord Time="2005-04-23T22:21:52.8593056-07:00"
    Source="TransportRead" Type="System.ServiceModel.BufferedMessage"
xmlns="http://schemas.microsoft.com/ServiceModel/2004/06/Management/MessageTrace">
  <s:Envelope xmlns:s="http://schemas.xmlsoap.org/soap/envelope/">
    <s:Header>
      <ActivityId xmlns="http://schemas.microsoft.com/2004/09/ServiceModel/Diagnostics">
        uuid:98b6ad9c-49a8-4ea8-97fc-e6107d025880</ActivityId>
    </s:Header>
    <s:Body s:encodingStyle="http://schemas.xmlsoap.org/soap/encoding/">
      <q1:Add xmlns:q1="http://Microsoft.ServiceModel.Samples"
        xmlns:xsi="http://www.w3.org/2001/XMLSchema-instance"
        xmlns:xsd="http://www.w3.org/2001/XMLSchema">
        <n1 xsi:type="xsd:double" xmlns="">100</n1>
        <n2 xsi:type="xsd:double" xmlns="">15.99</n2>
      </q1:Add>
    </s:Body>
  </s:Envelope>
</MessageLogTraceRecord>
```

The Service Trace Viewer

Raw traces can be hard to understand. To assist in viewing and analyzing traces, Indigo includes a tool named SvcTraceViewer. You can open multiple trace files in SvcTraceViewer. You can thus combine the activity from multiple programs and systems into a single view and thereby trace control flow and activities from one process to another.

The SvcTraceViewer user interface was shown earlier in Figure 11-1. The activity pane on the left shows the activity IDs contained in the trace. The event pane at the upper right shows events for the selected activity. The event detail pane at the lower right shows details for the selected event. When one or more activities are selected in the activity, the corresponding events are displayed in the event pane. When an event is selected in the event pane, the event's details are shown in the detail pane. If the event is a logged message, the detail pane allows the logged message to be viewed.

The detail pane provides two or more tabs for viewing details about the selected event. The Browser View tab shows event details as XML. The Stylesheet tab shows event details in table form. If the event being viewed is the logging of a message, a third tab named Message is available that shows the logged message. Figure 11-2 shows a logged message being viewed.

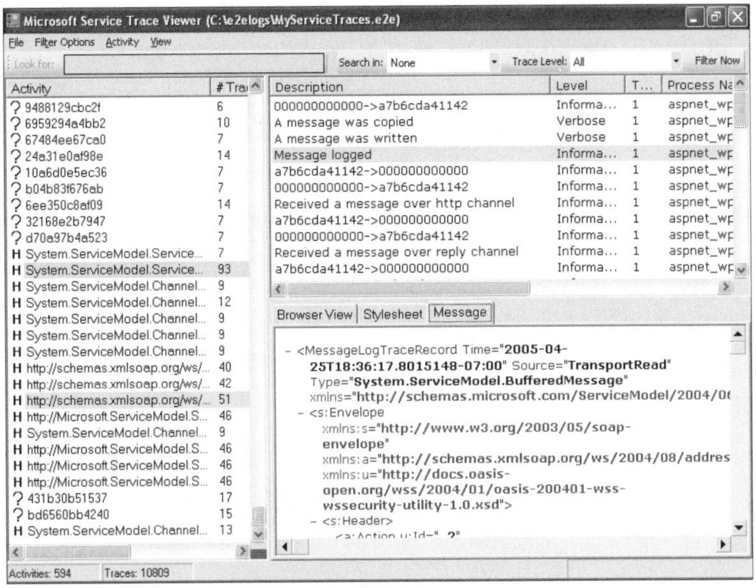

Figure 11-2 SvcTraceViewer tool

Programming Management

Indigo's management features are not enabled by default. Configuration file settings are used to enable end-to-end tracing, message logging, and the Indigo WMI provider. Inspection and control of Indigo runtime information is done programmatically through the Windows System Management API.

Configuring End-to-End Tracing

End-to-end tracing can be enabled in configuration settings in the *<system.diagnostics>* section of a client or service configuration file. Unlike most configuration sections used with Indigo, the *<system.diagnostics>* section is outside the *<system.serviceModel>* element.

To enable end-to-end tracing, you include a trace source and trace listener definition like the one that follows. Follow these rules:

- In the *<source>* element, the *name* attribute must be set to *"E2e"*.

- In the *<source>* element, the *switchValue* attribute should be set to *"None"*, *"Critical"*, *"Error"*, *"Warning"*, *"Information"*, or *"Verbose"* to set the level of information logged.

- In the *<listeners>* section, an *<add>* element defines the listener type. In this chapter's examples, they are of type *System.Diagnostics.XmlWriterTraceListener*.

- In the *<listeners>* section, the *<add>* element defines the location and filename of the log file with an *initializeData* attribute.

```xml
<?xml version="1.0" encoding="utf-8" ?>
<configuration xmlns="http://schemas.microsoft.com/.NetConfiguration/v2.0">
    <system.serviceModel>
        ...
    </system.serviceModel>
    <system.diagnostics>
        <!-- Add the E2e Trace Source -->
        <sources>
            <source name="E2e" switchValue="Verbose" >
                <listeners>
                    <add name="xml"
                         type="System.Diagnostics.XmlWriterTraceListener"
                         initializeData="\E2eLogs\ServiceTraces.e2e" />
                </listeners>
            </source>
        </sources>
        <trace autoflush="true" />
    </system.diagnostics>
</configuration>
```

Configuring Message Logging

Message logging is enabled through configuration file settings in the *<system.serviceModel>* section of a client or service configuration file.

To enable message logging, you include a *<messageLogging>* element like the one shown here. The *<messageLogging>* element is part of the *<diagnostics>* section of *<system.serviceModel>*.

```xml
<?xml version="1.0" encoding="utf-8" ?>
<configuration xmlns="http://schemas.microsoft.com/.NetConfiguration/v2.0">
    <system.serviceModel>
        ...
        <diagnostics>
            <!-- log all messages received or sent at the transport or
            service model levels -->
            <messageLogging logEntireMessage="true"
                            maxMessagesToLog="300"
                            logMessagesAtServiceLevel="true"
                            logMalformedMessages="true"
                            logMessagesAtTransportLevel="true" />
        </diagnostics>
    </system.serviceModel>
</configuration>
```

The *<messageLogging>* element contains these attributes:

- *logEntireMessage (boolean)*   If this attribute is set to *true*, messages are logged in their entirety. If set to *false*, only the headers of the message are logged.

- *maxMessagesToLog (integer)*   Sets a maximum number of messages that are logged. The default is 1000. A value of −1 means the number of messages logged is limited only by available disk space.

- *logMessagesAtServiceLevel (boolean)*   If this attribute is set to *true*, messages are logged at the service level. If an incoming message was encrypted, it is now decrypted. If this attribute is set to false, messages are not logged at the service level.

- *logMalformedMessages (boolean)*   If this attribute is set to *true*, malformed messages are logged. If it is set to *false*, malformed messages are not logged.

- *logMessagesAtTransportLevel (boolean)*   If this attribute is set to true, messages are logged at the transport level (before decryption). If an incoming message was encrypted, it remains encrypted at this point. If this attribute is set to *false*, messages are not logged at the transport level.

You can also define an *IndigoMessageLogTraceSource* trace source in the *<system.Diagnostics>* section of the configuration file, as shown next. The settings allow you to change the location where message are logged and to set a limit on the amount of disk space available for message logging.

```xml
<?xml version="1.0" encoding="utf-8" ?>
<configuration xmlns="http://schemas.microsoft.com/.NetConfiguration/v2.0">
    <system.serviceModel>
        ...
    </system.serviceModel>
    <system.diagnostics>
        <source name="IndigoMessageLogTraceSource" switchValue="Verbose">
            <listeners>
                <add name="multifile"
                    type="System.ServiceModel.Diagnostics.MessageWriterTraceListener,
                        System.ServiceModel, Version=2.0.0.0, Culture=neutral,
                    PublicKeyToken=b77a5c561934e089"
                    initializeData=".\Client\"
                    maxDiskSpace="1000" />
            </listeners>
        </source>
    <system.diagnostics>
</configuration>
```

The *<add>* element under *<listeners>* contains these attributes:

- *initializeData (string)*   The location to log messages to. The default location is %WINDIR%\system32\LogFiles\Messages.

- *maxDiskSpace (integer)*   The maximum amount of disk space that logged messages can take up.

Analyzing Traces with the SvcTraceViewer Tool

The SvcTraceViewer tool organizes and presents the information contained in end-to-end traces. It provides a unified view of activities, events, and logged messages.

Opening Traces

You open an end-to-end trace file in SvcTraceViewer by selecting Open from the File menu or by pressing Ctrl+O. You can open more than one trace file at a time. When this is the case, SvcTraceViewer shows a combined view of the information.

SvcTraceViewer displays three panes of information. The activity pane on the left shows activities for the end-to-end trace file(s) that have been opened. The event pane at the top right shows events for the selected activity. The detail pane at the bottom right shows details for the selected event.

Locating Errors

Activities are listed in the SvcTraceViewer's activity pane. To locate activities containing errors, look for activity IDs that are highlighted. Click on a highlighted activity to see its events. In the events pane, failed events are also highlighted. Click on a highlighted event to see its failure details.

Viewing Logged Messages

Events and message are correlated. When an event of type *Logged Message* is selected in the event pane, the detail pane provides a view of the message. You can also view logged messages directly as files, but inspecting them through SvcTraceViewer provides the context of where the message occurred in the flow of events.

Viewing Activity Trees

Indigo can show sequences of related activities—for example, by pairing the activity of a request message with its reply message. To view an activity tree, select Activity Tree from the View menu. Activities are displayed in an outline form. Expand an outline to see related activities.

The Service Configuration Editor

You can use the Service Configuration Editor tool, SvcConfigEditor.exe, to view and modify configuration file settings. You might find it more convenient to use this tool than to modify configuration files by hand.

When you launch SvcConfigEditor, you have three choices:

- Choose Open Exe Configuration to work with configuration files for a self-hosted service or its client.

- Choose Open COM+ Configuration to work with configuration files for a COM+ integration service or its client.

- Choose Open Web-Hosted Configuration to work with configuration files for a service hosted in IIS or its client.

After you make a selection, a dialog box prompts you to open a client or service program file, such as an .exe file. Figure 11-3 shows the appearance of the SvcConfigEditor tool once a file is open.

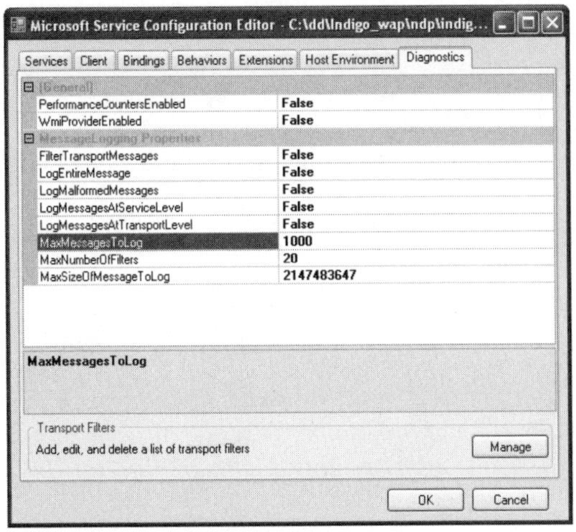

Figure 11-3 The SvcConfigEditor tool

Tabs in the display allow you to specify the following kinds of configurations:

- **Service**   *<service>* sections that define services, including service endpoint definitions
- **Client**   A *<client>* section that defines client endpoint definitions
- **Bindings**   Binding configuration sections
- **Behaviors**   Service behaviors
- **Extensions**   Configuration settings that define extensions to Indigo
- **Host Environment**   Definition of a service host
- **Diagnostics**   Enabling and configuration of management settings

When you add or edit configuration elements, additional dialog boxes appear as needed for details. Figure 11-4 shows a service endpoint being added for a service that is being edited from the Service tab.

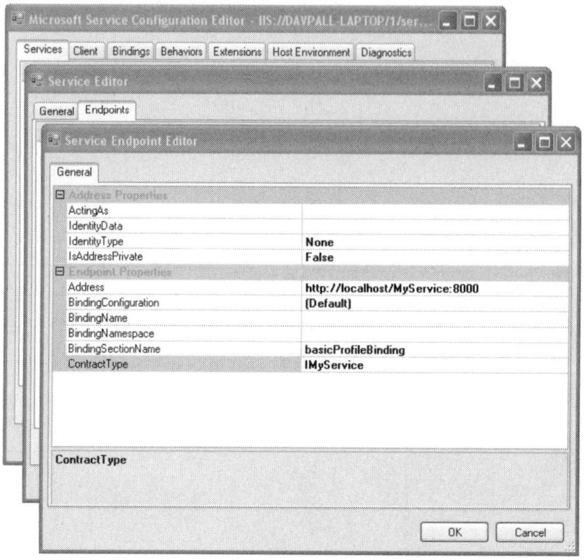

Figure 11-4 Modifying the configuration using the SvcConfigEditor tool

Enabling the Indigo WMI Provider

The Indigo WMI provider is enabled through configuration file settings. To enable the WMI provider, you include a *<diagnostics>* element in the *<system.serviceModel>* section and set its *wmiProviderEnabled* attribute to *true*, as shown here.

```xml
<?xml version="1.0" encoding="utf-8" ?>
<configuration xmlns="http://schemas.microsoft.com/.NetConfiguration/v2.0">
    <system.serviceModel>
        ...
        <diagnostics wmiProviderEnabled="true" />
    </system.serviceModel>
</configuration>
```

Accessing Indigo Runtime Information Through WMI

When the Indigo WMI provider is enabled, you can access runtime information about services through management tools or program code. To access the WMI information programmatically, use the System.Management API or the WMI scripting API.

The WMI namespace for Indigo runtime information is *"root/Indigo"*. You can explore the information under this root location using WMI tools. The following code shows how to iterate through all running services and extract the name of each service.

```
ManagementScope scope = new ManagementScope("root/Indigo");
ObjectQuery query = new ObjectQuery("select * from Service");
ManagementObjectSearcher searcher = new ManagementObjectSearcher(scope, query);
```

```
ManagementObjectCollection queryCollection = searcher.Get();
ManagementObjectCollection.ManagementObjectEnumerator e = queryCollection.GetEnumerator();
while (e.MoveNext())
{
    Console.WriteLine(e.Current["FriendlyName"]);
}
```

Programming Exercise: Classified Ad Service

In this programming exercise, we will create a service and a client for a newspaper classified ad service. The service will accept orders for classified ads and return the price of running the ad. The price of the ad will be affected by the ad category, the number of lines of text in the ad, and the number of days the ad will run.

We will enable end-to-end tracing and message logging for the service. After we run the service and client, we will examine the trace logs and messages. To see how errors are reported in traces, we will deliberately introduce a failure.

This exercise has 11 development steps:

1. Create the service program.
2. Create the .svc file.
3. Create a configuration file for the service.
4. Build the service.
5. Create a virtual directory for the service.
6. Test the service with a browser.
7. Create the client.
8. Generate proxy code for the client.
9. Create a configuration file for the client.
10. Build the client.
11. Create a tracing directory.

Step 1: Create the Service Program

We'll first create the service program, which will compile to a DLL library assembly. Launch your development environment and create a new C# console application project named *service*. Enter the code in Listing 11-2.

To perform these tasks using Microsoft Visual Studio:

1. Select New, Project from the File menu. Under Project Type, select Windows under Microsoft Visual C#. Under Templates, select Class Library. In the Name box, type **service**, in the Location box, specify any path you want, and in the Solution Name box, type **classified**. Click OK to generate and open the new project.

2. Replace the generated code in Program.cs with the code shown in Listing 11-2.

Your service project will need to reference System.ServiceModel.dll and System.Runtime.Serialization.dll.

To perform these tasks using Visual Studio:

1. Right-click References in the Solution Explorer window and select Add Reference.

2. In the Add Reference dialog box, on the .NET tab, select System.ServiceModel.dll and click OK.

3. Add another reference in the same manner for System.Runtime.Serialization.dll.

Listing 11-2   Classified Ad Service: Program.cs

```
using System;
using System.ServiceModel;

namespace ProgrammingIndigo
{
    [ServiceContract(Namespace = "http://ProgrammingIndigo")]
    public interface IClassified
    {
        [OperationContract]
        decimal SubmitAd(DateTime date, int daysToRun, string section,
            string[] description);
    }

    public class ClassifiedService : IClassified
    {
        public decimal SubmitAd(DateTime date, int daysToRun, string section,
            string[] adtext)
        {
            switch(section)
            {
                case "auto":
                    return 1.00M * adtext.Length * daysToRun;
                case "employment":
                    return 2.00M * adtext.Length * daysToRun;
                case "realestate":
                    return 3.00M * adtext.Length * daysToRun;
                default:
                    throw new ArgumentOutOfRangeException();
            }
        }
    }
}
```

Step 2: Create the .svc File

An .svc file is needed to identify the Indigo service to IIS. Using an editor or development environment, create a text file named Service.svc. Enter the code shown in Listing 11-3.

To perform these tasks using Visual Studio:

1. Right-click the service project and select Add, New Item. Select Text File and click Add. Rename the text file Service.svc.

2. Enter the code in Listing 11-3 into Service.svc.

Listing 11-3   Classified Ad Service: Service.svc

```
<%@Service language=c# Debug="true" class="ProgrammingIndigo.ClassifiedService" %>
<%@Assembly Name="service" %>
```

Step 3: Create a Configuration File for the Service

A Web.config file is needed to specify endpoints and bindings for the service. Using an editor or development environment, create a text file with the code shown in Listing 11-4. Save the code under the name Web.config in the same folder in which the service program and .svc file are located.

To perform these tasks using Visual Studio:

1. Right-click the service project and select Add, New Item. Select Application Configuration File and click Add. Name the file Web.config.

2. Enter the code in Listing 11-4 into Web.config.

Listing 11-4   Classified Ad Service: Web.config

```
<?xml version="1.0" encoding="utf-8" ?>
<configuration xmlns="http://schemas.microsoft.com/.NetConfiguration/v2.0">
    <system.serviceModel>
        <services>
            <service
                serviceType="ProgrammingIndigo.ClassifiedService">
                <endpoint address=""
                        bindingSectionName="basicProfileBinding"
                        contractType="ProgrammingIndigo.IClassified" />
            </service>
        </services>

        <!-- Enable message logging -->
        <diagnostics>
            <messageLogging logEntireMessage="true"
                        maxMessagesToLog="300"
                        logMessagesAtServiceLevel="true"
```

```
                                logMalformedMessages="true"
                                logMessagesAtTransportLevel="true" />
        </diagnostics>

    </system.serviceModel>

    <system.web>
       <compilation debug="true" />
    </system.web>

     <system.diagnostics>

         <!-- Enable end-to-end tracing -->
         <sources>
            <source name="E2e" switchValue="Verbose" >
                <listeners>
                    <add name="xml"
                        type="System.Diagnostics.XmlWriterTraceListener"
                        initializeData="c:\logs\service.e2e" />
                </listeners>
            </source>
         </sources>

         <trace autoflush="true" />

     </system.diagnostics>
  </configuration>
```

Step 4: Build the Service

Build the service program to create Service.dll. Resolve any typographical errors.

To perform the task using Visual Studio, select Build Solution from the Build menu to generate Service.dll.

Step 5: Create a Virtual Directory for the Service

Like ASP.NET applications, services hosted in IIS reside in virtual directories. Follow this procedure to set up a virtual directory for the service.

1. Create a folder on your computer named classified.

2. From the Start menu, launch Control Panel. Select Administrative Tools, Internet Information Services. Navigate to Web Sites, Default Web Sites. Right-click and select New, Virtual Directory. Specify the name **classified** and associate it with the classified folder created in step 1. Before exiting IIS Manager, check step 3.

3. Navigate to Web Sites, Default Web Sites. The classified directory should be listed. Right-click it and select Properties. On the Directory Security tab, click Edit.

4. In the Authentication Methods dialog box, Anonymous Access should be selected; if it isn't, select it.

5. Close all dialog boxes by clicking OK, and close IIS.

6. Copy the Service.svc and Web.config files to the classified folder. Underneath classified, create a \bin subdirectory and copy Service.dll into it. You should have the following directory-file structure.

```
\classified
    service.svc
    web.config
    \bin
        service.dll
```

Step 6: Test the Service with a Browser

Before going on to the client, we want to test that the service can be accessed. Launch Internet Explorer. On the address bar, specify the URL *http://localhost/classified/service.svc* and press ENTER. If the resulting page does not list any errors, proceed to step 7. If there are problems, check the following.

- If the page returned by the browser describes compilation errors, check the code entered in the preceding steps. The compilation error display should highlight the offending code for you.

- If the resulting page describes HTTP errors, make sure your system has IIS enabled. You should be able to access *http://localhost* in a browser without receiving an error. If IIS seems to be properly enabled, review the virtual directory setup in the prior steps. If this also fails, look for clues in Control Panel, Administrative Tools; check the Event Log; or try an IISRESET.

The service is now ready. Next we need a client program to access it.

Step 7: Create the Client

Create the client program. Launch your development environment and create a new C# console application project named *client*. Enter the code in Listing 11-5.

To perform these tasks using Visual Studio:

1. Select New, Project from the File menu. Under Project Type, Select Windows under Visual C#. Under Templates, select Console Application. In the Name box, type **client**, in the Location box, type any path you want, and in the Solution Name box, type **classified**. Click OK to generate and open the new project.

2. Replace the generated code in Program.cs with the code shown in Listing 11-5.

Your client project will need to reference System.ServiceModel.dll.

To perform the task using Visual Studio:

1. Right-click References in the Solution Explorer window and select Add Reference.

2. In the Add Reference dialog box, on the .NET tab, select System.ServiceModel.dll and click OK.

Build the client, which will create Client.exe.

Listing 11-5   Classified Ad Client: Program.cs

```
using System;
using System.ServiceModel;

namespace ProgrammingIndigo
{
    class Client
    {
        static void Main()
        {
            using (ClassifiedProxy proxy = new ClassifiedProxy("default"))
            {
                DateTime startDate = DateTime.Today;
                int daysToRun;
                string section;
                string[] description;
                decimal cost;

                daysToRun = 1;
                section = "auto";
                description = new string[2];
                description[0] = "1978 Compact, Green";
                description[1] = "$800 or best offer";

                cost = proxy.SubmitAd(startDate, daysToRun, section, description);

                Console.WriteLine("Cost for {0} ad x {1} lines x {2} days: {3}",
                    section, description.Length, daysToRun, cost);

                daysToRun = 5;
                section = "auto";
                description = new string[4];
                description[0] = "2005 Sedan, Midnight Blue";
                description[1] = "A/C, power windows, CD player";
                description[2] = "leather upholstery.";
                description[3] = "All serious offers considered.";

                cost = proxy.SubmitAd(startDate, daysToRun, section, description);

                Console.WriteLine("Cost for {0} ad x {1} lines x {2} days: {3}",
                    section, description.Length, daysToRun, cost);
```

```
        daysToRun = 14;
        section = "employment";
        description = new string[4];
        description[0] = "Programmer needed";
        description[1] = "Experience building";
        description[2] = "distributed systems";
        description[3] = "required. C# exp a plus.";

        cost = proxy.SubmitAd(startDate, daysToRun, section, description);

        Console.WriteLine("Cost for {0} ad x {1} lines x {2} days: {3}",
            section, description.Length, daysToRun, cost);

        Console.Write("Press ENTER to cause a failure: ");
        Console.ReadLine();

        daysToRun = 1;
        section = "invalid";
        description = new string[2];
        description[0] = "This ad is invalid";
        description[1] = "and should trigger an error";

        cost = proxy.SubmitAd(startDate, daysToRun, section, description);

        Console.WriteLine("Cost for {0} ad x {1} lines x {2} days: {3}",
            section, description.Length, daysToRun, cost);

        proxy.Close();
    }

    Console.WriteLine();
    Console.WriteLine("Press <ENTER> to terminate client.");
    Console.ReadLine();
    }
  }
}
```

Step 8: Generate Proxy Code for the Client

We will now generate client proxy code by accessing the service's MEX endpoint with the Svcutil tool. From a command window, change the directory to the location where your client project and source files reside. Run the following Svcutil command:

```
svcutil http://localhost/classified/service.svc /out:proxy.cs
```

The file Proxy.cs will be generated, containing the service contract and a proxy class for accessing the service.

Add Proxy.cs to your client project.

To perform the task using Visual Studio:

Right-click the project in the Solution Explorer window and select Add, Existing Item. Select Proxy.cs from the File Open dialog box and click OK to add it to the client project.

Step 9: Create a Configuration File for the Client

A Client.exe.config file is needed to specify the service endpoint and binding to use. Using an editor or development environment, create a text file with the code shown in Listing 11-6. Save the code under the name Client.exe.config.

To perform these tasks using Visual Studio:

1. Right-click the service project and select Add, New Item. Select Application Configuration File and click Add.

2. Name the file App.config. (It will be copied to Client.exe.config at build time.)

Enter the code in Listing 11-6 into App.config.

Listing 11-6   Classified Ad Client: App.config

```xml
<?xml version="1.0" encoding="utf-8" ?>
<configuration xmlns="http://schemas.microsoft.com/.NetConfiguration/v2.0">
    <system.serviceModel>

        <client>
          <endpoint configurationName="default"
             address="http://localhost/classified/service.svc"
             bindingSectionName="basicProfileBinding"
             contractType="IClassified" />
        </client>

    </system.serviceModel>

    <system.diagnostics>

        <!-- Enable end-to-end tracing -->
        <sources>
            <source name="E2e" switchValue="Verbose" >
                <listeners>
                    <add name="xml"
                        type="System.Diagnostics.XmlWriterTraceListener"
                        initializeData="c:\logs\client.e2e" />
                </listeners>
            </source>
        </sources>

        <trace autoflush="true" />

    </system.diagnostics>

</configuration>
```

Step 10: Build the Client

Build the client program to create Client.exe. Resolve any typographical errors.

To perform the task using Visual Studio, select Build Solution from the Build menu to generate Client.exe.

Step 11: Create a Tracing Directory

We must create a directory with appropriate permissions for end-to-end tracing. The activity for the client and service will be logged to the directory c:\logs in files named client.e2e and service.e2e.

Create a directory named logs on the C drive. If you are unable use the directory c:\logs, be sure to change all references to c:\logs in the client and service configuration files. Give the user Network Service write access to the logs directory by following these steps:

1. In Windows Explorer, right-click the logs directory and select Sharing And Security.

2. Select the Security tab.

3. Click the Add button. Enter the username **Network Service** and click OK.

4. Under the Allow column, select the Write check box and click OK.

Deployment

We're now ready to try things out. Run the client from your development environment or from a command line. You should see output like that shown in Figure 11-5, showing the ads submitted to the service and the prices returned.

Figure 11-5   Classified ad client

Now press ENTER on the client to send a request to the service with an invalid parameter. As coded, the service generates an exception. The failure is reported on the client as an *Invalid-OperationException* with the message "the server did not reply".

Press ENTER again on the client to shut it down. We can now examine the trace logs and logged messages to review the activity of the service and client.

Analyzing the End-to-End Traces

The c:\logs directory should contain two trace files, client.e2e and service.e2e. To view the traces, launch the SvcTraceViewer tool and open either file. You can also open both files for a combined view of events.

Figure 11-6 shows the SvcTraceViewer tool with service.e2e opened. One of the activities in the left pane is highlighted, indicating that an error has occurred. Click on the failed activity to view its events in the upper right pane. One of the events is *Tracing an exception*. Click on the exception event to view its details in the lower right pane. You can study the exception and surrounding events to determine what led to the error. Examining the event immediately before the error shows that the method *SubmitAd* was executed. Examining the exception event shows that an *ArgumentOutOfRangeException* exception occurred.

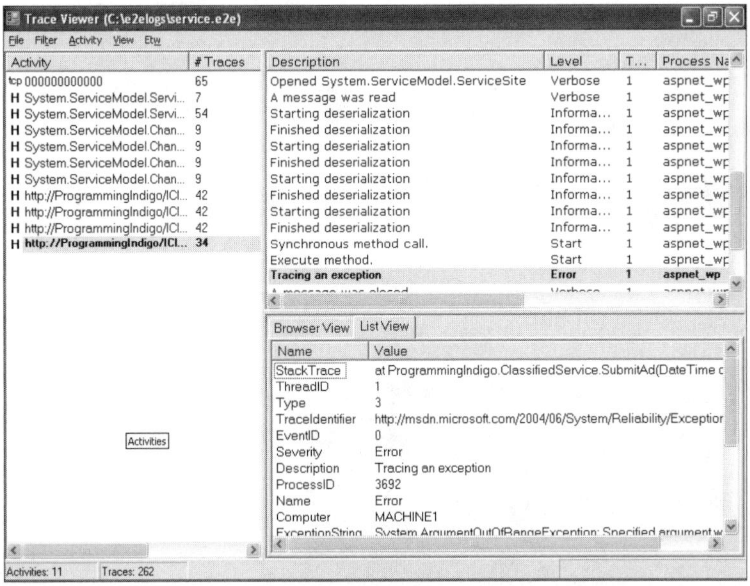

Figure 11-6   Viewing an exception in SvcTraceViewer

Analyzing the Logged Messages

The messages sent between the client and service were logged to the \LogFiles\Messages directory under the Windows System32 directory. The messages can be viewed directly using Internet Explorer, Notepad, or an XML viewing tool. Logged messages are also viewable in the SvcTraceViewer tool for Message Logged events.

Listing 11-7 shows the final message logged, which was the request that failed to receive a response from the service. You can see that the request that caused a problem contained an invalid parameter—a section named "invalid" instead of the expected categories "auto," "employment," or "real estate."

Listing 11-7   Logged Request Message

```
<MessageLogTraceRecord Time="2005-04-18T22:33:08.3872272-07:00"
   Source="ServiceLevelRequestIn" Type="System.ServiceModel.BufferedMessage" xmlns=
   "http://schemas.microsoft.com/ServiceModel/2004/06/Management/MessageTrace">
  <s:Envelope xmlns:s="http://schemas.xmlsoap.org/soap/envelope/">
   <s:Header>
     <ActivityId xmlns="http://schemas.microsoft.com/2004/09/ServiceModel/Diagnostics">
        uuid:9f94fb4e-8eb6-4f6b-aa56-01a2edb13547</ActivityId>
     <To s:mustUnderstand="1" xmlns="http://schemas.xmlsoap.org/ws/2004/08/addressing"
        xmlns:s="http://schemas.xmlsoap.org/soap/envelope/">
        http://davpall-laptop.redmond.corp.microsoft.com/classified/service.svc</To>
     <Action s:mustUnderstand="1" xmlns="http://schemas.xmlsoap.org/ws/2004/08/
        addressing" xmlns:s="http://schemas.xmlsoap.org/soap/envelope/">
        http://ProgrammingIndigo/IClassified/SubmitAd</Action>
   </s:Header>
   <s:Body>
     <SubmitAd xmlns="http://ProgrammingIndigo">
        <date>2005-04-18T00:00:00-07:00</date>
        <daysToRun>1</daysToRun>
        <section>invalid</section>
        <description x:Id="1" x:ItemType="x:string" x:Size="2"
           xmlns:x="http://schemas.microsoft.com/2003/10/Serialization/"
           xmlns:xsi="http://www.w3.org/2001/XMLSchema-instance">
          <Item x:Id="2" xmlns="">This ad is invalid</Item>
          <Item x:Id="3" xmlns="">and should trigger an error</Item>
        </description>
     </SubmitAd>
   </s:Body>
  </s:Envelope>
</MessageLogTraceRecord>
```

Summary

This chapter covered Indigo's management features: end-to-end tracing, message logging, and the Indigo WMI provider. All of the management features are turned off by default and can be enabled through configuration file settings.

End-to-end tracing records events as an Indigo program runs. The events are written to an end-to-end trace file in a logs directory. The location and name of the log file is defined in configuration settings. Network Service must be given write access to the logs directory. The Svc-TraceViewer tool is used to view end-to-end traces.

Message logging saves copies of messages sent or received by an Indigo program. Messages are logged under the Windows System32 directory in a folder named /LogFiles/Messages.

Each message is logged as an individual XML file. Messages can be logged at the transport and service levels. Logged messages can also be viewed with the SvcTraceViewer tool.

The SvcConfigEditor tool provides a GUI for editing configuration files.

Indigo contains a WMI provider that allows inspection and control of services as they are running. The information can be accessed programmatically through the System.Management API or through external management tools.

In our programming exercise, we created a newspaper classified ad service and caused a deliberate failure. We analyzed the failure using SvcTraceViewer, the end-to-end trace log for the service, and logged messages.

Chapter 12

Deployment and Troubleshooting

Each problem that I solved became a rule which served afterwards to solve other problems.

—René Descartes

It takes more than proper design and development to result in a successful solution. The software must be deployed to production systems and configured correctly for its environment. Problems arising in deployment or while in production need to be corrected in a timely manner.

After completing this chapter, you will:

- Know how to prepare machines for Indigo.
- Know how to install, configure, and upgrade Indigo applications.
- Understand techniques for troubleshooting problems.
- Be familiar with failures and their possible causes.

Understanding Deployment

Deployment activities include preparing machines for Indigo, installing Indigo applications, configuring applications, launching applications, monitoring applications, and upgrading applications.

Preparing a Machine for Indigo

Before you can install Indigo applications on a machine, you should make sure you are using a supported operating system and have already installed Indigo and the software Indigo requires. The supported operating systems for Indigo are Microsoft Windows XP SP2, Windows Server 2003, and Windows "Longhorn."

Software Required for Indigo

To run Indigo programs, your system must have the following software installed:

- .NET Framework 2.0

- If you are hosting services in Microsoft Internet Information Services (IIS): IIS 5.1, 6.0, or 7.0 and Microsoft ASP.NET 2

- If you are using the Microsoft Message Queue (MSMQ) transport: MSMQ 3.5

- Indigo, which is part of the WinFX Windows Application Pack (WAP)

- Any Windows hot fixes described in the Indigo release notes that apply to your operating system version

Installing Internet Information Services

To install IIS, you launch Add Or Remove Programs from Control Panel and select Add/Remove Windows Components. Select the option for IIS, which will be displayed as Internet Information Services on client operating systems and Application Server on server operating systems.

To check that IIS has been installed successfully, create a small HTML page named Test.htm in your %SystemDrive%\inetpub\wwwroot folder using the following code. Test access to the page by navigating to the address *http://localhost/test.htm* in a Web browser. The response page should display "IIS is working!"

```
<html>
<body>
IIS is working!
</body>
</html>
```

Installing ASP.NET

ASP.NET is included with the .NET Framework 2.0, but it isn't installed by default. To install ASP.NET, first make sure IIS and the .NET Framework 2.0 are installed. From a command window, run the *aspnet_regiis –i* command. (Make sure you are using the .NET Framework 2.0 version of this command.)

For security reasons, installing ASP.NET on server operating systems does not enable it. To enable ASP.NET on a server operating system, launch IIS from Control Panel, Administrative Tools. Expand the outline and select Web Service Extensions. Select ASP.NET 2.0 in the right pane, and click the Allow button.

To check that ASP.NET has been installed successfully, create a small text file named Test.apx in your %SystemDrive%\inetpub\wwwroot folder using the following code. Test access to the page by navigating to the address *http://localhost/test.aspx* in a Web browser. The response page should display "ASP.NET is working!" and show the current date and time.

```
<html>
<body>
ASP.NET is working! <%= DateTime.Now.ToString() %>
</body>
</html>
```

Installing Indigo

Indigo is part of the WinFX Windows Application Pack (WAP). If you are running Windows "Longhorn," WAP is part of the operating system. If you are running Windows XP SP2 or Window Server 2003, WAP is available as a download. You install the WAP release by running a Microsoft installer (.msi) file.

The order of installation matters in the case of Indigo, IIS, and ASP.NET. If you will be hosting services in IIS, you should install IIS and ASP.NET *before* installing Indigo. Indigo will register itself with IIS and ASP.NET when it is installed. If you install IIS and ASP.NET after Indigo, this registration will not occur and .svc files will not be recognized. However, you can still register Indigo with IIS and ASP.NET by running the command *xws_reg −i* from a command window.

Firewall Setup

If your Indigo applications will need to communicate through a firewall using HTTP or TCP, you must enable the ports your application will be using or authorize the application itself with your firewall software.

If you're using the Windows Firewall included with Windows XP SP2, you enable a port in the firewall as follows:

1.   Launch the Windows Firewall applet from Control Panel.

2.   On the Exceptions tab, click Add Port.

3.   Type a descriptive name and a port number, and select the TCP option.

4.   Click the Change Scope button, select an appropriate scope, and click OK.

5.   Repeat steps 2 through 4 for additional ports that need to be enabled.

6.   Click OK to close the firewall applet.

An alternative to enabling ports in the firewall is to enable application programs to access the firewall. In Windows, you enable a program in the firewall as follows:

1.   Launch the Windows Firewall applet from Control Panel.

2.   On the Exceptions tab, click Add Program.

3. Select a program name from the list or click Browse and navigate to the location of your program file.

4. Click the Change Scope button, select an appropriate scope, and click OK.

5. Repeat steps 2 through 4 for additional programs that need to be enabled.

6. Click OK to close the firewall applet.

You can also configure the firewall in scripts by using the *netsh* command. The *netsh* command shown here enables port 9000 for all applications.

```
netsh firewall add portopening protocol = TCP port = 9000 name =
   "My app using port 9000" mode = Enable profile = ALL
```

Proxy Setup

By default, Indigo applications use the system's proxy settings (usually configured with Microsoft Internet Explorer) for HTTP communication. To view or change the proxy settings, follow these steps:

1. Launch Internet Explorer.

2. Select Internet Options from the Tools menu.

3. On the Connections tab, click LAN Settings.

4. Change the proxy settings to suit your environment, and then click OK.

If you don't want to align Indigo's proxy settings with the system proxy settings, you can specify a proxy in an Indigo program's configuration file.

Installing Indigo Applications

Indigo programs are simple to deploy. As with other .NET applications, all you have to do is copy the assemblies and their configuration files to the system they will run on if the service is an EXE program. Additional steps are necessary in the case of Indigo programs that are hosted in IIS or are Microsoft Windows NT services. Services hosted in IIS can be deployed as assemblies or as source code that is compiled on demand.

Installing an Indigo Service Hosted in IIS

Services hosted in IIS are defined by an .svc file that resides in a virtual directory. The .svc file defines the service class for the service. A Web.config file contains the configuration settings for the service. The program code for the service can be deployed in binary or source form.

To deploy a service in binary form, you place one or more assemblies in a bin directory underneath the virtual directory. If the assemblies are located in a nonstandard location instead of a bin, the .svc file can reference them with a *<%@service src="<file>"%>* directive. The following file structure shows a service deployed in binary form.

```
\MyService
    MyService.svc
    web.config
    \bin
        MyService.dll
```

To deploy a service in source form, you can place source code in the .svc file itself (inline code) or in a separate source file. If the source code is located in a separate file, the .svc file can reference it with a *<%@service name="<file>"%>* directive. For more information on hosting in IIS, see Chapter 10. The following file structure shows a service deployed in source code form.

```
\MyService
    MyService.svc
    web.config
    MyService.cs
```

Use the following procedure to install a service hosted in IIS:

1. Create a virtual directory for the service, as described in the following section. The virtual directory should have an application name specified, execute permissions set to Scripts, and anonymous access enabled.

2. Place the service's .svc and Web.config files in the virtual directory.

3. Place any assembly DLL files referenced by the .svc file for the service in a bin directory under the virtual directory.

4. Place any source files referenced by the .svc file for the service in the virtual directory.

5. Test the service by navigating to it in a Web browser. The address is determined by the machine name, virtual directory name, and .svc filename, for example, *http://server.contoso.com/hr/401k.svc*. If SSL transport security is in use, specify an *https://* scheme in the address.

Creating a Virtual Directory

A virtual directory is required for services hosted in IIS. To create a virtual directory manually, follow these steps:

1. Launch the Internet Information Services applet from Control Panel, Administrative Tools.

2. Right-click on Default Web Site and select New, Virtual Directory to launch the Virtual Directory Creation Wizard.

3. Specify a virtual directory name and associate it with a disk directory. After completing the Virtual Directory Wizard, the Virtual Directory dialog box will be displayed, as shown in Figure 12-1.

4. Check that Application Name is empty, and click Create to create an application.

5. Make sure the Execute Permissions value is set only to Scripts.

6. Select the Directory Security tab and click Edit. Check that the appropriate authentication mode is specified. Unless you are using a specific HTTP authentication mode for transport security, anonymous access should be selected.

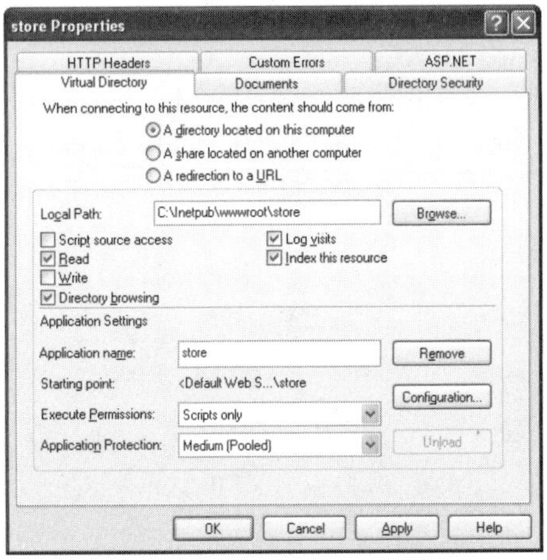

Figure 12-1 Virtual Directory dialog box

You can also create virtual directories by using scripts. The batch file shown here creates a virtual directory named MyService.

```
@echo off
iisreset /stop
mkdir %SystemDrive%\inetpub\wwwroot\MyService\bin
cscript.exe %SystemDrive%\inetpub\adminscripts\adsutil.vbs CREATE w3svc/1/root/
MyService "IIsWebVirtualDir"
cscript.exe %SystemDrive%\inetpub\adminscripts\adsutil.vbs SET w3svc/1/root/MyService/
Path %SystemDrive%\inetpub\wwwroot\MyService
cscript.exe %SystemDrive%\inetpub\adminscripts\adsutil.vbs SET w3svc/1/root/MyService/
AppRoot "w3svc/1/Root/MyService"
cscript.exe %SystemDrive%\inetpub\adminscripts\adsutil.vbs APPCREATEPOOLPROC w3svc/1/root/
MyService
iisreset /start
```

Installing an Indigo Windows NT Service

Indigo programs that are written to be Windows NT services require installation. To install a Windows NT service, launch a command window and run the *installutil* command, specifying the name of a program file.

```
installutil MyIndigoService.exe
```

After installation, the service should appear in the Services applet of Control Panel under its service name (which might be different from the program name). You can start or stop the service or configure it for automatic startup by using the Services applet. You can also start and stop the service by using the *net start* and *net stop* commands.

```
net start MyIndigoWindowsNTService
```

To uninstall a Windows NT service, stop the service using the Services applet or the *net stop* command and run the *installutil* command with the *−u* option.

```
net stop MyIndigoWindowsNTService
installutil -u MyIndigoService.exe
```

For information on how to host an Indigo program in a Windows NT service, see Chapter 10.

Security Setup

Secure services might require that certificates or user accounts be created. You can create test certificates by using the *makecert* command. Production certificates are issued by a certificate authority.

If SSL transport security is in use, you must assign a certificate in the Control Panel's Internet Information Services applet. After obtaining a certificate for a server, follow these steps to assign the certificate:

1. Launch the Internet Information Services applet from Control Panel, Administrative Tools.

2. Right-click on Default Web Site and select Properties. The Web Sites Properties dialog box appears.

3. On the Directory Security tab, click the Server Certificate button. The Web Server Certificate Wizard launches. Click Next.

4. Select Assign An Existing Certificate, and then click Next. A list of certificates like the one shown in Figure 12-2 is displayed. Select the appropriate certificate.

5. Complete the wizard.

6. Once the service has been deployed, test access to the service with a browser, specifying an *https://* scheme in the address (for example, *https://MyMachine/MyService/service.svc*).

Figure 12-2   IIS Web Server Certificate Wizard

Configuring Indigo Applications

Configuration files play a major role in Indigo solutions. In a distributed solution, much of the heavy lifting is done not in the individual programs but in what takes place between the programs: communication, security, and transaction coordination. In a typical service, program code contains application logic and configuration file settings define endpoints, bindings, and security settings. This division of labor provides a great deal of flexibility at deployment time.

Adding or Changing Service Endpoints

Endpoints for a service are contained in the *<service>* section of the service's configuration file. Each endpoint is defined by a separate *<endpoint>* element. It's easy to modify existing endpoints or add new ones for a service, but you must observe several rules. For detailed information about endpoint definitions, see Chapter 4.

You can't necessarily use any binding with a service. Several factors restrict the choice of binding:

- The binding must support the messaging pattern of the service. For example, you can't use the *NetProfileMsmq* binding with a two-way service.

- The binding must support the reliable session, security, and transaction requirements of the service.

- The developer might have specified explicit binding requirements in the program code. For example, the code might require a particular interop profile.

- Your interoperability requirements might restrict you to the *BasicProfile* binding or one of the *WSProfile* bindings.

- If you require durable communication for reliability purposes, you are restricted to the MSMQ transport, which is the only transport mode that provides this capability.

Cross-Machine Considerations

When a client needs to access a service from another machine, any absolute endpoint addresses or base addresses in the client and service configuration files should specify a fully qualified domain name (FQDN), for example:

```
<client>
    <endpoint configurationName="TaxService"
            address="http://tax.adventureworks.com/TaxService/service.svc"
            bindingSectionName="wsProfileBinding"
            contractType="ITax" />
</client>
```

If the service is self-hosted, an FQDN address must also be specified in the service endpoint definition, as shown next. This is not necessary in a service hosted in IIS because the address is not specified in configuration file settings.

```
<services>
    <service serviceType="AdventureWorks.TaxService" >
        <endpoint address="http://tax.adventureworks.com/TaxService/service.svc"
                bindingSectionName="wsProfileBinding"
                contractType="AdventureWorks.ITax" />
    </service>
<services>
```

Specifying Endpoint Identity

When a client accesses a remote machine with Windows security enabled, the default identity specified for the service is Network Service. If the service being accessed is hosted in IIS, its identity is Network Service and the client can access the service. If the service being accessed is self-hosted, it might be running under some other identity. The client can specify service identity by including an *<addressProperties>* element in its endpoint definition. Both user principal names and system principal names can be specified. The following code specifies a user principal name. Notice that the domain and account name are separated by a double back-slash.

```
<client>
    <endpoint
        configurationName="DefaultEndpoint"
        address="http://localhost:8000/MyService/"
        bindingSectionName="wsProfileBinding"
        bindingConfiguration="MyBinding"
        contractType="ISampleService" >
        <addressProperties identityData="mydomain\\jeffsmith" identityType="Upn"/>
    </endpoint>
</client>
```

Launching Indigo Applications

You can launch Indigo applications in the following ways, depending on your service's hosting environment.

- Services hosted in IIS don't need to be launched. IIS activates them automatically when an incoming message is received.

- You can configure services hosted in Windows NT services to start up automatically, by using the Control Panel's Services applet.

- Services that are EXE programs must be explicitly launched.

Monitoring Indigo Applications

Several facilities are available for monitoring the status of running Indigo programs:

- You can monitor and configure Indigo applications at runtime by using Windows Management Interface (WMI).

- You can trace client and service activity by using end-to-end tracing via *System.Diagnostics* or Event Tracing for Windows (ETW).

- You can log messages to disk for later analysis.

- Some errors are written to the event log.

- You can monitor performance counters.

For information on how to enable end-to-end tracing and WMI, see Chapter 11.

Upgrading Indigo Applications

One tenet of service orientation is that services are autonomous. The temporary unavailability of a service shouldn't cause the rest of a distributed solution to fail. If developers write their clients and services to this standard, taking down a service briefly to upgrade it shouldn't cause any disruption. However, stopping a service will disrupt any current client connections and sessions.

Deploying Upgraded Services

In the case of self-hosted services, deploying an upgrade usually involves the following:

1. Stopping the service program

2. Performing any uninstallation required (such as uninstalling a Windows NT service)

3. Copying a new version of the program and its configuration file onto the server

4. Performing any setup required (such as installing a Windows NT service)

5. Starting up the upgraded service

For services hosted in IIS, all you do to upgrade a service is copy the .svc, Web.config, and source or assembly files to the virtual directory and its bin subdirectory. This causes ASP.NET to spin up the new edition of the service automatically. This is the least disruptive way to upgrade a service.

Upgrading Service Contracts

Because a service might contain multiple service contracts, one strategy for upgrading a service contract is to add a new contract but continue to support the original contract for compatibility reasons. If you follow this practice and upgrade a service contract, you can configure endpoints for the old and new contracts. For example, consider the following configuration for a service with a single service contract named *ITaxService*.

```
<services>
    <service serviceType="ProgrammingIndigo.TaxService"
            behaviorConfiguration="TaxServiceBehavior">
        <endpoint address="http://myserver.contoso.com/taxservice"
                bindingSectionName="wsProfileBinding"
                contractType="ProgrammingIndigo.ITaxService" />
    </service>
</services>
```

Let's say a developer adds a newer service contract to the service named *ITaxService2* and leaves the original *ITaxService* service contract in place. At deployment time, an additional endpoint can be added for the new *ITaxService2* service contract. The *contractType* attribute of each *<endpoint>* element identifies the service contract the endpoint connects to. The updated configuration file settings for two service contracts is shown here.

```
<services>
    <service serviceType="ProgrammingIndigo.TaxService"
            behaviorConfiguration="TaxServiceBehavior">
        <endpoint address="http://myserver.contoso.com/taxservice"
                bindingSectionName="wsProfileBinding"
                contractType="ProgrammingIndigo.ITaxService" />
        <endpoint address="http://myserver.contoso.com/taxservice2"
                bindingSectionName="wsProfileBinding"
                contractType="ProgrammingIndigo.ITaxService2" />
    </service>
</services>
```

Upgrading Data Contracts

Data contracts have a built-in versioning system. Parameters in the *[DataMember]* attribute allow you to specify a version number and whether a member is optional. For guidelines on upgrading data contracts without breaking compatibility, see Chapter 5.

Troubleshooting Indigo

Troubleshooting software problems resembles detective work and is particularly challenging with distributed systems. Being familiar with the available diagnostic tools and the general types of failures that can occur is necessary for effective troubleshooting.

Tools and Techniques

The following tools and troubleshooting techniques are useful in diagnosing problems.

Divide and Conquer: When Clients and Services Can't Communicate

When a client and service aren't communicating, it can be unclear whether the service or the client is the problem. A good first step is to focus on the service and see if it can be communicated with by other means. If the service is hosted in IIS, test access to the service in a browser, first locally and then from a remote machine. You can also test a service by attempting to access it with the Svcutil tool. If the service can be accessed successfully in these ways, turn your attention to the client.

Compare Configuration Settings

A perfectly valid service and a perfectly valid client might fail to communicate if they disagree about any of these areas:

- Service, data, or message contract definitions

- Addresses

- Bindings

To resolve any of these differences, have the client regenerate client proxy code and configuration settings with the Svcutil tool. For information about addresses and bindings, see Chapter 4. For information about contracts, see Chapter 5.

Use Fault Reporting for Debugging

Unhandled exceptions in a service operation are generally difficult to observe. You can enable the *returnUnknownExceptionsAsFault* behavior in a configuration file, as shown here. Turning on this behavior allows unhandled exceptions to be reported to clients as faults.

```
<behaviors>
    <behavior configurationName="ParcelServiceBehavior"
            returnUnknownExceptionsAsFaults="true" >
    </behavior>
</behaviors>
```

This behavior is typically not needed in a production system, so turn it off after debugging. For information about enabling the *ReturnUnknownExceptionsAsFaults*, see Chapter 5.

Use End-to-End Tracing to Understand Events Leading to Failure

Some errors might not have obvious explanations. Intermittent errors can be difficult to explain until investigation reveals conditions for failure or a pattern to the failures. End-to-end tracing puts failures in context by showing the events leading up to an error. Viewing traces in the SvcTraceViewer tool is like looking under the hood of a car. For information about enabling end-to-end tracing, see Chapter 11.

Use Message Logging to Understand What's Being Communicated

If you're not in control of both ends of communication, you might be in the dark about what is being sent by the remote client or service. Message logging allows you to store sent and received messages for later inspection. Message logging can reveal that a problem is due to incorrect or unexpected message content or message structure. For information about enabling message logging, see Chapter 11.

Exceptions

In addition to the general exceptions any .NET programs might throw, Indigo programs might throw exceptions specific to Indigo. Table 12-1 lists the Indigo exception types and general descriptions. Always look at the message accompanying an exception to determine the exact nature of the error.

Table 12-1   Indigo Exception Types

Exception Type	Description
AddressAccessDeniedException	An attempt was made to use an address improperly, such as mixing the wrong scheme and transport.
AddressAlreadyInUseException	An attempt was made to listen on an address that is already in use.
AggregateException	This exception contains multiple exceptions that were aggregated.
ChannelConnectException	An error occurred during an attempt to make a connection on a channel.
ChannelException	An error occurred within a channel.
ChannelIOException	An error occurred while a channel was performing I/O.
ChannelListenException	An error occurred in a listener channel.
ConnectionRefusedException	A connection to a machine was refused.
EndpointNotFoundException	An expected endpoint was not found.
ExpiredSecurityTokenException	A security token has expired.
FilterInvalidBodyAccessException	The filter engine attempted to access the body of a message in an invalid way.
FilterNodeQuotaExceededException	The filter engine exceeded a node quota.
InvalidBodyAccessException	An attempt was made to access the body of a message in an invalid way.
InvalidMessageContractException	An invalid message contract was encountered.
InvalidSettingsException	Invalid settings were encountered.
MessageException	A message contains an error.
MessageIOException	An error occurred during the sending or receiving of a message.
MultipleFilterMatchesException	More than one filter engine rule matches a message.
MessageSecurityException	An error occurred during processing of the security information in a message.
MonikerSyntaxException	The service moniker specified by a COM+ application is invalid.
NavigatorInvalidBodyAccessException	An attempt to access an area of the body failed during navigation in the filter engine.
NavigatorNodeQuotaExceededException	A quota was exceeded during navigation in the filter engine.
NodeQuotaExceededException	A quota was exceeded during XPath processing in the filter engine.
PipeException	An error occurred during named pipe communication.
ProtocolException	An error occurred during validation of a messaging protocol.
QueryException	A query contained an error.
QuotaExceededException	A quota was exceeded.
SessionFaultedException	A fault occurred in a session.

Table 12-1 Indigo Exception Types

Exception Type	Description
SessionKeyExpiredException	A session key has expired.
SecurityNegotiationException	An error occurred during security negotiation.
SecurityTokenException	A security token caused an error.
SecurityTokenValidationException	A security token failed to be validated.
WrappedDispatcherException	An error occurred during message dispatching.
WbemException	An error occurred during interfacing with WMI.

Runtime Errors

In addition to exceptions, the following problems can occur during program execution.

Client Receives No Response from Service

If a client does not receive a response from a service, any of the following could be the cause:

- The client has the incorrect address for the service.

- The client and service have differences in their service contract.

- The client and service are not using the same bindings.

Error While Trying to Deserialize Parameter *<parameter-name>*, Expected It to be of type *<type>*

The client and service might have different definitions of service contract operations, or the parameter types might be mismatched. Check the service contract definitions on the client and service, or regenerate the client service contract using the Svcutil tool.

Encountered Unexpected Node *<parameter-name>* While Deserializing Parameters

The client and service might have different definitions of service contract operations, or the number of parameters might be mismatched. Check the service contract definitions on the client and service, or regenerate the client service contract using the Svcutil tool.

Configuration Errors

The following errors can occur during the processing of configuration file settings and .svc files.

Parser Error: Unable to create type <service-class>.

This error occurs when an.svc file for a hosted service specifies a class parameter that cannot be found at runtime. Check that the class value specified in the .svc file's *<%@service%>* directive matches the type of the service class in code and has the correct spelling, case, and namespace.

Configuration system failed to initialize

The configuration file settings are invalid and cannot be loaded for processing. This can be caused by missing elements, elements out of sequence, or misspelled elements.

Could not find Channel element for configuration name <name> and contractType <type>

This error occurs on clients when a proxy is created and the expected endpoint configuration information is not found in the configuration file. This error can occur for the following reasons:

- The *<endpoint>* element's *configurationName* parameter does not match the configuration name specified in the proxy constructor. Check that the *configurationName* parameter matches the value specified in the proxy constructor in code. When a proxy is created with the default constructor, the endpoint configuration name should be *"default"*.

- The *<endpoint>* element's *contractType* parameter does not match the name of the service contract. Check the spelling, case, and namespace of the *contractType* value.

Could not resolve type <type>, contract cannot be created.

The configuration file for the service has an incorrect endpoint definition in its *<service>* section. The *contractType* parameter has specified a type that is not found in the service assembly. Check the spelling, case, and namespace of the *contractType* value.

Configuration section system.serviceModel/bindings/<binding-type> could not be created. Machine.config is missing information. To fix, run xws_reg.exe -i.

The configuration file for the service has an incorrect endpoint definition in its *<service>* section. The *bindingSectionName* parameter has specified an unrecognized binding type. Check the spelling and case of the *bindingSectionName* value.

Configuration Error: Parser Error Message: There is no binding named <binding-configuration-name> at system.serviceModel/bindings/ <binding-type>. Invalid value for bindingConfiguration.

The configuration file for the service has an incorrect endpoint definition in its *<service>* section. The *bindingConfiguration* parameter has specified a binding configuration name that does not appear in the configuration file. Check that the *bindingConfiguration* name specified has a corresponding binding configuration.

Configuration Error: Parser Error Message: Unrecognized attribute '<attribute-name>'. Note that attribute names are case-sensitive.

The configuration file for the service contains an incorrect attribute. Locate the attribute name listed in the error message and check its spelling, case, and placement.

Service validation error: Service has zero application (non-infrastructure) endpoints, this might be because no configuration file was found for your application, or because there was a problem with the serviceType in the configuration file.

The configuration file for the service does not define any endpoints for the service. This error can occur for the following reasons:

- There is no *<service>* section for the service.

- There is a *<service>* section for the service but it specifies the wrong class name in its *serviceType* parameter.

- There are no *<endpoint>* definitions in the *<service>* section.

- The *<endpoint>* definition in the service section specifies the wrong type in its *contractType* parameter.

Configuration Error: Parser Error Message: There is no serviceBehavior named <behavior-name>.

The configuration file for the service has an incorrect service behavior name in its *<service>* section. The *serviceBehavior* parameter has specified a service behavior configuration that does not appear in the configuration file. Check that the *serviceBehavior* name specified has a corresponding *<behavior>* section.

Summary

This chapter covered deploying and troubleshooting Indigo. Setting up a machine for Indigo involves installing required software and installing Indigo. You should install software in sequence or you might have to run commands to register Indigo with IIS and ASP.NET. Installing Indigo applications is simple and is similar to installing other .NET applications. Services hosted in IIS must be deployed to a virtual directory. The way services launch is determined by their hosting model. You can monitor services at runtime using management features. Upgrading service programs, service contracts, and data contracts is straightforward if you observe certain guidelines.

Techniques for troubleshooting Indigo solutions include identifying the failing program, comparing client and service configuration settings, enabling fault reporting, using end-to-end tracing, and using message logging. The chapter also described exceptions and runtime errors in Indigo.

Part IV
Case Studies

In this part:

Chapter 13

Case Study: Enterprise Order Processing

One of the primary reasons next generation Web services came into being is to make it possible to create interoperable applications that are enterprise-ready. In this chapter, an enterprise order processing application is developed.

After completing this chapter, you will:

- Understand how Indigo can be applied in an e-commerce setting.

- Understand how MSMQ and HTTP communication, reliable sessions, transport and SOAP security, and transactions can be used together in a solution.

- Know how Indigo services can be combined with an ASP.NET client.

The files for this solution can be downloaded from the Web as described in the Introduction.

The Problem

In this case study, we'll build an order processing solution for an enterprise. The solution will encompass a Web storefront, an order entry service to approve orders, a payment service at a credit agency to authorize payments, and an order processing service to accept approved orders.

Our fictitious enterprise is a company called Adventure Works, Inc., which sells mountain bikes. Adventure Works wants to complement its existing sales channels (bike stores and catalog sales) with an e-commerce solution. Selling online is attractive to Adventure Works for several reasons: it will bring in more customers who prefer to use the Web to make purchases, and selling online will cost less than other sales channels.

Business solutions follow some common patterns, but organizations often have a unique combination of requirements and priorities. Adventure Works has identified the following key requirements:

- An attractive, easy-to-use Web site for browsing the company's product line and placing online orders securely. The site should resemble the existing product catalog.

- A service-oriented approach to the back-end processing of orders.

- A straightforward way to quickly reconfigure how the solution is deployed.

- Ability to scale any part of the solution in response to increased activity.

- Ability to verify payment of online orders with a credit agency. Only orders with authorized payments should be passed on to systems on the intranet for processing. Communication with the credit agency must be secure.

- Ability to handle the temporary unavailability of systems in the enterprise due to maintenance, backups, or upgrades. Unavailability should not prevent orders from being taken from customers and stored.

The Solution

With the problem definition in place, we can design a service-oriented solution. We must identify service boundaries, determine the roles of services and clients, choose a messaging pattern, and design contracts, bindings, and service settings.

Service Boundaries

The solution for Adventure Works starts with an interactive e-commerce site where customers place orders and ends with delivery of orders to its intranet. The requirements suggest four parts to the solution:

- E-commerce Web site

- Order Entry service

- Payment service

- Order Processing service

The Web site will accept orders from customers and pass them on to the Order Entry service, which will sit in the perimeter network, also known as the demilitarized zone (DMZ), outside the intranet firewall. The Order Entry service will send payments to the credit agency for authorization. Authorized orders will be sent to the Order Processing service, which is on the intranet. The Order Processing service will integrate with the other systems in the enterprise to fulfill the order. (Note that we won't consider this final aspect in this chapter.)

The communication needed is a mix of one-way and two-way messaging, as shown in Figure 13-1.

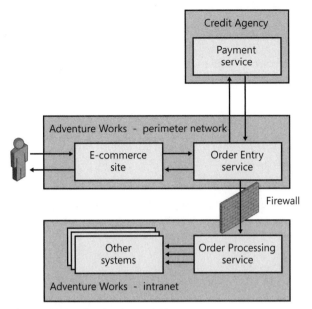

Figure 13-1   Service boundaries

Communication follows this path:

1. When a customer places an order through the e-commerce site, the order is sent to the Order Entry service, which sits in the perimeter network.

2. The Order Entry service submits the payment part of the order to a Payment service at a separate organization, a credit agency.

3. The Payment service responds with an approval code or declines the payment.

4. If the order is approved, the Order Entry service sends the order to the Order Processing service in the intranet. The Order Processing system might not always be available, so a durable means of communication is necessary.

5. The Order Entry service responds to the e-commerce site, which informs the customer that the order has either been accepted or declined.

6. The Order Processing service receives the order and passes it along to other systems in the intranet to fulfill the order.

Service Contracts

The Order Entry service needs a simple service contract with a single operation for submitting orders. *SubmitOrder* accepts an *Order* object and returns an Order ID string or a decline code.

```
[ServiceContract(Namespace = "http://AdventureWorks")]
public interface IOrderEntry
{
```

```
    [OperationContract(IsOneWay = false)]
    string SubmitOrder(Order order);
}
```

The Payment service provides a service contract for authorizing payments. *AuthorizePayment* accepts a *Payment* object and returns an approval code or a decline code.

```
[ServiceContract(Session=true)]
public interface IPayment
{
    [OperationContract(IsOneWay = false)]
    string AuthorizePayment(Payment payment);
}
```

The Order Processing service needs a service contract with a single operation for submitting orders. *SubmitOrder* accepts an approved *Order* object. This is a one-way service operation that does not return a response.

```
[ServiceContract(Namespace="http://AdventureWorks")]
public interface IOrderProcessing
{
    [OperationContract(IsOneWay=true)]
    void SubmitOrder(Order order);
}
```

Data Contracts

Although the service contracts pass only two complex data types, *Order* and *Payment*, *Order* contains additional classes. Data contracts are needed for the following:

- *Order*   The master class that represents an order
- *Payment*   The payment information for an order
- *Contact*   An instance for the Bill To and Ship To parts of an order
- *OrderItem*   Each instance is a line item of detail for an order

Binding

Bindings are needed with characteristics that meet the solution requirements. The application has these requirements:

- The Order Entry service needs a binding that is secure, supports request-reply messaging, and makes sense in the enterprise's perimeter network. The binding we will use is *WSProfile*.

- The Payment service needs a binding that is secure, supports request-reply messaging, and is appropriate for use by two organizations across the Internet. The binding we will use is *WSProfile*.

- The Order Processing service needs a binding that supports one-way communication, stores messages durably, and tolerates sender and receiver not being online at the same time. This indicates a need to use queuing. The binding we will use is *NetProfileMsmq*.

Service Behaviors

The Order Entry service will implement the *IOrderEntry* service contract. *PerCall* instancing will be used because a single *SubmitOrder* service operation is all that is needed to submit an order.

The Payment service will implement the *IPayment* service contract. We will use *PrivateSession* instancing to allow clients to maintain a session per connection to the credit agency.

The Order Processing service will implement the *IOrderProcessing* service contract. We will use *PerCall* instancing because a single *SubmitOrder* service operation is all that is needed to submit an order.

Program Design

The solution consists of four applications: an e-commerce site, an Order Entry service, a Payment service, and an Order Processing service.

E-Commerce Site

The e-commerce site is implemented as a Microsoft ASP.NET application and is deployed in the perimeter network. The site has a page for shopping and a page for placing orders. Figure 13-2 shows the appearance of the shopping page.

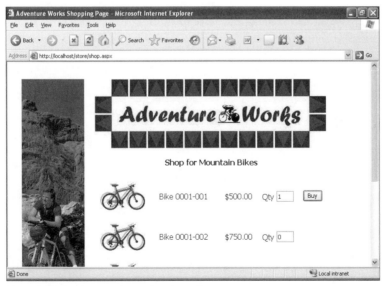

Figure 13-2 E-commerce site shopping page

After selecting items from the shopping page and clicking Buy, the customer is taken to the order page (Figure 13-3). When a customer submits an order, the application functions as a client of the Order Entry service and submits an order.

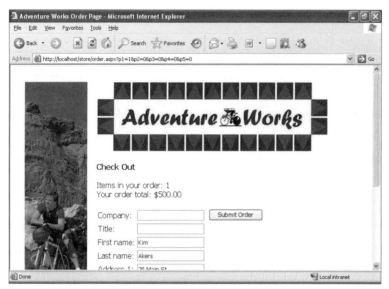

Figure 13-3   E-commerce site order page

Order Entry Service

The Order Entry service is implemented as an Indigo service. The service is hosted in Microsoft Internet Information Services (IIS) and is deployed in the perimeter network. The Order Entry service can be scaled using the same techniques used to scale Web applications, such as Web farms and routers.

Payment Service

The Payment service is implemented as an Indigo service. It is hosted in IIS and is deployed in the perimeter network of another organization, a credit agency. The Payment service can also be scaled using the same techniques used for scaling Web applications.

Order Processing Service

The Order Processing service is implemented in Indigo. The service is an EXE program that is deployed in the intranet. The service receives messages from a durable queue, which allows the service to be safely taken out of service from time to time without losing orders. The service can be scaled by running more than one instance. Multiple instances of the service can safely read from the same queue, increasing the throughput of order processing. This is an example of the Competing Consumers design pattern.

Implementing the Solution

Now we can proceed to implementation. The structure of the solution is shown in Table 13-1. For space reasons, we will keep each application's implementation to a minimum. The online store will be stateless and will not have the notion of a saved shopping cart, customer sign-on, or sessions. The Order Entry and Payment services will contain minimal business logic. The Order Processing service will merely write orders that it receives to disk for inspection.

Table 13-1   Enterprise Order Processing Solution Structure

Project	Program Files	Location	Description
Store	*.aspx, Web.config	/store	ASP.NET application
OrderEntry	Service.cs, Web.config	/OrderEntry	Indigo service
CreditAgency	Service.cs, Web.config	/CreditAgency	Indigo service
OrderProcessing	Service.cs, Web.config	/OrderProcessing	Indigo service

Online Store ASP.NET Application

The Adventure Works online store is an ASP.NET application that contains two primary pages, Shop.aspx and Order.aspx. Shop.aspx is the catalog browsing page (shown earlier in Figure 13-2). The online store consists of these files:

- **Shop.aspx**   Web page for browsing product catalog

- **Order.aspx**   Web page for placing an order

- **ProxyOrderEntry.cs**   Generated proxy code for the Order Entry service

- **Web.config**   Configuration file

- ***.jpg**   Images for the shopping and order pages

The code for Shop.aspx is shown in Listing 13-1. When a customer selects one or more bikes and clicks the Buy button, he is taken to the second page, Order.aspx. The quantity and part numbers of selected items are passed to Order.aspx as part of the Web request.

Listing 13-1   Shop.aspx

```
<%@ Page language="c#"%>
<%@ Import Namespace="System.Net" %>
<%@ Import Namespace="System.IO" %>
<%@ Import Namespace="System.ServiceModel" %>
<%@ Import Namespace="System.Runtime.Serialization" %>
<%@ Assembly src="proxyOrderEntry.cs" %>

<script runat="server" lang="c#">

private void Page_Load(object sender, System.EventArgs e)
{
}
</script>
```

```
<HTML>
<HEAD>
<title>Adventure Works Shopping Page</title>
<style type="text/css">
h1 {font-family: times; font-size: 72pt}
p {font-family: tahoma}
input {font-family: tahoma}
td {font-family: tahoma}
p.sansserif {font-family: sans-serif}
</style>
</HEAD>
<body>
<table border=0 cellspacing=20>
<tr><td valign=top><img src="biker1.jpg"/></td>
<td>

<img src="logo.jpg"><p>
   <form action="order.aspx" method="get">
   <p align=center><B>Shop for Mountain Bikes</B></p>
   <table border=0 cellpadding=10>
   <tr>
      <td><img src="bike1.jpg">  </td>
      <td>Bike 0001-001</td>
      <td align=right>$500.00</td>
      <td>Qty <input type="text" size=2 name="p1" value="0"/>    
         <input type="submit" ID="Submit" text="Buy" value=" Buy "/></td>
   </tr>
   <tr>
      <td><img src="bike1.jpg">  </td>
      <td>Bike 0001-002</td>
      <td align=right>$750.00</td>
      <td>Qty <input type="text" size=2 name="p2" value="0"/></td>
   </tr>
   <tr>
      <td><img src="bike1.jpg">  </td>
      <td>Bike 0001-003</td>
      <td align=right>$1,000.00</td>
      <td>Qty <input type="text" size=2 name="p3" value="0"/></td>
   </tr>
   <tr>
      <td><img src="bike1.jpg">  </td>
      <td>Bike 0001-004</td>
      <td align=right>$1,500.00</td><td>Qty <input type="text" size=2
         name="p4" value="0"/></td>
   </tr>
   <tr>
      <td><img src="bike1.jpg">  </td>
      <td>Bike 0001-005</td>
      <td align=right>$2,000.00</td>
      <td>Qty <input type="text" size=2 name="p5" value="0"/></td>
   </tr>
   <tr><td></td><td></td><td></td><td></td></tr>
   </table>
```

```
</form>
</td></tr>
</table>
</body>
</HTML>
```

The second page of the online store is Order.aspx, which collects contact and payment information and submits orders (as shown earlier in Figure 13-3).

The code for Order.aspx is shown in Listing 13-2. The directives at the top of Order.aspx reference Indigo System.ServiceModel.dll and System.Runtime.Serialization.dll. They also reference a ProxyOrderEntry.cs source file, which contains proxy code for the Order Entry service that was generated by the Svcutil tool.

When a user submits an order, the code in Order.aspx creates a proxy to the Order Entry service and submits an order. The response from Order Entry contains an order number or a decline code.

Listing 13-2   Order.aspx

```
<%@ Page language="c#"%>
<%@ Import Namespace="System.Net" %>
<%@ Import Namespace="System.IO" %>
<%@ Import Namespace="System.ServiceModel" %>
<%@ Import Namespace="System.Runtime.Serialization" %>
<%@ Assembly src="proxyOrderEntry.cs" %>

<script runat="server" lang="c#">

    //*************
    //*  Payment   *
    //*************
    //Representation of a payment.

    [DataContract(Namespace="Microsoft.Xws.Test.Integration.IndiEnterprise")]
    public class Payment
    {
    [DataMember]     public string Company;
    [DataMember]     public string Prefix;
    [DataMember]     public string FirstName;
    [DataMember]     public string MiddleName;
    [DataMember]     public string LastName;
    [DataMember]     public string Suffix;
    [DataMember]     public string Address1;
    [DataMember]     public string Address2;
    [DataMember]     public string City;
    [DataMember]     public string Region1;
    [DataMember]     public string Region2;
    [DataMember]     public string Phone1;
    [DataMember]     public string Phone2;
    [DataMember]     public string Email;
    [DataMember]     public string Authorization;
```

```
[DataMember]     public string Confirmation;
[DataMember]     public string PaymentMethod;
[DataMember]     public string Account;
[DataMember]     public string ExpDate;
[DataMember]     public double Amount;
}


//*************
//*  Contact  *
//*************
//Representation of a contact.

[DataContract(Namespace="Microsoft.Xws.Test.Integration.IndiEnterprise")]
public class Contact
{
[DataMember]     public string Company;
[DataMember]     public string Prefix;
[DataMember]     public string FirstName;
[DataMember]     public string MiddleName;
[DataMember]     public string LastName;
[DataMember]     public string Suffix;
[DataMember]     public string Address1;
[DataMember]     public string Address2;
[DataMember]     public string City;
[DataMember]     public string Region1;
[DataMember]     public string Region2;
[DataMember]     public string Phone1;
[DataMember]     public string Phone2;
[DataMember]     public string Email;
}


//**************
//*  Customer  *
//**************
//Representation of a customer.

[DataContract(Namespace="Microsoft.Xws.Test.Integration.IndiEnterprise")]
public class Customer
{
[DataMember]     public string CustomerID;
[DataMember]     public string Company;
[DataMember]     public string Prefix;
[DataMember]     public string FirstName;
[DataMember]     public string MiddleName;
[DataMember]     public string LastName;
[DataMember]     public string Suffix;
[DataMember]     public string Address1;
[DataMember]     public string Address2;
[DataMember]     public string City;
[DataMember]     public string Region1;
[DataMember]     public string Region2;
[DataMember]     public string Phone1;
[DataMember]     public string Phone2;
```

```csharp
[DataMember]    public string Email;
}



//***********
//*  Order   *
//***********
//Order header. Each order has 1 or more line items.

[DataContract(Namespace="Microsoft.Xws.Test.Integration.IndiEnterprise")]
public class Order
{
[DataMember]    public string OrderID;
[DataMember]    public Contact BillTo;
[DataMember]    public Contact ShipTo;
[DataMember]    public DateTime OrderDate;
[DataMember]    public OrderItem[] Items;
[DataMember]    public double Subtotal;
[DataMember]    public double Tax;
[DataMember]    public double Total;
[DataMember]    public Payment payment;
[DataMember]    public string CrmCustomerID;
[DataMember]    public string ErpOrderID;
}



//***************
//*  OrderItem   *
//***************
//Order line item.

[DataContract(Namespace="Microsoft.Xws.Test.Integration.IndiEnterprise")]
public class OrderItem
{
[DataMember]    public int Qty;
[DataMember]    public string PartNo;
[DataMember]    public string Description;
[DataMember]    public double UnitPrice;
[DataMember]    public double ExtPrice;
}



[ServiceContract]
interface ISampleContract
{
[OperationContract]
string Echo(string text);
[OperationContract]
void MakeUpper(ref string text);
}



private void Page_Load(object sender, System.EventArgs e)
```

```
    {
        double subtotal = 0.00D;
        int bike1, bike2, bike3, bike4, bike5;

        bike1 = Convert.ToInt32(Request.QueryString["p1"]);
        bike2 = Convert.ToInt32(Request.QueryString["p2"]);
        bike3 = Convert.ToInt32(Request.QueryString["p3"]);
        bike4 = Convert.ToInt32(Request.QueryString["p4"]);
        bike5 = Convert.ToInt32(Request.QueryString["p5"]);
        if (bike1>0) subtotal += bike1 * 500.00D;
        if (bike2>0) subtotal += bike2 * 750.00D;
        if (bike3>0) subtotal += bike3 * 1000.00D;
        if (bike4>0) subtotal += bike4 * 1500.00D;
        if (bike5>0) subtotal += bike5 * 2000.00D;
        itemCount.Text = Convert.ToString(bike1+bike2+bike3+bike4+bike5);
        orderSubtotal.Text = subtotal.ToString("c");

        if(Page.IsPostBack)
        {
            try
            {
                OrderEntryProxy orderEntryService =
                    new OrderEntryProxy("OrderEntryEndpoint");
                ProgrammingIndigo.Order order = new ProgrammingIndigo.Order();

                order.OrderID = "web";

                order.BillTo = new ProgrammingIndigo.Contact();
                order.BillTo.Company = Company.Text;
                order.BillTo.Prefix = Prefix.Text;
                order.BillTo.FirstName = FirstName.Text;
                order.BillTo.LastName = LastName.Text;
                order.BillTo.Address1 = Address1.Text;
                order.BillTo.Address2 = Address2.Text;
                order.BillTo.City = City.Text;
                order.BillTo.Region1 = Region1.Text;
                order.BillTo.Region2 = Region2.Text;
                order.BillTo.Phone1 = Phone1.Text;
                order.BillTo.Phone2 = Phone2.Text;
                order.BillTo.Email = Email.Text;

                order.ShipTo = new ProgrammingIndigo.Contact();
                order.ShipTo.Prefix = order.BillTo.Prefix;
                order.ShipTo.FirstName = order.BillTo.FirstName;
                order.ShipTo.MiddleName = "";
                order.ShipTo.LastName = order.BillTo.LastName;
                order.ShipTo.Company = order.BillTo.Company;
                order.ShipTo.Address1 = order.BillTo.Address1;
                order.ShipTo.Address2 = order.BillTo.Address2;
                order.ShipTo.City = order.BillTo.City;
                order.ShipTo.Region1 = order.BillTo.Region1;
                order.ShipTo.Region2 = order.BillTo.Region2;
                order.ShipTo.Phone1 = order.BillTo.Phone1;
                order.ShipTo.Phone2 = order.BillTo.Phone2;
                order.ShipTo.Email = order.BillTo.Email;
```

```
order.Subtotal = subtotal;
order.Tax = 0.00D;
order.Total = order.Subtotal + order.Tax;

int items = 0;
if (bike1>0) items++;
if (bike2>0) items++;
if (bike3>0) items++;
if (bike4>0) items++;
if (bike5>0) items++;

order.Items = new ProgrammingIndigo.OrderItem[items];

int item = 0;

if (bike1>0)
{
    order.Items[item] = new ProgrammingIndigo.OrderItem();
    order.Items[item].PartNo = "0001-001";
    order.Items[item].Description = "Bike 1";
    order.Items[item].Qty = bike1;
    order.Items[item].UnitPrice = 500.00D;
    order.Items[item].ExtPrice = bike1*500.00D;
    item++;
}

if (bike2>0)
{
    order.Items[item] = new ProgrammingIndigo.OrderItem();
    order.Items[item].PartNo = "0001-002";
    order.Items[item].Description = "Bike 2";
    order.Items[item].Qty = bike2;
    order.Items[item].UnitPrice = 750.00D;
    order.Items[item].ExtPrice = bike2*750.00D;
    item++;
}

if (bike3>0)
{
    order.Items[item] = new ProgrammingIndigo.OrderItem();
    order.Items[item].PartNo = "0001-003";
    order.Items[item].Description = "Bike 3";
    order.Items[item].Qty = bike3;
    order.Items[item].UnitPrice = 1000.00D;
    order.Items[item].ExtPrice = bike3*1000.00D;
    item++;
}

if (bike4>0)
{
    order.Items[item] = new ProgrammingIndigo.OrderItem();
    order.Items[item].PartNo = "0001-004";
    order.Items[item].Description = "Bike 4";
    order.Items[item].Qty = bike4;
    order.Items[item].UnitPrice = 1500.00D;
```

```
        order.Items[item].ExtPrice = bike4*1500.00D;
        item++;
    }

    if (bike5>0)
    {
        order.Items[item] = new ProgrammingIndigo.OrderItem();
        order.Items[item].PartNo = "0001-005";
        order.Items[item].Description = "Bike 5";
        order.Items[item].Qty = bike5;
        order.Items[item].UnitPrice = 2000.00D;
        order.Items[item].ExtPrice = bike5*2000.00D;
        item++;
    }

    ProgrammingIndigo.Payment payment = new ProgrammingIndigo.Payment();
    order.payment = payment;
    payment.LastName = order.BillTo.LastName;
    payment.FirstName = order.BillTo.FirstName;
    payment.Address1 = order.BillTo.Address1;
    payment.Address2 = order.BillTo.Address2;
    payment.City = order.BillTo.City;
    payment.Region1 = order.BillTo.Region1;
    payment.Region2 = order.BillTo.Region2;
    payment.PaymentMethod = "Visa";
    payment.Account = "441453423443200234";
    payment.ExpDate = "12/05";
    payment.Amount = order.Total;

    order.OrderDate = System.DateTime.Now;

    string orderID = orderEntryService.SubmitOrder(order);
    order.OrderID = orderID;


    if (order.OrderID=="DECLINE")
    {
        btnSubmit.Visible = true;
        action.Text = "Order Declined";
        orderConfirmation.Text =
            "We're sorry, your order has been declined." +
            "<br>" +
            "Please try again.";
    }
    else
    {
        btnSubmit.Visible = false;
        action.Text = "Order Complete";
        orderConfirmation.Text =
            "Your order has been placed. Your order number is " +
            order.OrderID +
            ".<br>" +
            "Thank you for your business!";
    }
```

```
            }
            catch(Exception ex)
            {
                btnSubmit.Visible = true;
                action.Text = "Unable to Complete Your Order";
                orderConfirmation.Text = ex.GetType().Name + " - " + ex.Message;
            }
        }
        else
        {
            action.Text = "Check Out";
        }
    }

</script>
<HTML>
    <HEAD>
        <title>Adventure Works Order Page</title>
        <style type="text/css">
            h1 {font-family: times; font-size: 72pt}
            p {font-family: tahoma}
            input {font-family: tahoma}
            td {font-family: tahoma}
            p.sansserif {font-family: sans-serif}
        </style>
    </HEAD>
    <body>

    <table border="0" cellspacing="20">
        <tr>
            <td valign="top">
                <img src="biker1.jpg"/>
            </td>
            <td>

            <a href="shop.aspx">
                <img src="logo.jpg" border="0">
            </a>
            <p>
                <form runat="server">
            <p>
                <b>
                    <asp:Literal ID="action" Runat="server" />
                </b>
            </p>
                <asp:Literal ID="orderConfirmation" Runat="server" />
            <p>
                Items in your order:
                <asp:Literal ID="itemCount" Runat="server" /><br>
                Your order total:
                <asp:Literal ID="orderSubtotal" Runat="server" />
            <p>
```

```
<table border="0">
   <tr>
      <td>Company:</td>
      <td>
            <asp:TextBox ID="Company" Runat="server" />  
            <asp:Button ID="btnSubmit" Text="Submit Order" Runat="server" />
      </td>
      </tr>
   <tr>
      <td>Title:</td>
      <td>
            <asp:TextBox ID="Prefix" Runat="server" />
      </td>
   </tr>
   <tr>
      <td>First name:</td>
      <td>
            <asp:TextBox ID="FirstName" text="Kim" Runat="server" />
      </td>
   </tr>
   <tr>
      <td>Last name:</td>
      <td>
            <asp:TextBox ID="LastName" text="Akers" Runat="server" />
      </td>
   </tr>
   <tr>
      <td>Address 1:</td>
      <td>
            <asp:TextBox ID="Address1" text="25 Main St." Runat="server" />
      </td>
   </tr>
   <tr>
      <td>Address 2:</td>
      <td>
            <asp:TextBox ID="Address2" text="" Runat="server" />
      </td>
   </tr>
   <tr>
      <td>City:</td>
      <td>
            <asp:TextBox ID="City" text="Redmond" Runat="server" />
      </td>
   </tr>
   <tr>
      <td>Region 1:</td>
      <td>
            <asp:TextBox ID="Region1" text="WA" Runat="server" />
      </td>
   </tr>
   <tr>
      <td>Region 2:</td>
      <td>
            <asp:TextBox ID="Region2" Runat="server" />
      </td>
   </tr>
```

```
     <tr>
        <td>Phone 1:</td>
        <td>
              <asp:TextBox ID="Phone1" text="425-555-1234" Runat="server" />
        </td>
     </tr>
     <tr>
        <td>Phone 2:</td>
        <td>
              <asp:TextBox ID="Phone2" text="" Runat="server" />
        </td>
     </tr>
     <tr>
        <td>Email:</td>
        <td>
              <asp:TextBox ID="Email" text = "" Runat="server" />
        </td>
     </tr>
   </table>
 <br>

 </form>
   </td>
   </tr>
   </table>

 </body>
 </HTML>
```

At deployment time, the .aspx and Web.config files are deployed to a virtual directory named Store. The service.dll assembly is deployed to OrderEntry\bin. The address for the online store is *http://<machine-name>/Store/shop.aspx*.

The online store can be deployed securely using Secure Sockets Layer (SSL). This involves creating a certificate for the server and assigning the certificate using IIS Manager. With SSL in place, the address for the service is *https://<machine-name>/Store/shop.aspx*.

Order Entry Service

The OrderEntry project contains program code in Service.cs, configuration settings in Web.config, and hosting instructions in Service.svc. It also contains client code for the Payment and Order Processing services in the files ProxyCreditAgency.cs and ProxyOrderProcessing.cs, which were generated by the Svcutil tool.

The code in Service.cs is shown in Listing 13-3. The *IOrderEntry* contract is implemented by the *OrderEntryService* class. The *SubmitOrder* service operation interacts with two other services when an order is received. The payment part of the order is sent to the Payment service for authorization, and a response is received that authorizes or declines the payment. If the payment is authorized, the order is queued to the Order Processing service. A response is then sent to the client indicating whether the order was accepted.

At deployment time, the Service.svc and Web.config files are deployed to a virtual directory named OrderEntry. The Service.dll assembly is deployed to OrderEntry\bin. The address for the service is *http://<machine-name>/OrderEntry/service.svc*.

Listing 13-3   Order Entry Service: Service.cs

```
//*********************************************************************************
//*                                                                              *
//*                        Order Entry Service                                   *
//*                                                                              *
//*********************************************************************************
// This Order Entry service receives orders from the web storefront and approves them.
// Payment is verified with a credit agency.
// If an order is approved, it is queued into the enterprise for processing.

using System;
using System.Configuration;
using System.Messaging;
using System.Runtime.Serialization;
using System.ServiceModel;
using System.Transactions;

namespace ProgrammingIndigo
{
    //***********************
    //*                     *
    //*   Service Contract   *
    //*                     *
    //***********************

    //******************
    //*  IOrderEntry   *
    //******************
    // Order Entry service contract.

    [ServiceContract(Namespace = "http://AdventureWorks")]
    public interface IOrderEntry
    {
        [OperationContract(IsOneWay = false)]
        string SubmitOrder(Order order);
    }

    //*********************
    //*                   *
    //*   Data Contracts   *
    //*                   *
    //*********************

    //*************
    //*  Contact  *
    //*************
    // Representation of a contact.

    [DataContract]
    public class Contact
```

```
{
    [DataMember]
    public string Company;
    [DataMember]
    public string Prefix;
    [DataMember]
    public string FirstName;
    [DataMember]
    public string MiddleName;
    [DataMember]
    public string LastName;
    [DataMember]
    public string Suffix;
    [DataMember]
    public string Address1;
    [DataMember]
    public string Address2;
    [DataMember]
    public string City;
    [DataMember]
    public string Region1;
    [DataMember]
    public string Region2;
    [DataMember]
    public string Phone1;
    [DataMember]
    public string Phone2;
    [DataMember]
    public string Email;
}


//**************
//*  Customer  *
//**************
// Representation of a customer.

[DataContract]
public class Customer
{
    [DataMember]
    public string CustomerID;
    [DataMember]
    public string Company;
    [DataMember]
    public string Prefix;
    [DataMember]
    public string FirstName;
    [DataMember]
    public string MiddleName;
    [DataMember]
    public string LastName;
    [DataMember]
    public string Suffix;
    [DataMember]
    public string Address1;
```

```
    [DataMember]
    public string Address2;
    [DataMember]
    public string City;
    [DataMember]
    public string Region1;
    [DataMember]
    public string Region2;
    [DataMember]
    public string Phone1;
    [DataMember]
    public string Phone2;
    [DataMember]
    public string Email;
}


//***********
//*  Order  *
//***********
// Order header. Each order has 1 or more line items.

[DataContract]
public class Order
{
    [DataMember]
    public string OrderID;
    [DataMember]
    public Contact BillTo;
    [DataMember]
    public Contact ShipTo;
    [DataMember]
    public DateTime OrderDate;
    [DataMember]
    public OrderItem[] Items;
    [DataMember]
    public double Subtotal;
    [DataMember]
    public double Tax;
    [DataMember]
    public double Total;
    [DataMember]
    public Payment payment;
    [DataMember]
    public string CrmCustomerID;
    [DataMember]
    public string ErpOrderID;
}


//***************
//*  OrderItem  *
//***************
// Order line item.
```

```csharp
[DataContract]
public class OrderItem
{
    [DataMember]
    public int Qty;
    [DataMember]
    public string PartNo;
    [DataMember]
    public string Description;
    [DataMember]
    public double UnitPrice;
    [DataMember]
    public double ExtPrice;
}


//****************************
//*                          *
//*  Service Implementation  *
//*                          *
//****************************
// Service class that implements the IOrderEntry service contract.

public class OrderEntryService : IOrderEntry
{
    static Object syncObject = new object();
    static int NextOrderNo = 1001;

    //*****************
    //*  SubmitOrder  *
    //*****************
    // Accept an order.
    // Return value is order number if accepted, or "DECLINE" if declined

    [OperationBehavior(AutoEnlistTransaction = true, AutoCompleteTransaction = true)]
    public string SubmitOrder(Order order)
    {
        string orderID;
        string approvalCode;

        // Get payment approval.

        using (PaymentProxy proxy = new PaymentProxy("UnsecurePaymentEndpoint"))
        {
            approvalCode = proxy.AuthorizePayment(order.payment);
            order.payment.Authorization = approvalCode;
            proxy.Close();
        }

        // If payment declined, return without further processing.

        if (approvalCode == "DECLINE")
            return approvalCode;

        // Payment approved - assign order number.
```

```
            lock (syncObject)
            {
                orderID = NextOrderNo.ToString();
                NextOrderNo++;
            }

            order.OrderID = orderID;
            order.OrderDate = DateTime.Today;

            // Queue approved order into the enterprise for processing.
            using (OrderProcessingProxy proxy =
                new OrderProcessingProxy("OrderProcessingEndpoint"))
            {
                //Create a transaction scope.
                using (TransactionScope scope =
                    new TransactionScope(TransactionScopeOption.Required))
                {
                    proxy.SubmitOrder(order);
                    scope.Complete();
                }
                proxy.Close();
            }

            return orderID;
        }

    }
}
```

The configuration file for the Order Entry service is Web.config, shown in Listing 13-4. The configuration defines endpoints in both the *<client>* and *<service>* sections. The endpoint definitions in the *<service>* section define the service endpoint for the Order Entry service. The endpoint definitions in the *<client>* section define the endpoints used to access the Payment service and the Order Processing service. Order Entry is a client of these two services.

Listing 13-4   Order Entry Service: Web.config

```
<?xml version="1.0" encoding="utf-8" ?>
<configuration xmlns="http://schemas.microsoft.com/.NetConfiguration/v2.0">

    <system.serviceModel>

        <client>
        <!-- Use a behavior to configure the client certificate
            to present to the service. -->
            <endpoint configurationName="SecurePaymentEndpoint"
                    address="http://localhost/CreditAgency/service.svc/secure"
                    bindingSectionName="wsProfileBinding"
                    bindingConfiguration="SecurePaymentBinding"
                    behaviorConfiguration="ClientCertificateBehavior"
                    contractType="IPayment">
            <!--addressProperties identityData="MyDomain\\MyUser" identityType="Upn"/-->
            </endpoint>
```

```xml
        <endpoint configurationName="UnsecurePaymentEndpoint"
                address="http://localhost/CreditAgency/service.svc/unsecure"
                bindingSectionName="wsProfileBinding"
                bindingConfiguration="UnsecurePaymentBinding"
                contractType="IPayment">
    </endpoint>
        <!-- Define NetProfileMsmqEndpoint -->
        <endpoint configurationName="OrderProcessingEndpoint"
                address="net.msmq://localhost/private$/OrderProcessing"
                bindingSectionName="netProfileMsmqBinding"
                bindingConfiguration="nonSecuredMsmqBinding"
                contractType="IOrderProcessing" />
        <endpoint configurationName="OrderProcessingEndpointHttp"
                address="http://localhost:8000/OrderProcessing"
                bindingSectionName="wsProfileBinding"
                contractType="IOrderProcessing" />
</client>

<services>
    <service
        serviceType="ProgrammingIndigo.OrderEntryService"
        behaviorConfiguration="OrderEntryBehavior">
        <endpoint address=""
                bindingSectionName="wsProfileBinding"
                contractType="ProgrammingIndigo.IOrderEntry" />
    </service>
</services>

<bindings>
    <wsProfileBinding>
        <!--
         This configuration defines the SecurityMode as WSSecurityOverHttp and
         the WSSecurity.AuthenticationMode to Certificate.
         -->
        <binding configurationName="SecurePaymentBinding"
                securityMode="WSSecurityOverHttp"
                reliableSessionEnabled="true">
            <wsSecurity authenticationMode="Certificate" />
        </binding>
        <binding configurationName="UnsecurePaymentBinding"
                reliableSessionEnabled="true">
        </binding>
    </wsProfileBinding>
    <netProfileMsmqBinding>
        <binding configurationName="nonSecuredMsmqBinding"
                msmqAuthenticationMode="None"
                msmqProtectionLevel="None">
        </binding>
    </netProfileMsmqBinding>
</bindings>

<behaviors>
    <behavior configurationName="OrderEntryBehavior"
            returnUnknownExceptionsAsFaults="True" />
    <behavior configurationName="ClientCertificateBehavior">
```

```
<!--
        The channelSecurityCredentials behavior allows one to
         define a certificate to present to a service.
        A certificate is used by a service to authenticate the
        client and provide message protection.
        This configuration references the "client.com"
        certificate installed during the setup instructions.
-->
<channelSecurityCredentials x509AuthenticationRevocationMode="NoCheck">
    <clientX509Certificate findValue="contoso.com"
        storeLocation="LocalMachine" storeName="My" x509FindType=
        "FindBySubjectName" />
</channelSecurityCredentials>
        </behavior>
    </behaviors>

</system.serviceModel>

<system.web>
    <compilation debug="true" />
</system.web>

</configuration>
```

Payment Service

The CreditAgency project contains program code in Service.cs, configuration settings in Web.config, and hosting instructions in Service.svc.

The code in Service.cs is shown in Listing 13-5. The *IPayment* contract is implemented by the *PaymentService* class. The *AuthorizePayment* service operation accepts a payment and responds with an approval code or a decline code.

At deployment time, the Service.svc and Web.config files are deployed to a virtual directory named CreditAgency. The Service.dll assembly is deployed to CreditAgency\bin. The address for the service is *http://<machine-name>/CreditAgency/service.svc*.

Listing 13-5   Payment Service: Service.cs

```
//************************************************************************************
//
*                                                                                   *
//
*                               Payment Service                                     *
//
*                                                                                   *
//
//************************************************************************************
// This Order Entry service receives orders from the Web storefront and approves them.
// Payment is verified with a credit agency.
// If an order is approved, it is queued into the enterprise for processing.
```

```csharp
using System;
using System.Configuration;
using System.Runtime.Serialization;
using System.ServiceModel;

namespace ProgrammingIndigo
{
    //***********************
    //*                     *
    //*   Service Contract  *
    //*                     *
    //***********************

    //**************
    //*  IPayment  *
    //**************
    // Order Entry service contract.

    [ServiceContract(Session=true)]
    public interface IPayment
    {
        [OperationContract(IsOneWay = false)]
        string AuthorizePayment(Payment payment);
    }

    //*********************
    //*                   *
    //*   Data Contracts  *
    //*                   *
    //*********************

    //*************
    //*  Payment  *
    //*************
    // Representation of a payment.

    [DataContract]
    public class Payment
    {
        [DataMember]
        public string Company;
        [DataMember]
        public string Prefix;
        [DataMember]
        public string FirstName;
        [DataMember]
        public string MiddleName;
        [DataMember]
        public string LastName;
        [DataMember]
        public string Suffix;
        [DataMember]
        public string Address1;
        [DataMember]
        public string Address2;
```

```csharp
    [DataMember]
    public string City;
    [DataMember]
    public string Region1;
    [DataMember]
    public string Region2;
    [DataMember]
    public string Phone1;
    [DataMember]
    public string Phone2;
    [DataMember]
    public string Email;
    [DataMember]
    public string Authorization;
    [DataMember]
    public string Confirmation;
    [DataMember]
    public string PaymentMethod;
    [DataMember]
    public string Account;
    [DataMember]
    public string ExpDate;
    [DataMember]
    public double Amount;
}


//*************
//*  Contact  *
//*************
// Representation of a contact.

[DataContract]
public class Contact
{
    [DataMember]
    public string Company;
    [DataMember]
    public string Prefix;
    [DataMember]
    public string FirstName;
    [DataMember]
    public string MiddleName;
    [DataMember]
    public string LastName;
    [DataMember]
    public string Suffix;
    [DataMember]
    public string Address1;
    [DataMember]
    public string Address2;
    [DataMember]
    public string City;
    [DataMember]
    public string Region1;
```

```csharp
    [DataMember]
    public string Region2;
    [DataMember]
    public string Phone1;
    [DataMember]
    public string Phone2;
    [DataMember]
    public string Email;
}


//**************
//*  Customer  *
//**************
// Representation of a customer.

[DataContract]
public class Customer
{
    [DataMember]
    public string CustomerID;
    [DataMember]
    public string Company;
    [DataMember]
    public string Prefix;
    [DataMember]
    public string FirstName;
    [DataMember]
    public string MiddleName;
    [DataMember]
    public string LastName;
    [DataMember]
    public string Suffix;
    [DataMember]
    public string Address1;
    [DataMember]
    public string Address2;
    [DataMember]
    public string City;
    [DataMember]
    public string Region1;
    [DataMember]
    public string Region2;
    [DataMember]
    public string Phone1;
    [DataMember]
    public string Phone2;
    [DataMember]
    public string Email;
}


//***********
//*  Order  *
//***********
```

```
//Order header. Each order has 1 or more line items.

[DataContract]
public class Order
{
    [DataMember]
    public string OrderID;
    [DataMember]
    public Contact BillTo;
    [DataMember]
    public Contact ShipTo;
    [DataMember]
    public DateTime OrderDate;
    [DataMember]
    public OrderItem[] Items;
    [DataMember]
    public double Subtotal;
    [DataMember]
    public double Tax;
    [DataMember]
    public double Total;
    [DataMember]
    public Payment payment;
    [DataMember]
    public string CrmCustomerID;
    [DataMember]
    public string ErpOrderID;
}


//***************
//*  OrderItem  *
//***************
//Order line item.

[DataContract]
public class OrderItem
{
    [DataMember]
    public int Qty;
    [DataMember]
    public string PartNo;
    [DataMember]
    public string Description;
    [DataMember]
    public double UnitPrice;
    [DataMember]
    public double ExtPrice;
}


//***************************
//*                         *
//*  Service Implementation  *
//*                         *
```

```
//*****************************
// Service class that implements the IPayment service contract.

[ServiceBehavior(InstanceMode=InstanceMode.PrivateSession)]
public class PaymentService : IPayment
{
    static Object syncObject = new object();
    static int NextApprovalCode = 37001;

    //***********************
    //*  AuthorizePayment   *
    //***********************
    // Authorize a payment.
    // Payment is rejected if missing name or address information.

    public string AuthorizePayment(Payment payment)
    {
        string approvalCode = "";
        bool approved = false;

        // Reject an order without a name or address.

        if (payment.FirstName=="" || payment.LastName=="" ||
            payment.Address1 == "" || payment.City == "")
            approved = false;
        else
            approved = true;

        if (approved)
        {
            // Increment approval code number.
            lock (syncObject)
            {
                approvalCode = NextApprovalCode.ToString();
                NextApprovalCode++;
            }
        }
        else
            approvalCode = "DECLINE";

        return approvalCode;
    }

}
}
```

The configuration file for the Payment service is Web.config, shown in Listing 13-6. The configuration defines service endpoints in a <*service*> section. The payment service provides both a secure and a nonsecure endpoint for access. The secure endpoint has the address *http://localhost/CreditAgency/service.svc/secure* and requires X.509 certificate authentication. The nonsecure endpoint has the address *http://localhost/CreditAgency/service.svc/unsecure*.

Listing 13-6   Payment Service: Web.config

```xml
<?xml version="1.0" encoding="utf-8" ?>
<configuration xmlns="http://schemas.microsoft.com/.NetConfiguration/v2.0">
    <system.serviceModel>

        <services>
            <service
                    serviceType="ProgrammingIndigo.PaymentService"
                    behaviorConfiguration="PaymentServiceBehavior">
                <!-- use base address provided by host -->
                <endpoint address="secure"
                        bindingSectionName="wsProfileBinding"
                        bindingConfiguration="SecurePaymentBinding"
                        contractType="ProgrammingIndigo.IPayment" />
                <endpoint address="unsecure"
                        bindingSectionName="wsProfileBinding"
                        bindingConfiguration="UnsecurePaymentBinding"
                        contractType="ProgrammingIndigo.IPayment" />
            </service>
        </services>

        <bindings>
            <wsProfileBinding>
                <!--
                    This configuration defines the SecurityMode as WSSecurityOverHttp and
                    the WSSecurity.AuthenticationMode to Certificate.
                -->
                <binding configurationName="SecurePaymentBinding"
                        securityMode="WSSecurityOverHttp"
                        reliableSessionEnabled="true">
                    <wsSecurity authenticationMode="Certificate" />
                </binding>
                <binding configurationName="UnsecurePaymentBinding"
                        reliableSessionEnabled="true">
                </binding>
            </wsProfileBinding>
        </bindings>

        <behaviors>
            <behavior
                configurationName="PaymentServiceBehavior"
                returnUnknownExceptionsAsFaults="true" >
                <!--
                    The serviceSecurityCredentials behavior allows
                    one to define a service certificate.
                    A service certificate is used by a client to authenticate
                    the service and provide message protection.
                    This configuration references the "localhost" certificate
                    installed during the setup instructions.
                -->
                <serviceSecurityCredentials x509AuthenticationMapToWindows="false">
                    <serviceX509Certificate findValue="localhost"
                        storeLocation="LocalMachine" storeName="My" x509FindType=
                        "FindBySubjectName" />
```

```
            </serviceSecurityCredentials>
          </behavior>
       </behaviors>
    </system.serviceModel>
    <system.web>
       <compilation debug="true" />
    </system.web>
 </configuration>
```

Order Processing Service

The OrderProcessing project contains program code in Service.cs and configuration settings in App.config (which is renamed Service.exe.config at deployment time). The program is a self-hosted EXE.

The code in Service.cs is shown in Listing 13-7. The *IOrderProcessing* contract is implemented by the *OrderProcessingService* class. The *SubmitOrder* service operation is a one-way operation that accepts orders from a durable queue and does not send a response. The static *Main* function contains the code to host the service.

At deployment time, the Service.exe and Service.exe.config files can be run from any location. No virtual directories are involved because the service is self-hosted. The address for the service is *http://<machine-name>/OrderProcessing*.

Listing 13-7   Order Processing Service: Service.cs

```
//
// ******************************************************************************
//
// *                                                                            *
//
// *                        Order Processing Service                            *
//
// *                                                                            *
//
// ******************************************************************************
// This service receives orders from the Order Entry service for processing in the
// enterprise.
// This implementation merely logs received orders to disk in the form of files.
// In an actual implementation, orders would likely be written to a database and
// there would be orchestration of multiple systems in the enterprise to fill
// the order.

using System;
using System.Configuration;
using System.IO;
using System.Messaging;
using System.Runtime.Serialization;
using System.ServiceModel;
using System.Transactions;
```

```
namespace ProgrammingIndigo
{
    //***********************
    //*                     *
    //*   Service Contracts *
    //*                     *
    //***********************


    //*********************
    //*  IOrderProcessing *
    //*********************
    // Order Processing service contract.

    [ServiceContract(Namespace="http://Adventureworks")]
    public interface IOrderProcessing
    {
        [OperationContract(IsOneWay=true)]
        void SubmitOrder(Order order);
    }


    //********************
    //*                  *
    //*   Data Contracts *
    //*                  *
    //********************


    //*************
    //*  Payment  *
    //*************
    // Representation of a payment.

    [DataContract]
    public class Payment
    {
        [DataMember]
        public string Company;
        [DataMember]
        public string Prefix;
        [DataMember]
        public string FirstName;
        [DataMember]
        public string MiddleName;
        [DataMember]
        public string LastName;
        [DataMember]
        public string Suffix;
        [DataMember]
        public string Address1;
        [DataMember]
        public string Address2;
        [DataMember]
        public string City;
        [DataMember]
        public string Region1;
        [DataMember]
```

```
    public string Region2;
    [DataMember]
    public string Phone1;
    [DataMember]
    public string Phone2;
    [DataMember]
    public string Email;
    [DataMember]
    public string Authorization;
    [DataMember]
    public string Confirmation;
    [DataMember]
    public string PaymentMethod;
    [DataMember]
    public string Account;
    [DataMember]
    public string ExpDate;
    [DataMember]
    public double Amount;
}


//*************
//*  Contact  *
//*************
// Representation of a contact.

[DataContract]
public class Contact
{
    [DataMember]
    public string Company;
    [DataMember]
    public string Prefix;
    [DataMember]
    public string FirstName;
    [DataMember]
    public string MiddleName;
    [DataMember]
    public string LastName;
    [DataMember]
    public string Suffix;
    [DataMember]
    public string Address1;
    [DataMember]
    public string Address2;
    [DataMember]
    public string City;
    [DataMember]
    public string Region1;
    [DataMember]
    public string Region2;
    [DataMember]
    public string Phone1;
    [DataMember]
    public string Phone2;
```

```csharp
        [DataMember]
        public string Email;
    }


//*************
//*  Customer  *
//*************
// Representation of a customer.

[DataContract]
public class Customer
{
    [DataMember]
    public string CustomerID;
    [DataMember]
    public string Company;
    [DataMember]
    public string Prefix;
    [DataMember]
    public string FirstName;
    [DataMember]
    public string MiddleName;
    [DataMember]
    public string LastName;
    [DataMember]
    public string Suffix;
    [DataMember]
    public string Address1;
    [DataMember]
    public string Address2;
    [DataMember]
    public string City;
    [DataMember]
    public string Region1;
    [DataMember]
    public string Region2;
    [DataMember]
    public string Phone1;
    [DataMember]
    public string Phone2;
    [DataMember]
    public string Email;
}


//**********
//*  Order  *
//**********
// Order header. Each order contains 1 or more line items.

[DataContract]
public class Order
{
    [DataMember]
    public string OrderID;
    [DataMember]
```

```
    public Contact BillTo;
    [DataMember]
    public Contact ShipTo;
    [DataMember]
    public DateTime OrderDate;
    [DataMember]
    public OrderItem[] Items;
    [DataMember]
    public double Subtotal;
    [DataMember]
    public double Tax;
    [DataMember]
    public double Total;
    [DataMember]
    public Payment payment;
    [DataMember]
    public string CrmCustomerID;
    [DataMember]
    public string ErpOrderID;
}


//***************
//*  OrderItem   *
//***************
// Order line item.

[DataContract]
public class OrderItem
{
    [DataMember]
    public int Qty;
    [DataMember]
    public string PartNo;
    [DataMember]
    public string Description;
    [DataMember]
    public double UnitPrice;
    [DataMember]
    public double ExtPrice;
}


//****************************
//*                          *
//*  Service Implementation  *
//*                          *
//****************************
// Service class that implements the IOrderProcessing service contract.

public class OrderProcessingService : IOrderProcessing
{
    //*****************
    //*  SubmitOrder  *
    //*****************
    // Accept an order.
```

```
[OperationBehavior(AutoEnlistTransaction = true, AutoCompleteTransaction = true)]
public void SubmitOrder(Order order)
{
    Console.WriteLine("Received order " + order.OrderID);
    StoreOrder(order);
}


//****************
//*  StoreOrder  *
//****************
// Store a received order.

void StoreOrder(Order order)
{
    TextWriter tw = File.CreateText("order-" + order.OrderID + ".txt");
    tw.WriteLine("ORDER      Order No. {0}  Order Date: {1}",
        order.OrderID, order.OrderDate.ToString("d"));
    tw.WriteLine();
    tw.WriteLine("BILL TO:  {0} {1}", order.BillTo.FirstName,
        order.BillTo.LastName);
    tw.WriteLine("          {0} {1}", order.BillTo.Address1,
        order.BillTo.Address2);
    tw.WriteLine("          {0} {1} {2}", order.BillTo.City,
        order.BillTo.Region1, order.BillTo.Region2);
    tw.WriteLine("          {0} {1} {2}", order.BillTo.Phone1,
        order.BillTo.Phone2, order.BillTo.Email);
    tw.WriteLine();
    tw.WriteLine("SHIP TO:  {0} {1}", order.ShipTo.FirstName,
        order.ShipTo.LastName);
    tw.WriteLine("          {0} {1}", order.ShipTo.Address1,
        order.ShipTo.Address2);
    tw.WriteLine("          {0} {1} {2}", order.ShipTo.City,
        order.ShipTo.Region1, order.ShipTo.Region2);
    tw.WriteLine("          {0} {1} {2}", order.ShipTo.Phone1,
        order.ShipTo.Phone2, order.ShipTo.Email);
    tw.WriteLine();
    tw.WriteLine("Qty  Part No    Description
        Unit Price  Ext Price");
    tw.WriteLine("---  ----------  ------------------------------  ----------
        ---------");
    foreach(OrderItem orderItem in order.Items)
    {
        tw.WriteLine("{0,3}  {1,-10}  {2,-32}  {3,10}  {4,9}",
            orderItem.Qty, orderItem.PartNo, orderItem.Description,
            orderItem.UnitPrice.ToString("c"),
            orderItem.ExtPrice.ToString("c"));
    }
    tw.WriteLine();
    tw.WriteLine("                                                ----------");
    tw.WriteLine("                                        Subtotal {0,10}",
        order.Subtotal.ToString("c"));
    tw.WriteLine("                                        Tax      {0,10}",
        order.Tax.ToString("c"));
    tw.WriteLine("                                        Total    {0,10}",
        order.Total.ToString("c"));
```

```
        tw.Close();
}


//*******************
//*  Hosting Code  *
//*******************
// Host the service in a console application (exe).

public static void Main()
{
    // Get the OrderProcessing MSMQ queue name from app settings in
    // configuration and create the queue if necessary.
    string queueName = ConfigurationManager.AppSettings["queueName"];
    if (!MessageQueue.Exists(queueName))
        MessageQueue.Create(queueName, true);

    // Get base address from app settings in configuration
    Uri baseAddress = new Uri(ConfigurationManager.AppSettings["baseAddress"]);

    // Create a ServiceHost<T> for the OrderProcessingService type.
    using (ServiceHost<OrderProcessingService> serviceHost =
        new ServiceHost<OrderProcessingService>(baseAddress))
    {
        // Open the ServiceHost to create listeners and start
        // listening for messages.
        serviceHost.Open();

        // The service can now be accessed.
        Console.WriteLine("The order processing service is ready.");
        Console.WriteLine("Press <ENTER> to terminate service.");
        Console.WriteLine();
        Console.ReadLine();

        // Close the ServiceHost to shut down the service.
        serviceHost.Close();
    }
}

}

}
```

The configuration file for the Order Processing service is App.config, which is shown in Listing 13-8. It is renamed Service.exe.config at deployment time. The configuration defines endpoints in the *<service>* section. The endpoint definitions in the *<service>* section define two endpoints for the service. The primary endpoint uses the MSMQ transport and is the normal endpoint used to send orders to the service. The service also provides a secondary HTTP endpoint to provide an alternative means of accessing the service.

Listing 13-8   Order Processing Service: App.config

```xml
<?xml version="1.0" encoding="utf-8" ?>
<configuration xmlns="http://schemas.microsoft.com/.NetConfiguration/v2.0">

    <appSettings>
        <!-- use appSetting to configure MSMQ queue name -->
        <add key="queueName" value=".\private$\OrderProcessing" />
        <add key="baseAddress" value="http://localhost:8000/OrderProcessing" />
    </appSettings>

    <system.serviceModel>
        <services>
            <service
                serviceType="ProgrammingIndigo.OrderProcessingService">
                <!-- Define NetProfileMsmqEndpoint -->
                <endpoint address="http://localhost:8000/OrderProcessing"
                          bindingSectionName="wsProfileBinding"
                          contractType="ProgrammingIndigo.IOrderProcessing" />
                <endpoint address="net.msmq://localhost/private$/OrderProcessing"
                          bindingSectionName="netProfileMsmqBinding"
                          bindingConfiguration="nonSecuredMsmqBinding"
                          contractType="ProgrammingIndigo.IOrderProcessing" />
            </service>
        </services>

        <bindings>
            <netProfileMsmqBinding>
                <binding configurationName="nonSecuredMsmqBinding"
                         msmqAuthenticationMode="None"
                         msmqProtectionLevel="None">
                </binding>
            </netProfileMsmqBinding>
        </bindings>

    </system.serviceModel>
</configuration>
```

Setup Procedures

This solution requires the following setup procedures. You can run the solution with or without security. The following steps assume you are running everything on a single machine. If you are deploying to a multiple-machine configuration, you must change the addresses in configuration files and run the security setup steps on the appropriate machines.

Set up the Online Store application:

1.   Create a virtual directory named Store for the online store.

2.   Copy the .aspx, .cs, and Web.config files to the virtual directory.

3.   Test that you can access the service from a browser at *https://localhost/Store/shop.aspx.*

Set up security for the Online Store application:

1. Skip this procedure if you are not using security.

2. Run the Setup.bat script in the Source project directory to create a certificate. This runs the following *makecert* command:

```
makecert -sr LocalMachine -ss My -n CN=ProgrammingIndigo-HTTPS-Server -sky exchange
    -sk ProgrammingIndigo-HTTPS-Key
```

3. Launch IIS. Right-click on Default Web Site and select Properties. On the Directory Security tab, click Server Certificate to start the Web Server Certificate Wizard.

4. Complete the wizard screens. Select the Assign A Certificate option and select the ProgrammingIndigo-HTTPS-Server certificate from the list of certificates.

5. Test that you can access the service from a browser at *https://localhost/Store/shop.aspx*.

Set up the Order Entry service:

1. Build the OrderEntry.sln solution using Microsoft Visual Studio 2005 or the *msbuild* command.

2. Create a virtual directory named OrderEntry for the service.

3. Copy the Service.svc and Web.config files to the virtual directory, and copy Service.dll to its \bin subdirectory.

4. Test that you can access the service from a browser at *http://localhost/OrderEntry/service.svc*.

Set up the Payment service:

1. Build the CreditAgency.sln solution using Visual Studio 2005 or the *msbuild* command.

2. Create a virtual directory named CreditAgency for the service.

3. Copy the Service.svc and Web.config files to the virtual directory, and copy Service.dll to its \bin subdirectory.

4. Test that you can access the service from a browser at *http://localhost/CreditAgency/service.svc*.

Set up security for the Payment service:

1. Skip this procedure if you are not using security.

2. Run the Setup.bat script in the CreditAgency project to create client and service certificates.

3. Test that you can still access the service from a browser at *http://localhost/CreditAgency/service.svc*.

Set up the Order Processing service:

1. Build the OrderProcessing.sln solution using Visual Studio 2005 or the *msbuild* command.

2. Create an MSMQ queue named OrderProcessing.

3. From the Start menu, select Run and type **compmgmt.msc**.

4. Expand Services and Applications in the outline, and navigate to Message Queuing.

5. Right-click Private Queues and select New, Private Queue.

6. Type the name **OrderProcessing** for the queue, and select the Transactional check box. Close the dialog box to create the queue.

7. Test that you can run the service by launching Service.exe. You should see console output confirming that the service is running.

Executing the Solution

The solution is now ready to use. To use the solution and verify its operation, perform the following steps:

1. In a Web browser, type the address of the online store: **http://<*machine-name*>/Store/shop.aspx**. Specify **https:** in the address if you set up SSL security for the online store. You should see a page like that shown earlier in Figure 13-2.

2. Make a purchase by changing the quantity of one or more items to a number greater than 0. Click the Buy button to proceed to the order page. Change the contact information and click Submit Order to place an order.

3. What happens next is invisible to the user. While the user is waiting for a response, the order is passed to the Order Entry service, which verifies payment with the Payment service. If the payment is declined (which occurs if name or address information is missing), the response to the Web store indicates a declined order and the user is informed that the order was not accepted. If the payment is accepted, the order is sent to the Order Processing service via a durable queue. The response to the Web store indicates approval, and the user is informed of her order number.

4. Go to the Order Processing project's service\bin directory and launch Service.exe. If you have sent one or more approved orders into the system, you see the order numbers displayed as the Order Processing service receives them. You should see console output similar to that shown in Figure 13-4. The orders are written to text files named Order-<*order-number*>.txt.

Figure 13-4   Order Processing console output

5. Open the Order*.txt files created by the Order Processing service and verify that they contain the orders submitted to the online store. Listing 13-9 shows an example of an order file.

Listing 13-9   Order Text File

```
ORDER      Order No. 1005  Order Date: 4/15/2005

BILL TO:  Jay Adams
          100 Main St.
          Redmond WA
          425-555-1234

SHIP TO:  Jay Adams
          100 Main St.
          Redmond WA
          425-555-1234

Qty  Part No    Description                             Unit Price  Ext Price
---  ---------- -------------------------------         ----------  ---------
  1  0001-001   Bike 1                                     $500.00    $500.00
  1  0001-002   Bike 2                                     $750.00    $750.00
  1  0001-003   Bike 3                                   $1,000.00  $1,000.00

                                                                    ----------
                                                        Subtotal    $2,250.00
                                                        Tax             $0.00
                                                        Total       $2,250.00
```

This case study has illustrated secure, reliable, transacted enterprise order processing using Indigo. Let's consider how our solution has met the requirements identified by Adventure Works:

- We met the interactive Web store requirement by creating an ASP.NET application. Because Indigo can be used from any managed code environment, it is no problem for the ASP.NET application to also function as a client of the Order Entry service.

- We met the service-oriented approach requirement by designing the solution with service orientation in mind and implementing most parts of the solution as Indigo services.

- We met the requirement for easy reconfiguration and rapid deployment by using Indigo. Addresses, bindings, and security are controlled by configuration files.

- We met the scalability requirement by our choice of implementation technologies. ASP.NET and the two services hosted in IIS can be scaled using traditional Web techniques. The queue-based Order Processing service can run in multiple instances for parallel processing of incoming orders.

- We met the requirement to verify payments with another organization by connecting the Order Entry service with the credit agency's Payment service.

- We met the requirement to handle temporary unavailability of systems in the enterprise through the use of durable queuing. The Order Processing service can be taken in and out of service as needed but it will not lose orders.

If this were a production system, we would take some additional steps in our implementation. All of the client code should use *try* and *catch* logic to handle fault conditions, such as the unavailability of another service, a disruption in communication, or a security failure.

Summary

Our enterprise order processing case study put Indigo to the test in an enterprise setting. Requirements included an interactive online store, an order processing facility in the perimeter network, communication with another organization to authorize payments, and an order processing facility in the intranet.

The solution combines an interactive ASP.NET Web application with Indigo services, and the two technologies are easy to integrate. We used HTTP communication outside the intranet and used MSMQ communication to pass orders into the intranet. The online store supports HTTPS transport security, and the credit agency supports X.509 certificate security. The use of durable queuing allows the solution to provide a continuous e-commerce presence to customers even when systems in the intranet are taken offline.

Chapter 14
Case Study: Digital Whiteboard

In many client/service applications, clients are isolated from each other. In peer-to-peer applications, clients interact with each other and may share resources. In this chapter, a digital whiteboard application will be created to illustrate a peer-to-peer style application.

After completing this chapter, you will:

- Build a sample application that uses Indigo in a desktop productivity setting with collaboration between multiple parties.

- Understand how HTTP communication, IIS hosting, duplex contracts, reliable sessions, instancing, and events can be used together in a solution.

- Understand how Indigo can be used in the context of an interactive Microsoft Windows Forms application.

The files for this sample application can be downloaded from the Web as described in the Introduction.

The Problem

In this case study, we'll build a digital whiteboard that can be viewed and modified simultaneously by multiple remote participants. The application will allow people who are geographically separated to meet virtually and have an experience similar to being in a room together and sharing a whiteboard. The application will do this by providing desktop clients for displaying and editing the whiteboard and a central service for keeping all clients informed of changes. To facilitate the conversation that accompanies drawing on a whiteboard, the application will also allow participants to send text messages.

Whiteboards are useful in face-to-face meetings for brainstorming and conveying ideas visually. Figure 14-1 shows an example of whiteboard scribbling that might result from a meeting. Items commonly drawn on whiteboards include lines, rectangles, filled rectangles, ellipses, and text. Our digital whiteboard application must be able to represent these basic drawing elements. It must also present users with a simple interface that is easy to use, even for first-time users.

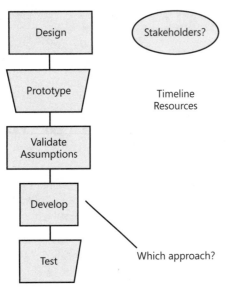

Figure 14-1   Sample whiteboard scribbling in the real world

The digital whiteboard is a shared resource, and the solution's behavior must reinforce that concept. Everyone involved in the meeting should see the same whiteboard at all times. Anyone should be able to make a change to the whiteboard, and everyone's view of the whiteboard should be updated accordingly.

Meeting participants should be free to join or leave the meeting as they wish. When participants join a meeting, they should get the same updated view of the whiteboard even if they enter the meeting late. Because the participants are not meeting face to face, it must be clear who is participating in a meeting and who is drawing on the board.

The solution must have these elements:

- Multiple participants who are separated geographically can collaborate in a virtual meeting using the metaphor of a whiteboard.

- A desktop graphical interface must facilitate viewing and editing of a shared digital whiteboard.

- The digital whiteboard must be able to represent lines, rectangles, ellipses, and text.

- Participants must be able to communicate using text messages that are external to the whiteboard itself.

- The desktop interface must be simple and easy to use.

- Participants should be free to join or leave the meeting as they wish.

- Participants must know who else is in the meeting and who is drawing on the board.

The Solution

With the problem definition in place, we can design a service-oriented solution. We must identify service boundaries, determine the roles of services and clients, choose a messaging pattern, and design contracts, bindings, and service behaviors.

Service Boundaries

Although the digital whiteboard application will feel like a peer-to-peer solution to the people using it, a client/server design makes sense and solves a number of problems that would otherwise be complicated to address. Figure 14-2 shows a design in which desktop clients interact with a whiteboard service on a central server. Using a central server provides a common reference point for all clients to communicate with, so only one address is needed in the entire solution: the address of the server. A client/server design also simplifies the job of passing on whiteboard changes to all meeting participants because all participants are clients of the service. When a client makes a change, such as drawing a rectangle, the service passes on the change to all clients.

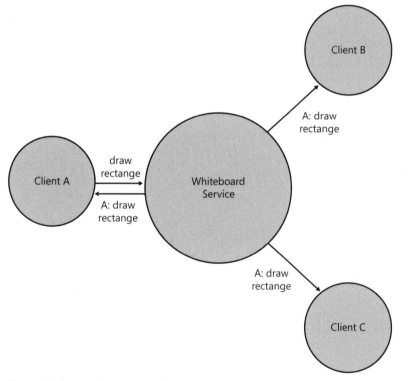

Figure 14-2   Service boundaries

This solution requires duplex communication because most actions by a single client will require the service to respond by initiating communication with all clients. The whiteboard service on the central server must provide service operations for joining and leaving a meeting, finding out what's on the whiteboard, making changes to the whiteboard, and sending text messages. The clients must provide service operations for being informed about changes to the whiteboard, receiving text messages, and being notified that someone new has joined the meeting.

Service Contracts

The duplex messaging pattern will require a pair of service contracts: the whiteboard service contract and the client callback contract to the desktop clients. We'll call the service contract *IWhiteboardDuplex* and the client callback contract *IWhiteboardDuplexCallback*.

The whiteboard service will provide these operations:

- *Join* A client signaling that it wants to join the meeting
- *Leave* A client signaling that it wants to leave the meeting
- *ChangeBoard* A client making a change to the whiteboard, such as drawing a circle
- *GetBoardHistory* A client requesting the history of changes to the whiteboard
- *ClearAll* A client clearing the entire whiteboard
- *Undo* A client rolling back the last change made to the whiteboard
- *Announce* A client announcing its arrival to other clients

The operations for adding images or text to the whiteboard often require similar information, such as starting and ending coordinates. For this reason, we'll use a single operation, *ChangeBoard*, for most whiteboard changes, along with a structure named *BoardAction*, which we'll define in the next section.

The whiteboard client will provide these service operations in its callback contract:

- *ChangeBoard* The service telling each client to update its rendering of the whiteboard to reflect a client change
- *AnnounceNewParty* The service telling each client that a new participant has joined the meeting

The following pair of service contracts defines these operations. The service contract specifies that sessions are required. (These are necessary for duplex communication.)

```
// IWhiteboardDuplex
// Service contract for the service side of the duplex conversation.

[ServiceContract(Namespace = "http://ProgrammingIndigo", Session = true,
    CallbackContract = typeof(IWhiteboardDuplexCallback))]
public interface IWhiteboardDuplex
{
    [OperationContract(IsOneWay = false, IsInitiating=true, IsTerminating=false)]
```

```
    int Join(string name);
    [OperationContract(IsOneWay = true, IsInitiating = false, IsTerminating=true)]
    void Leave();
    [OperationContract(IsOneWay = true, IsInitiating = false, IsTerminating = false)]
    void ChangeBoard(BoardAction boardAction);
    [OperationContract(IsOneWay = false, IsInitiating = false, IsTerminating = false)]
    List<BoardAction> GetBoardHistory();
    [OperationContract(IsOneWay = true, IsInitiating = false, IsTerminating = false)]
    void ClearAll();
    [OperationContract(IsOneWay = true, IsInitiating = false, IsTerminating = false)]
    void Undo();
    [OperationContract(IsOneWay = true, IsInitiating = false, IsTerminating = false)]
    void Announce();
}

// IWhiteboardDuplexCallback
// Service contract for the client callback side of the duplex conversation.

public interface IWhiteboardDuplexCallback
{
    [OperationContract(IsOneWay = true)]
    void ChangeBoard(BoardAction boardAction);
    [OperationContract(IsOneWay = true, IsInitiating = false, IsTerminating = false)]
    void AnnounceNewParty(List<Party> parties);
}
```

Let's review the fine details of the service contract. The service contract expects a client to call these operations in a specific order: a call to *Join* followed by multiple calls to various service operations and then a call to *Leave*.

The *Join* operation starts a new session for a client. The operation is marked as *IsInitiating=true*, which means a new instance and session will be started when this operation is called.

The *Leave* operation ends a session for a client. The operation is marked as *IsTerminating=true*, which means the instance and session will be terminated after this operation is called.

The service-side *ChangeBoard* operation informs the server that a client is making a change to the board. The server then calls the same client-side operation for each client to keep its views up to date. *ChangeBoard* depends on a *BoardAction* structure to communicate changes to the whiteboard.

Data Contracts

Several data contracts are defined in the service, most notably a *BoardAction* structure. *BoardAction* is passed from a client to a service to indicate a change to the whiteboard. It is also passed from the service to all clients to propagate a change.

```
// A board action code defines an action to be shared with other parties.

public enum BoardActionCode {
    Clear,                    // Clear the whiteboard and history of changes.
```

```
    Undo,                       // Undo the last change to the whiteboard.
    DrawLine,                   // Draw a line.
    DrawRectangle,              // Draw a rectangle.
    DrawFilledRectangle,        // Draw a filled rectangle.
    DrawCircle,                 // Draw a circle.
    DrawText,                   // Draw text.
    EraseRectangle,             // Erase a rectangular area.
    SendMessage,                // Send a message.
    Announce                    // Announce a new party.
};

// A party contains information about a participant, such as his name.

[DataContract(Namespace = "http://ProgrammingIndigo")]
public class Party
{
    [DataMember]
    public string Name;
}

// A board action identifies an action to take and supporting detail needed for
// the action, such as coordinates.

[DataContract(Namespace="http://ProgrammingIndigo")]
public class BoardAction
{
    [DataMember]
    public int Party;                // The party number of the originator of the action.
    [DataMember]
    public BoardActionCode Action;   // The action to take.
    [DataMember]
    public long X1;                  // Starting position X coordinate.
    [DataMember]
    public long Y1;                  // Starting position Y coordinate.
    [DataMember]
    public long X2;                  // Ending position X coordinate.
    [DataMember]
    public long Y2;                  // Ending position Y coordinate.
    [DataMember]
    public string TextMessage;       // Text message.
}
```

Let's take a look at the members of the *BoardAction* data contract:

- *Party*   The client's party number, which is used to indicate the originator of the action. The service assigns a party number to each client when it joins the conversation.

- *Action*   The action to take, such as drawing a line. The *BoardActionCode* enumeration lists the possible action codes.

- *X1* and *Y1*   The coordinates of the starting point for the action.

- *X2* and *Y2*   The coordinates of the ending point for the action.

- *TextMessage*   Text related to the action, if any.

Binding

A binding is needed that specifies appropriate transport, session, and delivery assurances. Our application has these requirements:

- Cross-machine, cross-organization communication
- Duplex messaging pattern
- Reliable sessions
- Exactly-once, in-order delivery assurances

The *WSProfileDualHttp* binding fulfills these requirements. HTTP communication is a good transport choice because participants are likely to be in different locations. Reliable sessions will provide the stateful client sessions that our design calls for as well as delivery assurances. We want messages to arrive exactly once and in order so that requests are handled fairly. We won't implement any security in this application, but if security were needed, it would simply be a matter of configuring the binding.

Service Behaviors

The service class will implement the *IWhiteboardDuplex* service contract. Service behaviors must specify appropriate instancing and concurrency modes for the solution. Here are the service settings we will use:

```
[ServiceBehavior(
    InstanceMode = InstanceMode.PrivateSession,
    ConcurrencyMode=ConcurrencyMode.Single)]
public class WhiteboardService : IWhiteboardDuplex
{
    ...
}
```

The *[ServiceBehavior]* attribute specifies the use of private session instancing, a requirement for duplex communication. The service will create a separate instance for each client connection.

Program Design

In this solution, the client is highly visible to users while the service is invisible. The client side of the solution will be a desktop Windows Forms application that the user interacts with. The service side of the solution will be hosted in Microsoft Internet Information Services (IIS) and will be completely out of sight.

Client Program Design

Figure 14-3 shows the main form for the client program. The solution is able to represent the basic diagramming elements of lines, rectangles, filled rectangles, ellipses, and text, and it has a simple user interface.

The application's functions are available as menu items and buttons. The menu is structured as follows:

- **File menu**   Contains options for clearing the whiteboard and exiting the application.

- **Edit menu**   Contains options for undoing an operation and refreshing the display. These functions are also available as buttons on the left side of the display.

- **Connect menu**   Contains options for joining or leaving the whiteboard meeting. These functions are also available as buttons near the top of the display.

- **Tools menu**   Contains options for setting the drawing mode to drawing lines, rectangles, filled rectangles, ellipses, and text, or setting it to erase. These functions are also available as drawing tool buttons on the left side of the display.

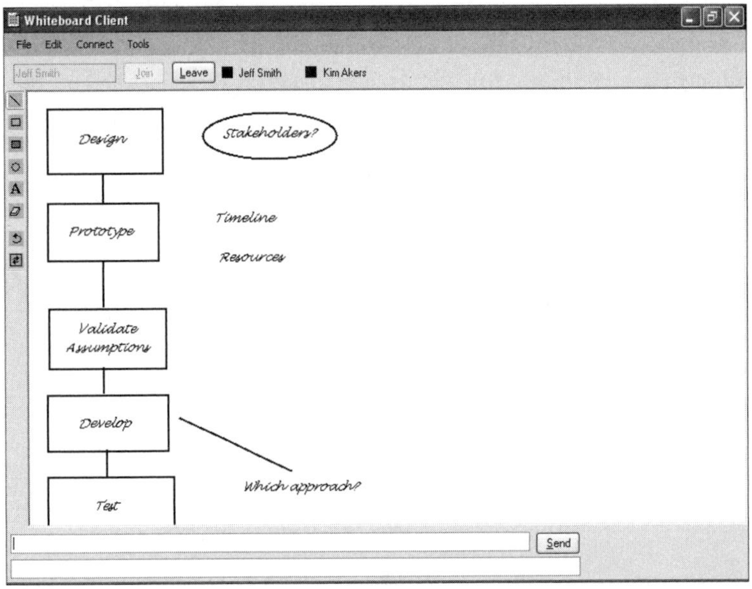

Figure 14-3   Digital whiteboard client

To get started, users enter a name at the top right of the form and click the Join button (or select Join from the Connect menu). This connects them to the service and allows them to view and modify the whiteboard. To leave the whiteboard, users click the Leave button (or select Leave from the Connect menu), which disconnects them from the service.

Once a user connects to the server, the display is updated to reflect the current appearance of the whiteboard. At the top of the screen, each participant's name and drawing color are listed. Participants are assigned different colors, which allows anyone viewing the whiteboard to tell who drew what.

To draw a line, rectangle, filled rectangle, or ellipse on the whiteboard, or to erase a rectangular region, a user selects the appropriate tool, presses the mouse button on a starting position, moves the mouse to an ending position, and releases the mouse button. To draw text, the user clicks on a position. If text has been entered in the Send Message text box, that text is inserted. Otherwise, the user is prompted to enter text, which is then inserted. When a user makes a drawing or text change to the board, that change is sent to the service. The service then informs all clients (including the originating client) of the change, and the clients update their whiteboard displays accordingly. If a participant makes a change to the whiteboard, she doesn't see the graphic display update until a round-trip communication has occurred and a notification has been received from the service.

The client can also send and receive text messages. At the bottom of the display are two text boxes, shown in Figure 14-4. The upper text box accepts text to send and is accompanied by a Send button. When the Send button is clicked, the message is sent to the service and then on to each client. When a client receives a text message, it is displayed in the lower text box. Text messages are sent to all clients, just as whiteboard changes are.

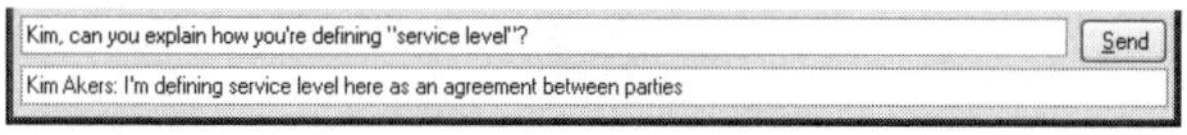

Kim, can you explain how you're defining "service level"?   Send
Kim Akers: I'm defining service level here as an agreement between parties

Figure 14-4   Sending and receiving text messages

Service Program Design

The service program defines several contracts, including the *IWhiteboardDuplex* and *IWhiteboardDuplexCallback* service contracts and the *BoardAction* data contract. The service program also implements the *IWhiteboardDuplex* service contract in a class named *WhiteboardService*.

The primary function of the service is to allow the clients to collaborate by serving as the central point of communication. When a client informs the service about a change to the whiteboard, the service must pass on the change to all of the clients. To do its job, the service must keep track of all clients and be able to send a message to all of the clients more or less simultaneously. Keeping track of the meeting participants is relatively simple. The service will use private session instancing so that each client that joins a meeting gets a dedicated instance of the service class. But the service also needs a way to send one message to multiple clients in a one-to-many fashion.

To send a message to all clients, we need to be inventive, because Indigo doesn't currently contain an out-of-the-box feature for multicasting or publish-subscribe–style communication. In this case, we can use a static Microsoft .NET event as a mechanism to help trigger communication to the clients. When a client joins a whiteboard meeting, the service instance will subscribe a handler to the .NET event. When a client leaves the whiteboard meeting, the instance will unsubscribe its handler from the .NET event. Whenever the service has a message to send to all clients, it will raise the event. The handlers in each instance will execute in response, sending a message back to their respective clients over their duplex callback connections. Figure 14-5 illustrates how the event is used to trigger communication to the clients.

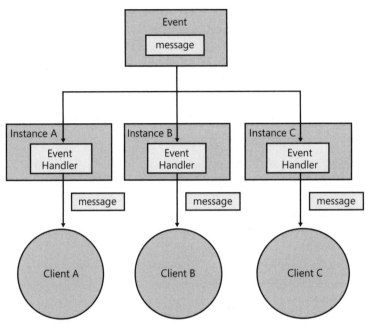

Figure 14-5   Using an event to trigger communication to multiple clients

Implementing the Solution

Now we can proceed to implementation. The primary files that make up the solution are listed in Table 14-1.

Table 14-1   Digital Whiteboard Solution Structure

Project	File	Class	Assembly
Client	Form1.cs	*Form1*	Client.exe
Client	FormText.cs	*FormText*	Client.exe
Client	Proxy.cs	*WhiteboardDuplexProxy*	Client.exe
Client	App.config	N/A	N/A
Service	Service.cs	*WhiteboardService*	Service.dll
Service	Web.config	N/A	N/A

Form1.cs

Form1.cs, along with Form1Designer.cs and Form1.resx, defines the main form for the client in the class *Form1*. Form1.cs is shown in Listing 14-1. Much of the code in Form1.cs is dedicated to providing the user interface.

The variables declared in the *Form1* class are used for communication and to maintain state. They serve these functions:

- *Proxy* An instance of the generated class *WhiteboardDuplexProxy*, which allows the client to communicate with the whiteboard service.

- *Site* A *ServiceSite* representing an instance of *Form1* that implements the client callback contract service operations.

- *BoardHistory* A list of *BoardAction* variables that tracks the history of changes made to the whiteboard. This information is stored so the client can redraw the whiteboard when the form needs repainting.

- *MaxParties* An integer constant that sets the maximum number of meeting participants. This is currently set to 8.

- *Online* A Boolean variable indicating whether the client has joined the whiteboard meeting and has made a connection to the service.

- *MouseDown*, *MouseDownX*, and *MouseDownY* A Boolean variable that tracks whether the mouse button has been pressed and long variables that indicate the starting coordinates of a drawing operation.

- *MouseUp*, *MouseUpX*, and *MouseUpY* A Boolean variable that tracks whether the mouse button has been released and long variables that indicate the ending coordinates of a drawing operation.

Listing 14-1 Client: Form1.cs

```
//*******************************
//*                             *
//*  Digital Whiteboard Client  *
//*                             *
//*******************************

using System;
using System.Collections.Generic;
using System.Data;
using System.Drawing;
using System.ServiceModel;
using System.Security.Principal;
using System.Windows.Forms;

namespace client
{
    //***********
    //*         *
    //*  Form1  *
    //*         *
    //***********
    // This is the main form of the whiteboard client.
    // This class also implements the IWhiteboardDuplexCallback client-side
    // service operations for the duplex conversation.

    [ServiceBehavior(ConcurrencyMode=ConcurrencyMode.Single)]
    public partial class Form1 : Form, IWhiteboardDuplexCallback
```

```
{
    WhiteboardDuplexProxy proxy;
    ServiceSite site;

    List<programmingindigo.BoardAction> BoardHistory = new
        List<programmingindigo.BoardAction>();

    const int MaxParties = 8;
    System.Drawing.Color[] PartyColor;
    int party = 0;

    bool online = false;

    bool MouseDown = false;
    long MouseDownX;
    long MouseDownY;

    bool MouseUp = false;
    long MouseUpX;
    long MouseUpY;

    public Form1()
    {
        InitializeComponent();

        PartyColor = new Color[MaxParties];
        PartyColor[0] = Color.Black;
        PartyColor[1] = Color.Blue;
        PartyColor[2] = Color.Green;
        PartyColor[3] = Color.Red;
        PartyColor[4] = Color.Purple;
        PartyColor[5] = Color.Orange;
        PartyColor[6] = Color.Brown;
        PartyColor[7] = Color.Gray;
    }


    //****************
    //*              *
    //*  Form_Load   *
    //*              *
    //****************
    // Form load routine.
    // Get current Windows identity, remove domain, and set as default party name.

    private void Form1_Load(object sender, EventArgs e)
    {
        string name = WindowsIdentity.GetCurrent().Name;
        int pos = name.IndexOf("\\");
        if (pos != -1)
            name = name.Substring(pos + 1);
        textBoxName.Text = name;
        textBoxName.Focus();
    }
```

```csharp
private void Form1_Paint(object sender, PaintEventArgs e)
{
    //pictureBoxWhiteboard.Invalidate();
    //RefreshWhiteboard();
}

void RefreshWhiteboard()
{
    foreach (programmingindigo.BoardAction action in BoardHistory)
    {
        ApplyChangeToBoard(action);
    }
}

private void pictureBoxWhiteboard_Paint(object sender, PaintEventArgs e)
{
    RefreshWhiteboard();
}


//*******************************
//*                             *
//*  Mouse Operation Handlers   *
//*                             *
//*******************************

// Mouse down.
// If the text tool is selected, insert text at the mouse down point.
// If a drawing tool is selected, remember the mouse down location.

private void pictureBoxWhiteboard_MouseDown(object sender, MouseEventArgs e)
{
    if (!online)
        return;

    if (menuToolsText.Checked)
    {
        string textToInsert = textBoxChatSend.Text;
        textBoxChatSend.Text = "";
        if (textToInsert.Length==0)
        {
            FormText form = new FormText();
            if (form.ShowDialog()==DialogResult.Cancel)
                return;
            textToInsert = form.textBoxText.Text;
        }
        programmingindigo.BoardAction boardAction = new
            programmingindigo.BoardAction();
        boardAction.Party = party;
        boardAction.Action =
            ProgrammingIndigo1.BoardActionCode.DrawText;
        boardAction.X1 = e.X;
        boardAction.Y1 = e.Y;
        boardAction.X2 = 0;
        boardAction.Y2 = 0;
```

```
            boardAction.TextMessage = textToInsert;
            proxy.ChangeBoard(boardAction);
            return;
        }

        //Drawing tool selected.

        MouseDown = true;
        MouseDownX = e.X;
        MouseDownY = e.Y;
    }

    // Mouse up.
    // If a drawing tool is selected, transmit a drawing action to the service.

    private void pictureBoxWhiteboard_MouseUp(object sender, MouseEventArgs e)
    {
        if (!online)
            return;
        if (MouseDown)
        {
            MouseUp = true;
            MouseUpX = e.X;
            MouseUpY = e.Y;

            programmingindigo.BoardAction boardAction =
                new programmingindigo.BoardAction();
            boardAction.Party = party;
            if (menuToolsLine.Checked)
                boardAction.Action =
                    ProgrammingIndigo1.BoardActionCode.DrawLine;
            else if (menuToolsRectangle.Checked)
                boardAction.Action =
                    ProgrammingIndigo1.BoardActionCode.DrawRectangle;
            else if (menuToolsFilledRectangle.Checked)
                boardAction.Action =
                    ProgrammingIndigo1.BoardActionCode.DrawFilledRectangle;
            else if (menuToolsCircle.Checked)
                boardAction.Action =
                    ProgrammingIndigo1.BoardActionCode.DrawCircle;
            else if (menuToolsEraser.Checked)
                boardAction.Action =
                    ProgrammingIndigo1.BoardActionCode.EraseRectangle;
            else
                boardAction.Action =
                    ProgrammingIndigo1.BoardActionCode.DrawLine;
            boardAction.X1 = MouseDownX;
            boardAction.Y1 = MouseDownY;
            boardAction.X2 = MouseUpX;
            boardAction.Y2 = MouseUpY;
            proxy.ChangeBoard(boardAction);

            MouseDown = false;
            MouseUp = false;
        }
```

```
}

void ClearNames()
{
    labelPlayerColor1.Visible = false;
    labelPlayerColor2.Visible = false;
    labelPlayerColor3.Visible = false;
    labelPlayerColor4.Visible = false;
    labelPlayerName1.Visible = false;
    labelPlayerName2.Visible = false;
    labelPlayerName3.Visible = false;
    labelPlayerName4.Visible = false;
}


//*********************
//*                   *
//*  Button clicked   *
//*                   *
//*********************

// Button clicked: Join.
// Run the equivalent menu item function.

private void buttonJoin_Click(object sender, EventArgs e)
{
    menuConnectJoin_Click(sender, e);
}


// Button clicked: Leave.
// Run the equivalent menu item function.

private void buttonLeave_Click(object sender, EventArgs e)
{
    menuConnectLeave_Click(sender, e);
}


// Button clicked: Send.
// Send a text message to the other participants.

private void buttonSend_Click(object sender, EventArgs e)
{
    Cursor = Cursors.WaitCursor;
    programmingindigo.BoardAction boardAction = new
        programmingindigo.BoardAction();
    boardAction.Action =
        ProgrammingIndigo1.BoardActionCode.SendMessage;
    boardAction.Party = party;
    boardAction.TextMessage = textBoxName.Text + ": " +
        textBoxChatSend.Text;
    proxy.ChangeBoard(boardAction);
    textBoxChatSend.Text = "";
    Cursor = Cursors.Default;
}
```

```
//*********************************
//*                               *
//*  Menu item selection - File   *
//*                               *
//*********************************


// File menu item selected: Clear All.
// Clear the whiteboard.

private void menuFileClearAll_Click(object sender, EventArgs e)
{
    proxy.ClearAll();
}


// File menu item selected: Refresh.
// Clear and redraw the whiteboard.

private void menuFileRefresh_Click(object sender, EventArgs e)
{
    RefreshWhiteboard();
}


// File menu item selected: Exit.
// Exit the application.

private void menuFileExit_Click(object sender, EventArgs e)
{
    Close();
    Environment.Exit(0);
}


//*********************************
//*                               *
//*  Menu item selection - Edit   *
//*                               *
//*********************************


// Edit menu item selected: Undo.
// Undo the last change to the whiteboard.

private void menuEditUndo_Click(object sender, EventArgs e)
{
    proxy.Undo();
}


// Edit menu item selected: Refresh.
// Clear and redraw the whiteboard.

private void menuEditRefresh_Click(object sender, EventArgs e)
{
    RefreshWhiteboard();
}
```

```
//**********************************
//*                                *
//*   Menu item selection - Connect *
//*                                *
//**********************************

// Connect menu item selected: Join.
// Connect to the whiteboard server and join the conversation.

private void menuConnectJoin_Click(object sender, EventArgs e)
{
    Cursor = Cursors.WaitCursor;
    site = new ServiceSite(this);
    proxy = new WhiteboardDuplexProxy(site, "default");
    party = proxy.Join(textBoxName.Text);
    online = true;
    menuConnectJoin.Enabled = false;
    menuConnectLeave.Enabled = true;
    textBoxName.Enabled = false;
    buttonJoin.Enabled = false;
    buttonLeave.Enabled = true;
    Application.DoEvents();
    BoardHistory = proxy.GetBoardHistory();
    RefreshWhiteboard();
    proxy.Announce();
    Cursor = Cursors.Default;
}

// Connect menu item selected: Leave.
// Leave the conversation and disconnect from the whiteboard server.

private void menuConnectLeave_Click(object sender, EventArgs e)
{
    if (online)
    {
        Cursor = Cursors.WaitCursor;
        ClearNames();
        online = false;
        proxy.Leave();
        menuConnectJoin.Enabled = true;
        menuConnectLeave.Enabled = false;
        textBoxName.Enabled = true;
        buttonJoin.Enabled = true;
        buttonLeave.Enabled = false;
        textBoxName.Focus();
        Cursor = Cursors.Default;
    }
}

//**********************************
//*                                *
//*   Menu item selection - Tools  *
//*                                *
//**********************************
```

```csharp
// Tools menu item selected: Draw Line.
// Check the menu item and the equivalent toolbar button.

private void menuToolsLine_Click(object sender, EventArgs e)
{
    menuToolsLine.Checked = true;
    menuToolsRectangle.Checked = false;
    menuToolsFilledRectangle.Checked = false;
    menuToolsCircle.Checked = false;
    menuToolsEraser.Checked = false;
    menuToolsText.Checked = false;
    toolStripDrawLine.Checked = true;
    toolStripDrawRectangle.Checked = false;
    toolStripDrawFilledRectangle.Checked = false;
    toolStripDrawCircle.Checked = false;
    toolStripEraser.Checked = false;
    toolStripText.Checked = false;
}

// Tools menu item selected: Draw Rectangle.
// Check the menu item and the equivalent toolbar button.

private void menuToolsRectangle_Click(object sender, EventArgs e)
{
    menuToolsLine.Checked = false;
    menuToolsRectangle.Checked = true;
    menuToolsFilledRectangle.Checked = false;
    menuToolsCircle.Checked = false;
    menuToolsEraser.Checked = false;
    menuToolsText.Checked = false;
    toolStripDrawLine.Checked = false;
    toolStripDrawRectangle.Checked = true;
    toolStripDrawFilledRectangle.Checked = false;
    toolStripDrawCircle.Checked = false;
    toolStripEraser.Checked = false;
    toolStripText.Checked = false;
}

// Tools menu item selected: Draw Circle.
// Check the menu item and the equivalent toolbar button.

private void menuToolsCircle_Click(object sender, EventArgs e)
{
    menuToolsLine.Checked = false;
    menuToolsRectangle.Checked = false;
    menuToolsFilledRectangle.Checked = false;
    menuToolsCircle.Checked = true;
    menuToolsEraser.Checked = false;
    menuToolsText.Checked = false;
    toolStripDrawLine.Checked = false;
    toolStripDrawRectangle.Checked = false;
    toolStripDrawFilledRectangle.Checked = false;
    toolStripDrawCircle.Checked = true;
    toolStripEraser.Checked = false;
    toolStripText.Checked = false;
```

```
}

// Tools menu item selected: Eraser.
// Check the menu item and the equivalent toolbar button.

private void menuToolsEraser_Click(object sender, EventArgs e)
{
    menuToolsLine.Checked = false;
    menuToolsRectangle.Checked = false;
    menuToolsFilledRectangle.Checked = false;
    menuToolsCircle.Checked = false;
    menuToolsEraser.Checked = true;
    menuToolsText.Checked = false;
    toolStripDrawLine.Checked = false;
    toolStripDrawRectangle.Checked = false;
    toolStripDrawFilledRectangle.Checked = false;
    toolStripDrawCircle.Checked = false;
    toolStripEraser.Checked = true;
    toolStripText.Checked = false;
}


private void Form1_FormClosing(object sender, FormClosingEventArgs e)
{
    if (online)
    {
        proxy.Leave();
        proxy.Close();
    }
}


// Tools menu item selected: Filled Rectangle.
// Check the menu item and the equivalent toolbar button.

private void menuToolsFilledRectangle_Click(object sender, EventArgs e)
{
    menuToolsLine.Checked = false;
    menuToolsRectangle.Checked = false;
    menuToolsFilledRectangle.Checked = true;
    menuToolsCircle.Checked = false;
    menuToolsEraser.Checked = false;
    menuToolsText.Checked = false;
    toolStripDrawLine.Checked = false;
    toolStripDrawRectangle.Checked = false;
    toolStripDrawFilledRectangle.Checked = true;
    toolStripDrawCircle.Checked = false;
    toolStripEraser.Checked = false;
    toolStripText.Checked = false;
}

// Tools menu item selected: Text.
// Check the menu item and the equivalent toolbar button.

private void menuToolsText_Click(object sender, EventArgs e)
```

```
    {
        menuToolsLine.Checked = false;
        menuToolsRectangle.Checked = false;
        menuToolsFilledRectangle.Checked = false;
        menuToolsCircle.Checked = false;
        menuToolsEraser.Checked = false;
        menuToolsText.Checked = true;
        toolStripDrawLine.Checked = false;
        toolStripDrawRectangle.Checked = false;
        toolStripDrawFilledRectangle.Checked = false;
        toolStripDrawCircle.Checked = false;
        toolStripEraser.Checked = false;
        toolStripText.Checked = true;
    }

    // Toolbar button clicked: Line tool.
    // Call the equivalent menu click function.

    private void toolStripDrawLine_Click(object sender, EventArgs e)
    {
        menuToolsLine_Click(sender, e);
    }

    // Toolbar button pressed: Draw Rectangle.
    // Call the equivalent menu click function.

    private void toolStripDrawRectangle_Click(object sender, EventArgs e)
    {
        menuToolsRectangle_Click(sender, e);
    }

    // Toolbar button pressed: Draw Filled Rectangle.
    // Call the equivalent menu click function.

    private void toolStripDrawFilledRectangle_Click(object sender, EventArgs e)
    {
        menuToolsFilledRectangle_Click(sender, e);
    }

    // Toolbar button pressed: Draw Circle.
    // Call the equivalent menu click function.

    private void toolStripDrawCircle_Click(object sender, EventArgs e)
    {
        menuToolsCircle_Click(sender, e);
    }

    // Toolbar button pressed: Text.
    // Call the equivalent menu click function.

    private void toolStripText_Click(object sender, EventArgs e)
    {
        menuToolsText_Click(sender, e);
    }
```

```
// Toolbar button clicked: Eraser tool.
// Call the equivalent menu click function.

private void toolStripEraser_Click(object sender, EventArgs e)
{
    menuToolsEraser_Click(sender, e);
}

// Toolbar button clicked: Undo.
// Call the equivalent menu click function.

private void toolStripUndo_Click(object sender, EventArgs e)
{
    menuEditUndo_Click(sender, e);
}

// Toolbar button clicked: Refresh.
// Call the equivalent menu click function.

private void toolStripRefresh_Click(object sender, EventArgs e)
{
    menuEditRefresh_Click(sender, e);
}


//***********************
//*                     *
//*  Service Operations *
//*                     *
//***********************

// Service operation - AnnounceNewParty
// Announce a new party has joined. Update the list of colors and names.

public void AnnounceNewParty(List<programmingindigo.Party> partyNames)
{
    ClearNames();
    int partyNo = 0;
    foreach (programmingindigo.Party party in partyNames)
    {
        SetName(partyNo++, party.Name);
    }
}

void SetName(int party, string name)
{
    switch (party)
    {
        case 0:
            labelPlayerColor1.BackColor = PartyColor[party];
            labelPlayerColor1.Visible = true;
            labelPlayerName1.Text = name;
            labelPlayerName1.Visible = true;
            break;
```

```
                case 1:
                    labelPlayerColor2.BackColor = PartyColor[party];
                    labelPlayerColor2.Visible = true;
                    labelPlayerName2.Text = name;
                    labelPlayerName2.Visible = true;
                    break;
                case 2:
                    labelPlayerColor3.BackColor = PartyColor[party];
                    labelPlayerColor3.Visible = true;
                    labelPlayerName3.Text = name;
                    labelPlayerName3.Visible = true;
                    break;
                case 3:
                    labelPlayerColor4.BackColor = PartyColor[party];
                    labelPlayerColor4.Visible = true;
                    labelPlayerName4.Text = name;
                    labelPlayerName4.Visible = true;
                    break;
                default:
                    // We only list the first 4 parties.
                    break;
            }
        }


        // Service operation - ChangeBoard.
        // Update the board to reflect a change by a participant and add to history.

        public void ChangeBoard(programmingindigo.BoardAction action)
        {
            // Store board action in history unless it is a Clear, Undo, or
            // SendMessage action.
            switch (action.Action)
            {
                case ProgrammingIndigo1.BoardActionCode.Clear:
                case ProgrammingIndigo1.BoardActionCode.Undo:
                case ProgrammingIndigo1.BoardActionCode.SendMessage:
                    break;
                default:
                    BoardHistory.Add(action);
                    break;
            }
            ApplyChangeToBoard(action);
        }


        void ApplyChangeToBoard(programmingindigo.BoardAction action)
        {
            long width, height;
            int originParty = action.Party;
            Pen pen = new Pen(PartyColor[originParty], 2);
            Graphics g = pictureBoxWhiteboard.CreateGraphics();
            switch (action.Action)
            {
                // ---- draw a line ----
                case ProgrammingIndigo1.BoardActionCode.DrawLine:
                    g.DrawLine(pen, action.X1, action.Y1, action.X2, action.Y2);
```

```
        break;
// ---- draw a rectangle ----
case ProgrammingIndigo1.BoardActionCode.DrawRectangle:
    if (action.X2 < action.X1)
        width = action.X1 - action.X2;
    else
        width = action.X2 - action.X1;
    if (action.Y2 < action.Y1)
        height = action.Y1 - action.Y2;
    else
        height = action.Y2 - action.Y1;
    g.DrawRectangle(pen, action.X1, action.Y1, width, height);
    break;
// ---- draw a circle ----
case ProgrammingIndigo1.BoardActionCode.DrawCircle:
    if (action.X2 < action.X1)
        width = action.X1 - action.X2;
    else
        width = action.X2 - action.X1;
    if (action.Y2 < action.Y1)
        height = action.Y1 - action.Y2;
    else
        height = action.Y2 - action.Y1;
    g.DrawEllipse(pen, action.X1, action.Y1, width, height);
    break;
// ---- erase a rectangular area ----
case ProgrammingIndigo1.BoardActionCode.EraseRectangle:
    if (action.X2 < action.X1)
        width = action.X1 - action.X2;
    else
        width = action.X2 - action.X1;
    if (action.Y2 < action.Y1)
        height = action.Y1 - action.Y2;
    else
        height = action.Y2 - action.Y1;
    g.FillRectangle(new SolidBrush(Color.White), action.X1, action.Y1,
        width, height);
    break;
// ---- draw a filled rectangle ----
case ProgrammingIndigo1.BoardActionCode.DrawFilledRectangle:
    if (action.X2 < action.X1)
        width = action.X1 - action.X2;
    else
        width = action.X2 - action.X1;
    if (action.Y2 < action.Y1)
        height = action.Y1 - action.Y2;
    else
        height = action.Y2 - action.Y1;
    g.FillRectangle(new SolidBrush(PartyColor[originParty]),
        action.X1, action.Y1, width, height);
    break;
// ---- draw text ----
case ProgrammingIndigo1.BoardActionCode.DrawText:
    {
        String drawString = action.TextMessage;
```

```
                    Font drawFont = new Font("Lucida Handwriting", 10,
                        FontStyle.Italic);
                    SolidBrush drawBrush = new
                        SolidBrush(PartyColor[originParty]);
                    float x = action.X1;
                    float y = action.Y1;
                    g.DrawString(drawString, drawFont, drawBrush, x, y);
                }
                break;
            // ---- send a message ----
            case ProgrammingIndigo1.BoardActionCode.SendMessage:
                {
                    string newText = action.TextMessage;
                    int newTextLength = newText.Length;
                    textBoxChatReceive.Text = newText;
                    textBoxChatReceive.ForeColor =
                        PartyColor[originParty];
                }
                break;
            // ---- clear the board ----
            case ProgrammingIndigo1.BoardActionCode.Clear:
                BoardHistory.Clear();
                pictureBoxWhiteboard.Refresh();
                RefreshWhiteboard();
                break;
            // ---- undo the last change to the whiteboard ----
            case ProgrammingIndigo1.BoardActionCode.Undo:
                int count = BoardHistory.Count;
                if (count > 0)
                    BoardHistory.RemoveAt(count - 1);
                pictureBoxWhiteboard.Refresh();
                RefreshWhiteboard();
                break;
            // ---- unknown operation ----
            default:
                break;
        }
    }

    private void Form1_Activated(object sender, EventArgs e)
    {
        Application.DoEvents();
        RefreshWhiteboard();
    }

    }

}
```

Near the bottom of the class are the methods implementing the two client-side service operations, *AnnounceNewParty* and *ChangeBoard*. The service will call *AnnounceNewParty* to indicate that a new meeting participant has joined the whiteboard meeting. The service will call *ChangeBoard* to inform the client that the whiteboard has changed or that there is a text message.

Not listed here is the form designer source file for this form, Form1.Designer.cs. That file is included in the download files for this chapter.

Proxy.cs

The Proxy.cs file contains the generated client code for the whiteboard service. The proxy is generated using the Svcutil tool.

In addition to defining the service and the data contracts needed to interact with the service, the generated code includes a *WhiteboardDuplexProxy* proxy class. The client creates an instance of the class to communicate with the service.

Client.exe.config

The client configuration file, Client.exe.config, is shown in Listing 14-2. In the Microsoft Visual Studio project, this file is named App.config; it is copied and renamed at build time to Client.exe.config. The configuration file defines the endpoint and binding used to access the service. The client endpoint configuration is named *default*. The endpoint specifies a *WSProfileDualHttp* binding. Security has been disabled in the binding configuration.

Listing 14-2   Client.exe.config

```xml
<?xml version="1.0" encoding="utf-8" ?>
<configuration xmlns="http://schemas.microsoft.com/.NetConfiguration/v2.0">
    <system.serviceModel>

        <client>
            <endpoint configurationName="default"
                      address="http://localhost/whiteboard/service.svc"
                      bindingSectionName="wsProfileDualHttpBinding"
                      bindingConfiguration="DuplexBinding"
                      contractType="IWhiteboardDuplex" />
        </client>

        <bindings>
            <wsProfileDualHttpBinding>
                <binding configurationName="DuplexBinding"
                         securityMode="None"/>
            </wsProfileDualHttpBinding>
        </bindings>

    </system.serviceModel>

</configuration>
```

Service.cs

Service.cs is shown in Listing 14-3. This code contains the following:

- Service contract definitions for the duplex contract pair *IWhiteboardDuplex* and *IWhiteboardDuplexCallback*

- A data contract definition for the *BoardAction* data structure used to communicate board changes and the related *BoardActionCode* enumeration

- An event named *BoardActionEvent*, an event arguments structure named *BoardActionEventArgs*, and an event handler named *BoardActionEventHandler*

- A class named *WhiteboardService*, which implements the service-side service operations for the *IWhiteboardDuplex* service contract

The *WhiteboardService* class implements the *Join*, *Leave*, *ChangeBoard*, *GetBoardHistory*, *ClearAll*, *Undo*, and *Announce* service operations. Clients call *Join* to join the whiteboard meeting and *Leave* to leave the meeting. *Join* creates a service instance, and *Leave* releases the instance. Clients call *ChangeBoard* to indicate a whiteboard change or to send a text message, which the service propagates to all clients. Clients call *Undo* to repeal the latest whiteboard change, or *ClearAll* to wipe the whiteboard clean. Clients call *Announce* to send an announcement to clients that they are joining the whiteboard meeting.

Listing 14-3   Service.cs

```
//********************************
//*                              *
//*  Digital Whiteboard Service  *
//*                              *
//********************************

using System;
using System.Collections;
using System.Collections.Generic;
using System.Drawing;
using System.Runtime.Serialization;
using System.ServiceModel;

namespace ProgrammingIndigo
{
    //*********************
    //*                   *
    //*  Data Contracts   *
    //*                   *
    //*********************
    // Data contracts for structures passed to or from service operations.

    // A board action code defines an action to be shared with other parties.

    public enum BoardActionCode {
        Clear,                  // Clear the whiteboard and history of changes
```

```
    Undo,                       // Undo the last change to the whiteboard
    DrawLine,                   // Draw a line
    DrawRectangle,              // Draw a rectangle
    DrawFilledRectangle,        // Draw a filled rectangle
    DrawCircle,                 // Draw a circle
    DrawText,                   // Draw text
    EraseRectangle,             // Erase a rectangular area
    SendMessage,                // Send a message
    Announce                    // Announce a new party
};

// A party contains information about a participant, such as his name.

[DataContract(Namespace = "http://ProgrammingIndigo")]
public class Party
{
    [DataMember]
    public string Name;
}


// A board action identifies an action to take and supporting detail needed for
// the action, such as coordinates.

[DataContract(Namespace="http://ProgrammingIndigo")]
public class BoardAction
{
    [DataMember]
    public int Party;                   // The party number of the originator of
                                        // the action.
    [DataMember]
    public BoardActionCode Action;      // The action to take.
    [DataMember]
    public long X1;                     // Starting position  X coordinate.
    [DataMember]
    public long Y1;                     // Starting position Y coordinate.
    [DataMember]
    public long X2;                     // Ending position X coordinate.
    [DataMember]
    public long Y2;                     // Ending position Y coordinate.
    [DataMember]
    public string TextMessage;          // Text message.
}



//***********************
//*                     *
//*   Service Contracts *
//*                     *
//***********************


// IWhiteboardDuplex
// Service contract for the service side of the duplex conversation.

[ServiceContract(Namespace = "http://ProgrammingIndigo", Session = true,
    CallbackContract = typeof(IWhiteboardDuplexCallback))]
```

```csharp
public interface IWhiteboardDuplex
{
    [OperationContract(IsOneWay = false, IsInitiating=true, IsTerminating=false)]
    int Join(string name);
    [OperationContract(IsOneWay = true, IsInitiating = false, IsTerminating=true)]
    void Leave();
    [OperationContract(IsOneWay = true, IsInitiating = false, IsTerminating=false)]
    void ChangeBoard(BoardAction boardAction);
    [OperationContract(IsOneWay = false, IsInitiating = false, IsTerminating=false)]
    List<BoardAction> GetBoardHistory();
    [OperationContract(IsOneWay = true, IsInitiating = false, IsTerminating=false)]
    void ClearAll();
    [OperationContract(IsOneWay = true, IsInitiating = false, IsTerminating=false)]
    void Undo();
    [OperationContract(IsOneWay = true, IsInitiating = false, IsTerminating=false)]
    void Announce();
}


// IWhiteboardDuplexCallback
// Service contract for the client callback side of the duplex conversation.

public interface IWhiteboardDuplexCallback
{
    [OperationContract(IsOneWay = true)]
    void ChangeBoard(BoardAction boardAction);
    [OperationContract(IsOneWay = true,
        IsInitiating = false, IsTerminating = false)]
    void AnnounceNewParty(List<Party> parties);
}


//************
//*          *
//*  Events  *
//*          *
//************
// Event used to communicate between client instances.

public class BoardActionEventArgs : EventArgs
{
    public BoardAction Action;
}




//**********************
//*                    *
//*  WhiteboardService  *
//*                    *
//**********************
// Service class which implements the whiteboard service contract.

[ServiceBehavior(
    InstanceMode = InstanceMode.PrivateSession,
    ConcurrencyMode=ConcurrencyMode.Single)]
public class WhiteboardService : IWhiteboardDuplex
{
```

```
static Object syncObject = new object();

const int MaxParties = 8;
static int ActiveParties = 0;
static List<Party> parties = new List<Party>();

static List<BoardAction> BoardHistory = new List<BoardAction>();

public static event BoardActionEventHandler BoardActionEvent;
public delegate void BoardActionEventHandler(object sender,
    BoardActionEventArgs e);
BoardActionEventHandler boardActionHandler = null;

IWhiteboardDuplexCallback callback = null;

int party;
string name;


//**********
//*        *
//* Join *
//*        *
//**********
// Service operation - join the conversation.

public int Join(string name)
{
    this.name = name;

    callback =
        OperationContext.Current.GetCallbackChannel<IWhiteboardDuplexCallback>();
    boardActionHandler = new
        BoardActionEventHandler(BoardActionHandler);
    lock (syncObject)
    {
        BoardActionEvent += BoardActionHandler;

        party = -1;
        int count = parties.Count;
        for (int n = 0; n < count; n++)
        {
            if (Convert.ToString(parties[n].Name) == name)
            {
                party = n;
                n = count;
            }
        }

        if (party == -1)
        {
            Party newParty = new Party();
            newParty.Name = name;
            parties.Add(newParty);
            party = ActiveParties;
```

```
        }

        if (ActiveParties>=MaxParties)
            throw new Fault<string>
            ("the maximum number of participants has been exceeded");
        ActiveParties++;
    }

    return party;
}


//***********
//*         *
//*  Leave  *
//*         *
//***********
// Service operation - leave the conversation.

public void Leave()
{
    lock (syncObject)
    {
        ActiveParties--;
        BoardActionEvent -= BoardActionHandler;
    }

    if (ActiveParties == 0)
    {
        BoardHistory.Clear();
    }
    else
    {
        BoardAction boardAction = new BoardAction();
        boardAction.Action = BoardActionCode.SendMessage;
        boardAction.Party = 0;
        boardAction.TextMessage = name + " has left the conversation";
        PublishBoardAction(boardAction);
    }
}


//*********************
//*                   *
//*  GetBoardHistory  *
//*                   *
//*********************
// Service operation - get board history.
// Return a board history so clients late to the conversation can
// fully re-create the whiteboard display.

public List<BoardAction> GetBoardHistory()
{
    return BoardHistory;
}
```

```
//*****************
//*               *
//*  ChangeBoard  *
//*               *
//*****************
// Service operation - board change.
// Propagate to other clients to keep their displays in sync.

public void ChangeBoard(BoardAction boardAction)
{
    BoardHistory.Add(boardAction);
    PublishBoardAction(boardAction);
}


//**************
//*            *
//*  ClearAll  *
//*            *
//**************
// Service operation - clear board and history.
// Propagate to other clients to keep their displays in sync.

public void ClearAll()
{
    BoardHistory.Clear();
    BoardAction boardAction = new BoardAction();
    boardAction.Action = BoardActionCode.Clear;
    boardAction.Party = 0;
    PublishBoardAction(boardAction);
}


//**********
//*        *
//*  Undo  *
//*        *
//**********
// Service operation - undo last change.
// Propagate to other clients to keep their displays in sync.

public void Undo()
{
    int count = BoardHistory.Count;
    if (count == 0)
        return;
    BoardHistory.RemoveAt(count - 1);
    BoardAction boardAction = new BoardAction();
    boardAction.Action = BoardActionCode.Undo;
    boardAction.Party = 0;
    PublishBoardAction(boardAction);
}



//**************
//*            *
//*  Announce  *
```

```
//*              *
//*************
// Service operation - announce new party.
// Propagate to other clients to keep their displays in sync.

public void Announce()
{
    BoardAction boardAction = new BoardAction();
    boardAction.Action = BoardActionCode.Announce;
    boardAction.Party = 0;
    PublishBoardAction(boardAction);
}


//*************************
//*                       *
//*  PublishBoardAction   *
//*                       *
//*************************
// Create an event to notify other clients of a new board action.

void PublishBoardAction(BoardAction action)
{
    BoardActionEventArgs e = new BoardActionEventArgs();
    e.Action = action;
    BoardActionEvent(this, e);
}


//*************************
//*                       *
//*  BoardActionHandler   *
//*                       *
//*************************
// Respond to a BoardActionEvent event.
// Inform this instance's client about the board action.

public void BoardActionHandler(object sender, BoardActionEventArgs e)
{
    switch (e.Action.Action)
    {
        case BoardActionCode.Announce:
            callback.AnnounceNewParty(parties);
            break;
        default:
            callback.ChangeBoard(e.Action);
            break;
    }
}


}


}
```

Service.svc

Service.svc defines the service to IIS and is shown in Listing 14-4. It identifies the service type, *ProgrammingIndigo.WhiteboardService*, and the assembly where the code resides, service (bin\service.dll). Service.svc, Web.config, and bin\service.dll will be placed in a virtual directory named whiteboard.

Listing 14-4   Service.svc

```
<%@Service language="c#" Debug="true" class="ProgrammingIndigo.WhiteboardService" %>
<%@Assembly Name="service" %>
```

Web.config

Web.config is the configuration file for the service and is shown in Listing 14-5. The configuration file defines an endpoint and binding for the service. The endpoint configuration specifies a *WSProfileDualHttp* binding. Security has been disabled in the binding configuration.

The address of the service is determined by the machine name, virtual directory name (whiteboard), and .svc filename (Service.svc). When the client and service are on the same machine, the service's endpoint address is *http://localhost/whiteboard/service.svc*.

Listing 14-5   Web.config

```
<?xml version="1.0" encoding="utf-8" ?>
<configuration xmlns="http://schemas.microsoft.com/.NetConfiguration/v2.0">
    <system.serviceModel>
        <services>
            <service
                serviceType="ProgrammingIndigo.WhiteboardService"
                behaviorConfiguration="WhiteboardServiceBehavior">
                <!-- use base address provided by host -->
                <endpoint address=""
                        bindingSectionName="wsProfileDualHttpBinding"
                        bindingConfiguration="DuplexBinding"
                        contractType="ProgrammingIndigo.IWhiteboardDuplex,
                            service" />
            </service>
        </services>

        <bindings>
            <wsProfileDualHttpBinding>
                <binding configurationName="DuplexBinding"
                        securityMode="None"/>
            </wsProfileDualHttpBinding>
        </bindings>

        <behaviors>
            <behavior
                configurationName="WhiteboardServiceBehavior"
```

```
                    returnUnknownExceptionsAsFaults="true" >
            </behavior>
        </behaviors>

    </system.serviceModel>

    <system.web>
        <compilation debug="true" />
    </system.web>

</configuration>
```

Deploying the Solution

Once you build the solution, you can deploy the program and configuration files and use the solution.

Service Deployment

To set up the service, follow these steps to set up a virtual directory for the IIS-hosted service:

1. Create a folder for deployment of the service, and then create a virtual directory for it named whiteboard.

2. Place Service.svc and Web.config in the whiteboard folder.

3. Place Service.dll in a bin subdirectory underneath the whiteboard folder.

4. Test that the service can be accessed by navigating to the following address using a Web browser: *http://localhost/whiteboard/service.svc*. You should receive a page confirming successful access to the service without compilation errors.

Client Deployment

To set up the client, follow these steps:

1. Copy Client.exe and Client.exe.config to client machines.

2. If clients are running from different machines than the service, edit their Client.exe.config files and change the name *localhost* in the endpoint address to the fully qualified machine name of the server where the service is hosted.

Once the service and clients are deployed, the solution can be used.

1. On a client machine, launch Client.exe. Once it initializes, enter a name at the top right, and then click the Join button to connect to the service. Once your name appears at the top of the screen, you can access the whiteboard.

2. Launch one or more additional instances of the client by repeating step 1, specifying a different name each time.

3. The solution is now ready for use. As new parties join the whiteboard meeting, the list of names at the top of each client should be updated. Whenever a participant makes a change to the whiteboard, the other clients' displays should be updated to match. Clients should be able to send text messages that all other clients see.

4. To shut down the solution, click the Leave button on each of the client programs. Each program can then be closed. There is no need to shut down the service.

Flow of Communication

Let's follow a partial whiteboard session to understand the message flow. Figure 14-6 shows a sequence diagram of a whiteboard session.

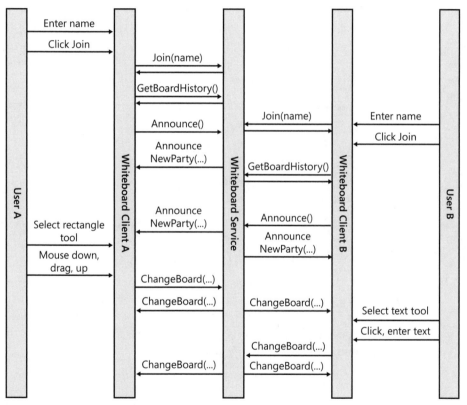

Figure 14-6   Whiteboard session sequence diagram

Here's what takes place during each step of the session:

1. User A launches the whiteboard client on a computer. User A enters a user name and clicks Join. In response, Client A creates an instance of the *WhiteboardDuplexProxy* class and invokes the *Join* operation, specifying the client name. This causes a message to be sent to the whiteboard service.

2. If the whiteboard service is not already running, IIS activates the service. On the service, a new service instance is created for Client A. The *Join* service operation executes. It adds an event handler to the *BoardActionEvent* event. *Join* adds the client name to a list of parties and responds to the client with a party number (0).

3. Client A invokes the *GetBoardHistory* service operation using the proxy. The service responds with a list of *BoardAction* objects, each describing a change in state of the whiteboard. In this case, the list is empty because no whiteboard activity has occurred yet. Client A stores the board history in its *BoardHistory* object and redraws the client view of the board, which is currently empty.

4. Client A invokes the *Announce* service operation using the proxy. The service creates a *BoardAction* object describing the announcement and raises a *BoardActionEvent* event. The event triggers execution by all of the event handlers that have subscribed to the event. At the moment, the instance for Client A is the only subscriber. The event handler uses the duplex callback to invoke the client's *AnnounceNewParty* service operation. A message is sent to Client A.

5. On Client A, the *AnnounceNewParty* service operation executes in response to the message from the service. Client A displays User A's name and drawing color at the top of the window as the sole party in the meeting.

6. User B launches the whiteboard client on a computer. User B enters a user name and clicks Join. In response, Client B creates an instance of the *WhiteboardDuplexProxy* class and invokes the *Join* operation, specifying the client name. This causes a message to be sent to the whiteboard service.

7. On the service, a new service instance is created for Client B. The *Join* service operation executes. It adds an event handler to the *BoardActionEvent* event. *Join* adds the client name to a list of parties and responds to the client with a party number (1).

8. Client B invokes the *GetBoardHistory* service operation using the proxy. The service responds with a list of *BoardAction* objects, each describing a change in state of the whiteboard. In this case, the list is empty because no whiteboard activity has occurred yet. Client B stores the board history in its *BoardHistory* object and redraws the client view of the board, which is currently empty.

9. Client B invokes the *Announce* service operation using the proxy. The service creates a *BoardAction* object describing the announcement and raises a *BoardActionEvent* event. The event triggers execution by all of the event handlers that have subscribed to the event. The instances for Client A and Client B are subscribers, so both of their event handlers execute. Each event handler uses the duplex callback to invoke its client's *AnnounceNewParty* service operation. A message is sent to Client A and to Client B.

10. On both Client A and Client B, the *AnnounceNewParty* service operation executes in response to the messages sent by the service. On both clients, the display at the top of the window is updated to show the names and drawing colors for User A and User B.

11. User A decides to draw a box on the whiteboard. User A clicks the rectangle drawing tool. On the whiteboard display area, User A presses down the mouse button, moves the mouse down and right diagonally, and releases the mouse button. In response, Client A constructs a *BoardAction* object and invokes the *ChangeBoard* service operation using the proxy. A message is sent to the service.

12. On the service, the *ChangeBoard* service operation executes in the instance for Client A. The service stores the board change in its history list and then raises a *BoardActionEvent* event. The event triggers execution by all of the event handlers that have subscribed to the event. The instances for Client A and Client B are subscribers, and both of their event handlers execute. Each event handler uses the duplex callback to invoke its client's *ChangeBoard* service operation. A message is sent to Client A and to Client B.

13. On both Client A and Client B, the *ChangeBoard* service operation executes in response to the messages sent by the service. On both clients, the *BoardAction* is added to the history list and a rectangle is drawn in black, User A's drawing color. All clients have now updated their displays to reflect the change made by User A.

14. User B decides to add some text to the whiteboard. User B clicks the text tool. On the whiteboard display area, User B clicks on the whiteboard area. The client prompts User B for text, and User B enters some. In response, Client B constructs a *BoardAction* object and invokes the *ChangeBoard* service operation using the proxy. A message is sent to the service.

15. On the service, the *ChangeBoard* service operation executes in the instance for Client B. The service stores the board change in its history list and then raises a *BoardActionEvent* event. The event triggers execution by all of the event handlers that have subscribed to the event. The instances for Client A and Client B are subscribers, and both of their event handlers execute. Each event handler uses the duplex callback to invoke its client's *ChangeBoard* service operation. A message is sent to Client A and to Client B.

16. On both Client A and Client B, the *ChangeBoard* service operation executes in response to the messages sent by the service. On both clients, the *BoardAction* is added to the history list and text is added to the whiteboard in blue, User B's drawing color. All clients have now updated their displays to reflect the change made by User B.

Summary

In our digital whiteboard case study, we applied Indigo to a collaboration application. Using the metaphor of a whiteboard, the application allows participants who are geographically separated to engage in a virtual meeting.

The solution design prescribes desktop GUI clients using a central service as a communication hub for clients. When a client informs the service of a change to the whiteboard, the service passes on that change to all clients. A .NET event is used as a mechanism to trigger communication of messages to all clients nearly simultaneously. Duplex messaging is required so clients as well as the service can initiate communication.

The whiteboard service is implemented in a *WhiteboardService* class and hosted in IIS. The client is implemented in a Windows Forms application.

We executed the solution to interactively observe the system in operation. We followed a specific session in detail, noting message flow.

Chapter 15

Case Study: Elevator Control System

Real-time applications frequently require programming that is asynchronous, responsive, and adaptable. In this chapter, real-time programming with Indigo is illustrated by creating an elevator control system.

After completing this chapter, you will:

- Know how to build a sample application that uses Indigo for real-time machinery control.

- Understand how TCP communication, duplex contracts, reliable sessions, and initiating and terminating service operations can be used together in a solution.

- Understand how Indigo can be used in the context of a Microsoft Windows Forms application.

The files for the sample application can be downloaded from the Web, as described in the Introduction.

The Problem

In this case study, we'll build an elevator control system for a building with multiple elevators. For the sake of brevity, our system will be simple, lacking AI algorithms, weight sensors, and other sophistications of modern elevator systems.

A single elevator is a fairly efficient and autonomous device. Many employ a simple strategy:

1. Keep moving up, stopping at floors with going-up requests, until all going-up requests have been serviced.

2. Keep moving down, stopping at floors with going-down requests, until all going-down requests have been serviced.

3. Repeat.

This explains why an elevator will pass your floor without stopping if you are waiting to go up and the elevator is going down. Not surprisingly, this is known as the **elevator algorithm**. The elevator algorithm has found application in other areas, such as disk I/O scheduling.

In a building with a bank of multiple elevators, as depicted in Figure 15-1, this strategy is unsatisfactory. The elevators can service passengers much more efficiently if their movements are coordinated. A control system is needed to monitor the position and direction of the cars and dispatch up and down requests to the optimal elevator car.

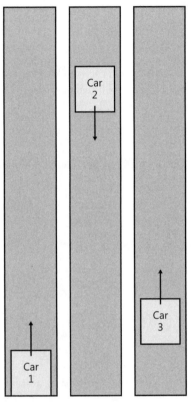

Figure 15-1 Bank of elevators

Elevators have to respond to two kinds of requests: destination calls and hall calls. A **destination call** occurs when someone inside an elevator car presses a floor button on the control panel. A **hall call** occurs when someone in a hallway presses the elevator up or elevator down button. Destination calls always have to be serviced by a specific elevator—the one containing the passenger who pressed the button—but hall calls can be serviced by any elevator. This is where the control system comes in. The control system decides which elevator "sees" a hall call.

A control system could micromanage all elevator actions, but in this case we want to retain the autonomous behavior of each elevator. The individual elevators can continue to use the elevator algorithm, but the control system will determine which elevator to dispatch hall calls to. This approach allows the elevators to provide some level of service even if the control system is offline. We'd like to consider each elevator, and the control system, as self-contained modules—convenient boundaries for designing a service-oriented solution.

The problem to be solved has these elements:

- There are n elevator cars and one control system.

- Elevator cars can be placed in service or taken out of service at any time.

- When in service, each elevator car needs to be able to communicate with the control system. The control system needs to be aware of the position and direction of travel of each elevator car.

- When in service, elevators respond to destination calls and hall calls autonomously, moving in an up direction/down direction cycle as long as requests are pending. Elevators remain stationary when there are no requests.

- Each elevator maintains its own list of requests. Elevators become aware of destination requests when a passenger presses a floor button on the elevator's control panel. Elevators become aware of hall calls via the control system.

- When a hall call is made, the control system needs to efficiently determine which of the in-service elevators should be assigned the call.

The Solution

With the problem definition in place, we can design a service-oriented solution. We need to identify service boundaries, determine the roles of services and clients, choose a messaging pattern, and design contracts, bindings, and service settings.

Service Boundaries

In this case study, we'll stipulate that each elevator, and the control system, can be treated as a self-contained, autonomous unit. This makes it a simple matter to determine the service boundaries. Because there is one control system and multiple elevators, making the control system a service and the elevators stateful clients of the service makes sense. Figure 15-2 illustrates the service boundaries.

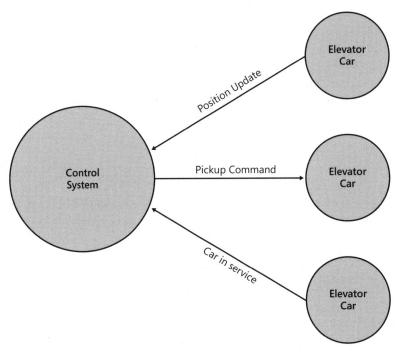

Figure 15-2   Service boundaries

A two-way messaging pattern is needed: elevator cars need to report their position and direction of travel to the control system, and the control system needs to inform elevator cars about hall calls. There's nothing synchronous about this communication, so duplex communication is the best fit. This allows the elevator cars and the control system to send communication to each other freely as events transpire.

Service Contracts

The duplex messaging pattern requires a pair of service contracts: the interface to the control system and the client callback interface to the elevator cars.

The control system provides the following operations:

- *CarInService*: An elevator car signaling that it is now in service
- *CarNotInService*: An elevator car signaling that it is now out of service
- *CarUpdate*: An elevator car updating its location and direction of travel

The elevator car will provide a single operation:

- *Pickup*: The control system signaling an elevator car to pick up on additional floors

The following service contract defines these operations. It specifies that sessions, which are necessary for duplex communication, are required.

```
[ServiceContract(Session=true, CallbackContract=typeof(IElevatorCar))]
public interface IControl
{
    [OperationContract(IsInitiating=true, IsTerminating=false)]
    int CarInService();
    [OperationContract(IsTerminating=true, IsInitiating=false)]
    void CarNotInService();
    [OperationContract]
    void CarUpdate(int floor, bool goingUp, bool pickingUp);
}

public interface IElevatorCar
{
    [OperationContract]
    void Pickup(bool[] upRequests, bool[] downRequests);
}
```

Let's review the fine details of the service contract. The service contract expects an elevator car client to call these operations in a specific order: first a call to *CarInService*, followed by multiple calls to *CarUpdate*, and lastly a call to *CarNotInService*.

The *CarInService* operation starts a new session for a car that is being placed in service. The operation is marked as *IsInitiating=true*, meaning a new instance and session will be started when this operation is called. The control system assigns a car number to the elevator, which is the operation's return value.

The *CarNotInService* operation ends a session for a car that is being taken out of service. The operation is marked as *IsTerminating=true*, meaning the instance and session will be terminated after this operation is called.

The *CarUpdate* operation informs the control system of a car's current location and direction of travel.

When the control system needs to respond to a passenger making a hall call, the client callback service contract comes into play. After deciding which car is in the best position to service a hall call, the control system calls the chosen elevator car's *Pickup* service operation, passing two arrays containing new going-up and going-down requests for the car.

Binding

A binding is needed that specifies appropriate transport, session, and delivery assurances. Our application has these requirements:

- Cross-machine communication
- Duplex messaging pattern
- Reliable sessions
- Exactly-once, in-order delivery assurances

NetProfileDualTcpBinding fulfills the above requirements. TCP communication is a good choice here because the elevators and control system are likely on different computers but don't need to communicate over the Internet. Reliable sessions provide the stateful client sessions our design calls for as well as delivery assurances. We want messages to arrive exactly once and in order so that requests are handled fairly.

Service Behaviors

The service class will implement the *IControl* service contract. Service behaviors must specify appropriate instancing and concurrency modes for the solution. Here are the service settings we will use.

```
[ServiceBehavior(InstanceMode=InstanceMode.PrivateSession,
    RunOnUIThread=true, ConcurrencyMode=ConcurrencyMode.Multiple)]
public class Control : IControl
{
    ...
}
```

The *[ServiceBehavior]* attribute specifies the use of private session instancing, a requirement for duplex communication. It also indicates that the service is running on a UI thread because a WinForms application is creating the service.

Program Design

The solution will contain two programs: an elevator program, Elevator.exe, and a control system program, Control.exe. There will be one instance of Control.exe but multiple instances of Elevator.exe—one for each elevator.

You likely don't have access to actual elevator equipment for this exercise, so we'll settle for a simulation. The state of the elevator system will be apparent from the programs' displays.

We'll choose an eight-story building with a bank of up to three elevators as the setting for the solution. The number of floors and maximum number of elevators will be set by constants.

Elevator

The elevator program, Elevator.exe, will represent a single elevator car. It can handle destination calls on its own, responding when a passenger presses a floor button.

The elevator program consists of these elements:

- *FormElevator*: The display form and startup class of the program. *FormElevator* creates an instance of the *ElevatorCar* class.

- *ElevatorCar*: The class that implements the elevator car. This class tracks a list of requests and spawns a worker thread that moves the elevator based on requests.

The *ElevatorCar* class is a client of the *Control* service. When the elevator car is put in service, taken out of service, changes location, or becomes idle, the control service is notified. The elevator and the control service are in communication about once a second.

The user interface of the elevator program is shown in Figure 15-3. The user can press Start and Stop buttons to put the elevator in or out of service. Floor buttons can be pressed to make destination calls.

Figure 15-3   Elevator program user interface

One instance of Elevator.exe is launched for each elevator car.

Control System

The control system program, Control.exe, is the intelligent dispatcher for the elevator system.

The program consists of these elements:

- *FormControl*: The display form and startup class of the program. *FormControl* creates an instance of the *Control* class.

- *Control*: The class that implements the control system. This class tracks a list of requests and runs a worker thread that moves the elevator based on requests.

FormControl also simulates the building's up/down hallway buttons and shows the location and direction of each elevator that is in service. When the user presses a floor's up or down button, *FormControl* calls a method of the *Control* class to register a hall call. The hall call in turn is assigned to one of the in-service elevators.

The *Control* class is also the implementation class for the *IControl* service contract. Elevator cars act as clients of the service, announcing when they go into or out of service, and regularly checking in to update their status and obtain new hall calls.

The user interface of the control program is shown in Figure 15-4. At the top of the form are Start and Stop buttons to start or stop the service. The URI of the service is displayed. The remainder of the form shows the overall status of the elevator system. This includes the location and direction of each elevator car and a graphical depiction of the elevator car. The form also provides the up and down hallway buttons for each floor.

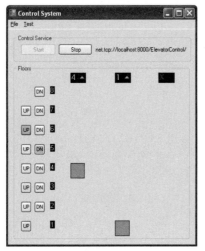

Figure 15-4   Control program user interface

Only one instance of Control.exe is launched. It can accommodate multiple elevator clients.

Implementing the Solution

Now we can proceed to implementation. The structure of the solution is shown in Table 15-1.

Table 15-1   Elevator Solution Structure

Project	File	Class	Assembly
Elevator	ElevatorCar.cs	*ElevatorCar*	Elevator.exe
Elevator	FormElevator.cs	*FormElevator*	Elevator.exe
Control	Control.cs	*Control*	Control.exe
Control	FormControl.cs	*FormControl*	Control.exe

ElevatorCar.cs

ElevatorCar.cs, which contains the *ElevatorCar* class, is shown in Listing 15-1. The caller of the class (*FormElevator*) calls the *Run* method to start up the elevator and the *Stop* method to shut it down. *Run* spawns a worker thread, establishes a proxy channel to the control service, and informs the service that this elevator car is now in service. *Stop* does the opposite: it informs the control service that this car is now out of service, closes the channel, and aborts the worker thread.

The class tracks the elevator's car number, in-service status, current location, direction of travel, idle/moving state, and requests. A number of these are public to allow the caller of the class, *FormElevator*, to show elevator status on its form. When the *ElevatorCar* class takes an action that should cause a display refresh, the Boolean variable *UpdateDisplay* is set to *true*. When *FormElevator* updates its display, *UpdateDisplay* is set to *false*.

Requests are stored in two arrays, one for up requests and one for down requests. When the elevator is moving to a new floor, it checks the request array matching its current direction of travel to decide if it should stop and open its doors and pause.

Listing 15-1   ElevatorCar.cs

```csharp
using System;
using System.ServiceModel;
using System.Threading;
using ProgrammingIndigo.Elevator;

namespace ProgrammingIndigo.Elevator
{
    //**************  service contract
    //*              *
    //*   IControl   *
    //*              *
    //**************

    [ServiceContract(Session = true, CallbackContract = typeof(IElevatorCar))]
    public interface IControl
    {
        [OperationContract(IsInitiating = true, IsTerminating = false)]
        int CarInService();
        [OperationContract(IsTerminating = true, IsInitiating = false)]
        void CarNotInService();
        [OperationContract]
        void CarUpdate(int floor, bool goingUp, bool pickingUp);
    }

    public interface IElevatorCar
    {
        [OperationContract]
        void Pickup(bool[] upRequests, bool[] downRequests);
    }

    //******************
    //*                *
    //*   ElevatorCar  *
    //*                *
    //******************
```

```
    // Service implementation class.

public class ElevatorCar : IElevatorCar
{
   public bool UpdateDisplay = false;       // Set to true to update the display form.
     public static ManualResetEvent workerThreadRunning = new
        ManualResetEvent(false);

     IControl controlSystem = null;         // Proxy to control system service.

     const int TimeToMoveOneFloor = 500;    // Amount of time to move one floor.
     const int TimeToStopAtFloor = 2000;    // Amount of time to wait at one floor.

     public const int NumberOfFloors = 8;   // Number of floors in the building.

   int ElevatorID = 1;                      // This car's elevator ID.
   bool InService = false;                  // True = car in service.
   bool Idle = true;                        // True = not currently servicing any requests.
   public bool GoingUp = true;              // True = going up.
   public bool PickingUp = false;           // True = picking up.
   public int CurrentFloor = 1;             // Current floor.
   Thread elevatorThread = null;            // Thread for elevator service routine.
   int RequestCount = 0;                    // Number of requests.
   int UpRequestCount = 0;                  // Number of going up requests.
   int DownRequestCount = 0;                // Number of going down requests.
   public bool[] UpRequests = new bool[NumberOfFloors+1];
      // Array of going up requests.
   public bool[] DownRequests = new bool[NumberOfFloors + 1];
      // Array of going down requests.

   // Constructor.

   public ElevatorCar()
   {
      UpdateDisplay = true;                 // Flag for a display update.
   }

     //*********
     //*       *
     //*  Run  *
     //*       *
     //*********
        // This method runs when the user starts the elevator car from the UI.
        // It creates a proxy to the control system service and
        // starts the elevator routine running on a worker thread.

   public int Run()
   {
      EndpointAddress address =
         new EndpointAddress("net.tcp://localhost:8000/ElevatorControl/");
      NetProfileDualTcpBinding binding = new NetProfileDualTcpBinding();
      binding.TcpPortSharingEnabled = true;
      binding.SecurityMode = NetProfileDualTcpSecurityMode.None;
      ServiceSite site = new ServiceSite(this);
      controlSystem = ChannelFactory.CreateDuplexChannel<IControl>(site,
```

```
        address, binding);
    ElevatorID = controlSystem.CarInService();
    InService = true;
    elevatorThread = new Thread(new ThreadStart(ElevatorRoutine));
    elevatorThread.Start();
    return ElevatorID;
}
```

```
//**********
//*        *
//*  Stop  *
//*        *
//**********
// This method runs when the user stops the elevator car from the UI.
// It signals the elevator routine to stop and
// waits for the worker thread to shut down.

public void Stop()
{
    InService = false;
    workerThreadRunning.WaitOne();
}
```

```
//************   service operation
//*          *
//*  Pickup  *
//*          *
//************
// This is the one service operation the elevator car implements.
// The control system calls Pickup to tell this elevator car about one or more
// hall calls.

public void Pickup(bool[] upRequests, bool[] downRequests)
{
    for (int i = 1; i <= 8; i++)
    {
        // Store the up and down requests.
        if (upRequests[i] && !UpRequests[i])
        {
            UpRequests[i] = true;
            UpRequestCount++;
            RequestCount++;
        }
        if (downRequests[i] && !DownRequests[i])
        {
            DownRequests[i] = true;
            DownRequestCount++;
            RequestCount++;
        }
    }
}
```

```
//***************
//*             *
//*  IsGoingTo  *
```

```
    //*              *
    //***************
    // Return true if there are any up or down requests for the specified floor.

public bool IsGoingTo(int floor)
{
    return (UpRequests[floor] || DownRequests[floor]);
}

    //***************
    //*             *
    //*  GoToFloor  *
    //*             *
    //***************
    // Create a request to move to a floor.

public void GoToFloor(int floor)
{
    if (floor == CurrentFloor)
       return;

       // Determine the direction of the request.

    bool upRequest = true;

    if (floor==1)
       upRequest = true;
    else if (floor==NumberOfFloors)
       upRequest = false;
    else if (floor < CurrentFloor)
       upRequest = false;

       //Store an up request or down request.

    if (!upRequest)
    {
       if (DownRequests[floor]) return;
       DownRequests[floor] = true;
       DownRequestCount++;
       RequestCount++;
       UpdateDisplay = true;
    }
    else
    {
       if (UpRequests[floor]) return;
       UpRequests[floor] = true;
       UpRequestCount++;
       RequestCount++;
       UpdateDisplay = true;
    }
}

    //********************
    //*                  *
    //*  ReportPosition  *
```

```
//*                     *
//*********************
//Report position, direction, and state to the elevator control system.

void ReportPosition()
{
     if (controlSystem == null) return;
     controlSystem.CarUpdate(CurrentFloor, GoingUp, PickingUp);
}


//*********************
//*                   *
//*   ElevatorRoutine *
//*                   *
//*********************
// Elevator routine.
// Runs on a worker thread and moves the elevator to service requests.

void ElevatorRoutine()
{
   try
   {
        workerThreadRunning.Set();
        while (InService)
        {
            ReportPosition();
            if (Idle)
            {
                if (RequestCount > 0)
                {
                    Idle = false;
                    SetDirection();
                }
                else
                {
                    System.Threading.Thread.Sleep(100);
                }
            }
            else
            {
                if (MoreAhead() == 0)
                {
                    ChangeDirection();
                    StopIfNeeded();
                    Idle = true;
                }
                else
                {
                    if (GoingUp && MoreAhead() > 0)
                        MoveUp();
                    else if (!GoingUp && MoreAhead() > 0)
                        MoveDown();
                    StopIfNeeded();
                }
            }
```

```
        }
        controlSystem.CarNotInService();
    }
    finally
    {
        workerThreadRunning.Reset();
    }
}
```

```
//************
//*          *
//*  MoveUp  *
//*          *
//************
// Move up a floor.

void MoveUp()
{
    System.Threading.Thread.Sleep(TimeToMoveOneFloor);
    CurrentFloor++;
    UpdateDisplay = true;
    if (CurrentFloor == NumberOfFloors)
        GoingUp = false;
}
```

```
//**************
//*            *
//*  MoveDown  *
//*            *
//**************
// Move down a floor.

void MoveDown()
{
    System.Threading.Thread.Sleep(TimeToMoveOneFloor);
    CurrentFloor--;
    UpdateDisplay = true;
    if (CurrentFloor == 1)
        GoingUp = true;
}
```

```
//*********************
//*                   *
//*  ChangeDirection  *
//*                   *
//*********************
// Change direction of the elevator car.

void ChangeDirection()
{
    GoingUp = !GoingUp;
    ChangeDirectionIfNeeded();
}
```

```
//***********************
//*                     *
//*   ChangeDirection   *
//*                     *
//***********************
// Change direction of the elevator car if at the top or bottom floor.

void ChangeDirectionIfNeeded()
{
   if (CurrentFloor == 1)
      GoingUp = true;
   if (CurrentFloor == NumberOfFloors)
      GoingUp = false;
}


   //*******************
   //*                 *
   //*   StopIfNeeded  *
   //*                 *
   //*******************
   // Stop the elevator at the curent floor if there is a hall call for it to
   // take on passengers.

void StopIfNeeded()
{
   if (GoingUp || CurrentFloor == 1 || CurrentFloor==NumberOfFloors)
   {
      if (UpRequests[CurrentFloor])
      {
         PickingUp = true;
             ReportPosition();
         UpRequests[CurrentFloor] = false;
         UpRequestCount--;
         RequestCount--;
         if (RequestCount == 0)
                 Idle = true;
         OpenDoors();
         WaitAtFloor();
         CloseDoors();
         PickingUp = false;
         UpdateDisplay = true;
      }
   }
      if (!GoingUp || CurrentFloor == NumberOfFloors || CurrentFloor == 1)
      {
      if (DownRequests[CurrentFloor])
      {
         PickingUp = true;
             ReportPosition();
         DownRequests[CurrentFloor] = false;
         DownRequestCount--;
         RequestCount--;
         if (RequestCount == 0)
                 Idle = true;
         OpenDoors();
```

```
            WaitAtFloor();
            CloseDoors();
            PickingUp = false;
            UpdateDisplay = true;
        }
    }
}


//*******************
//*                 *
//*  SetDirection   *
//*                 *
//*******************
// Stop the direction of the elevator car based on where the most requests are.

void SetDirection()
{
    int RequestsAbove = 0;
    int RequestsBelow = 0;
    for (int floor = CurrentFloor + 1; floor <= NumberOfFloors; floor++)
    {
        if (UpRequests[floor] || DownRequests[floor])
        {
            RequestsAbove++;
        }
    }

    for (int floor = CurrentFloor - 1; floor >= 1; floor--)
    {
        if (UpRequests[floor] || DownRequests[floor])
        {
            RequestsBelow++;
        }
    }

    if (RequestsAbove > RequestsBelow)
    {
        GoingUp = true;
        Idle = false;
        PickingUp = false;
    }
    else if (RequestsBelow > 0)
    {
        GoingUp = false;
        Idle = false;
        PickingUp = false;
    }
    else
    {
        Idle = true;
    }
}


//***************
//*             *
```

```
//*   MoreAhead   *
//*               *
//***************
// Return the number of requests ahead in the current direction the
// elevator car is moving.

int MoreAhead()
{
   if (GoingUp)
   {
      return MoreAheadGoingUp();
   }
   else
   {
      return MoreAheadGoingDown();
   }
}

int MoreAheadGoingUp()
{
   int count = 0;
   for (int floor = CurrentFloor + 1; floor <= NumberOfFloors; floor++)
   {
      if (UpRequests[floor] || DownRequests[floor])
      {
         count++;
      }
   }
   return count;
}

int MoreAheadGoingDown()
{
   int count = 0;
   for (int floor = CurrentFloor - 1; floor >= 1; floor--)
   {
      if (UpRequests[floor] || DownRequests[floor])
      {
         count++;
      }
   }
   return count;
}

   //***************
   //*             *
   //*  OpenDoors  *
   //*             *
   //***************
   // Open the elevator doors. No implementation.

void OpenDoors()
{
}
```

```
//*****************
//*               *
//*  CloseDoors   *
//*               *
//*****************
// Close the elevator doors. No implementation.

void CloseDoors()
{
}


//*****************
//*               *
//*  WaitAtFloor  *
//*               *
//*****************
// Wait at a floor to allow passenger time to enter or exit the elevator car.

void WaitAtFloor()
{
    System.Threading.Thread.Sleep(TimeToStopAtFloor);
}

    }
}
```

FormElevator.cs

FormElevator.cs, which contains the *FormElevator* class, is shown in Listing 15-2. *FormElevator* creates an instance of the *ElevatorCar* class, calls its methods to start or stop the elevator car, and shows its status on the form.

The form's *Activated* event for the class runs a continuous loop that sleeps briefly and then updates the display if needed.

Listing 15-2   FormElevator.cs

```
#region Using directives

using System;
using System.Collections.Generic;
using System.ComponentModel;
using System.Data;
using System.Drawing;
using System.Windows.Forms;

#endregion

namespace ProgrammingIndigo.Elevator
{
    partial class FormElevator : Form
    {
        ElevatorCar elevator = null;
```

```
bool initialized = false;

public FormElevator()
{
    InitializeComponent();
}

private void FormElevator_Load(object sender, EventArgs e)
{

}

private void FormElevator_Activated(object sender, EventArgs e)
{
    if (initialized) return;
    initialized = true;
    Application.DoEvents();
    while (true)
    {
        Application.DoEvents();
        if (elevator != null && elevator.UpdateDisplay)
        {
            UpdateDisplay();
            elevator.UpdateDisplay = false;
        }
        System.Threading.Thread.Sleep(100);
    }
}

private void buttonStart_Click(object sender, EventArgs e)
{
    Cursor = Cursors.WaitCursor;
    Application.DoEvents();

    elevator = new ElevatorCar();
    int carNo = elevator.Run();
    labelCarNo.Text = carNo.ToString();
    Text = "Elevator No. " + carNo.ToString();

    buttonStart.Enabled = false;
    buttonStop.Enabled = true;
    Cursor = Cursors.Default;
}

void UpdateDisplay()
{
    buttonCurrentFloor.Text = elevator.CurrentFloor.ToString();
    if (elevator.GoingUp)
    {
        labelGoingUp.ForeColor = Color.LawnGreen;
        labelGoingDown.ForeColor = Color.Black;
    }
    else
    {
        labelGoingDown.ForeColor = Color.LawnGreen;
        labelGoingUp.ForeColor = Color.Black;
```

```
        }

        for (int floor = 1; floor <= ElevatorCar.NumberOfFloors; floor++)
        {
            //Illuminate elevator control panel buttons.

            Color buttonForeColor = Color.White;
            Color buttonBorderColor = Color.White;
            if (elevator.IsGoingTo(floor))
            {
                buttonForeColor = Color.Gold;
                buttonBorderColor = Color.Gold;
            }
            switch (floor)
            {
                case 1:
                    button1.ForeColor = buttonForeColor;
                    button1.BorderColor = buttonBorderColor;
                    break;
                case 2:
                    button2.ForeColor = buttonForeColor;
                    button2.BorderColor = buttonBorderColor;
                    break;
                case 3:
                    button3.ForeColor = buttonForeColor;
                    button3.BorderColor = buttonBorderColor;
                    break;
                case 4:
                    button4.ForeColor = buttonForeColor;
                    button4.BorderColor = buttonBorderColor;
                    break;
                case 5:
                    button5.ForeColor = buttonForeColor;
                    button5.BorderColor = buttonBorderColor;
                    break;
                case 6:
                    button6.ForeColor = buttonForeColor;
                    button6.BorderColor = buttonBorderColor;
                    break;
                case 7:
                    button7.ForeColor = buttonForeColor;
                    button7.BorderColor = buttonBorderColor;
                    break;
                case 8:
                    button8.ForeColor = buttonForeColor;
                    button8.BorderColor = buttonBorderColor;
                    break;
            }
        }

    }

    private void menuItemExit_Click(object sender, EventArgs e)
    {
        Environment.Exit(0);
```

```csharp
        }

        private void button1_Click(object sender, EventArgs e)
        {
            elevator.GoToFloor(1);
        }

        private void button2_Click(object sender, EventArgs e)
        {
            elevator.GoToFloor(2);
        }

        private void button3_Click(object sender, EventArgs e)
        {
            elevator.GoToFloor(3);
        }

        private void button4_Click(object sender, EventArgs e)
        {
            elevator.GoToFloor(4);
        }

        private void button5_Click(object sender, EventArgs e)
        {
            elevator.GoToFloor(5);
        }

        private void button6_Click(object sender, EventArgs e)
        {
            elevator.GoToFloor(6);
        }

        private void button7_Click(object sender, EventArgs e)
        {
            elevator.GoToFloor(7);
        }

        private void button8_Click(object sender, EventArgs e)
        {
            elevator.GoToFloor(8);
        }

        private void buttonStop_Click(object sender, EventArgs e)
        {
            Cursor = Cursors.WaitCursor;
            buttonStop.Enabled = false;
            Application.DoEvents();

            elevator.Stop();

            buttonStart.Enabled = true;
            Cursor = Cursors.Default;
        }
    }
}
```

Not listed here is the form designer source file for this form, FormElevator.Designer.cs. That file is included in the download files for this chapter.

Control.cs

Control.cs is shown in Listing 15-3. It defines the *IControl* service contract, a *NetProfileDualTcp* binding, and the *Control* class, which implements the service. The *Control* class implements the three service operations—*CarInService*, *CarUpdate*, and *CarNotInService*.

The caller of the class (*FormControl*) creates a service specifying *Control* as the implementation class. When an elevator client calls the service's *CarInService* service operation, a new instance of the class is created.

The *Control* class tracks the overall status of the elevator system in static variables, including location and direction of elevator cars that are in service and arrays of new up and down hall calls. Some of these variables are public so the hosting class, *FormControl*, can show the elevator system's status on its form.

In addition to service operations, the *Control* class provides a *HallCall* method. When a hallway up or down button is pressed on *FormControl*, *HallCall* is invoked to register the request.

Listing 15-3   Control.cs

```
#region Using directives

using System;
using System.Collections.Generic;
using System.ServiceModel;
using System.Threading;

#endregion

namespace ProgrammingIndigo.Elevator
{
    //**************   service contract
    //*               *
    //*   IControl    *
    //*               *
    //**************

    [ServiceContract(Session=true, CallbackContract=typeof(IElevatorCar))]
    public interface IControl
    {
        [OperationContract(IsInitiating=true, IsTerminating=false)]
        int CarInService();
        [OperationContract(IsTerminating=true, IsInitiating=false)]
        void CarNotInService();
        [OperationContract]
            void CarUpdate(int floor, bool goingUp, bool pickingUp);
    }
```

```
    public interface IElevatorCar
    {
        [OperationContract]
        void Pickup(bool[] upRequests, bool[] downRequests);
    }



//*************    service implementation class
//*             *
//*   Control   *
//*             *
//*************

[ServiceBehavior(InstanceMode=InstanceMode.PrivateSession,
    RunOnUIThread=true, ConcurrencyMode=ConcurrencyMode.Multiple)]
public class Control : IControl
{
    public const int MaxCars = 3;
    public const int NumberOfFloors = 8;

  int carNo;
                        // Elevator car number for this instance.

    public static bool UpdateDisplay = false;
        // Set to true to flag a display refresh.
    static int NoCars = 0;
                        // Number of elevator cars.

    // Elevator car tracking information.

    public static int[] CarLocation = new int[MaxCars+1];
    public static bool[] CarGoingUp = new bool[MaxCars+1];
    public static bool[] CarPickingUp = new bool[MaxCars + 1];

    // Hall call requests.

    public static bool[,] HallCallUp = new bool[MaxCars + 1, NumberOfFloors + 1];
    public static bool[,] HallCallDown = new bool[MaxCars + 1, NumberOfFloors + 1];

    static IElevatorCar[] Callback = new IElevatorCar[MaxCars+1];
    // Duplex callback to elevator car.


    //*****************    service operation
    //*               *
    //*  CarInService *
    //*               *
    //*****************
    // A new elevator car is in service. Store the callback to the client and
    // assign an elevator car ID.

    public int CarInService()
    {
        int car = 0;
```

```
       for (int c = 1; c <= NoCars; c++)
       {
           if (CarLocation[c] == 0)
           {
               car = c;
               break;
           }
       }
       if (car == 0)
       {
           car = ++NoCars;
       }
       this.carNo = car;
       Callback[carNo] =
           OperationContext.Current.GetCallbackChannel<IElevatorCar>();
    Console.WriteLine("Car " + car + " in service");
    CarLocation[car] = 1;
    return car;
}


//********************  service operation
//*                 *
//*  CarNotInService *
//*                 *
//********************
// An elevator car is going out of service.

public void CarNotInService()
{
   Console.WriteLine("Car " + carNo + " out of service!");
   CarLocation[carNo] = 0;
}


//**************  service operation
//*           *
//*  CarUpdate *
//*           *
//**************
// An elevator car is updating its location and direction.
// Send back any new hall calls that have been assigned to this car.

  public void CarUpdate(int floor, bool goingUp, bool pickingUp)
{
   Console.WriteLine("Car " + carNo + " at floor " +
      floor + ", going up=" + goingUp);
   CarLocation[carNo] = floor;
   CarGoingUp[carNo] = goingUp;
   CarPickingUp[carNo] = pickingUp;

   // If elevator is picking up at this floor,
   // clear all requests for this floor and direction.
```

```
        for (int f = 1; f <= NumberOfFloors; f++)
        {
            if (pickingUp && goingUp && floor == f)
            {
                for (int car = 1; car <= MaxCars; car++)
                {
                    HallCallUp[car, f] = false;
                }
            }
            else if (pickingUp && !goingUp && floor == f)
            {
                for (int car = 1; car <= MaxCars; car++)
                {
                    HallCallDown[car, f] = false;
                }
            }
        }
        UpdateDisplay = true;
}


//**************
//*            *
//*  HallCall  *
//*            *
//**************
// Register a hall call.

public static void HallCall(int floor, bool goingUp)
{
    int car = SelectCar(floor, goingUp);
    if (car != 0)
    {
        if (goingUp)
        {
            HallCallUp[car, floor] = true;
        }
        else
        {
            HallCallDown[car, floor] = true;
        }
    }

        bool[] upRequests = new bool[NumberOfFloors + 1];
        bool[] downRequests = new bool[NumberOfFloors + 1];

        // If elevator is picking up at this floor,
        // clear all requests for this
        // floor and direction.

        for (int f = 1; f <= NumberOfFloors; f++)
        {
            upRequests[f] = HallCallUp[car, f];
```

```
                        HallCallUp[car, f] = false;
                        downRequests[f] = HallCallDown[car, f];
                        HallCallDown[car, f] = false;
                    }
                Callback[car].Pickup(upRequests, downRequests);
        }

    //***************
    //*             *
    //*  SelectCar  *
    //*             *
    //***************
    // Select the best available car to handle a hall call.

    static int SelectCar(int floor, bool goingUp)
    {
     int bestDistance = 8;
     int bestCar = 0;
     int distance = 0;

        // Try to find a car going in the same direction.
        // If there is more than one car to choose from, select the one
        // with the shortest distance to go.

        for (int car = 1; car <= MaxCars; car++)
        {
            int location = CarLocation[car];
            if (location != 0 && CarGoingUp[car]==goingUp)
            {
                if (location < floor)
                {
                    distance = floor - location;
                }
                else
                {
                    distance = location - floor;
                }
                if (distance < bestDistance)
                {
                    bestDistance = distance;
                    bestCar = car;
                }
            }
        }

        // If we failed to find a car moving in the same direction,
        // assign to any car. If there is more than one car to
        // choose from, select the one
        // with the shortest distance to go.

        if (bestCar == 0)
        {
            for (int car = 1; car <= MaxCars; car++)
```

```
        {
            int location = CarLocation[car];
            if (location != 0)
            {
                if (location < floor)
                {
                    distance = floor - location;
                }
                else
                {
                    distance = location - floor;
                }
                if (distance < bestDistance)
                {
                    bestDistance = distance;
                    bestCar = car;
                }
            }
        }
    }

    Console.WriteLine("Assigning hall call " + floor +
        "," + goingUp + " to car " + bestCar);
    return bestCar;
}

}


}
```

FormControl.cs

FormControl.cs, which contains the *FormControl* class, is shown in Listing 15-4. *FormControl* creates an instance of the *Control* class and shows its status on the form.

The form's *Activated* event for the class runs a continuous loop that sleeps briefly and then updates the display.

Listing 15-4 FormControl.cs

```
#region Using directives

using System;
using System.Collections.Generic;
using System.ComponentModel;
using System.Data;
using System.Drawing;
using System.ServiceModel;
using System.Windows.Forms;

#endregion
```

```csharp
namespace ProgrammingIndigo.Elevator
{
    partial class FormControl : Form
    {
        ServiceHost<Control> controlService = null;
        bool initialized = false;
        System.Random random = new System.Random();
        bool TestRandom = false;

        public FormControl()
        {
            InitializeComponent();
        }

        private void menuItemFileExit_Click(object sender, EventArgs e)
        {
            Environment.Exit(0);
        }

        private void buttonStart_Click(object sender, EventArgs e)
        {
            Cursor = Cursors.WaitCursor;
            Application.DoEvents();
            buttonStart.Enabled = false;
            buttonStop.Enabled = true;
            Uri uri = new Uri("net.tcp://localhost:8000/ElevatorControl/");
            NetProfileDualTcpBinding binding = new NetProfileDualTcpBinding();
            binding.SecurityMode = NetProfileDualTcpSecurityMode.None;
            controlService = new ServiceHost<Control>();
            controlService.AddEndpoint(typeof(IControl), binding, uri);
            controlService.Open();
            labelUri.Text = uri.ToString();
            Cursor = Cursors.Default;
        }

        private void buttonStop_Click(object sender, EventArgs e)
        {
            Cursor = Cursors.WaitCursor;
            Application.DoEvents();
            controlService.Close();
            controlService = null;
            buttonStart.Enabled = true;
            buttonStop.Enabled = false;
            Cursor = Cursors.Default;
        }

        private void label5_Click(object sender, EventArgs e)
        {

        }

        private void label4_Click(object sender, EventArgs e)
        {
```

```
}

private void label3_Click(object sender, EventArgs e)
{

}

private void label2_Click(object sender, EventArgs e)
{

}

private void label1_Click(object sender, EventArgs e)
{

}

private void label6_Click(object sender, EventArgs e)
{

}

private void label7_Click(object sender, EventArgs e)
{

}

private void label8_Click(object sender, EventArgs e)
{

}

private void buttonUp1_Click(object sender, EventArgs e)
{
   buttonUp1.BackColor = Color.Gold;
   Control.HallCall(1, true);
}

private void buttonUp2_Click(object sender, EventArgs e)
{
   buttonUp2.BackColor = Color.Gold;
   Control.HallCall(2, true);
}

private void buttonDown2_Click(object sender, EventArgs e)
{
   buttonDown2.BackColor = Color.Gold;
   Control.HallCall(2, false);
}

private void buttonUp3_Click(object sender, EventArgs e)
{
   buttonUp3.BackColor = Color.Gold;
   Control.HallCall(3, true);
```

```
    }

    private void buttonDown3_Click(object sender, EventArgs e)
    {
        buttonDown3.BackColor = Color.Gold;
        Control.HallCall(3, false);
    }

    private void buttonUp4_Click(object sender, EventArgs e)
    {
        buttonUp4.BackColor = Color.Gold;
        Control.HallCall(4, true);
    }

    private void buttonDown4_Click(object sender, EventArgs e)
    {
        buttonDown4.BackColor = Color.Gold;
        Control.HallCall(4, false);
    }

    private void buttonUp5_Click(object sender, EventArgs e)
    {
        buttonUp5.BackColor = Color.Gold;
        Control.HallCall(5, true);
    }

    private void buttonDown5_Click(object sender, EventArgs e)
    {
        buttonDown5.BackColor = Color.Gold;
        Control.HallCall(5, false);
    }

    private void buttonUp6_Click(object sender, EventArgs e)
    {
        buttonUp6.BackColor = Color.Gold;
        Control.HallCall(6, true);
    }

    private void buttonDown6_Click(object sender, EventArgs e)
    {
        buttonDown6.BackColor = Color.Gold;
        Control.HallCall(6, false);
    }

    private void buttonUp7_Click(object sender, EventArgs e)
    {
        buttonUp7.BackColor = Color.Gold;
        Control.HallCall(7, true);
    }

    private void buttonDown7_Click(object sender, EventArgs e)
    {
        buttonDown7.BackColor = Color.Gold;
        Control.HallCall(7, false);
```

```csharp
}

private void buttonDown8_Click(object sender, EventArgs e)
{
    buttonDown8.BackColor = Color.Gold;
    Control.HallCall(8, false);
}

private void FormControl_Activated(object sender, EventArgs e)
{
    if (initialized) return;
    initialized = true;
    while (true)
    {
        Application.DoEvents();
        if (controlService != null)
        {
            Control.UpdateDisplay = false;
            UpdateDisplay();
                if (TestRandom)
                    RandomHallCall();
                System.Threading.Thread.Sleep(500);
        }
    }
}

void UpdateDisplay()
{
    //Update location and direction of each elevator's indicators.
    for (int car = 1; car <= Control.MaxCars; car++)
    {
        Color color;
        string direction = "";
        string location =  "";
        int position = 324;
        bool visible;
        Color carColor = Color.DarkGray;
            //string carState = "closed";
            if (Control.CarLocation[car] == 0)
        {
            location = "x";
            direction = "";
            color = Color.Red;
            visible = false;
        }
        else
        {
            position = 364 - (Control.CarLocation[car] * 40);
            location = Control.CarLocation[car].ToString();
            color = Color.LawnGreen;
            visible = true;
            if (Control.CarPickingUp[car])
            {
                carColor = Color.White;
```

```
                    //carState = "open";
            }
        if (Control.CarGoingUp[car])
        {
            direction = "5";       // up arrow in Webdings font
        }
        else
        {
            direction = "6";       // down arrow in Webdings font
                    }
            }
            switch (car)
            {
                case 1:
                        labelCar1Floor.Text = location;
                        labelCar1Direction.Text = direction;
                        labelCar1Floor.ForeColor = color;
                        labelCar1.Visible = visible;
                        labelCar1.BackColor = carColor;
            //labelCar1.Text = carState;
            if (position!=0)
                            MoveCar(ref labelCar1, position);
                        //labelCar1.Top = position;
                        break;
                case 2:
                        labelCar2Floor.Text = location;
                        labelCar2Direction.Text = direction;
                        labelCar2Floor.ForeColor = color;
                        labelCar2.Visible = visible;
                        labelCar2.BackColor = carColor;
            //labelCar2.Text = carState;
            if (position != 0)
                            MoveCar(ref labelCar2, position);
                        //labelCar2.Top = position;
                        break;
                case 3:
                        labelCar3Floor.Text = location;
                        labelCar3Direction.Text = direction;
                        labelCar3Floor.ForeColor = color;
                        labelCar3.Visible = visible;
                        labelCar3.BackColor = carColor;
            //labelCar3.Text = carState;
            if (position != 0)
                            MoveCar(ref labelCar3, position);
            //labelCar3.Top = position;
                        break;
            }
        }

        //Clear up and down buttons that have been serviced.

        for (int floor = 1; floor <= Control.NumberOfFloors; floor++)
        {
            int upCount = 0;
```

```
int downCount = 0;
for (int car = 1; car <= Control.MaxCars; car++)
{
    if (Control.CarLocation[car] ==
        floor && Control.CarGoingUp[car])
            upCount++;
    if (Control.CarLocation[car] ==
        floor && !Control.CarGoingUp[car])
            downCount++;
}
if (upCount>0)
{
    switch (floor)
    {
        case 1:
            buttonUp1.BackColor = SystemColors.Control;
            break;
        case 2:
            buttonUp2.BackColor = SystemColors.Control;
            break;
        case 3:
            buttonUp3.BackColor = SystemColors.Control;
            break;
        case 4:
            buttonUp4.BackColor = SystemColors.Control;
            break;
        case 5:
            buttonUp5.BackColor = SystemColors.Control;
            break;
        case 6:
            buttonUp6.BackColor = SystemColors.Control;
            break;
        case 7:
            buttonUp7.BackColor = SystemColors.Control;
            break;
    }
}
if (downCount > 0)
{
    switch (floor)
    {
        case 2:
            buttonDown2.BackColor = SystemColors.Control;
            break;
        case 3:
            buttonDown3.BackColor = SystemColors.Control;
            break;
        case 4:
            buttonDown4.BackColor = SystemColors.Control;
            break;
        case 5:
            buttonDown5.BackColor = SystemColors.Control;
            break;
        case 6:
            buttonDown6.BackColor = SystemColors.Control;
```

```
                                        break;
                                    case 7:
                                        buttonDown7.BackColor = SystemColors.Control;
                                        break;
                                    case 8:
                                        buttonDown8.BackColor = SystemColors.Control;
                                        break;
                                }
                            }
                        }
                    }

            void MoveCar(ref Label labelCar, int position)
            {
                int startY = 0, finalY = 0;
                if (labelCar.Location.Y == position) return;
                startY = labelCar.Top;
                finalY = position;
                if (startY < finalY)
                {
                    for (int y = startY; y <= finalY; y += 10)
                    {
                        labelCar.Top = y;
                        Application.DoEvents();
                    }
                }
                else
                {
                    for (int y = startY; y >= finalY; y -= 10)
                    {
                        labelCar.Top = y;
                        Application.DoEvents();
                    }
                }
            }

            private void FormControl_Load(object sender, EventArgs e)
            {

            }

            private void groupBox2_Enter(object sender, EventArgs e)
            {

        }

        private void menuItemTestRandom_Click(object sender, EventArgs e)
        {
            TestRandom = !TestRandom;

        }
```

```
void RandomHallCall()
{
    int floor, direction;
    bool goingUp;
    floor = random.Next(Control.NumberOfFloors) + 1;
    direction = random.Next(2);
    goingUp = (direction == 0) ? true : false;
    if ((goingUp && floor == Control.NumberOfFloors ||
        goingUp && floor == 1))
        goingUp = !goingUp;
    switch (direction)
    {
        case 0:
            switch (floor)
            {
                case 1:
                    buttonUp1.BackColor = Color.Gold;
                    break;
                case 2:
                    buttonUp2.BackColor = Color.Gold;
                    break;
                case 3:
                    buttonUp3.BackColor = Color.Gold;
                    break;
                case 4:
                    buttonUp4.BackColor = Color.Gold;
                    break;
                case 5:
                    buttonUp5.BackColor = Color.Gold;
                    break;
                case 6:
                    buttonUp6.BackColor = Color.Gold;
                    break;
                case 7:
                    buttonUp7.BackColor = Color.Gold;
                    break;
            }
            break;
        case 1:
            switch (floor)
            {
                case 2:
                    buttonDown2.BackColor = Color.Gold;
                    break;
                case 3:
                    buttonDown3.BackColor = Color.Gold;
                    break;
                case 4:
                    buttonDown4.BackColor = Color.Gold;
                    break;
                case 5:
                    buttonDown5.BackColor = Color.Gold;
```

```
                        break;
                    case 6:
                        buttonDown6.BackColor = Color.Gold;
                        break;
                    case 7:
                        buttonDown7.BackColor = Color.Gold;
                        break;
                    case 8:
                        buttonDown8.BackColor = Color.Gold;
                        break;
                }
                break;
        }
        Control.HallCall(floor, goingUp);
    }


    }
}
```

Not listed here is the form designer source file for this form, FormElevator.Designer.cs. That file is included in the download files for this chapter.

Launching the Executables

Once the solution is built, the executables can be launched. This is the startup procedure:

1. Launch Control.exe. Once it initializes, click Start to start the service.

2. Launch one to three instances of Elevator.exe. Once they initialize, click Start on each to put the cars into service. As the cars go into service, the control system shows the cars becoming available.

The solution is now ready for use. At this point, you can freely press floor buttons on the elevator cars' control panels to make destination calls, or you can press up/down buttons on the control system display to make hall calls. Hall calls are dispatched to an appropriate elevator based on proximity and direction of movement.

To shut down the solution, press Stop on each elevator car. Then stop the control system. Each of the programs can then be closed.

Flow of Communication

Let's follow an elevator session to understand the message flow. Figure 15-5 shows a sequence diagram of an elevator session.

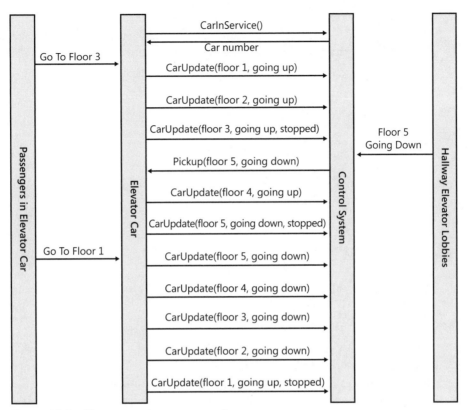

Figure 15-5   Elevator session sequence diagram

Here's what takes place during each step of the session:

1. Elevator.exe is launched, and the Start button is pressed. This creates an instance of the *ElevatorCar* class and calls its *Run* method, which creates a proxy channel to the control service and spawns a worker thread. The worker thread invokes the *CarInService* operation, which sends a message to the control service.

```
public int Run()
{
EndpointAddress address =
    new EndpointAddress("net.tcp://localhost:8000/ElevatorControl/");
NetProfileDualTcpBinding binding = new NetProfileDualTcpBinding();
binding.SecurityMode = NetProfileDualTcpSecurityMode.None;
ServiceSite site = new ServiceSite(this);
controlSystem =
    ChannelFactory.CreateDuplexChannel<IControl>(site, address, binding);
ElevatorID = controlSystem.CarInService();
InService = true;
elevatorThread = new Thread(new ThreadStart(ElevatorRoutine));
elevatorThread.Start();
return ElevatorID;
}
```

2. The control service, upon receiving the message from the elevator client, instantiates a new instance of the *Control* class because *CarInService* is an instantiating service operation. As *CarInService* executes, a car number is assigned and returned to the elevator client.

```
public int CarInService()
{
    int car = 0;
    for (int c = 1; c <= NoCars; c++)
    {
        if (CarLocation[c] == 0)
        {
            car = c;
            break;
        }
    }
    if (car == 0)
    {
        car = ++NoCars;
    }
    this.carNo = car;
    Callback[carNo] = OperationContext.Current.GetCallbackChannel<IElevatorCar>();
    Console.WriteLine("Car " + car + " in service");
    CarLocation[car] = 1;
    return car;
}
```

3. The elevator's worker thread now runs a loop in which it idles, moves up, or moves down depending on the requests it has. Idling or moving up or down one floor takes one second. Stopping at a floor, opening doors, waiting, and closing doors takes three seconds. After each of these events, the *CarUpdate* service operation is called, informing the control system of the car's current floor location and direction of service.

```
void SyncWithControlSystem()
{
    if (controlSystem == null) return;
    bool[] upRequests = new bool[NumberOfFloors + 1];
    bool[] downRequests = new bool[NumberOfFloors + 1];
    controlSystem.CarUpdate(CurrentFloor, GoingUp, PickingUp);
}
```

4. In response to the request from the elevator client, the control system executes its *CarUpdate* method. *CarUpdate* updates its tracking information about the elevator car.

```
public void CarUpdate(int floor, bool goingUp,
    out bool[] upRequests, out bool[] downRequests)
{
    Console.WriteLine("Car " + carNo + " at floor " +
        floor + ", going up=" + goingUp);
    CarLocation[carNo] = floor;
    CarGoingUp[carNo] = goingUp;
    upRequests = new bool[NumberOfFloors+1];
    downRequests = new bool[NumberOfFloors+1];
```

```
              // Clear all requests for this floor if this car's
              // floor and direction match.
              for (int f = 1; f <= 8; f++)
              {
                    if (goingUp && floor == f)
                    {
                          for (int car = 1; car <= MaxCars; car++)
                          {
                                HallCallUp[car, f] = false;
                          }
                    }
                    else if (!goingUp && floor == f)
                    {
                          for (int car = 1; car <= MaxCars; car++)
                          {
                                HallCallDown[car, f] = false;
                          }
                    }
                    upRequests[f] = HallCallUp[carNo, f];
                    downRequests[f] = HallCallDown[carNo, f];
                    HallCallUp[carNo, f] = false;
                    HallCallDown[carNo, f] = false;
              }
              UpdateDisplay = true;
        }
```

5. Any time a hallway up or down button is pressed on the control system form, the *Control* class's *HallCall* method is called. This method determines which elevator car is best suited to handle the call and stores the pending request in memory. The control system communicates with the selected car by calling the *Pickup* operation of its client callback contract.

```
public static void HallCall(int floor, bool goingUp)
{
    int car = SelectCar(floor, goingUp);
    if (car != 0)
    {
        if (goingUp)
        {
            HallCallUp[car, floor] = true;
        }
        else
        {
            HallCallDown[car, floor] = true;
        }
    }

    bool[] upRequests = new bool[NumberOfFloors + 1];
    bool[] downRequests = new bool[NumberOfFloors + 1];

    // If elevator is picking up at this floor, clear all
    // requests for this floor and direction.
    for (int f = 1; f <= NumberOfFloors; f++)
    {
        upRequests[f] = HallCallUp[car, f];
```

```
                HallCallUp[car, f] = false;
                downRequests[f] = HallCallDown[car, f];
                HallCallDown[car, f] = false;
            }
            Callback[car].Pickup(upRequests, downRequests);
        }
```

6. Any time a floor number button is pressed on an elevator's control panel, the elevator adds a destination call to its list of pending requests. The request must be satisfied on the elevator where the button was pressed, so the control system is not involved.

```
public void GoToFloor(int floor)
{
    if (floor == CurrentFloor)
    {
        return;
    }
    bool upRequest = true;
    if (floor==1)
        upRequest = true;
    else if (floor==NumberOfFloors)
        upRequest = false;
    else if (floor < CurrentFloor)
    {
        upRequest = false;
    }
    if (!upRequest)
    {
        if (DownRequests[floor]) return;
        DownRequests[floor] = true;
        DownRequestCount++;
        RequestCount++;
        UpdateDisplay = true;
    }
    else
    {
        if (UpRequests[floor]) return;
        UpRequests[floor] = true;
        UpRequestCount++;
        RequestCount++;
        UpdateDisplay = true;
    }
}
```

7. Pressing the Stop button takes the elevator out of service. This invokes *CarNotInService*. No further communication occurs unless Start is pressed again, so the channel can be safely closed. The elevator's worker thread is no longer needed and can be aborted.

```
public void Stop()
{
    InService = false;
    workerThreadRunning.WaitOne();
}
```

8. The control service, upon receiving the message from the elevator client, executes *Car-NotInService* and then terminates the elevator car's instance because *CarNotInService* is a terminating service operation.

```
public void CarNotInService()
{
        Console.WriteLine("Car " + carNo + " out of service!");
        CarLocation[carNo] = 0;
}
```

Summary

The elevator control system case study applies Indigo to the problem of simplified elevator scheduling where a control system and elevator cars must communicate. Elevator cars can handle destination calls autonomously, but hall calls must be dispatched by the control system to the elevator that is in the best position to respond to the call rapidly.

In this solution design, the elevator cars and the control system are natural service boundaries. The control system is a service that hosts client elevators. Two-way communication is needed. The duplex messaging pattern allows the control system and the elevator to freely communicate as events transpire.

The elevator is implemented in an *ElevatorCar* class and hosted by a Windows Forms *Form_Elevator* class that builds into Elevator.exe. The control system is implemented in a *Control* class and hosted by a Windows Forms *FormControl* class that builds into Control.exe.

Executing the solution allows us to interactively observe the system in operation during a specific session.

Index

Symbols

* (asterisk), 173, 174, 186, 341
. (period), 138
/ (forward slash), 92

A

absolute addresses, 106, 242, 430
access. *See* authentication; authorization; security
access points. *See* endpoints
accounts. *See also* authentication; authorization
    authorization and, 299
    Username authentication and Windows NT, 294
actions
    message contract, 186
    service operation, 173, 174
activation
    hosting layer and, 12
    IIS hosting automatic, 370, 431. *See also* IIS hosting
Active Directory, 94, 111
ActiveXMessageFormatter, 116
activities, 403, 404, 408
activity IDs, 403, 408
Actor parameter, 188
AddEndpoint method, 253
address attribute, 106, 216, 254
    address parameter, 381
Address property, 270
AddressAccessDeniedException exceptions, 435
AddressAlreadyInUseException exceptions, 435
address-binding-contract endpoints. *See* endpoints
addresses, 91–94
    address agnostic services, 8
    cross-machine, 430
    determining endpoint, 105
    digital whiteboard case study, 515
    endpoints and, 33, 72, 91, 242. *See also* endpoints
    exposing MEX endpoints, 104
    formats, 35, 92–94
    IIS-hosted services, 380, 427
    interoperability and WSDL, 327
    programming, 104–106
    runtime errors, 436
    self-hosting vs. IIS hosting, 370

    specifying base, 105
    specifying relative, 106
    specifying, in code, 106
    specifying, in configuration files, 106
    types of, 91
AddressingMode property, 111
addressProperties element, 431
AddressProperties property, 301
administrators, authorization and, 299
AggregateException exceptions, 435
AllowConcurrentTransactions parameter, 258, 259
anonymous access. *See also* Anonymous authentication
    enabling, 77, 231
    interoperable catalog service exercise, 355
    virtual directories and, 427, 428
Anonymous authentication. *See also* anonymous access
    anonymous client determination, 302
    client impersonation levels and, 298
    overview, 289
    specifying, 294
    transport security and, 296
application configuration files (App.config), 14, 15, 52, 83, 153. *See also* configuration files
application developers, this book and, xx
application programming interface (API). *See* imperative programming; object model
Application Server, IIS as, 424
applications. *See* programs
architecture
    Indigo, 12
    service orientation, 4
ArgumentOutOfRangeException exception, 420
arrays
    implicit data contracts and, 166
    message bodies as, 187
ASMX Web services
    client program interoperability with Indigo service programs, 328–331
    interoperability and first-generation, 322
    interoperability of Indigo client programs with, 331–334
    interoperable catalog service exercise client program, 359–364

About the Author

David Pallmann is a former program manager of usability for Microsoft Code Name "Indigo" who created samples and applications for Indigo in that role. Previously, as the technical lead for integration and scenarios, he was responsible for integration-testing Indigo and for ensuring that key scenarios could be satisfied by implementing enterprise applications and design patterns. David is now a principal consultant with Neudesic LLC. He has over 25 years of experience in designing and developing software, much of it related to distributed computing. Before working at Microsoft, David served as chief technology officer of NQL Inc., where he created a variety of bot and intelligent agent technologies. He and his wife Becky have three children. David can be contacted at dpallmann@hotmail.com.

What do you think of this book?
We want to hear from you!

Do you have a few minutes to participate in a brief online survey? Microsoft is interested in hearing your feedback about this publication so that we can continually improve our books and learning resources for you.

To participate in our survey, please visit:

www.microsoft.com/learning/booksurvey

And enter this book's ISBN, 0-7356-2151-9. As a thank-you to survey participants in the United States and Canada, each month we'll randomly select five respondents to win one of five $100 gift certificates from a leading online merchant.* At the conclusion of the survey, you can enter the drawing by providing your e-mail address, which will be used for prize notification *only*.

Thanks in advance for your input. Your opinion counts!

Sincerely,

Microsoft Learning

Microsoft | Learning

Learn More. Go Further.